The Evolution of Primate Behavior
Alison Jolly

On the Origins of Language
Philip Lieberman

The Ascent of Man
David Pilbeam

Primate Evolution
Elwyn L. Simons

The Macmillan Series in Physical Anthropology
Elwyn L. Simons and David Pilbeam, editors
other volumes in preparation

Alice M. Brues

UNIVERSITY OF COLORADO

PEOPLE AND RACES

The Macmillan Series in Physical Anthropology

MACMILLAN PUBLISHING CO., INC.
New York

COLLIER MACMILLAN PUBLISHERS
London

Macmillan Publishing Co., Inc.
866 Third Avenue, New York, New York 10022

Collier Macmillan Canada, Ltd.

Library of Congress Cataloging in Publication Data

Brues, Alice Mossie, (date)
   People and races.

   (The Macmillan series in physical anthropology)
   Bibliography: p.
   Includes index.
   1. Race.   2. Physical anthropology.   I. Title.
GN269.B78   573   76-1880
ISBN 0-02-315670-8

Printing: 3 4 5 6 7 8   Year: 2 3

ISBN   0-02-315670-8

to the memory of my father

Charles T. Brues

who taught me to think biologically
at a very early age

Preface

This book is based on a course entitled *Human Races,* which I have given since 1968 at the University of Colorado. Though the course is officially of "advanced undergraduate" level, enrollment is not limited to anthropology majors and it has no formal prerequisites. Therefore, it does not take for granted any background in genetics or any of the special fields on which it touches. Everything that is necessary to understand the subject, beyond a general high-school comprehension of the world, is incorporated in the course itself. The book retains all this. Thus I have reason to hope that it can be read with understanding and interest not only by anthropology students but by students in other fields, or by anyone with college-level curiosity. I must emphasize to my readers what I always tell the class at the first meeting; this is *physical,* not cultural anthropology, and the social and political problems associated with race will be mentioned only incidentally. Few students seem to drop the course after this announcement. I believe that in a period in which the word "race" has become politically and emotionally charged, most people welcome an opportunity to discuss the perfectly simple physical differences that distinguish populations of geographically different ancestry. The very air of conspiracy with which some people avoid talking about racial differences is enough to give the impression that these differences are in some way sinister. I do not feel this way. Racial differences need not be thought of as something puzzling or uncomfortable about strangers: they can also be something interesting about your friends.

The subject matter of this book has been effectively reviewed by successive classes of students, who have showed by their facial expressions and sometimes bodily postures whether it was clear and interesting to them. I have not inflicted any of this manuscript on my everyday colleagues, so none of them are in any way responsible for its failings. I am indebted to Dr. E. L. Simons and Dr. David Pilbeam of Yale University for their critical review as editors of this series. Mr. Kenneth Scott of Macmillan has provided numerous useful comments, as well as relaying to me the anonymous reviews by which publishers like to raise the anxiety levels of their authors.

The assembling of the "people-pictures" in Chapters 3, 13, and 14 has been a major task in itself. I have tried particularly to show a representative sample of the students, academicians, and political leaders which all races and nationalities are producing in increasingly conspicuous numbers. The acknowledgment of sources accompanying the pictures indicates the number of individuals and organizations from whom I received help in this effort. Where no specific acknowledgment is made, the pictures were either taken by myself or sent to me by the individuals represented. I am indebted to a number of United States political leaders for professional quality portraits appearing in this volume. The reader must forgive some pictures of lesser quality that were necessary to complete the world portrait gallery. For assistance in obtaining photos or for information about the persons represented, I am especially indebted to Madeleine Mitchell, Chief, Public Inquiries Unit, United Nations; Diane Pierson and Josephine D'Orsi of the American Museum of Natural History; Lorna Condon of the Peabody Museum; Edgar Schewe of the Wistar Press; Paul Clifford of Wide World Photos; Martha Blaine of the Oklahoma Historical Society; and Dr. Norman Tindale. Thanks are also due to the Division of Physical Anthropology of the United States National Museum, particularly Dr. J. L. Angel and Dr. Lucille Hoyme, for helping me select and photograph skulls in the museum collections, some of which are reproduced in Chapter 7.

Most of the work of transforming a messy manuscript into a neat copy was done by Debbie Otterstrom of the University of Colorado Anthropology Department, who deserves not only thanks for her patience but praise for her skill.

Lastly, my thanks go to the administration of the University of Colorado for granting me a semester of sabbatical leave during the most critical period of writing this book.

A. M. B.

Contents

Introduction

This book will be almost entirely about human beings and the differences between them, and about human races and the differences between them. Let the reader understand at the start that we are interested in physical and genetic differences primarily, and only very indirectly in how people differ because of their culture and upbringing.

It is conventional to start with definitions of the terms to be used. We will not define a human being because each of our readers knows one of them with a special immediacy. *Race* has been considered a hard word to define, though it is probably no more so than many other commonly used words that refer to collections of events or objects. A race is: *a division of a species which differs from other divisions by the frequency with which certain hereditary traits appear among its members.* Among these traits are features of external appearance that make it possible to recognize members of different populations by visual inspection with greater or less accuracy. Members of such a division of a species share ancestry with one another to a greater degree than they share it with individuals of other races. Finally, races are usually associated with particular geographic areas.

We have not said how large these divisions we call races are, or how many of them there are. This is a matter of choice, depending on how much detail is desired. Thus at one time we may speak of major races of continental scale, considering Europeans and their widely scattered relatives and descendants as a single unit. In another connection, we may distinguish various races *within* Europe. This is no more significant than turning the turret of a microscope to change the magnification.

It is important to realize that we can describe races only on the basis of differences between *populations*. The frequency with which a trait occurs in a population can be evaluated only if we have a statistical sample. A single individual is not a race, and no single individual will match in every respect the average of the population from which he comes; most individuals, in fact, are quite non-average in one way or another. If we try to make fine distinctions in describing differences between populations in different parts of Europe, for instance, we will find that the differences between populations are rather small, and are confusingly overlaid with a great deal of individual variation. In this case, certain individuals could not be identified with any particular area, and we might say of a man, "He could come from almost anywhere." However, if we had a *sample* of a number of individuals from the same area, we would be more confident about deciding where the population came from: and the larger the sample, the greater would be our confidence. We might say, "There couldn't be so many people who look like this anywhere but in Nation X." If we were to compare two very different population groups, such as Norwegians and Tanzanians, we might find an overlap in single traits, but not in the total appearance of any individual. Out of a thousand of each group, we could easily find a swarthy Norwegian whose skin color was similar to that of an unusually fair Tanzanian. And we could find a Norwegian with the kind of bushy hair that occurs sporadically among Europeans, and comes within the limits of variation of African blacks. But this hair form is not correlated with skin color in European populations, and it would be a one-in-a-hundred-thousand chance to find the two variants in the same individual. Still to be taken into account would be many differences in facial features between the two races. In this case we would probably not mistake our aberrant Norwegian for a Tanzanian, though we might reasonably guess that he was from any of a number of other places, and confess that he was an anthropological puzzle. Races, then, even quite distinct ones, cannot be clearly defined in terms of one or a few characteristics; they must be defined in terms of their normal combinations of characteristics.

The hereditary nature of the traits that are significant for distinguishing races is shown by the fact that when populations move from one part of the world to another, the descendants continue to resemble their ancestors. Some Americans look European, and some look African, because their ancestors came from these regions many generations ago. If American-born descendants of Japanese are taller and heavier than their parents, we do not say that their racial characteristics have changed; we conclude that height and weight are only partly correlated with race because they are also affected by environment. Obviously there is a correlation between physical appearance and geographical area of residence or ancestry, but if there is a causal relation, it is not so simple or immediate that the children of Old World settlers in the New World grow up to look like American Indians. The nature of the relation between area and race will prove to be a very interesting one.

The importance of common ancestry in determining racial characteristics is also shown by intergradations between races wherever populations have been incompletely separated in the past. This effect, combined with the individual variation within groups, makes it impossible to set definite boundaries to races, in most cases. In a simpler and more innocent world, before people had moved about so much and had settled in territories far from their original homes, we might have made a leisurely trip away from home, in any direction, and observed a changing appearance of the people we saw, that would have given us a realistic view of racial differences. A few hundred miles away we might have noticed that certain variations we knew among the people of our own village—blond, brunet; tall, short; beaky nose or turned-up nose—were commoner or rarer than we were accustomed to. We might have seen a number of individuals who would look rather unusual back home. As we went further, we might begin to see individuals who looked like no one we had ever seen at home; and farther away still, we might find a population in which *nobody* looked like *anybody* back home. At what point in these travels could we say we had met a different race? We had observed an increasing racial difference from the population at our starting point, but where would we draw lines between races?

If we recognize as distinct races only populations so different that no individual of one of them could ever be mistaken for a member of the other, most of the people in the world would not belong to *any* of our races. Only when people whose ancestors originally came from widely separated areas have later been brought into contact with one another by travel or migration, do we have a situation in which clearly different elements in a single community (that is, elements with little or no overlap of physical appearance) can be defined as separate races. This is an abnormal, and largely a recent, phenomenon, that has given rise in some areas to attempts to define race in a legal way. However, if we look at races in their natural habitats, continuity is the rule rather than the exception.

How then can we define a particular race? The answer is that we cannot. We can try to define the word *race* itself, but individual races, like many other biological phenomena, can only be *described.* Some have said that for this reason we should not name races, although we can measure degrees of racial difference between populations. It is quite likely, however, that we will continue to name races in the future, just as we name colors—though colors intergrade infinitely, and people often cannot agree on which word to apply to a particular hue. Other sciences have similar problems of terminology. Biologists give names to "biomes"—characteristic plant-animal associations of different areas—which intergrade everywhere at their boundaries. And a geographer speaks of "climates," although a climate is only a statistical generalization derived from a tremendous variety of weather events that occur with different frequency in different areas. Yet it is meaningful to say that the climate of Colorado is colder than that of Florida, even though there are many days in each year when it gets warmer in Denver than it does in Jacksonville.

Sometimes races are grouped into "primary" races, which are unique or extreme in certain respects, and "secondary" races, which appear to be intermediate between neighboring populations. This is a relative matter, because nearly all populations have some distinctive features that cannot be explained in terms of a mixture between any of their neighbors. One indirect inference from this kind of classification is generally wrong: the notion that at some time in the past races were "purer," that is, more distinct from one another and more uniform within themselves, than they now are. This may be true, to a degree, in some cases: for example, in Europe during the last few thousand years. In the Neolithic period, populations were smaller, there was probably more uninhabited territory between tribes, and regional differences may have been clearer at that time than they are now. But it is not safe to extrapolate this further backward. Alternating periods of migration and isolation have probably occurred throughout human history, with race formation (that is, accentuation of regional differences) at some times and places, and race mixture at other times and places.

One common misconception about race is that it is unique to man. On the contrary, nearly every widespread animal species has geographical varieties, just as the human species does. Visitors who have seen the semitame bears of the national parks of the western United States may wonder why this species is officially known as the "black" bear, when so many of the bears are some shade of brown. This is simply a racial difference. In the eastern race of this species, which the early European colonists first encountered and named, most bears were black. However, farther west, large numbers of lighter colored bears, including those of reddish hues, occur; and because the eastern race is largely extinct now, the name is not entirely appropriate. These color variants within the "black" bear population are reminiscent of hair color variation in man in another way: they appear in different *proportions* in different areas, and not only does a single local population of the species include individuals of different colors, but different shades of color may appear within a single family of mother and cubs.

Zoologists have given considerable attention to geographical variation in animal species. Sometimes they use the term *subspecies* instead of *race*. This is largely a matter of terminology: the word *subspecies* has sometimes been used in reference to man. Intensive study of widespread species has shown that many characteristics, less obvious to casual observation than coat color, are equally diversified geographically. Measurements of the skull, which are individually variable but which also show average differences between collections from different areas, have often been studied, simply because the mammal collector usually brings the skull and the skin back to the museum and leaves the rest of the animal behind. Early anthropologists, studying skulls of different races of man, also found numerous regional differences. Recently, biochemical differences between races have been studied in many species, including man. Often, as we come to know more about various animals, we find that what we once considered separate species actually intergrade with one another, and are merely races. This shows that man's pattern of one species and many races is less distinctive than we once thought.

We may ask, "If a species which formerly had a restricted range spreads over a wide area, how long will it take for racial differences to develop?" The answer seems to be, "Not necessarily very long." In 1852, English sparrows were introduced to North America from England and Germany. Unafraid of man, and willing to live in closer proximity to man's activities than most other birds, they had a tremendous potential for expansion, and soon increased to millions, scattered over most of the continent. A careful study of sparrow populations at the present time shows a variety of regional differences, particularly in color but also in body size and proportions (Johnston and Selander, 1964). The color variations tend toward lighter and darker variations of the typical plumage in most cases, but in two populations, a distinct yellowish or rufous color appears on the under parts. As in man, individual differences in various traits overlie the regional differences, so that individual specimens, in many cases, cannot be definitely assigned to a particular region. But in the case of sparrows from Hawaii, not a single specimen from the island collection could be mistaken for one from the continent, or vice versa. We would call this a very marked racial difference. The period of time during which this amount of regional differentiation took place, from the introduction of the sparrows to North America until the date of collection of the specimens used in the study, was 111 years—a maximum of 111 generations for sparrows, and on the average, fewer, because many sparrows live to breed for more than one season. On the human scale, this would be about three thousand years—not a very long time in the history of our species.

Can we make a clear distinction between racial differences and species differences? Not *absolutely* clear, in all cases. Members of the same species must be able to interbreed and produce fertile offspring: this is essential in order to maintain the species as a genetic entity. If two groups do not so interbreed, they are considered distinct species. But there are instances where groups that *can* interbreed do not normally do so, even though they are in frequent contact; mere differences in courtship behavior are sometimes responsible for this. Insofar as differences in culture, acting on either a conscious or unconscious level, have at some times and places discouraged mating between different races, we can say that the possibility has existed that human races might become species: but the possibility has never been realized. When related populations are long separated from one another, whether by physical barriers or otherwise, they eventually develop differences that make it impossible for them to interbreed. When this happens, what were once races have become species. This is an important process in evolution. But such a process seems to take a long time, and under present conditions of contact and interaction between different human races, there is no indication that it is likely ever to occur in man.

It is important to distinguish certain differences between human groups which, although they may *correlate* with race, are not the same thing. Sometimes the name of a nation is used as if it were a designation of race, as, the "Irish race" or the "German race." If the boundaries of these nations were quite permanent and well-sealed against immigration, the populations within them might in time come to be genetically meaningful units. However, national boundaries have often shifted in the past, and people have crossed boundaries, either in groups as invaders, or individually as immigrants; so there may be more difference, genetically, between different parts of a single nation than between adjacent parts of different nations. In the case of some large modern nations like the United States, extremely divergent races are present under a single flag. It is unwise, therefore, to use terms that confuse nationality with race. Languages do not define races either, though common language is sometimes evidence of common ancestry, and may be a guide to understanding the history of population movements and racial affinities. Language differences also inhibit communication and may thus discourage intermarriage. But languages can be imposed on groups by political means: the "Latin languages" of Europe do not define a "Latin" race; these languages are relicts of the Roman Empire, which, at its greatest extent, included a rather diverse lot of people. And in some areas, languages that are not detectably related may be spoken by peoples whose physical type is quite similar, as among the Plains Indian tribes of North America. Nor does religion define race, though in some areas there may, for historical reasons, be racial differences between adherents of different religions. And race is not culture, though different racial groups in an area may have cultures that are different to a greater or less degree. Many dubious statements have been made in the past about causal relations between race and culture. If we define race in genetic terms, the only meaningful relation between race and culture would be one that was the result of inherited differences in temperament and aptitude, which determined to some extent the various modes of thought and action of various populations.

Whether such relations exist is an interesting question, but one that is extremely difficult to answer, at least at the present time. The learned patterns of behavior that we call culture represent adaptations of groups to particular environments; because culture is largely ruled by tradition, it is sometimes an adaptation to an environment that no longer exists in its original form. And because environment in the full sense of the word is not the same for different social classes in the same community, it is not surprising that differences in culture between races may persist for a long time after the races have come in contact with one another. Thus, it is easy to believe that behavioral differences are genetic in origin, as are physical differences. But we need to know much more about the ways in which behavior patterns develop in groups and in individuals before we can speak with assurance about any genetic factors in human behavior.

What do we mean by a *racial trait,* or *racial characteristic?* Without exception, traits that are found to differ in frequency of occurrence or degree of development between races are also found to differ among individuals within races. However, a trait that differed between individuals but in no way correlated with geographical area would obviously be of no interest in describing races. If all populations all over the world had the same average stature, stature would not be a racial trait at all. If it could be shown that stature variations between populations were entirely the result of nutrition or other extrinsic factors, we would consider stature not to be a racial trait on grounds of lack of *hereditary* difference between races. However, stature *is* a racial trait, although the amount of racial variation compared to individual variation is not very large in this case. Hair form is more clearly diagnostic of race, because one variety, the wooly type, is nearly universal in some parts of the world and very rare in others. Thus, there are degrees to which various sorts of variation may be spoken of as "racial" traits. Yet, surprisingly, just as there are virtually no variations in man that are *totally* "racial," so there is virtually none that is not at least *slightly* "racial" in the sense that some average differences can be detected between populations of different areas.

It will be clear from what we have said so far that there is no single characteristic that is shared by all individuals of one race and denied to everyone else. Still less is there any single simple quality, which one race possesses and another does not, that bestows a "package deal" of physical and behavioral traits on some people and not on others. This is a disappointment to those who wish the world were simple.

2 The Discovery of Race

No less than fifty thousand years ago there were human beings of essentially modern type. Coexisting with them were the people we now call Neanderthal Man, who are now generally believed to have been simply a race of the people who were our ancestors. We would expect, on the basis of what we know of other animals, that whenever the human species spread over an area a thousand or more miles across, some racial differences would have been present. But even if there were, at this period few people would have been aware of the existence of racial differences. Through most of man's history, few people ever moved more than a short distance from their place of birth. They had no way to travel except on foot, no way to carry belongings except on their backs. In addition, it was usually hazardous for them to move away from their homes and their tribes. A few miles from home, they no longer knew the game trails, the fishing spots, or the places where useful plants could be gathered in season. Still farther away, the whole landscape might be forbidding; not because it lacked food altogether, but because its resources were not of a kind that their own culture taught them how to use. Even if adjacent territories had no inhabitants who might resent or repel intruders, migration was unrewarding and dangerous, to be undertaken only when life was threatened by a deadly quarrel with a fellow tribesman. In such times one rarely encountered a group of people who were racially different from himself to any but a slight degree. The tribe on the other side of the hill might be somewhat different in customs and dress, and speak a different dialect or even a different language, but in physical appearance they would not be greatly different. Many previous centuries of living side by side in a stable world would ensure that such neighbors had intermarried sufficiently to be genetically similar. In some parts of the world there are people of simple culture who still live in this way. It is not true, however, that such tribes have always liked their physically similar neighbors. Many tribes refer to themselves by the word in their language that simply means "men," thus implying that their neighbors are slightly less than human. Some regard neighbor tribes with horror because they do not observe the same taboos; or they accuse each other of unspeakable (and imaginary) vices. Intermittent hostilities may sometimes occur between such groups; fortunately casualties are not high when the weaponry of the combatants is primitive and evenly matched. This situation might be said to have all the ingredients of racism—except race.

Man's knowledge of the racial variety of his own species had to wait for the development of motives for travel. Oddly enough, trade, in its early stages, did require extended travel. In early periods, trade goods could be carried over great distances by exchange between one tribe and another, with none of the traders going farther than the boundary of his own tribal territory. Anyone who was tempted to bypass the numerous middlemen knew all too well that outside his own tribe, no one was much concerned with his safety. Cruising along a coast in a boat was less hazardous than adventuring by land, and probably some of the first people to see races noticeably different from themselves were traveling in this way. One could always hope to push off to sea again if things got threatening. Until well into modern times in many parts of the world, overland travel remained dangerous, and travelers moved in groups, armed to protect themselves if necessary.

About five thousand years ago, a few societies became sufficiently complex to develop a ruling class which, having tasted the pleasure of having other people do their work for them, aspired to increasing the numbers of their subjects. By this time it was possible to support and feed some individuals from the taxes of others in order to undertake excursions, in which the functions of trade, war, and pillage were not clearly separated, into other people's territories. Thus the ancient empires of Egypt and the Near East began to develop. At about the same time, written records were first made, so that we can document the sometimes monotonous history of invasions and conquests that followed. During this time invading forces began to encounter strange peoples, who differed from themselves in culture, speech, and dress, and often to a greater or less degree in physical appearance also. Defeated soldiers or unlucky civilians were brought back as captives, to be displayed to the wondering home folks, and later put to work. In this way Egyptians of the ancient dynasties, themselves brunet whites of the type still living around the Mediterranean Sea, came to know black Africans from areas south of Egypt—even the small-statured Pygmies—and the hook-nosed people of the Near East. The artists who decorated Egyptian tombs and temples have left graphic evidence of their knowledge of these various races. There is no indication in the Old Testament that the people whose traditions it records were aware of races greatly different from themselves, though perhaps they were simply not interested in describing human variations. At a much later time, some passages in Genesis were interpreted to mean that the three sons of Noah—Ham, Shem, and Japheth—became the respective ancestors of the black Africans, the brunet Near Eastern-ers, and the blond Europeans. However, the Biblical account traces these supposed descendants only a few hundred miles in these various directions, indicating that the scriptural story was intended to explain the existence of different tribes of similar racial type rather than different races in the modern sense of the word.

The ancient Greeks knew about Ethiopians, a term used then and later to mean any of the black peoples of Africa. In the ninth century B.C. Homer refers to the Ethiopians as a remote, almost mythical people who lived far to the south. In a more matter-of-fact way he also describes a black, wooly-haired man as a warrior in the camp of the Trojan warrior, Odysseus (*Odyssey*, 19:246–248). The name *Ethiopian* means the "scorched ones," indicating that the Greeks supposed their color to be a suntan carried to the utmost degree. Four hundred years later, Greek art depicted typical black Africans in unmistakable detail (Figure 1). At this time Herodotus, the great Greek historian and geographer, mentions not only the Ethiopians but also nomads north of the Black Sea, who were called Scythians, and who were described as light-eyed and fiery-haired (Herodotus, *ca.* 435 B.C.). The latter term has sometimes been trans-lated as "red-haired" although red hair in the strict sense seems never to occur in *all* members of any population. The term may simply have meant bright or yellowish, like a flame: or perhaps the Greeks were so impressed by a few heads of really red hair that they characterized the whole population by it. In any case, these Scythians were obviously blond compared with the Greeks. Herod-otus also refers, correctly, to people in India who were "as black as the Ethiopians." At this time the Greeks were beginning to have hostile relations with the Near Eastern empires, which, incidentally, used black African mercenaries against them; a century later, Alex-ander the Great led Greek troops through Persia and as far as India. By the end of the fourth century B.C., then, the Caucasian popula-tions of the Mediterranean and Near Eastern areas knew one an-other well enough so that sophisticated city folks of one group would probably have recognized a member of the other group. Both

Figure 1 A Greek vase, fifth to sixth century B.C., depicting the head of an Ethiopean. (Courtesy Staatlichen Museen, Pruessischer Kulturbesitz, Antikenabteilung.)

knew black Africans by sight, though those Africans who remained in their native lands may have had very little knowledge of lighter-skinned races. The Mediterranean and Near Eastern populations also knew, or had heard of, blond people in the north, and black-skinned natives of India.

Soon after this the Roman Empire put under one government a variety of races, in an area extending from Britain in the west to the Sahara Desert in the south, and to the old empires of the Near East and Persia in the east. Racial differences were apparently of little interest to the Romans so long as people were politically malleable; in their writings they seldom comment on the racial variety they knew. By this time, perhaps, the presence of various travelers and foreigners in the Mediterranean area was taken for granted. Be-cause people at that time were less likely than now to adopt a standard form of dress, the presence of foreigners on the streets of Rome must have been conspicuous and picturesque. Roman artists show us that Ethiopians were known to them, as to the Greeks, though Roman rule did not extend into their native territory. As we have said, the Roman Empire pushed northward as well, into what were then savage domains. The Romans paid no compliments to the Germanic tribes they never conquered or to the Britons they conquered late. They described the Germans as the Greeks had described the Scythians: blue-eyed and red-haired (again, the red hair is probably exaggerated) and noted that the Scots were similar in appearance (Tacitus, *ca.* 100 A.D.). (Anyone of northwestern European ancestry who is inclined to look down on other peoples of the world will profit by reading the comments of the cultured Romans on the peoples of Germany and Britain, to whom civilization had not yet come.) In the East, the Romans had trade contacts with China, by which they received silk, nearly worth its weight in gold in Rome, a luxury which conservative Romans deplored. Rome's farthest military penetration was to southern Turkestan where, in 39 B.C., a unique confrontation took place between Roman legions and Chinese soldiers of the Han Dynasty (Goodrich, 1963). However, this first contact between Westerners and the peoples of central and east Asia was apparently not understood by the Romans. Almost a century later, a Roman author refers to the Chinese (the "silk people" as they were known) as tall, fair-haired, and blue-eyed. He apparently confused the Chinese with some unknown tribe, probably middlemen in the silk trade (Plinius Secundus, *ca.* 70 A.D.). He observed, correctly, that the Chinese avoided direct contact with foreigners.

A few centuries later, as the Empire weakened, the blond barbarians of northern Europe, for whom the Romans had such distaste, moved in various waves southward, invading first the borders of the Empire and then its center, taking over control locally and eventually destroying the Empire as a functioning state. In this period a wave of nomadic looters, called the Huns, came in from the East, across southern Russia. They are described in contemporary writings as Mongoloids, probably not unlike the Chinese (McGovern, 1939). But this hit-and-run invasion flickered out in France, leaving Europeans not much more aware of the races of Asia than they had been before. During this period of turmoil, there was no time for objective curiosity about human races. In the centuries that followed, Europe became politically fragmented among local rulers, some of whom were the heirs of the barbarians. Travel any distance from home once again became hazardous, and the people of Europe forgot the racial differences that the Romans had known; they marveled instead at tales of one-eyed men and other monsters supposedly inhabiting the far corners of the earth. The only new racial discovery by Europeans during this period was in the tenth century, when Viking adventurers saw Eskimos in Greenland—the first New World people whom Europeans had ever seen—and took no special note of them.

At this time, when Europe was withdrawn from the mainstream of history, the Near East underwent a political revival. The spread of Islam, beginning in the seventh century, was powered by military expansion; but the empire it founded, which extended from Spain to Persia, was maintained on a sound mercantile basis (Lewis, 1966).

Muslim merchants traveled directly to India, the East Indies, and China. The involuntary northward movement of black Africans, which had begun in Egyptian times, was systematized by the Arabs, who continued to dominate the slave trade for many centuries. They included among their slaves blond Europeans from the north, and have left us an interesting theory of the cause of racial differences. They believed that the development of the child in the womb was a sort of cooking process; that in cold northern climates the womb never became hot enough, leaving the infant pale, pasty, and blond; that in hot southern climates it scorched its contents, blackening the skin and crisping the hair (Lewis, 1971). To their way of thinking, only they themselves were "done" just right! The peoples of the Islamic empire thus knew most of the races that the peoples of the Roman Empire had known (though with less direct knowledge of northern Europe); they had greater familiarity with India, and had firsthand knowledge of the Chinese and related peoples of south Asia.

In this period of the Dark Ages of Europe, China also developed as an empire with wide commercial contacts. Chinese knowledge of racial differences in man was slowed by the fact that China was situated in the center of a region that was fairly homogeneous in racial composition, though early accounts record their knowledge of "different" groups, some of pygmy stature, in south central and Southeast Asia (Goodrich, 1963). Beginning in the second century A.D., Buddhist missionaries came to China from various areas, particularly India, where the racial type contrasted strongly with the Chinese themselves (Figure 2). In the eighth century, Syrians, Arabs, and Persians, as well as neighboring peoples of Mongoloid race, were living in Chinese cities; pottery figures of the T'ang Dynasty (about 1000 A.D.) depict caricatured foreigners of hooknosed Near Eastern type. Some of these strangers are shown riding camels—a clear indication that they came overland along the thou-

Figure 2 A Buddhist missionary from India in China in the thirteenth century A.D. (Detail from a Chinese figurine, courtesy Asian Art Museum of San Francisco, The Avery Brundage Collection.)

The Discovery of Race

sand-year-old "silk route." Old records describe some of the nomads on the northern borders of China as red-haired, as the Greeks
described the Scythians (McGovern, 1939). For many centuries the
more southern areas of Eurasia—China, India, the Middle East, and
the Mediterranean—had been occupied by peoples of agricultural
and settled habit. North of them, from the plains of central Europe
east to Siberia, lived nomads, quite mobile because of their use of
horses, and incompletely filling the land. The far-ranging blond
peoples who had been seen by the Chinese must have slipped
between other groups of nomads for two thousand miles, without
compromising their genetic identity.

Another demonstration of the swift movements of the northern
nomads came in the thirteenth century, when the Mongols of
central Asia, archetypes of the present races of central and eastern
Asia, expanded in the widest conquest the world had yet known:
they overran China, India, west Asia, and Eastern Europe as far as
Poland. A rather weary and superstitious Europe saw in the Mongols a divine scourge, and questioned whether these creatures of a
different race were indeed among the men whom God had created
on the sixth day, or were, instead, demons. *Tartars,* they called
them, after an ancient name for Hell, though their true name was
Tatar. Only half a century later, however, Marco Polo of Venice, a
city more sophisticated than most of Europe, followed the Asiatic
trade route to China and spent many years there, quite happily, in
the service of its Mongol rulers. From China he made further
excursions to Southeast Asia and India. The most tantalizing part of
his records is the lack of any but the most sketchy descriptions of
race. A merchant to the core, he marveled at the wealth of the East
but not at its genetics! In some respects, the racial horizons of
Europe seem to have been little affected by the incursions of the
Mongols or the travels of Marco Polo. A good indication of popular
knowledge of race sometimes comes from art. The Middle Ages
cherished a legend, still remembered today in some parts of the
world, that the three kings who gathered at the birth of Christ
represented a regathering of the three races that originated from the
sons of Noah. In a fifteenth century painting, these figures are
represented as a black African, a blond, blue-eyed Caucasian, and
an aquiline-nosed Near Easterner. The black king is represented so
well that the artist must have had a living model—evidence of the
presence of some Africans in Europe, at least near centers of trade.
The Asiatic king, shown with typical Near Eastern features, suggests that western Europeans at that time were either not really
aware of the presence of quite different races in central and eastern
Asia, or were unable to relate them to their scriptural traditions.

A great period of exploration, expansion of trade, and meeting of
distant peoples began in the Renaissance. The voyage of Columbus
was only one, and not the first, of many explorations that originated
in Europe, subsidized by various nations in the interest of trade,
and attracting the curious and adventurous. In the fourteenth century the Portuguese had begun to explore the coast of West Africa,

following routes that had been taken by the Carthaginians many centuries before, in search of the sources of the spices that had been coming overland through Asia at great cost. Spain sought a shortcut around the other side of the globe. Columbus thought himself half a world farther west than he was when he named the people of the New World "Indians." Anthropologically, he was not far wrong; these natives of the new continents were derived from the same basic stock as the people he would have found in the Spice Islands southeast of Asia. Soon Europe was literally inundated with information about new lands, new plants and animals, and new people. There was puzzlement and dismay. For a time, some of the larger anthropoid apes were tentatively identified as new races of man; and some of the new races encountered for the first time gave rise to pious concern because they were not accounted for by the records of the Holy Scriptures. It was suggested that there had been "Creations" other than the traditional one of Adam and Eve, producing different races for different continents (Morton, 1854). Though this theory was later used to promote ideas of racial inequality, it seems originally to have been an attempt to explain the abundance (and apparently long cultural history) of some of the peoples whom Europeans had newly come to know. At that time the accepted date for the Biblical great flood was 2348 B.C., which did not allow much time for the whole world to have been populated by the descendants of Noah.

Beginning in the sixteenth century, Europeans rapidly came to know nearly all the races of the world, and these races came to know Europeans, but not each other. Reconnaissance, invasion, and settlement of North and South America proceeded steadily from 1500 on. This was the first knowledge the American natives had of different races, because there had not been, in the Western Hemisphere, any of the marked racial differences that were found in the Old World. Until the coming of the Europeans—and very soon afterward their African slaves—the American Indians had known only the moderate tribal differences among themselves. Some seaborne stragglers from the Old World may have reached American shores previously in small numbers, but these were remembered only in legend. The first Europeans to meet New World natives accepted them casually—and of course erroneously—as Asian. As European infiltration proceeded inland from the Atlantic coast, the succession of tribes encountered were quite similar in physical features. The coastal explorers of Africa during this period did not encounter any unfamiliar races either, because the natives of that area had been known as occasional migrants to Europe for many centuries. In the sixteenth century, merchants going farther and farther down the African coast finally rounded the Cape and developed routes to India and Southeast Asia by sea, establishing the first regular direct contact between Europeans and the people of southern Asia. Magellan, circling the world from east to west, visited the East Indies and the Phillipines, and brought the island people of the western Pacific to European knowledge for the first time. In the seventeenth century, Australia was first visited, and its black people (who were immediately called by the universal term, *Indians*) were described. Another hundred years later, Cook mapped many of the smaller islands far-flung across the central Pacific. Then, last of all, in the eighteenth and nineteenth centuries, Europeans finally entered the interior of Africa, whose native races had been known to them since classical times. This was considered at the time to be the last great adventure of exploration, even though the Arabs had never lost contact with this area, and were still there plying the slave trade and greeting the visitors from western Europe with lethal suspicion.

All over the world, in the wake of the first European adventurers, came a mixed batch of their countrymen, to make their presence felt in many ways. In areas where people already lived by intensive agriculture, population was already dense, by contemporary standards. Europeans never entered these areas in large numbers, though they later obtained political control and economic power in some regions. But elsewhere, thinly populated lands drew Europeans like a vacuum. Some were fortune hunters, driven to violence by dreams of gold, who made the pale skin a symbol of terror in many lands. Many deadly conflicts between Europeans and native peoples, as late as the Sioux wars of the 1870's, were touched off by the lust for gold. Other men of the frontier were simple religious missionaries, better prepared for martyrdom than for the lack of interest they often encountered. And wherever there was uncultivated land and a climate congenial to Europeans, settlers came, fleeing a population explosion in Europe. Not at first, but slowly, conflicts developed between the increasing numbers of immigrants and the original inhabitants. It is easy to condemn the intruders; but in those days of slow and difficult travel they themselves were trapped as soon as they stepped off the boat. So the "palefaces" came to be known over half the world in many roles, of which the most hated have been the longest remembered.

After the beginning of the nineteenth century, the Europeans' knowledge of the various other races of the world depended largely on how the information obtained by a few travelers and explorers reached the layman. At the present time we take for granted not only that photography can accurately record all that the eye can see, but that mass printing can accurately reproduce photographs. This has been true only in the last century. Before that time the racial differences seen by the explorer were very poorly reported to the public. A remark, "These people are fine-looking and of dark complexion," might be the sole description of a new racial group. Sometimes a member of the traveling party with some artistic skill made sketches. If these sketches were rendered into woodcuts or lithographs by expert technicians, the results might be good. Rarely artists painted aboriginal peoples from the living subject (Figures 3 and 4). For the popular book trade of the time, original sketches by artists of indifferent talents were usually interpreted by engravers of mediocre skill. Frequently the final printed result was that the

Figure 3 (*left*) A Roanoke Chief (Virginia) Original watercolor by John White about 1587. (Courtesy William L. Clements Library, University of Michigan.)

Figure 4 (*above*) Eeh-Nis-Kin or Crystal Stone, a Blackfoot woman. Oil painting by George Catlin, about 1832. (Courtesy National Collection of Fine Arts, Smithsonian Institution.)

Figure 5 (*below left*) A caricature emphasizing non-European features of an African. (From Wood's *Natural History of Man*, 1870.)

Figure 6 (*below right*) A "Europeanized" version of an African. (From Wood's *Natural History of Man*, 1870.)

features of the alien races were either depicted in caricature form, exaggerating their difference from the European type with which the engraver was familiar (Figure 5), or that they were presented in an idealized form, which made all races slightly differing versions of a classical Caucasoid standard of beauty (Figure 6). (Even after photography came into use, with foolproof methods of translating the photograph into printed form, the same biases sometimes affected the choice of individuals to be photographed.) Since photography became simpler and moved out of the studio, increasing numbers of pictures have been taken and published, and the racial diversity of man has been abundantly displayed to the general public.

Races Large and Small

By the end of the eighteenth century, knowledge of the appearance of various peoples of the world was fairly complete (Figure 7). At this time European scholars began to speculate on these racial differences, attempt to put them into a systematic scheme, and suggest reasons why the human species had developed this regional diversity. Differences in skin color between races had always impressed the popular mind, and quite naturally this became incorporated into early attempts to classify races. Time does not permit us to discuss all the controversies and differing systems that developed. In general we can see that most of the problems these early classifiers struggled with were self-made, the result of a desire to create a system that was neater and more symmetrical than the data justified. The most influential of these racial classifications was that of Blumenbach, published while the American Revolution was just getting under way (Blumenbach, 1776; in Count, 1950). He divided all mankind into five major groups, which popularly came to be known as White, Yellow, Red, Brown, and Black. This scheme has

Figure 7 The view from a Victorian drawing-room: a missionary preaching to various races of the world. (From Wood's *Natural History of Man*, 1870.)

become firmly established in popular thinking and is often referred to after two hundred years. The color system is partially symbolic, because Blumenbach's "yellow" and "red" are really just shades of brown; the "whites" are not very white; and only the rarest of human beings is literally black. The persisting popular use of this color system is a tribute to the power of the indoctrinated mind to ignore the evidence of the senses. Actually, Blumenbach took into account numerous racial traits other than skin color, and was quite aware, as serious students of race have always been, that many populations of the world fall "between" races. These finer points of Blumenbach's anthropology tend to get lost in the popularized version. Also, since his time we have come to realize that some groups of people, though small in numbers, are quite as unique in characteristics as the larger races. Thus, there are more races than most people think there are. In part, of course, the number of races we recognize depends on how we group together, in major classifications, various combinations of local populations that are distinguishable but not radically different. No one, so far, has reduced the number of major races to less than three, however. We will recognize three racial groups that correspond in a general way to the old popular designations of "white, yellow, and black," and will discuss numerous varieties and subvarieties of these. Blumenbach's "red" race of the Americas shares many characteristics with the "yellow" of Asia, and the two are now generally classed together as a single, very widespread, major race. Most of Blumenbach's "brown" race would be included with them also. In addition, we shall call attention to other human populations, smaller in numbers, which cannot be honestly fitted into any simple scheme and should be considered races in their own right.

Most Americans are directly familiar with only those few racial groups of the world that have contributed significant numbers to the population of the United States. They know the range of variation in physical appearance among the nations of Europe, as represented by the minor racial differences existing between various parts of western and central Europe. (This awareness of regional differences in Europe is diminishing with each generation, however, as the European stocks become increasingly mixed with one another in the United States.) Eastern Europe and the Near East have contributed less to the United States population, and not all Americans have a clear idea of what people in these areas look like. The American concept of the peoples of Africa is based on the American Negro population, nearly all of whose ancestors (exclusive of mixture taking place on this continent) came from portions of the continent of Africa that were readily accessible to ships plying the Atlantic, and not even the most northern or most southern parts of this coast (Reed, 1969). Less than 2 per cent came from other parts of the African continent. Asia is represented, in the minds of most Americans, by the descendants of southern Chinese, largely from the area around Canton (most of whom came to this country in the last century), and a later immigration of Japanese. More recently other Asians—war brides, adopted orphans, and refugees—have come to the United States. These populations represent only a small part of Asia. Even American Indians are unfamiliar to Americans in many parts of the United States, though certain tribes are numerous and well-known in some Western states; and their mixed descendants, often Spanish-speaking, form a considerable part of the population in some parts of the Southwest. Popular knowledge of the physical traits of the American Indians has not been advanced by the movie and television industries, which often present us with "Indians" who are only Caucasians in dark make-up.

Anyone who spends much time on a university campus will see representatives of more races than the average American sees, because of the number of students from foreign countries; however, it is not very informative to see these individuals without knowing their nationality. Of course, travelers and servicemen know certain populations rarely represented in the United States, but few travelers have covered the world very thoroughly. The most available sources of knowledge about the physical appearance of foreign populations are newspapers and magazines. Often photographers of travel magazines and articles attempt to show scenery, activities, and "native costume," all of which distract from the physical features of the people. The pictures accompanying news articles are more likely to be portraits, and these—political figures of developing nations, for instance, and other persons of interest to an increasingly global-minded readership—can be a daily review of one's knowledge of human variation. Some of the illustrations in this book are taken from news sources.

Before we begin a detailed consideration of the many traits by which human races differ, we shall present a general overview of the distribution of human races, with the names customarily used for them. Some of these names will be familiar to our readers, some will not. In accordance with anthropological practice, we speak of populations of the world as they were distributed before the widespread migrations of Europeans, which outnumbered, and in some cases virtually eliminated, original inhabitants during the last four centuries. Maps of the world generally show the Western Hemisphere on the left and the Eastern Hemisphere on the right, with the Atlantic Ocean in the left center, as though the Pacific Ocean were a great barrier to man's movements and the Atlantic were not. However, this is not a true picture of human migration prior to the sixteenth century. The Pacific barrier was long ago bypassed by migration across the Bering Straits, from Siberia to Alaska, a migration which produced the strong racial affinity between Asia and the original inhabitants of the Western Hemisphere. Significant movements across the Atlantic from Europe to America did not occur until much later. Thus our anthropological map of the world shows Europe on the extreme left, Asia in left center, and the Pacific Ocean and the Americas completing the right side.

In a general way, major races correspond to continents, simply because separation of some kind is necessary if human populations are to develop and maintain genetic differences. But it is an error to interpret this too literally. There are no definite lines on our map (Figure 8) to indicate boundaries between races. In many areas there are transitional zones within which we find populations that clearly show genetic affinities to more than one race. In other areas the transition may be more abrupt, with peoples who consider themselves different—and who choose to remain so—living close together yet remaining genetically distinct. In a few cases, small population groups with distinct genetic characteristics may live in enclaves surrounded by people of a race different from their own. Such groups are very vulnerable to being absorbed by the populations surrounding them, yet occasionally situations like this may exist for a long time. Some of these populations have been indicated on the map (Figure 8) by asterisks.

The origins of the names attached to various races, large and small, are not consistent. The names we use for the major races end in *oid,* meaning *like.* In these instances, a term that originally applied to a specific smaller group has been extended to have a larger meaning. Because it was once believed that the Caucasus mountain region in southern Russia was the point of origin, or at least the area of purest manifestation, of the race sometimes called *white,* the word

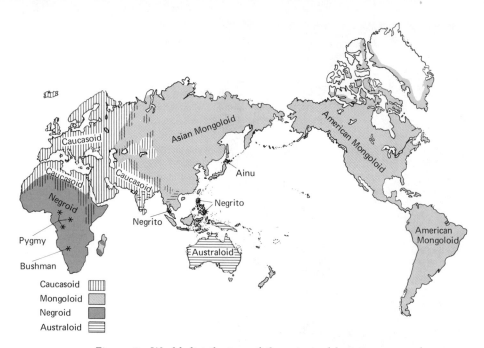

Figure 8 World distribution of the principal human races and some minor ones, as of 1500 A.D. The boundaries and areas of overlap are, by necessity, approximate.

Caucasoid, that is Caucasian-like, came to be applied to a major racial category (Figure 9). (The slightly different term, *Caucasian,* is in popular use with the same meaning.) Both terms are useful because, in contrast to *white* or *European,* they leave room for populations who do not live in Europe or are not very white. The term *Negroid* is an extended term referring to the dark-skinned populations of Africa, traditionally called *Negro,* and to other populations which are more or less genetically related to them (Figure 10). The *Mongols* are a population of north central Asia which became well-known in history as a result of their conquests in the thirteenth century, and their name, in the form *Mongoloid,* has been given not only to all the related people of a vast area of east and central Asia and the adjacent islands, but to the populations of the New World, who are more closely related to these Asians than to any other Old World racial group (Figure 11). *Australoid* is also an extended term (Figure 12). It includes not only the aboriginal inhabitants of Australia, but populations similar to them who live on nearby islands. Terms for the subgroups of the major races are derived from various sources: some are geographical, some are the names of language groups. Sometimes the name of a nation may be used to refer to areas and their populations; that is often convenient, but may lead to confusion when nations change their names or their boundaries. Other designations, particularly those of small groups, may be a

Figure 9 A Caucasoid: Margaret Thatcher, British political leader. (Wide World Photos.)

Figure 10 A Negroid: Former Ghanaian Prime Minister Kwame Nkrumah. (Wide World Photos.)

Figure 11 A Mongoloid: Senator Hiram Fong of Hawaii, of South Chinese ancestry.

Figure 12 An Australoid: Neville Bonner, Australian Senate member for Queensland. (Courtesy Australian Information Service.)

people's own name for themselves, or a name given to them by their neighbors.

In the center of our map is Asia, the largest continent, and the home of the *Asian Mongoloids,* the *yellow* race of older classifiers. These Mongoloids have straight black hair and dark brown eyes; their skin color varies from quite light to medium brown. Beard and body hair are usually meager or absent. The nose in Asian Mongoloids does not protrude, and because the cheek bones on either side are broad and massive, the face appears flat. Many other features will be discussed in later chapters. Local variations on the Mongoloid theme occupy central and east Asia: Turkestan and Tibet on the west, and north to Siberia; east to China, Japan, and the various countries of southeast Asia, and on to the Pacific islands of Indonesia, Micronesia, and Polynesia. The more southerly representatives of the Asian Mongoloids tend to be darker in color, and were the *brown* race of earlier classifiers. Within the territory of the Asian Mongoloids we find some local groups that are distinctly different: the *Ainu* and the *Negritoes* (see map, Figure 8), which will be discussed later. The Mongoloids, like other major racial groups, vary among themselves in ways that may indicate local absorption of other racial stocks, effects of selection in specific areas, or genetic drift; in many cases we can only guess which of these factors has been at work. Taken as a whole, the Asian Mongoloids are a numerous and successful race that occupies a tremendous range of climatic and ecological zones.

The road east out of Asia is in the high north, where Siberia comes within fifty miles of Alaska at the Bering Straits, and by this route the Americas were populated rather late in the history of man. Authorities do not agree in their estimates of the earliest coming of man to the New World: there appears to have been no substantial occupation of the hemisphere before about 10,000 B.C., though immigration may have taken place considerably earlier. There is some evidence of sporadic contacts by other routes between the Eastern and Western Hemispheres before historic times, but no indication that these contacts involved enough people to have any effect on physical type. The people of the New World are like the Mongoloids of Asia in many ways, and on the map we have designated them *American Mongoloids,* though we will often refer to them by the generally accepted, though inaccurate term, *American Indians.* Their skin color covers the same range as that of their Asian cousins, in spite of the imaginative term *red* which was long applied to them. The texture of the hair, and its usual sparsity on the male face and body, conforms to the Asian pattern. The most notable difference is that the American Mongoloids often have prominent noses, more Caucasoid than Mongoloid. Perhaps we should consider them to have "come of age" as a separate race after their long residence on their own continents. Both Asian and American Mongoloids may have changed since their separation. As we would expect, there are many local variants of the American Mongoloids over the vast area they occupy.

The Americas are the end of the line in this direction: until very recently the American Mongoloids had no neighbors. In the Old World, the Mongoloids have had contact with two other races. Some of the islands adjacent to Asia are, like the mainland, occupied by essentially Mongoloid peoples. However, this island territory abuts on that of the *Australoids,* who include the aborigines of Australia and the inhabitants of the Melanesian islands north and northeast of Australia. The Australoids differ markedly from the Mongoloids. Their skin color is darker, often quite black, their hair frequently curly in various degrees, and beard and body hair is abundant. Facial features, especially the wide nose, are very different. Though the Australoids are few in numbers now, we suspect that at one time they were more widely distributed and are a genetic element in some populations that are primarily of other races.

The other neighbors of the Mongoloids are *Caucasoids.* Though we tend to think of Caucasoids as European, they occupy a considerable part of Asia also. India, Pakistan, and Bangladesh are the easternmost extension of the Caucasoids: here they have Mongoloids living not only east but directly north of them. From India westward through the high plateaus of Afghanistan and Iran, and on the western shores of the Mediterranean—all technically parts of Asia—we find strictly Caucasoid peoples. North of Iran, extending through Turkestan north to western Siberia, is a zone that has long been occupied, jointly or successively, by populations of which some were Mongoloid, some Caucasoid, and some a mixture of the two. What *are* the distinctive features of the Caucasoids? Certainly not light eyes or hair, which many Caucasoids, even in Europe, do not have. Their most diagnostic feature is the nose, which has a narrow bony root that projects well forward of the eyes. This, combined with receding cheek bones, produces a facial contour strongly contrasted with that of the Mongoloids. In contrast, too, is the ample beard and body hair of Caucasoids. Other features are quite varied, including skin color, which approaches literal "whiteness' in some northern Europeans, but is light brown in most Caucasoids and ranges to very dark in some Caucasoids in India. Hair and eye color cover the whole range of the human species.

Africa is associated in most people's minds with the *Negroids* in the same way that Europe is associated with the Caucasoids. But the Negroids are the typical race only of that part of Africa south of Egypt and the Sahara Desert. Northern Africa is basically Caucasoid, and has been as far back as history records; its peoples are most closely related to the Europeans who live across the Mediterranean Sea from them. The physical characteristics of the Negroids are: dark brown to black skin, tightly curled hair, and distinctive facial features: large jaws and teeth, and a broad nose. This combination is most consistently seen in West Africa, from whence came the Negroids who were best known to Europeans at the time the word *Negro* came into use. In Ethiopia, and extending southward into the highlands of East Africa, more noticeable in some tribes than others, are facial features suggestive of some longstanding

Caucasoid admixture. Within black Africa there are also two small-statured races—the *Pygmy* and *Bushmen,* who are distinct from their larger neighbors.

This is a very short summary indeed of the complications of human classification and distribution. In Chapter 13, after we have systematically discussed the physical features by which human populations differ, we will consider the geography of human races in detail. Many more photographs will be found in that chapter.

Genetics and Human Variation

4

It is not possible to understand the differences of races from one another, or the constancy with which each group maintains its physical characteristics over many generations, without first considering the way in which physical traits are transmitted by heredity from parent to child. The fact that members of the same family resemble one another—within limits—has interested and puzzled man for centuries.

It was once believed that the heredity of an individual or of a race was carried in the blood. Even a few years ago some people feared that a blood transfusion, particularly from a person of a different race, might have an effect on their future offspring. The wide use of transfusions in recent years, accompanied by no more than the usual number of genetic surprises, seems to have put an end to this notion. Even now we hear the word *blood* used figuratively for heredity. But we now know that an individual's physical inheritance comes to him in the form of two microscopic packages, one from his mother and one from his father, which consist of solid cellular material. The nature of what is in these tiny packages has become known very slowly.

One of the difficulties of the "blood" theory of inheritance was that it did not explain the maintenance of human diversity from one generation to another. If the hereditary process consisted of mingling portions of two fluids into a homogeneous mixture, we would expect that all children of the same parents would be alike, except for difference in sex. This is obviously not the case. Furthermore, if the heredity of the individual represented a complete mixing of the heredity of the parents, and this process continued for a number of generations, individual differences within a population would gradually be lost as all the variations were slowly averaged out. Yet, though we may speak of a large population as a "melting pot," in a figurative sense, no homogeneous alloy has ever been formed; every known population continues to have a variety of different-looking people in it.

PARTICULATE INHERITANCE

The solution is found in the theory of *particulate inheritance*, which holds that the material of heredity consists of minute but indivisible units that are redistributed and recombined in the genetic process, but which are not altered or diluted by any combination in which they temporarily appear. (For example, we may deal and shuffle a deck of cards as often as we wish, and the deck always consists of aces, deuces, and three's, and so on; the shuffling never produces "$1\frac{1}{2}$'s" or "$3\frac{1}{4}$'s".) This explanation was first perceived a little over a hundred years ago, and further work since that time has clarified and extended the theory, without ever revealing any serious inconsistencies in it.

The particulate theory of inheritance was derived from a series of experiments on plants, and was published by Gregor Mendel in 1866. (See Bibliography.) He worked mainly with the garden pea, a plant that normally self-fertilizes its flowers, but permits artificial crosses between different plants. From these experiments Mendel derived basic laws of inheritance which have been found to apply not only to plants, but to animals of all kinds, from insects to man. It was necessary in early investigation to choose for study characteristics in which individuals of the same species showed clear-cut differences from one another, with no doubtful or intermediate classes. Thus, in his peas, Mendel found that some traits of the seeds were appropriate for study: color, whether green or yellow (there were only these two alternatives), and surface texture, whether wrinkled or smooth (he found no intermediates). In more complex organisms like man, traits often cannot be divided into distinct classes. However, certain reactions of the blood cells, which we call *blood groups*, are easily distinguished, and such traits can be used to show that human heredity follows the same genetic laws that Mendel formulated for plants.

An easy example may be taken from the "M–N" blood groups, in which every human may be classified as type M, N, or MN, according to whether his blood gives a positive test for one or both of two antigens, M and N. To study the inheritance of such traits in man, we must find families in which the parents show various different combinations of blood groups, and then tabulate the blood groups that appear in the children of these families. When the families are sorted out according to the blood group combinations of the parents, we find, as we might expect, that the parents' blood group will predict to some extent that of the children. In the case of the M–N blood-group system, with its three possible blood types, there are six possible family combinations, as shown in Table 1. (We do not specify which parent is father and which is mother, because in this case it makes no difference.)

Looking at this data from a common-sense viewpoint, we see no surprises in the first two types of family (M + M and N + N). In these cases the two parents are alike, and all the children resemble their parents. In the third and fourth types (M + MN and N + MN), the parents differ, and half the children take after one parent, and half take after the other. But in the fifth type, M + N, this does not occur. The children are all MN, apparently combining the blood groups of the two parents. Why were the children in this case not half M and half N? In the sixth type of family, MN + MN, we might logically expect that because the parents were of the same blood group, all the children would be MN like both parents, as in families of types one and two. Instead, we see the whole range of blood types of the M–N system in the children of these families, and half of them (the M and the N children), are not like either parent.

An important point to note in the family data is that where the children's blood groups are not all alike, the ratios tend to be very simple ones—halves and quarters. We can interpret this, as Mendel

TABLE 2 PHENOTYPES AND GENOTYPES OF THE
M-N BLOOD GROUPS

Phenotype (Blood group as tested)	Genotype (Underlying combination of two genes)
M	M + M or "MM"
N	N + N or "NN"
MN	M + N or "MN"

did, to indicate that the underlying mechanism is a simple one.

A successful hypothesis, which can explain all of these events, was derived by Mendel from his plant experiments. He proposed that for each distinct trait, every individual possessed two deter- miners, or *genes*, one of which he had received from his father, and one from his mother. One of these (and *only* one) he would pass on to any one of his children. Mendel further proposed that which of his two genes a parent passed on to any particular child was deter- mined purely by chance. In order to fit the blood-group data into such a scheme, we assume that an individual of M blood type has two M genes, that a person of N blood type has two N genes, and that person of MN type has one M and one N. We now have to distinguish between *phenotype*, the trait that we observe (in this case, the blood type evaluated in the laboratory), and *genotype*, the combi- nation of genes that we suppose to underlie it, as in Table 2.

These relations indicate that the gene M, when present, causes the production of the substance M that we detect in the blood, that gene N produces the substance N, and that the production of both substances occurs if both genes are present. We can now apply this knowledge of the genotypes to the explanation of the parent and child combinations that appear. A general division of genotypes is made into *homozygotes*, which have two similar genes (as MM or NN), and *heterozygotes*, which have two different genes, as MN.

To start with the most complicated case, as shown in Figure 13. If both parents are MN (heterozygotes), each may give either his M gene or his N gene to a particular child. Children who receive the father's M may receive from the mother either M or N: In the first case (No. 1 in the diagram), their blood type will be M (genotype MM); in the second case (No. 2 in the diagram), it will be MN. Other children will receive gene N from the father. These, accord- ing to whether they receive the mother's M (No. 3 in the diagram), or the mother's N (No. 4 in the diagram), will have blood group MN or N (genotype NN). Because the blood group that results in the child does not depend on which parent contributed a gene, "MN" and "NM" in Figure 13 are equivalent. Numerically, the chances of a child's receiving a particular combination are the same as coming

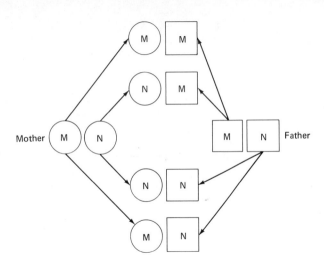

Figure 13 The recombinations of genes from two MN parents. Genes derived from the mother are indicated by circles; those from the father by squares.

up heads or tails in two tosses of a coin. The chances of getting heads in both tosses are one-fourth (compare this to MM). The chances of getting one head and one tail are one-half, regardless of which comes first (compare this to MN, regardless of which gene comes from which parent.) The last one-fourth chance is of getting tails in both tosses (compare this to NN). Of course, in any one family or small number of families, just as in a limited session of coin-tossing, the 25 per cent and 50 per cent *probabilities* would not produce this exact distribution of results, even if every family had just four children. But in a set of data including many families, these proportions would be closely approximated.

A simpler case is seen in the families where one parent is M (genotype MM), the other N (genotype NN). Here each child must receive an M gene from the MM parent and an N gene from the NN parent, and must have the blood type MN, exactly as the tabulation shows. In the third type, M + MN, each child in the family must receive an M from the first parent, and may receive either an M or an N from the second parent, thus giving two possible blood types, M and MN in about equal numbers. The fourth type of family, N + MN, is very similar to the third, with N and MN being two alternatives. In the first and second types of families, where only one of the two genes is present in either parent, all children will be alike and homozygous. Thus the hypothesis that explained the most complicated case explains also the simpler ones, as we might have expected.

The M–N blood-group system is relatively easy to study because an individual's phenotype always indicates exactly what his genotype is. But the matter is not always so simple, as in the case of the traits Mendel first studied. An instance of a trait in which genotypes are not completely known from phenotypes is found in the familiar A–B–O blood-group system. In this system we have three genes, A, B, and O, and four phenotypes, A, B, AB, and O. If there were a population in which only the A and B genes were present (there is not), there would be three phenotypes, A, B, and AB, which would show a pattern of inheritance exactly like that of the phenotypes M, N, and MN. However, the O gene bears a special relation to A and B, which confuses the picture. There are no phenotypes AO or BO. That is to say, blood of an individual with the AO genotype tests the same as that from an individual with genotype AA, and the BO genotype produces the same blood type as BB. This relation is called dominance. The A and B genes are said to be dominant to the O gene, and the O gene to be recessive to A and B. The presence of an O gene is completely concealed if an A or a B gene is present in the same individual. Only if a person has the genotype OO does his blood fall into the O blood group.

This dominance-recessiveness phenomenon has some odd results. For instance, it is possible for two individuals of A or B phenotype to have a child of blood group O. If both are heterozygotes, either AO or BO, some of their children—about one-fourth of the total—can combine an O gene from one parent with an O gene from the other parent and have genotype OO and blood group O (Figure 14). Often in human families, some trait will appear in a child which is present in neither parent, though the trait may be known to have occurred in the family in a previous generation. This reappearance of a character after it has apparently disappeared in intermediate generations, popularly called a throwback, is frequently the result of a recessive gene that produced no detectable effect in heterozygous parents but later is recognized in the homozygous child. This happens often enough that even people ignorant of genetics will say, "Oh yes, he must have got that from Grandpa Brown." Often, too, a child may show some trait resulting from a recessive gene which last showed itself so far back in the family that it has been completely forgotten.

Mendel, with carefully planned experiments, proceeded to dem-

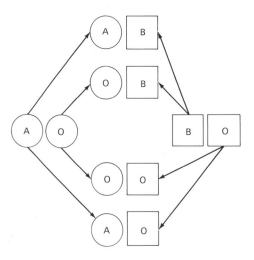

Figure 14 Emergence of a recessive: an O phenotype from A and B parents (third child from top).

onstrate that the genes continued to be passed on from generation to generation for as long as he wished to continue the experiments, and that the ratios of the various traits in the offspring continued to confirm the hypothesis he had set up. Of course he had an advantage in dealing with a plant that had a generation length of just one year, and so was able to trace many successive generations in a way that is not possible in human families. He also showed that various traits of the same plant—seed color and surface texture of the seed, for instance—were passed from parent to offspring independently of one another. A cross between plants, one of which had smooth green seeds, and the other wrinkled yellow seeds, and which were both taken from stocks that had bred true to type for a number of generations, could produce descendants combining the color and texture traits quite impartially, including plants with wrinkled green seeds and plants with smooth yellow seeds, as well as plants with the original combinations of traits. (We will spare our present readers the details of how this works out when dominance is involved in both gene pairs.) This principle, which Mendel called the *law of independent assortment*, is easy to see in man. Every family has discussed the features and complexions of its children, and looked for resemblances to one parent or the other (usually beginning when the baby is too small to resemble anybody). The usual conclusion is that though a child may "favor" one parent or the other in some of its more conspicuous characteristics, it usually has a combination of assorted bits of the phenotype of both parents, with some elements, as we have already mentioned, that can only be traced, if at all, to some ancestor further back. This independent inheritance of different traits also accounts for the fact that no ancestor is ever entirely duplicated in any of his descendants. In dealing with traits that are clearly defined, such as the blood groups, we can show this in man as clearly as in the experimental plant or animal. For instance, in a family in which the genes for the B blood group and those for the M blood group are known to have been introduced by the same ancestor, all the rest of the ancestors carrying only A, O, and N genes, we can show that in later generations the B and the M genes will be distributed independently among the descendants, with both appearing in the same individual only by chance (Figure 15).

CHROMOSOMES

Gregor Mendel lived in a small monastery in Germany, and his work was presented to and published by an obscure provincial scientific society. Thus its significance was not understood until 34 years later. Then, by repetition of Mendel's experiments and by similar experiments on many other plants and animals, it was found that a very basic law of inheritance had been discovered. Biologists

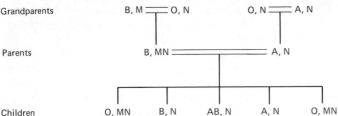

| Grandparents | B, M ⚌ O, N | | O, N ⚌ A, N |
| Parents | B, MN ══════════════ A, N |

| Children | O, MN | B, N | AB, N | A, N | O, MN |

Figure 15 Recombination of the A–B–O and M–N blood groups in three generations of a family. Only the fourth child shows the same combination of A-B-O and M-N blood groups as either parent or any of the grandparents. None of the children duplicates the first grandparent who introduced both B and M to the family.

who had studied tissues microscopically soon realized that Mendel's determiners of heredity, now named *genes,* behaved in a way remarkably similar to certain minute structures, called *chromosomes,* which had already been observed in animal and plant cells. (The name *chromosome* refers to their tendency to take on color from an artificial dye, and was given them on a purely descriptive basis, before their significance was understood.)

Chromosomes are found in the nucleus of the living cell, and one of their striking characteristics is that they occur in pairs. The number of pairs of chromosomes is very constant within a given species, though it may vary widely between species. When, during the process of growth, a body cell divides to form two daughter cells, the chromosomes are also duplicated; therefore, each daughter cell has a set of chromosomes just like the parent cell. (This fact alone suggested that chromosomes were very important.) But when cells divided to form germ cells—the special cells that are destined to come together from two parents to form a new individual— something different occurs. The chromosomes divide in such a way that each germ cell contains only one of each pair of chromosomes. If a normal body cell in a given species contains twelve chromosomes, the germ cell contains only six. But when a male and a female germ cell combine to form a new individual, twelve chromosomes are present in the combined unit, called the *zygote,* and so the new individual starts life with the normal number of chromosomes for his species, arranged in proper pairs. This had been observed in microscopic studies before Mendel's experiments became known.

A great advance was made when it was realized that if the genes were located in the chromosomes, all Mendel's laws of inheritance could be explained (Sutton, 1903). If chromosomes had places reserved in them for particular genes, then the matched pairs of chromosomes would carry matched pairs of genes, just as Mendel's laws required. When germ cells were formed, each germ cell, receiving only one chromosome of a given pair, would receive one and *only* one, of each pair of genes. Half the germ cells would have one of each pair, half the other. And when two germ cells came together to form a new individual, each individual would have one determiner from each of his parents, exactly as Mendel's theory anticipated. Thus the known manner of transmission of chromosomes from parent to child was exactly similar to the apparent transmission of genes.

The hypothesis of the gene as a unit located on a chromosome suggested another line of investigation. If two traits were determined by genes located in different chromosome pairs, this explained Mendel's law of *independent assortment;* but if they were located on the same pair of chromosomes, their inheritance would not be independent. Even though paired chromosomes sometimes break and recombine so as to trade corresponding portions with one another (a process called *crossing-over,* which is actually visible under the microscope), genes located close together on the same chromosome would more often than not be transmitted to the same germ cell and the same offspring; that is, Mendel's law of independent assortment would not hold true in these cases. Further investigation showed that this did sometimes occur: some genes were "linked" by location in the same chromosome and might remain together for a number of generations before a chromosome break at exactly the right point separated them. The phenomenon of *linkage* has not been important in human genetics, because man has so many pairs of chromosomes that the chances of two identifiable genes being located on the same chromosome are rather small, but some instances of linkage are known.

The gene, which originally was an abstraction (just as the atom once was), became more real in 1933, when attention was called to chromosomes in the salivary glands of certain flies. These chromosomes were of monstrous size, compared with chromosomes in other tissues of the body, and exhibited thick and thin portions like erratic strings of beads (Painter, 1933). Because the genetics of these insects was well-known, it was possible to correlate gene locations, as determined by studies of linkage, with these visible details. Eventually, after intensive study, the present concept of the gene was arrived at: a segment of a chromosome containing a special linear arrangement of molecules. Therefore, Mendel's different traits—such as green versus yellow seed color—can be thought of as the result of slightly different molecular patterns at particular points in a chromosome. This relationship of gene and chromosome is expressed by the term *locus,* which means the place in a chromosome where the gene affecting a particular trait is found. The various different molecular patterns which may occur at a particular locus are called *allelic genes* or *alleles.* Even the biochemical details of the way in which chromosomes duplicate themselves when new sets are required at the time of cell division, are now understood.

The modern concept of the gene is subtly altered by its having taken corporeal form. As an abstraction, it was a mere point on the chromosome; now it has a length, and we may ask what that length is. The answer is rather indefinite. It had been known for some time that a gene, brought into proximity with another by crossing-over, might appear to have its effect slightly altered—the *position effect*. Probably the chromosome should not be thought of as a chain of entirely distinct and independent "genes." The functional unit of the chromosome, which we recognize by its observable effect on the individual, cannot be defined exactly in terms of a specific number of adjacent molecules; and we cannot say, "Here one gene leaves off and another begins." We may sometimes speak of a *complex gene*, meaning a relatively long sequence of molecules, or we may refer to a *close linkage group*—meaning a sequence of which the parts sometimes, but only rarely, separate—and mean essentially the same thing by both terms. However, for most purposes, including discussion of human genetics—which is not nearly so well known as that of other animals—we can reasonably speak of genes as distinct units, though we realize that their unitary nature is slightly fuzzy.

THE RELATION OF GENE TO TRAIT

What is the relation of the gene, in any of its various stages of abstraction, to the *trait* which it controls? When the laws of heredity were first being worked out, the relationship was considered to be a simple one—largely because nothing was known about it. Actually it is extremely complex, involving the biochemistry and physiology of the whole organism. Most of the internal workings of the animal body are carried on, not in a mechanical fashion, but in a chemical one. The first step in the process by which energy is utilized by the body consists of the conversion of various foodstuffs into secondary products that can be absorbed and used. Only a few items in the diet, such as glucose, a form of sugar that occurs naturally in various fruits, can be used by the body immediately. Other substances must be chemically changed within the digestive system before they can be absorbed and used. These changes are brought about by *enzymes,* themselves chemical substances with rather complex molecules, which cause alterations in other organic substances by their mere presence, without being used up in the process. Without the highly efficient operation of enzymes, life would not be possible. A typical digestive enzyme is *lactase,* which is secreted by the small intestine and breaks down lactose (milk sugar) into a form in which it can be taken into the bloodstream through the wall of the intestine. Another important enzyme, probably the best known to the general public, is *insulin,* which is secreted into the bloodstream, and further breaks down sugars into forms that can be used for energy production by body cells. Some individuals may fail to produce one of these enzymes. An individual without lactase suffers severe indigestion after drinking milk, as the result of the fermen-

tation of undigested lactose; the individual who lacks insulin develops diabetes because of the accumulation of unused sugar in his blood.

The enzymes that are secreted into the digestive tract, or circulate in the blood, are only the beginning, however. Many enzymes are produced in, and remain within, individual cells; here they regulate transformations, often involving long chain reactions, by which substances necessary for the function of the cells are produced, or energy stored and released. The sum total of these processes is called *metabolism* (which essentially means *conversion*), and is made possible by a variety of enzymes present in each individual cell. Thus the normal functions of the body depend on the production of many separate enzymes, each responsible for one step in metabolism. The science dealing with these processes is called *biochemistry*, and the individual processes are referred to as *biochemical* or *metabolic*.

The relationship between genetics and biochemistry came to be understood through two lines of investigation. In 1909, it was shown that certain metabolic abnormalities in man appeared to be inherited in Mendelian fashion (Garrod, 1909). These "inborn errors of metabolism" can be traced to the absence of some enzyme necessary to normal metabolic processes. This can result in the accumulation of a useless or even dangerous substance in the body, or it can result in a lack of a substance which should have been produced. The genetic nature of these abnormalities suggested that absent genes might result in deficient enzymes. (The best known of metabolic errors in man, diabetes, is still not fully understood genetically, probably because dietary differences cause some susceptible individuals to develop the disease although others do not.)

A number of years later investigators, working with the one-celled organisms called bacteria, found genetic variants that were unable to utilize certain food substances present in the medium in which they were grown. (Bacteria do not reproduce in a standard sexual fashion; but they do have genes controlling their metabolism, and in some ways are easier to study than multicellular organisms.) Even these simple organisms, then, have individual variations. The differences in food utilization were found to be the result of different enzymes present in different strains. These observations again indicated that genes were closely related to enzymes; not that they were enzymes themselves, as first thought, but that they were permanent units in the cell, necessary for the production of enzyme molecules (Beadle and Tatum, 1941).

Production of an enzyme by a gene still leaves us rather far from the visible traits that Mendel, and many after him, have studied in living organisms—though in some cases we can trace the way in which the presence of the enzyme leads to an observed trait. The biochemical processes that are mediated by enzymes are often complicated, involving a series of steps that must take place in a definite order, with each step requiring the assistance of a separate enzyme. Thus, in the formation of *melanin*, the common dark pigment of skin, hair, and eyes, a series of colorless precursor substances is produced in a fixed order by the action of several enzymes. The process culminates in the formation, by the action of a final enzyme, of melanin pigment that is visible by its dark color. If an individual does not have the gene necessary to produce a certain key enzyme, he is an *albino*, i.e., an individual with no melanin in any part of the body. If he has the gene necessary to produce the essential enzyme, melanin will be formed; but other genes, by way of the enzymes they produce, may affect the amount of melanin formed, often acting differently in the hair, skin, and eyes of the same individual. In the case of the hair, still other genes determine whether the melanin formed is brown or red in color.

The example of albinism, incidentally, sheds some light on the meaning of dominance and recessiveness. Albinism is a recessive gene, i.e., an individual requires only one normal gene of a certain pair to have normal melanin formation, although most of us have two such normal genes. Because the amount of enzyme required for a biochemical reaction is very small, it is likely that in such cases one nonalbino gene can produce enough enzyme for the whole process of pigment formation to be carried out as usual. This is not always the case; in the inheritance of flower color in certain plants, for instance, the heterozygous individuals have pink flowers, intermediate between the red and white colors of the two homozygotes. Here, apparently, the exact amount of enzyme determines the shade of color. This leads to the idea that recessive genes are blanks which produce no functional enzyme at all. This may be generally if not always true.

The step-by-step action of enzymes means that often several or many genes must act together to produce a particular result. Another complication of what we once thought to be a simple relation between gene and trait is seen in the phenomenon called *pleiotropism*. This term describes the situation in which a single gene affects more than one process. In fact the normal-color (as opposed to albino) gene is an example of this, because it affects the color of all pigmented parts of the body, though we may think of the colors of different parts (skin, hair, and eye, for instance), as separate traits. It is probable that in many less obvious cases a single gene, through its enzyme, may affect a number of biochemical processes whose visible final results are not apparently related. For instance, in a number of mammals, including man, there occurs a condition in which the skin is unpigmented, the hair white, the eyes blue, and the individual congenitally deaf (Searle, 1968). This distinctive combination of traits is the result of a single gene that interferes with development at an early embryonic stage, and which acts similarly in a number of species.

Another type of gene interaction involves *polygenes*: that is, genes at more than one locus affecting the same trait. In the early days of genetics, the determination of size characteristics of the body appeared to present an exception to the theory of particulate inheritance. Such traits do not fall into distinct classes: they vary over a large range, from smallest to largest, and it is obvious that any kind of division into classes, such as small, medium, and large, is arbitrary. However, this can be interpreted in terms of a number of independent gene pairs at different loci. If the size characteristics of the adult animal are the result of the combined effect of alleles at several different loci, and if at each locus there is a choice of alleles, one that stimulates the growth of the body or of some part of it, and another that does not, animals carrying different combinations of these genes will be of a variety of sizes. If, for instance, there were three such loci, each carrying a pair of genes partially responsible for some body dimension, an individual with a total of six genes at these three loci might have any combination from six "small" genes and no "large" genes to six "large" genes and no "small" ones. If the genes at the various loci had exactly the same affect on size, there would then be a series of seven possible sizes, from smallest to largest. If, as is more likely, the alleles at different loci have somewhat different degrees of influence on size, and in addition some nongenetic factors (nutrition, health, and so on) affect body size as well, the theoretical division into seven size classes would blur, and therefore appear continuous. Careful study of crosses between large and small strains of various animals showed that size inheritance could in fact be explained in this way (Castle, 1929). Animal breeders had already developed large and small breeds of various domestic animals. Rabbits were one of the choices of the geneticist, because they were large enough to measure accurately but not too expensive to feed. It was suspected that these breeds differed from one another by more than one pair of genes involved in growth and size. When the strains were crossed, the first generation offspring were intermediate in size between the parent breeds, and rather uniform in size. But later generations of the mixed stock were variable in size, with a few individuals approaching the extreme sizes of the parent breeds. It is easy to see that the first generation hybrids would all have half of their size-determining genes from the small breeds, half from the large one, and would be of intermediate size. But if genes at several loci were inherited independently, individuals in later generations could differ from one another by having more or fewer of the genes from the large breed. As suggested earlier, let us assume a fairly simple case: with three loci involved. The chances are one out of two that an individual will receive a "large" gene as any one of his possible six genes, and the distribution of the body dimension within the hybrid population will resemble that of sets of six tosses of a coin. The smallest individuals would be those who drew six Tails on the six tosses; the next largest, those who drew five Tails and one Head, and so forth. The mathematical distribution of the seven possibilities of coin tosses is shown in Figure 16. It is a remarkable fact that this type of bell-shaped curve corresponds very closely to the distribution of size characteristics of hybrid populations, and therefore confirms the polygene hypothesis of size inheritance. Significant also is the fact that this curve resembles the normal distribu-

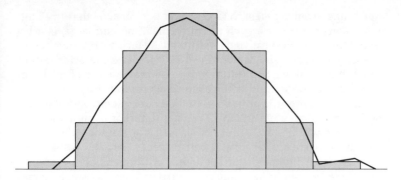

Figure 16   Comparison of the coin-tossing distribution $(x+y)^6$ with the stature distribution of 174 young American women.

tion of size characteristics in natural species, indicating that natural populations resemble the experimental hybrid ones in having a variety of alternate genes at many loci.

GENETICS OF SEX DIFFERENCES

So far we have discussed typical chromosome pairs in which the two chromosomes of any pair contain the same series of loci for various sets of alleles. Paired chromosomes can actually be seen to join company and lie side by side in the early part of the formation of a germ cell; this is the time when the exchange of portions called crossing-over takes place. At other times in the life of the various cells, the chromosomes are scattered around the nucleus of a cell without regard to pairing. At these times the chromosomes of a pair may be recognized by their appearance. The paired chromosomes are similar in size and shape, as we might expect from the fact that they contain the same loci in the same order. To study the chromosomes, we crush a single cell and examine the spread-out cell material under a microscope. Sometimes, after we have matched up and paired off the chromosomes in the cell, two are left which do not match, one being much larger than the other. In mammals this situation is found only in the cells of males. The unmatched chromosomes of the male consist of a larger chromosome, which is called the "X" and a smaller chromosome, which is called the "Y," whereas the female of the same species will have a matched pair of the X shape and size. This proved to be the explanation of how an individual's sex is determined, and why most organisms produce male and female offspring in approximately equal numbers. These sex chromosome pairs, XX in the female and XY in the male, divide, just as do other pairs, in the formation of germ cells. Each ovum contains one of the X chromosomes of the mother. A sperm cell receives from the father either his X or his Y. When ova and sperm combine, half of the zygotes have two X's and will produce a female; half have one X and one Y, and will produce a male.

The X chromosomes contain a series of loci with alleles, which have been studied in the same way as those in the *somatic* chromosomes (i.e., those other than sex chromosomes). Certain peculiarities of inheritance are found when a trait is determined by a gene in the X chromosome. A trait may occur in both sexes but be much more common in one sex than in the other. A familiar example is color-blindness in man. This trait is fairly common in males but quite rare in females. It is the result of a recessive allele carried in the X chromosome. The Y chromosome, which is quite different from the X, cannot carry either this gene or its dominant allele. Therefore, if a male receives the "color-blind" allele in his one X chromosome, it cannot be counteracted by a dominant allele, and he will be color-blind. The female, however, will not be color-blind unless she carries the recessive allele in both of her X chromosomes. If the recessive sex-linked allele is relatively uncommon, only 10 per cent gene frequency, this makes considerable difference. The number of males showing the recessive trait will be equal to the gene frequency, that is 10 per cent, but the number of affected females will be only one per cent (gene frequency squared). The sex-linked trait also shows a characteristic pattern in pedigrees. A son cannot inherit a sex-linked trait from his father, because only the daughters receive the father's X chromosome. The daughter of such a man will carry the sex-linked gene, but usually will not show the trait (she will show it only if she happened to receive a recessive gene from her mother as well as from her father). However, the trait is likely to reappear in one of the daughter's sons. Thus, the trait usually skips a generation, transmitted from grandfather to grandson through a female who is not herself affected.

The presence of sex-linked alleles, then, may cause certain traits to occur with different frequency in the two sexes. In general, however, those differences between the sexes that are fairly consistent are brought about in a different way. The Y chromosome has been a puzzle. As we have seen, it does not appear to carry alleles that are similar to those carried by the X, or capable of interacting with X chromosome alleles by dominance. Considerable search has been made for any distinctive genes carried by the Y chromosome only. If such genes existed, we should be able to find certain traits that were transmitted by a father to all his sons, and to his sons only, and through them to all his descendants in the male line. Inheritance of this kind has not been successfully demonstrated. Recently, however, we have learned more about the functions of the Y chromosome as a result of careful counts of chromosomes in many individuals. An individual's sex can be determined by examining a single cell to see whether the sex chromosome formula is XX or XY, although this is generally the hard way to do it. Extensive studies have revealed that there are rare individuals who do not have either of the conventional formulas. Although they often show some abnormalities (as do those with abnormal numbers of somatic chromosomes as well) they develop normally into one sex or the other insofar as basic anatomical differences go. An individual with a single X chromosome and no Y is anatomically female: one with two X's and a Y is anatomically male. These and other combinations show that the determination of sex does not depend at all on the number of X chromosomes, but depends on whether a Y chromosome is present. Thus the sole function of the Y chromosome, apparently, is to determine the sex of the individual.

The Y chromosome does not appear to affect development directly after the point in early embryonic life when it throws the switch to make the individual a male. Subsequently the gonad— testis or ovary, according to whether the individual is to be a male or a female—controls the development of sex differences. This becomes particularly conspicuous at the time of puberty, when the gonads produce the characteristic hormones that result in the development of what are called the secondary sex characteristics. The testicular hormone of the male stimulates the growth of body hair and beard, increases muscle size, and causes rapid growth of the larynx, making the voice change. The ovarian hormones in the female stimulate the growth of glandular tissue in the breast and cause deposition of fat in this and other areas of the body. In both sexes the actual reproductive organs increase in size at this time, also as a result of hormone secretion. These are only the most conspicuous of the changes brought about by the sex hormones. It is interesting to note that the whole process of developing the individual into one sex or the other is highly coordinated, starting with the primary effect of the Y chromosome in producing basic anatomical maleness, and ending with the continuing physiological effects of the sex hormones, which differ according to whether a testis or ovary has developed at the time of the primary differentiation. The control of secondary sex differences has been extensively studied in experimental animals, because hormones may be administered or withdrawn to ascertain their effects; but aside from such artificial procedures, sex differentiation, once started, continues automatically to completion.

Sometimes a second look may be required to determine whether or not a trait usually occurring only in males is sex-linked or is influenced by sex in some other way. A common example is baldness, which occurs in a distinctive form in many men, but only rarely and atypically in women. This might well be a sex-linked trait. But more careful study reveals that this type of baldness is often apparently inherited by a son from his father—which is not possible for a sex-linked trait. In some families this might occur if the mother happened, by coincidence, to be a carrier of the allele responsible. But enough data has been collected to show that this is not the case. Further clinical data from persons with abnormal hormonal balance has shown a complex situation. The predisposition to baldness is inherited as an ordinary nonsex-linked trait. But whether hair loss actually takes place in the susceptible individual

TABLE 3 SOME SEX DIFFERENCES

	Males	Females	Ratio Female Male
Stature	175.6 cm.	163.1 cm.	.93
Arm Length	76.5	69.8	.91
Sitting Height	91.3	86.4	.94
Shoulder Breadth	39.6	35.6	.90
Hip breadth	29.8	28.9	.97
Head Circumference	56.9	55.0	.97
Forehead Breadth	10.5	10.2	.97
Face Breadth	13.7	12.9	.94
Face Length	12.3	11.3	.91
Relative Arm Length	.436	.428	
Relative Sitting Height	.520	.530	
Shoulder Hip Index	.753	.813	

These figures are taken from a series of 126 males and 174 females, of American white ancestry, mostly brothers and sisters of the same families.

depends on the presence and kind of sex hormones. Such a trait is called *sex-limited*.

Sex differences must always be allowed for in comparing various traits between individuals and populations. All other things being equal genetically, the female will differ from the male in size characteristics as well as in development of hair, and so forth. Yet, in the interaction of sex and genetic variability, variation not related to sex may often override the six difference—as when, in the same population, we find a number of the tallest women to be taller than the shortest men. It is most important, of course, in collecting anthropological data, to keep the sexes separate in the records and in statistical analysis. This is most keenly appreciated by those who attempt to judge the body size of an ancient people by examination of skeletal remains. If we misjudge a few male skeletons as female, we may estimate the body size of the population to have been greater than it really was because of these "big women." It is interesting to examine the relative sex differences in various body dimensions. In most populations, average female stature is about 93 per cent of that of males. The difference is relatively greater in face length, particularly in dimensions of the lower jaw, and in measurements of hands and feet; in contrast the breadth across the forehead and the circumference of the head are more nearly equal in the two sexes. (Table 3). We can also evaluate sex difference by dividing the total amount of variation in a dimension into the portion associated with sex and the portion which is the result of other genetic causes. Then we can compare the amount of individual variation that is seen in the entire population with the smaller amount found within either sex taken separately. In a moderately heterogeneous white American population, the amount of variation in stature within one sex is about 58 per cent of the total amount of variation among all individuals regardless of sex, and thus the sex hormones account for only 42 per cent of total variability in body size in a single population. Compared with the variability of the entire human species, with all races considered together, sex differences would appear even less.

The distinctness of the sexes is usually overestimated by society. It is, to be sure, the only trait by which all human beings can be placed into one of two reasonably clear-cut categories. Shoe manufacturers are convinced that women's feet differ from men's feet in shape as well as in size; they do—but only after a number of years of wearing shoes constructed on this theory. And clothiers have extrapolated rather far from biology in decreeing that women's coats shall have the buttons on the left and the buttonholes on the right, and that men's coats shall be vice versa!

STUDYING GENETICS IN MAN

The human species presents all kinds of obstacles to the study of its genetics. It did not take long to find out that the rules are the same as for other animals and, for that matter, plants. In some respects, man seems to have more traits that are controlled polygenically— that is, by the combined action of alleles at several different loci— than do most of the species used for genetic experiments. Part of the difficulty is in the point of view. The research geneticist is interested in variable traits that can be studied to clarify genetic laws: he picks and chooses the traits he studies with this in mind. The anthropologist is interested in variable traits in man simply because they are variable, even though they may be quite unsuitable for strictly genetic study. Aside from this, however, there are objective problems in studying the genetics of man. For one thing, a human generation spans a long time. Experimental animals may have generation times of only one year or less, so that the investigator may study many successive generations in his breeding colony. In studying man, he deals with a species having a generation time the same as his own. Studying the genetics of elephants would present the same difficulty, but people are not so interested in elephants, and, in fact, the genetics of elephants is a virtually untouched field. Also, human matings cannot be programmed by the geneticist, so that he must go out and look for matings that happen to demonstrate some genetic point, rather than setting them up at will. And again, both as a result of the long generation and of the randomness of human matings, it is often impossible to know what recessive genes a human individual may carry. Mendel might never have discovered his laws if he had not dealt with a plant that normally self-fertilized its flowers and thus naturally produced a great preponderance of homozygous individuals. Experimental animals can be inbred for generations to approximate this condition of homozygosity; man, we have to take the way he is.

One way in which the problem of generation length can be solved to some extent in human genetics is by using traits that do not change at all with age. Blood groups and other serologic traits are present at birth and remain the same throughout the individual's life. Thus we can collect data of this kind on parents and children, often on grandparents as well, all at the same time. The data are comparable even though the subjects differ in age by many years. In contrast, the study of stature in families becomes difficult because by the time the children have attained their full growth the parents have often reached the age when they begin to shrink appreciably. So many traits of man change during the growth years, and again, in different ways, during adulthood, that simultaneous observations on family members of different ages introduce many unknown factors into the data. This, then, is a serious limitation on the kinds of traits that can be studied genetically in human families. Another way of avoiding the difficulties of the long generation in man is to study traits that are so obvious that they can be recorded on the basis of hearsay information about persons no longer living, traits observed in old photographs, or taken from medical records. Some defects and abnormalities can be studied over many generations in this way: hereditary disease conditions, albinism, extra fingers and toes, certain peculiar facial features, or even a fairly common condition such as baldness. Here again, however, the selection of traits for study is limited and rather depressingly pathological. Yet a compendium of human genetics shows that such are the traits on which most work in human genetics has been done (McKusick, 1968).

Another previously mentioned problem is that many interesting and important characteristics of man are determined polygenically, and cannot be explained by any single easily traced gene. Anthropologists have had help on this problem. Animal breeders, interested in such traits as body size, growth rates, and milk production, have had to deal with polygenically determined traits also, and have developed methods for studying them (Falconer, 1960). It is possible in such cases to determine the extent to which a trait is inherited without identifying particular alleles or loci. In many of these traits, in animals as well as man, the effects of multiple genes interact with environmental factors such as nutrition in such a way that the trait cannot be said to be entirely controlled by either heredity or environment. What is of interest is an estimate of *how much* of the total variation observed is due to genetic factors and how much to other factors. This could be done by totally standardizing external factors in the development and way of life of a population, and seeing how much variation is left. This is difficult to do even for domestic animals, impossible for man. An animal population so inbred that every member is genetically identical can be used to determine the effects of environment exactly. This is a common experimental approach. This of course is also impossible for man. But within a population having a variety of genotypes as well as a range of variation in environmental factors, we can observe whether genetically related individuals resemble each other more closely than unrelated individuals, and if so, how much more closely. Even this becomes complicated in man, because closely related persons generally share a home, that may be distinctive in diet and way of life, even as compared with other families in the same social class. In this case, some "family resemblances" may result from common experience and environment as well as from common heredity. The geneticist therefore looks for special cases, such as identical twins who have been separated at birth when one or both were adopted into other families. We are all familiar with the remarkable resemblance of identical twins in visible physical traits. In characteristics such as blood groups, which are precisely defined though not apparent to ordinary inspection, they are identical also. Such twins are in fact genetically identical, for they are the result of the splitting of a single fertilized ovum into two parts, each with the same set of genes, which then proceed to develop into separate individuals. Thus the rearing of identical twins in different families serves as an unplanned experiment, demonstrating how the same individual might have turned out if raised in two different ways. These studies have shown that not only physical characteristics, but such traits as temperament and aptitudes, have a genetic basis. In conjunction with the studies of identical twins reared apart, those reared together have been studied for comparison.

Other situations that have been studied are ordinary brothers and sisters reared together or apart; unrelated children adopted and reared in the same families, and so forth. These indirect approaches to human inheritance have given us much information that could not have been obtained in any other way. We must keep in mind certain features of this kind of study that may be misleading. The results of the study tell us how much of the total variation within the sample studied is due to inheritance and how much to environment: the *heritability* of a trait, a figure which may vary from 0 to 1.0, represents the inherited component taken as a fraction of the total variation. If the sample we have studied comes from a limited and rather uniform environment, the hereditary component will appear larger and the heritability higher than if we had used a sample that included environmental conditions of a more varied kind. Similarly, a sample from a population that was genetically uniform, though the individuals in it were not obviously related to one another, would make environment appear to be the prime source of variation—which, though true for this group, might not be true for a population having a normal amount of genetic variation. These problems have made heritability a rich source of partisan arguments.

POPULATION GENETICS

Genetics, as we have so far described it, makes it possible, in theory at least, to define all of an individual's hereditary characteristics. If all the genes of man and their exact effects were known, we could, by listing an individual's genes, give exact specifications as to how he was to be constructed. The genes do, in fact, give such instructions to the developing body, but only the living substance itself knows how to read the blueprint; science is far from understanding the code. The comprehensiveness of these genetic instructions to the growing organism is reflected in the remarkable likeness of identical twins. Even with our imperfect knowledge of the genetic code of man, however, we can define an individual to some degree. For instance, we can define individuals well enough in most cases to say whether or not it is possible for a person to have been the parent of a particular child; this answers legal questions of legitimacy, or of possible misidentification of a baby in a hospital nursery. It is a more complicated matter to define a human population. We know that any race or subrace, however defined, consists of many individuals who differ from one another in a variety of respects; and that when we compare different racial groups, we find that they share many traits, often differing from one another only in the frequency with which certain traits occur. For instance, blood group O occurs in all human races, group A in most of them; but the percentages of the two blood groups vary from one population to another. So describing a population genetically is somewhat more complicated than describing an individual genetically.

The term *population* has a special meaning to the geneticist. It is not merely a gathering; we would not consider the members of the United Nations Assembly as a population, though as anthropologists we would find them a very interesting group of people. But they are only temporarily gathered together. They will someday return to their own countries to grow old among their grandchildren, where they will be members of true *populations*. In their own homelands, each one is part of a group in which the members have a common genetic heritage, a group which, depending on circumstances, will remain genetically distinct for perhaps a very long time in the future. Even a community in the usual sense is not always the same as a population, though it may sometimes be. In a complex modern society, a city or state may consist of different social, religious, or ethnic groups that interact economically but tend not to intermarry with one another. Within a population in the genetic sense, however, we expect that any two individuals, though they may never meet, have a reasonable chance of someday having grandchildren, great grandchildren, or other descendants in common. Such a population, in a modern society, may be made up of people scattered over a large area, who share a genetic heritage and an ethnic identity with one another, and who at the same time are somewhat withdrawn socially from other people who are their actual neighbors. The definition of a population is a flexible one and does not imply any particular size, provided it is not so small that it regularly has to go outside itself for marriage partners. The largest population groups that are meaningful are subraces and races.

How do we define a population, with all its internal variability, in genetic terms? Of course, as in the case of individuals, we define it by phenotype, in respect to those traits we know to be hereditary but which we cannot attribute to specific, known genes. But the genetic definition of a population differs in another way: its variation can only be described *statistically*. For instance, we can take a sample of a population and examine each individual for some trait of simple genetic inheritance, such as the M–N blood groups; out of 100 individuals, we might find 35 M, 50 MN and 15 N blood types. Assuming that this is a reasonably accurate picture of the whole population (that is, our sample did not happen to pick up an undue number of any one blood group), this *distribution* of blood types defines the population in the same sense that a single blood type defines an individual. Furthermore, we may reduce the percentages of the three classes to only two numbers. In the case of the MN blood groups, as we have already discussed, we know the complete genotype for each phenotype: every M blood type has two M genes, every N blood type has two N genes, and every MN blood type has one M and one N. Therefore we can actually count the genes in this sample, and find that the 100 individuals have among them 120 M genes and 80 N genes. This can be reduced to a *gene frequency,* .60 M and .40 N, which is the simplest way of characterizing the population for this trait.

This is only a start; we will try to define populations in terms of as many traits as possible, because populations with the same M–N gene frequencies may be quite different in other respects. This gives a basic description of a population comparable to the description of an individual. Gene frequencies are not always as easy to obtain as in the M and N example. Even in the case of the A–B–O blood groups, we become involved in some guesswork. Because of dominance effects, we do not know in a given case whether an individual with an A or B phenotype is a homozygote or a heterozygote, and of course each homozygote adds twice as many A or B genes to the population count as does a heterozygote. However, there are ways of deriving an estimate of the gene frequency from the known phenotype frequency (this will be explained later), so that populations can be described in terms of gene frequency in the A–B–O system also. In the case of the many traits that are polygenic, or that for other reasons have not been analyzed in terms of specific genes, we continue to describe populations in terms of the distribution of phenotypes. We assume this to be roughly parallel to gene frequency distributions, and use it to estimate genetic differences between populations, though recognizing that it is not as accurate as data based on traits that are genetically defined. We should remember that no matter how fully we describe a population in terms of its gene frequencies, we have not set very strict limits on the genotype of any single individual. This is a confirmation in genetic terms of what we know about races and subraces in terms of observation. A particular gene combination may be *possible* in quite a number of different populations, but it is more likely to occur, and is therefore, in the long run, more common, in some populations than in others. Conversely, even if we have a large body of genetic information about an individual, there will be many degrees of certainty or uncertainty in the guess we might make about what population he came from. Figure 17, which shows graphically the gene frequencies and phenotype frequencies for the ABO and MN blood group systems in three populations from different parts of the world, indicates this clearly. The *populations* are certainly different from one another; even on the basis of these two traits alone we could tell them apart. But all we could say of an *individual*, knowing his ABO and MN phenotypes, is that he would be more likely to come from one of these populations than from another.

We described a natural population as one in which all individuals, if not potential mates, were potential in-laws or at least potential coancestors of children in some future generation. Ideally, within a single population, mating is at random: there are no isolated communities or exclusive social classes that separate it into smaller groups which do not freely intermarry. Few populations conform to this rule *exactly*, but many conform to it very nearly. If mating is random, the gene frequencies are related to the genotype frequencies in a predictable way.

As an example, suppose we take the population we described previously as having, at the M–N locus, gene frequencies of .6 M and .4 N. We speak of these frequencies as defining the *gene pool*. If we take an individual at random from this population, knowing nothing about his particular parents, all we can say is that any one allele he received had a .6 chance of being M and a .4 chance of being N. If the two alleles he received are different, he will be a heterozygous MN; if they are the same, he will be a homozygote, and obviously in this population he has a greater chance of being MM than NN. In this instance, the chances for the various genotypes—which we could verify by taking a large sample of individuals—would be 36 per cent MM, 48 per cent MN, and 16 per cent NN, or thereabouts, depending on how large and accurate a sample we took. (For those who like algebra, this may be expressed as $(M + N)^2 = M^2 + 2 MN + N^2$.) We could arrive at this result in a more complicated way: assume that the individuals of various genotypes in the parent population formed mating combinations at random, that is, without regard to each other's blood group genotype; then assume that each mating produced the expected combination of offspring genotypes. Then add up the whole lot. In fact this will give us the same result as calculating directly from the frequencies in the gene pool, because random mating is only a

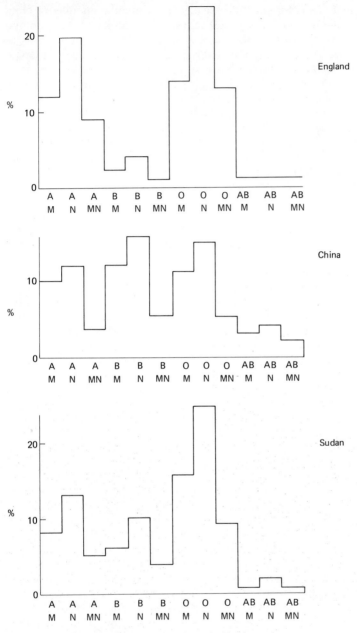

Figure 17 The relative numbers of individuals with various combinations of A-B-O and M-N blood types, in three racially different populations. Each combined phenotype is "most likely" in one of the three populations. But if each individual were assigned to his "most likely" population, more than half would be assigned wrongly. (Calculated from data assembled by Weiner, 1971.)

Gene Frequencies		Genotype Frequencies			Phenotype Frequencies	
O	A	OO	OA	AA	O (recessive)	A (dominant)
.1*	.9*	.01	.18	.81	.01	.99
.3*	.7*	.09	.42	.49	.09	.91
.5	.5	.25	.50	.25	.25	.75
.7	.3	.49	.42	.09	.49	.51
.9	.1	.81	.18	.01	.81	.19

* These frequencies do not actually occur in any living population.

complicated way of drawing alleles at random from the gene pool to produce new genotypes. Table 4 gives some sample frequencies of genotypes for particular gene frequencies. It is clear that there is a consistent, though not simple, relation of gene frequencies to genotype frequencies. The numbers of each homozygote will always be the *square* of the fraction which is the gene frequency, and the heterozygotes make up the remainder. In Table 4 we have shown genes A and O, rather than M and N, because the effect of dominance is an interesting and important one.

It will be seen that the dominant phenotype is always more common than the dominant gene, because it includes heterozygotes, and that the recessive phenotype is always rarer than the recessive gene. In fact, if a recessive gene is one-tenth of the gene pool (see first line in Table 4), the recessive *phenotype* will appear in only one out of a hundred individuals. These relations are constant for any given gene frequency; so if dominance relations are known, it is possible to work backwards from phenotype frequency to gene frequency. This is the basis for the type of calculation, previously mentioned, by which we infer gene frequencies from phenotype data. Thus, where the blood group phenotypes are 51 per cent A and 49 per cent O, this does not indicate that the *genes* are in about equal numbers. These are the expected proportions of phenotype for a population in which the gene frequencies are A (dominant) = 30 per cent, O (recessive) = 70 per cent. Some attention to these figures will clear up a misunderstanding that arose when the concept of genetic dominance was first introduced, and which may still puzzle some people when they first encounter the concept. For the purposes of experimental demonstrations we may do as Mendel did in his first experiments: cross individuals who are both homozygous, one for a dominant gene, and one for a recessive, and obtain offspring that are all heterozygous and show the dominant phenotype. The word *dominant,* which is a slightly loaded one, refers to this apparent "power." A hasty reading of this by someone who does not examine the small print may lead to the conclusion that after a few generations of mixture of different strains, the dominant trait will take over the whole population, and the recessive disappear. If this were the case, the history of man or any other species would show some surprisingly abrupt changes in physical characteristics. The reason this does not occur is that in a real population, with its random mating system, many of the individuals with dominant phenotypes are heterozygous in genotype: *carriers,* as they are called, of the recessive gene. For instance, where the gene frequency of A is .1, the phenotype A is .19, but only one-nineteenth of these A phenotypes are homozygous; the vast majority of the A's are heterozygous. Genetically, these heterozygous A's are a bluff; they will produce a large number of recessive offspring as well as many heterozygotes like themselves. If we calculate the likelihood of various matings in such a population, we find that the numbers of the various genotypes in the next generation will be exactly the same as in the present generation. The gene pool, which has remained the same all along, will produce the same proportions of the various genotypes and phenotypes again and again in successive generations. This principle of the permanence of the gene pool, and the constancy of the numbers of genotypes and phenotypes it produces, is called the *Hardy-Weinberg Law,* after its two discoverers, and is the basic law of population genetics.

The terms *homozygous* and *heterozygous,* which we have defined and used in respect to individuals, may be used of populations also. A population *homozygous* for an allele is one in which that allele is 100 per cent of the gene pool, and all individuals are homozygous for it. A population *heterozygous* at a given locus is one in which at least two alleles are present in appreciable numbers, so that heterozygous individuals occur. The visible effect of heterozygosity in a population is also called *polymorphism.* For instance, we would say the American "black" bear is *polymorphic* in respect to coat color, or, in a more general way, the human species is *polymorphic* for a large number of traits. This heterozygosity at many loci becomes extremely complicated to describe. If human populations were like experimental ones—derived from simple crosses of homozygous strains—gene frequencies at any one locus would always be 50–50, and the expected numbers of phenotypes could be expressed in simple fractions. However, in an ordinary polymorphic population, the gene frequencies at different loci can be decimal fractions anywhere between zero and one, and the relative numbers of the different phenotypic combinations of traits are infinitely varied. Some "possible individuals" may have such a small chance of appearing that they may not occur for a number of generations; but the possibility still exists so long as the required genes are in the gene pool.

One source of information about the inheritance of human variation is the study of the traits of persons whose known recent
ancestry includes two or more fairly distinct racial populations. In
these studies we avoid in part the problem of not knowing by direct
observation what the traits of ancestors now deceased may have
been. If the ancestral populations, judged by their presently living
close relatives, are fairly distinct in certain traits, our error in guess-
ing the characteristics of the actual ancestors is small compared to
the known difference between groups. A number of the original
expectations from these studies have not been realized. One phenomenon looked for was genetic dominance of the racial traits of
some populations over those of others. Instead, the general rule
seems to be that the phenotypic traits by which race is generally
judged are polygenic and show a blending inheritance, so that the
offspring of a racial cross are visibly intermediate in appearance.
Considerable attention was given at first to any effects of race
mixture on the vigor, fertility, or biological success of the descendants. Two possibilities are suggested by knowledge of other species.
It is known that when different inbred strains of a species are
crossed, the offspring may exhibit what is called "hybrid vigor,"
that is, they will be stronger than either parent stock, and often
larger in size. But in other cases, where the difference between the
two populations approaches the magnitude of a species difference,
progeny may be produced which show lessened vigor, often evi-
denced by reduced fertility. The study of human racial mixtures has
not been successful in demonstrating either of these effects, though
claims on both sides have been made. The effects, if any, appear to
be too small to show through the confusion resulting from differing
social situations of parent and offspring populations. Probably no
human races are sufficiently inbred to produce the hybrid vigor that
occurs when strains of domestic animals are crossed, nor are they
sufficiently different from one another physiologically for any *adverse* results to appear as a result of mixture.

The most consistent finding in studies of racially mixed populations is that Mendel's law of independent assortment of alleles
applies very well to the traits that distinguish races from one another. The first generation resulting from mixed marriages tends to
be relatively uniform in appearance, at least as much so as either of
the parent populations. In the second and later generations, however, the appearance of the descendants becomes more varied,
indicating that independent assortment of genes is occurring. This
results in some individuals having, at certain loci, two alleles that
originally came from the same parent race. In popular usage these
individuals would be spoken of as throwbacks to one of the ancestral types in a particular trait. If the phenotypes are polygenically
determined, there will be *degrees* of throwback. As a result, in

populations in which there has been mixture between two races that differ considerably in phenotype, and even within single families in these populations, there can be great variety of appearance in a single trait, ranging, at the two extremes, from complete resemblance to one parental race to complete resemblance to the other. In addition, the independent assortment of genes is clearly shown. The loci controlling racially different traits, including those for the several loci of polygenically controlled traits, appear to be thoroughly scattered among the 26 chromosome pairs. Thus a single individual of mixed ancestry may revert in appearance toward one race in one trait and toward another in another trait. In this way *combinations* of features are formed that do not correspond to either race. Furthermore, some individuals will revert sufficiently toward the same race—in those traits the layman considers indicative of race—that he will usually not be recognized as of mixed ancestry. Where there are social advantages or disadvantages attached to race, such individuals may deny mixed ancestry, and their children, also mixed, may be unaware of it.

Some persons claim to know "secret" signs by which they can "always tell" if a person is racially mixed. These signs may be obscure traits of some genetic significance that sometimes appear in individuals who are not recognized as mixed according to popular concepts of race. However, for any such sign to *always* appear, it would have to be polygenic, with so many alleles at different loci that every descendant had to receive at least one. Some confusion in thinking has been introduced by the "blood" concept of inheritance. According to this concept, every one of an individual's traits is supposed to be present in diluted form in all his descendants. Particulate inheritance does not allow this possibility. Perhaps another source of misconception is the attempt to see in racial differences something similar to the coordinated process that determines sex differences. In the development of sex characteristics, the Y chromosome acts like a pleiotropic gene to establish simultaneously a whole complex of phenotypic traits. The evidence from study of racial mixtures indicates that no single factor of this kind is involved in race differences. Race differences are the result of a large number of separately inherited traits scattered over many chromosomes, and as a result the combinations of traits that characterize races disintegrate in racially mixed populations. The degree of correlation of racial traits that we do see in mixed populations is a result of the way mixture takes place. For a long time after mixture begins, usually there are, within the mixed population, families and individuals of different proportions of ancestry. Only in rare cases does mixture take place so that all mixed individuals are of exactly half-and-half ancestry in the first generation. One such case is known: the population of Pitcairn Island, which started with all English fathers (the mutineers of H.M.S. Bounty) and all Polynesian mothers. More commonly in a recent racial mixture, some unmixed families of each race will remain for a number of generations. Eventually, after many generations, when the population has blended to form a random mixture of all of the alleles present in the two parent races, there will be a new race, characterized by gene frequencies intermediate between those of the two races that mixed to form it, and producing its own blend of various phenotypes, according to the Hardy-Weinberg Law.

The way in which traits are distributed to the descendants of racial mixtures indicates that all races of man have homologous chromosomes with the same arrangement of loci for various alleles—the normal situation in any single species. There was a time when it was thought that there might be a racial difference in chromosome number. It had been believed, on the basis of early studies, that the normal chromosome number of man was 48. This was not checked very carefully, because counting chromosomes is a tedious business. In 1956, new techniques began to indicate that this number was in error. For awhile it was considered possible that human chromosome number varied among individuals and possibly with race (Kodani, 1958). However, it now appears that 46 chromosomes is the normal count for all human populations.

GENETIC CHANGES

So far we have discussed genes as though they passed from one generation to another without changing. This is not strictly true. Sometimes a gene changes abruptly, in such a way that it no longer produces its previous effect. Such an event is called a *mutation,* and the altered gene is called a *mutant* gene. (The term *mutation* is sometimes used, less correctly, for the altered gene itself, and *mutant,* by science fiction writers, to whom all things are possible, for the individual who carries a mutant gene.) When a mutation occurs, the mutant is a new and different allele at the same locus. It is carried and distributed in inheritance just as the original allele was, and remains stable in its new form as it goes on to subsequent generations. Mutations are rare. Examples that have been extensively studied show that certain exceptional alleles are likely to mutate as often as once in every five thousand generations, but most are much less susceptible to mutation than this. This is fortunate, because a mutation can be harmful in many more ways than it can be helpful. Sometimes mutations are deadly. Any great amount of unpredictable genetic change by mutation would make it difficult for a species to remain adapted to its environment. Therefore species, as a rule, are able to retain their tried and successful genotypes without too many disturbing mutations.

Certain external conditions, such as exposure to X-rays or to the radiation from radioactive substances, can increase mutation rates. These influences seem to increase all mutation rates proportionately, rather than bringing about any particular kind of mutation. Also, there is no known environmental circumstance that causes mutations of such a kind as to be adaptive to that particular environment. Mutations are believed to be the result of ultramicroscopic damage to the molecular structure of the gene, or of a mistake in copying the structure of the gene when a cell divides. So it is not surprising that they either do not function at all, or do not function as the original gene did. Like misprints, they usually do not make sense. Only rarely, and by coincidence, is the mutation functional—like the misprint that gives a new and unintended meaning to a sentence.

When the process of mutation was first discovered, mutations that produced striking or harmful effects were the first to be observed. This gave a distorted picture of the mutation process. It is likely that there are far more mutations of moderate effect, which easily escape notice, especially in a polymorphic species like man. Unless the mutant gene is clearly dominant, in fact, it is hard to be sure that an unusual trait that seems to have appeared out of nowhere is not simply due to a recessive allele that has been carried in the family for a long time. For this reason mutation was first recognized not in man, but in plants and animals that had been under close observation for many generations. The most notorious instance of mutation in man is the hemophilia mutant which first surfaced in two of the sons of Queen Victoria of England. Hemophilia is the result of a sex-linked allele which does not affect the females who carry it but produces excessive and sometimes dangerous bleeding in affected males. In this case the mutation must have occurred somewhere in the female line of ancestry, probably shortly before it first showed itself in males. We now know that any sister of a male afflicted with hemophilia has a one-half chance of being a carrier of the trait. But according to nineteenth-century custom, Queen Victoria's daughters were regarded as choice matches for the royal houses of Europe, and eventually produced hemophiliac heirs to the thrones of Spain and Czarist Russia. In the latter case, the royal family was so demoralized by the illness of their afflicted son and heir to the throne, that the mutant allele perhaps facilitated the Russian Revolution.

Mutation, however, has an importance that goes beyond any specific effect on an individual. Genetically speaking, everything that distinguishes man or any other complex organism from the simplest one-celled animals, originated at some time in the past as a mutation. Without mutation, there would be no polymorphism, no variety of genotype, and no opportunity for the development either of new species in the course of evolution, or of geographical races in the history of a species. So, though every mutation involves a risk, sometimes a very serious one to an individual, the mutation process is essential to the species. Some ancient forms of life that became extinct may have done so because mutation did not supply them with ways of changing to adapt to changing environments. Mutation rates themselves are probably adaptive: high enough to provide a variety of genetic material, yet low enough not to disrupt the genotype too much. We are properly concerned about possible increases in mutation resulting from radioactive fallout. A complete cessation of mutation might in the long run be disastrous also.

What becomes of a mutant gene after it has appeared? It may disappear quite soon, as the result of chance. The first carrier of it may have no offspring, for reasons unrelated to the mutation. Also, not every gene an individual carries, whether an "old-fashioned" allele or a new mutant, is necessarily transmitted to any of his children, particularly if he has a small family. So the mutation may flicker out quite soon. However, if we think in terms of geological time—the thousands and even millions of years over which a species lives and develops—the one-in-many-thousand chance of the occurrence of a particular mutation in a single generation translates into a repeated production of the same mutant allele. By repeated mutation, then, substantial proportions of mutant genes of various kinds will be built up, and the larger the population of the species, the greater the actual numbers of the mutant alleles. Because we estimate the number of loci in the chromosomes of man to be numbered in the millions, the very low rate of mutation *per locus* still means that most of us have several mutant alleles that were newly produced in our own generation. What does this do to the Hardy-Weinberg law? Very little, really. We would never discover mutation by comparing the frequency of a trait between one generation and another; but it does produce slow changes in the gene pool.

Over a long period of time, the repeated occurrence of a particular mutation can make a species polymorphic, with the new trait fairly common. But a mutation is not always a trivial matter. Some mutant genes are disastrous to the individual who carries them because they result in physical deformity or serious metabolic defects. In man, even a mutation that affects only appearance may cause a person to withdraw from social contacts, and as a result, not produce offspring. In animals, instances are known where a mutant gene may cause death so early in embryonic development that there is no way of knowing that conception took place, except by the fact that the number of living offspring produced falls short of the normal number. Such mutant alleles are called *lethal,* if they always result in death; *sublethal,* if they increase the risk of death or failed reproduction. In either case, the mutant allele tends to disappear because it is not passed on to the next generation, at least not in normal numbers. In these cases a balance is struck between the repeated occurrence of a mutation and the elimination of mutant genes as a result of the disadvantage suffered by those who carry it. The less the disadvantage, the greater the number of mutant alleles that will remain in the gene pool at any given time. Some mutants may be trivial, either because the mutant can serve the same purpose as the normal allele, or perhaps because the normal allele was already "unemployed" because of some evolutionary change. The existence of mutants that are entirely neutral, that is, have no effect either good or bad on the individuals who carry them, is a subject for argument that we will not enter into here. If neutral mutations exist, they are of little interest to the anthropologist who is primarily concerned with the adaptation of man to his surroundings. Finally, some mutations, however rare they may be, are useful; these are the great mutations that make evolution possible.

NATURAL SELECTION

Mutation is only the first of several processes that change gene frequencies. Mutation is unique and essential, because it is the only process that can change the frequency of an allele from zero to something more than zero. And though the accumulation of mutations is slow, it is inevitable. However, once a species has become polymorphic at any locus by the process of mutation, other mechanisms come into play, the most notable and most interesting being *natural selection*. We have already discussed it in one of its forms: its role of eliminating lethal and sublethal mutants so that their numbers remain small in the gene pool.

The term *natural selection* was originated long ago by Charles Darwin, who saw that if hereditary differences existed between individuals of a species, and if some of these differences affected health, longevity, or reproductive success, the traits of the successful individuals would gradually come to be typical of the species (Darwin, 1859). Selective breeding of animals, for special economic purposes, or even just for novelty of appearance, had been going on for many centuries before Darwin, and is still going on. Though breeders today operate more efficiently because of their knowledge of modern genetics, the basic process is unchanged. It consists of finding, within an existing animal population, certain individuals that seem to be an improvement, or an interesting variation, on the norm. These individuals are then separated out and bred to one another. If the traits for which the parents were selected are hereditary ones, these traits in time become the characteristics of a new breed. In some cases, new types are produced intentionally by crossing breeds that already differ in several characteristics. Genetic segregation in their offspring results in new combinations of the various traits in individuals of later generations. Then, by selection from these hybrids, we can establish a stock that has some of the characteristics of one parent breed, some of the other.

In the case of the domestic dog, the process of creating various breeds by selection of this kind has gone on for so long that we do not know exactly what the original "dog" looked like. It has been suggested that the amount of variation that made possible the production of breeds of dogs as remarkably different as we now have, resulted originally from the crossing of more than one natural dog-like species. This is only a guess. It is certain that in many cases, where domestic breeds show traits different from any wild species, use was made of mutations that appeared from time to time. Mutant genes, such as those that produce bulldog jaws or dachshund legs, would be lethal or sublethal in the wild; but the unpredictable tastes of human beings have caused them to be propagated and multiplied. An example of a mutant gene that has appeared in many species and is commonly found in domestic animals is the gene that produces white-spotting—the condition in which the normal color of the animals is interrupted by white areas of various shapes and sizes. This trait is rarely seen in wild animals. Man, however, gets amusement and pleasure from seeing animals so marked. Therefore, he has increased, by selection, the frequency of spotting in certain breeds of domestic animals. It is not necessary to suppose that the mutation has occurred more often in domestic animals than in wild ones; it has simply been multiplied in domestic breeds as a result of human preferences.

A less dramatic process than the development of a new breed is the later slow improvement of it, or the maintenance of its standards after it has become established. To keep the stock breeding true to its desired characteristics, the breeder continually "culls" it: that is, eliminates individuals who differ from the type desired. This is very similar in effect to the natural elimination of harmful mutations, which we have already described; though in the artificial breeding program the trait eliminated may not be harmful to the animals in any normal sense. Sometimes the culling consists of eliminating mutant genes. Often it serves to eliminate recessives, a process that often takes a long time because recessive alleles may remain concealed for many generations.

Darwin's insight, which profoundly changed biological thinking, was that the processes by which man developed and maintained his breeds of domestic animals could take place entirely without the intervention of man, solely as a result of natural processes. The same two general types of selection can be recognized. *Stabilizing selection,* similar to the culling process of the breeder, maintains the type of a species by the elimination of individuals who are not adequate to the requirements of its environnment and way of life. However, in other situations there may be an opportunity for a species or a part of it to *improve* its success by genetic change in a particular direction. In this case selection can produce a new breed—eventually, in fact, a new species—different from the original one. It is only necessary that a few individuals differ from the norm of the population in some way that can be turned to advantage. If these individuals are successful in producing more offspring than others in their group, their descendants, carrying their genes, eventually come to outnumber other elements in the population.

Darwin used the term *survival of the fittest* to express briefly his concept of the action of natural selection. People sometimes take a quick look at this, guess what Darwin meant by *fitness,* and guess wrong, assuming that Darwin meant by fitness the same sort of thing that an athletic coach means by it. Biological fitness is more subtle than this. Every form of life has its own form of fitness, its own way of successfully surviving. Some of the fittest animals in the world, to judge by their abundance and their millions of years of survival, are the little builders of coral, who cannot even move from one place to another. Some species among all forms of animal life—insects, fish, mammals, birds—are predators. They make their living by the unexpected attack and the swift kill—one kind of fitness. But they are greatly outnumbered by animals who survive by the watchful eye and the sly escape—another kind of fitness. Humans are sometimes intrigued by the idea of male animals fighting for the favors of the female, and winning the opportunity to pass on their genes. However, it is commonly observed among domestic cats that the female mates with a mild-tempered male, while two more belligerent toms are so occupied with tearing each other apart that they fail to observe what is taking place on the sidelines. Too much showing-off of this kind is not biological fitness. In many animals, particularly in birds and mammals, protective behavior of the parents toward the young may be an important kind of fitness. The mother animal may risk her own life in defending her young, but in the long run she will succeed biologically because the offspring who carry her inheritance are preserved to the species. In animals with a social organization, any action by an individual on behalf of others related to him may constitute "fitness" for himself. In fact, too high a level of competition between members of the same species may be hazardous to the welfare of the entire group.

Many theories had been proposed before Darwin's time to account for the variety of species, their often remarkable adaptation to particular niches in the environment, and their development of complicated behavior patterns. The idea that the variety of nature was created in the beginning, in all its details, was already widely questioned, and had been for many centuries, in fact. People sought to explain the living world in terms of natural laws that were the same in the present as in the past. However, the many remarkable adaptations of animals and plants to various ways of life still challenged explanation. The ancient belief that the suntan of the skin in one generation could cause later generations to be *born* dark-skinned—one of the first theories of the cause of a racial difference—is typical of one class of explanation. To account for this in modern terms, we would have to suppose that some substance from the tanned skin circulates to the germ cells and produces mutation in only that molecule which regulates pigment formation. Many experiments have shown that such things do not occur.

A somewhat similar theory, with a supernatural slant, supposed that the "desires" or "strivings" of the parent affected the characteristics of their offspring. But the theory of natural selection stated that if hereditary variability indeed existed (which was easy to show), the entirely natural processes of life and survival would bring about an increase of traits that would adapt a species to its environment, and a decrease of traits that would not. In fact, it would require supernatural intervention to *prevent* natural selection from working in this way!

Darwin knew nothing of modern genetics: he lived too soon.

However, he fully appreciated the genetic nature of natural selection. The population in which natural selection was to operate not only had to have *individual variability;* this variability had to be *hereditary.* If all members of a population are exactly alike in any trait, there is no way in which selection can take place. And if differences do exist but are not hereditary, the different rates of survival and reproduction of different individuals will not affect the characteristics of later generations. Long ago, before Darwin published any of his work, farmers knew that if they wanted to grow large pumpkins, they should save seeds from the vine that produced the largest fruit. However, they were wrong in thinking that they could get even better results by taking seeds from the largest pumpkin on the vine. The fruit—with the exception of the tiny germ of each seed—is a part of the mother plant, like a leaf or a flower. If one pumpkin on a vine is larger than another on the same vine, it is not because of different heredity but because of accidental circumstances, such as its position on the stem or the weather during its growth. In general, however, these people had a good understanding of heredity—better than that of many city-bred people nowadays, who have had no experience at all with domestic animals and plants.

One thing that continued to puzzle Darwin, and which he never managed to explain adequately, was the *origin* of variation. He could see that it was in danger of being depleted by the selection process itself: that is, when selection had produced a population uniform for the best hereditary combination that the original variability allowed, variation would be greatly reduced, even eliminated, and no further change would occur. We now know that the constant, slow occurrence of mutation explains why the variation is never exhausted. Mutation continually renews the polymorphism of a species. (We also suspect that there are other reasons why natural species do not achieve genetic uniformity; this we will discuss later.) Now, of course, we interpret the process of natural selection in terms of genes rather than traits. This explains some inconsistencies. If we (or nature) wish to eliminate a trait produced by a dominant gene, it can be done easily and quickly. The dominant allele cannot hide. Every individual who carries it, even in the heterozygous form, is marked, and if selection acts against the dominant phenotype, this individual is affected. The breeder, in fact, can eliminate every unwanted dominant allele from his stock by one ruthless operation. The processes of nature are usually gentler—eliminating a few in this generation, and a few later. But the elimination of a *recessive* allele is always a slower process. The recessive allele can hide. It does not make itself known in the heterozygous individual who carries it, and if its gene frequency is low, most of the individuals who carry it *are* heterozygous. This makes it difficult to eliminate recessive genes in a breeding program, and slows their elimination by natural selection. The recessive allele, like some creature with underground habits, can survive undetected for generations, surfacing only occasionally. And for the same reasons, a recessive mutation, if it is desirable, cannot be promoted by the selective process as efficiently as a dominant mutation. Selection is also complicated when polygenes are involved. Pleiotropism, in which the same allele produces more than one effect, may result in an increase of one of the traits it produces when selection is really acting on another one. And where Darwin evaluated population changes in terms of visible traits—phenotypes—we now evaluate them in terms of genotypes and interpret the changes produced as the result of changes in gene frequencies within the gene pool.

How does natural selection affect the Hardy-Weinberg law? It does not invalidate the law, but puts it in the proper perspective. We see that the Hardy-Weinberg law operates under certain conditions, one of which is that the survival and reproduction of all genotypes are exactly equal. It tells us that gene frequencies do not change from generation to generation because of any interactions of the genes among themselves. But selection is "outside the law" in this sense. However, it is still important to know how the numbers of phenotypes will change as a result of the change in gene frequencies that selection brings about. Then we can predict, using the Hardy-Weinberg law as a basis, and making allowance for changes due to selection, how gene frequencies will change over a series of generations. Some examples of predictions of this kind are shown in graphic form in Figures 18, 19, and 20.

First we must define exactly what the effects of selection are. This is done by assigning *selection coefficients* to various possible phenotypes in the population. This means that we evaluate the relative contribution that the individuals of a given phenotype will make to the gene pool of the next generation, taking into account any advantages or disadvantages which affect either their survival or their reproduction. A simple way of doing this is to assign a percentage value to the survival/reproduction of a phenotype as compared with other phenotypes in the population. Dominance complicates selection. Therefore, for the first illustration we will assume that an allele has a blending affect, that is, that the heterozygote is intermediate between the two homozygotes in its survival value. Thus, if a certain gene A confers advantage in such a way that individuals of genotype AA have 10 per cent more offspring (in the long run) than individuals of the genotype aa; and those of genotype Aa have 5 per cent more than those of aa, the selection coefficients would be, for AA, 1.10; for Aa, 1.05; and for aa, 1.00.

The calculation of what happens when such selection is acting is easily done, especially if we have an obliging computer to assist us. We decide what gene frequency we wish to take as a starting point. On this basis we calculate the expected number of each genotype, on the assumption of random mating. Then, to express the contribution of each genotype to the next generation, we multiply the number of each genotype by its selection coefficient. Looking at the results, we find that one gene has been passed on to the next generation more generously than another. Because we are not for

TABLE 5   A WORK PAGE FOR A CALCULATION OF SELECTION

Initial Gene Frequency (Generation Zero)   A = .1   a = .9

Genotpyes		Selection Coefficients	Contribution to Next Generation	Genes Passed on to Offspring A	a	
AA	.01	x 1.10	= .011	.0110		
Aa	.18	x 1.05	= .189	.0945	.0945	
aa	.81	x 1.00	= .810		.8100	Total
				.1055	.9045 /	1.010

Adjusted Gene Frequency (Generation 1)   A = .1045   a = .8955

$$\left(\frac{.1055}{1.010}\right) \qquad \left(\frac{.9045}{1.010}\right)$$

the moment concerned with actual increase or decrease in population size (this is subject to many other influences), we reduce the new gene numbers to a percentage basis. The process can be repeated, with progressive change in the gene frequencies, for as many generations as we wish. An example of this sort of calculation is given in Table 5.

This shows the kind of effect we can expect during a single generation, with selection coefficients of moderate degree. The favored gene, A, has edged ahead by a little less than one half of 1 per cent. Proceeding in this way, we can project selection effects over a number of generations, demonstrating the effects of selection of various different degrees, as shown in Figure 18.

Dominance, as we have already mentioned, has its effect on the selection process. This effect is conspicuous in the elimination of the harmful mutant genes which arise from time to time. The dominant mutation is more readily eliminated because the dominant gene always makes itself known in the phenotype of the individual who carries it; it is totally exposed to the selection process and rapidly affected by it. The recessive mutation, which rarely expresses itself in the phenotype, is protected from selection. In a situation in which a new *desirable* allele has appeared, or one in which an allele already present has newly acquired an advantage because of some change of environment, the differing susceptibility of the dominant and the recessive gene to selection is also significant. At the same gene frequency, an *uncommon dominant* allele will be increased more rapidly by favorable selection than an *uncommon recessive*. Hence, it has been said that evolutionary changes will take place more rapidly if the "progressive" genes are dominant ones

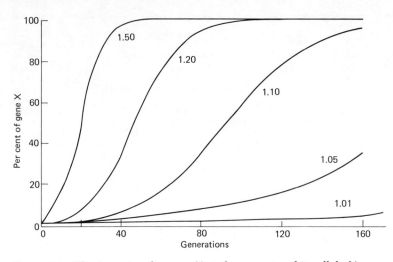

Figure 18   The increase of a gene X at the expense of its allele Y, with positive selection of various intensities. In every case selection is of a blending type, with the heterozygote intermediate in selective value between the two homozygotes. Each curve is designated by a number indicating the ratio of $\dfrac{\text{XX survival}}{\text{YY survival}}$ which produces it. Thus, the steepest curve of increase shown is that produced when the XX genotype has a 50 per cent advantage over the YY genotype.

than if they are recessive. Figure 19 contrasts these two cases in simulated form. It shows the expected rate of gene frequency increase for a new, and still rare, dominant gene favored by selection, and the rate for a new and rare recessive gene, which is also advantageous. In the two cases illustrated, the difference in selective advantage between the phenotypes is the same. In both cases the advantaged gene eventually outnumbers its rival. But the dominant gene increases much more rapidly at the beginning, and more slowly at the end. (The end of this sequence is, in effect, the case of a rare, undesirable recessive being difficult to eliminate completely.) The advantaged recessive gene is painfully slow in getting off the ground, and gains momentum only after it has attained a gene frequency of 50 per cent or more.

As we have seen in Figure 18, the larger the difference in selection coefficients between different genotypes, the faster gene frequencies will change. An important point is that rather minor selective differences can produce the same effect as major ones; it only requires more time. It is significant that at Darwin's time, geologists had recently shown that the history of the earth was far longer than the few hundred human generations indicated by religious tradition. Thus it appeared reasonable, as it had not previously, to explain the existing diversity of species in terms of relatively slow changes over a very long period.

The smoothness of the calculated curves in Figure 18 is of course

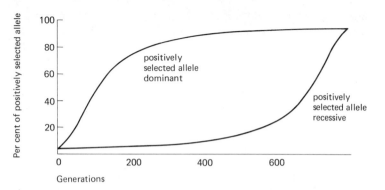

Figure 19 The increase of two alleles from a low frequency, with comparable positive selection, but one *dominant,* one *recessive.* In each case the selection coefficients of the two phenotypes differ as 1.04 to 1.0.

deceptive. Variation in external conditions—inevitable over a period of many generations—would cause changes in selective effects, which in turn would cause irregularities in the curves. This is a matter we will discuss later. Also, of course, in a population of limited size, there will be chance fluctuations in numbers of genes. Experimental work on selection has been done with animals of short generation time. Because of the limited size of the experimental populations, these experiments show gene frequency changes that form a zigzag rather than a straight line. However, the trend will resemble those of Figures 18 and 19, because the upward "zigs" outnumber the downward "zags." In either case, the process always goes step by step from one generation to the next. Every time a new generation is produced, the gene frequencies of the grandparents or of generations further back exist only as history. Each generation makes a new start from the gene frequencies of the generation just preceding it. If selective forces change, the change in the characteristics of the population may cease to go in the same direction as before; but there is no automatic tendency for gene frequencies to revert to what they were at some previous time. If they do revert, we seek an explanation in terms of another change of conditions.

Some obvious examples of differing selection under different conditions can be seen when natural selection is contrasted with selection in the same species under domestication. We have already referred to white-spotting as a trait which man has promoted in his domestic animals. In this case, selection tends to be in the opposite direction under wild conditions. In general, conspicuous coloring is a disadvantage to wild animals. If they blend into the background, they are safer from predation, and are more effective if they themselves are predators. Thus the white-spotting mutation, which has been selected positively in domestic animals, will be selected out if it appears in wild species. Only animals such as the skunk, who are safest when recognized, have developed conspicuous patterns incorporating white markings. Many domestic animals have been bred to differ from the wild species in a number of traits. Modern cattle, for instance, differ greatly from the long-horned rangy type of their original wild ancestors. Their horns were a nuisance to man: cattle could hurt not only people but each other with them, so when a hornless mutation appeared, man selected for it. A ponderous, blocky build produced more beef: so man selected the individuals who tended toward that shape. A belligerent disposition was hazardous to the handler: so animals of even temper were chosen for breeding. If an animal now appears who shows some of the traits of the original stock, he is called a "scrub" and eliminated, to preserve the "quality of the breed." But these modern highbred cattle need protection. They have lost, along with their horns and their meanness, their ability to protect their young against predators. Their heavy build increases their need for food and decreases their ability to range far in search of it. If these cattle were turned loose without human protection for a few generations, it would be the "scrubs" who would increase and multiply, and finally the herd would once again acquire the characteristics that had adapted it for taking care of itself in the first place. The *conditions,* then, which can change with time and differ from place to place, determine the relative success of various phenotypes and the likelihood of their survival. Whether the selection is made by man for his special purposes, or is an automatic result of natural environment, does not essentially change the process—though man's intervention may result in dramatic and rapid changes that may be in a different direction from any that would occur in nature.

Some successful species in stable environments have remained essentially unchanged, at least in external form, for millions of years. But others have exploited certain mutations which have produced genetic changes that are advantageous in many situations. Mammals, and especially the primates and man, have specialized in complex nervous systems, which allow very complicated and flexible behavior. In fossil material, the best indication of the development of behavior is the size of the brain, which can be inferred from a fossil skull. A most interesting and well-documented sequence is seen in the evolution of horses from the time of their earliest appearance 60 million years ago (Edinger, 1948). (Horses, unlike primates, were usually abundant animals in their time, thus the fossil record is very good.) There is a constant increase in brain size during this long period; the earliest forms were probably no brighter than a modern opossum, whereas contemporary horses, of course, are alert and quick-reflexed animals. We see the same process going on in other lineages during the same period. In these cases the difference between older and newer forms is far greater than any difference within single species, so that the change must have involved many mutations, which occurred and became established one after another. The selective force here was the endless competition between predators and their prey: the most intelligent predators were always the most successful of their species, and the most intelligent of their prey were the most successful of theirs.

Changes such as this are the material of evolution. In time they alter whole lineages until their origin is hardly recognizable. However, of more interest to the student of human races are the kinds of change that are adaptive to the various local environments encountered by a successful and widely ranging species such as man. Local variations within a species or group of related species are often clearly related to local circumstances. The color of the hair in mammals, for instance, sometimes shows a dramatic correlation with the background color of the environment in which they live. A white coat is almost unknown except in animals who often encounter snow in their habitat. In certain areas of the western United States, where very light sandy soils and very dark volcanic soils occur close together, the species living in each area conform to the color of the soil (Blair, 1943). Experiments have shown that this matching of color makes them far less liable to be captured by predatory birds, which hunt by sight and are their principal natural enemies (Dice, 1947). By referring to Figure 18, it is easy to see that genes that produced lightening or darkening of coat color could be quite rapidly increased or decreased in a population if predators eliminated animals that contrasted in color with their habitats. Any selection of this kind, which is specific to certain localities, will cause gene frequencies to become different in different populations of the same species. This is the type of selection we can expect to be important in producing *races* of any species. The workings of local selection can be extremely complicated. Not only color, but body size and shape, physiological adaptation to temperature stresses, timing of the reproductive cycle (so as to produce young at the season when food supplies will be most adequate for their growth), may be adapted to special local conditions. In the case of man, some of the more obvious impacts of the environment are modified by the development of clothing and shelter. But culture itself introduces new selective effects. Genes may increase or decrease in a population because they affect an individual's adaptation to invented devices and means of subsistence in a human culture, or because they affect his adaptation to the social group itself. We can still consider this "natural" selection, because it is not planned by an intelligent human agency. But we will not discuss here the specific evidence of selection in man, past and present. This will be more appropriate in the discussion of the variable traits of man, which will appear in later chapters.

HETEROZYGOTE ADVANTAGE

An interesting effect is produced when selection is favorable to individuals who are heterozygous at a locus, and unfavorable to those who are homozygous at the same locus, for either of the alleles involved. This effect is generally called *heterosis;* an older term was *overdominance.* This effect is not easily explained in terms of simplistic concepts of "good" and "bad" genes. We have already mentioned *hybrid vigor,* a phenomenon well-known in Darwin's time. Man had long attempted to produce superior breeds of domestic animals by careful selection, yet found that when the fence fell down and crossbred offspring were produced, they mocked the efforts of the breeders by being particularly fine and healthy specimens. In earlier days this could perhaps be written off as an example of the prosperity of the wicked, which scripture deplores and man constantly observes. Genetic explanation is not so easy. Although the hazards of inbreeding and the advantages of outbreeding have been abundantly verified and put into intensive use by modern agriculturists and animal breeders, there is still some disagreement about their explanation. Inbreeding *can* result in an accidental increase in undesirable alleles, a matter we will discuss at greater length later. However, obviously undesirable traits, even if recessive, can be removed by culling and it should be possible in time to eliminate them from a breeding stock. The effect called *inbreeding depression,* on the contrary, continues to get worse with time. It becomes most conspicuous during the process of producing the commerically valuable hybrid plants and animals. The parent strains that are maintained separately by the breeder are often sorry-looking specimens: but they are carefully preserved in the knowledge that the first generation cross between them will have superior qualities. The best explanation for this phenomenon of hybrid vigor is the interaction of alleles of which both are useful and neither one "bad." We have already suggested that dominance between alleles is often the result of the production of a functional enzyme by the dominant allele and the production of nothing, or nothing usable, by the recessive allele. If the enzyme is needed only in very small quantity—and this is characteristic of enzyme reactions—the heterozygote is at no disadvantage. Harm will result only if the functional allele is entirely displaced by the presence of *two* recessive genes. If this is a true explanation of dominance, it follows that in certain cases the presence of a second and different allele at a particular locus may add something by way of versatility or efficiency to the animal metabolism, without taking anything away. This affords a reasonable explanation of heterosis, which is probably the best explanation of hybrid vigor.

Heterosis produces a distinctive pattern in natural selection. A simple advantage of one allele over another, if the advantage itself is consistent over a period of time, will result in a consistent change of gene frequency. In this way the advantageous allele will eventually replace the disadvantageous one. The rate at which this takes place, as we have already explained, will vary with the amount of advantage, and with the presence, direction, and degree of dominance. But heterosis actually *prevents* the replacement of one allele by another within a population. In the extreme case, that is, if only heterozygotes could survive at all, the gene pool could never deviate from a 50-50 proportion of the two alleles, because every parent of every generation would have one of each. In a less extreme case the gene frequencies may vary. However, there will be a strong tendency for the gene frequency to return to an intermediate point. This is not because of any mystical "law of averages." It is because the selective advantage of one allele over the other *reverses itself* as the gene frequency changes. When the heterozygote is favored by selection over either homozygote, the total "success" of either gene depends on how often it is carried by homozygous individuals, and how often by heterozygous ones. We have already pointed out that the proportion of homozygotes varies with the frequency of an allele, but to an exaggerated degree. An allele with an 80 per cent gene frequency will produce 64 per cent homozygous individuals as compared with 32 per cent heterozygotes: if homozygotes have a selective disadvantage, this allele will be selected against when it is this common. Its rival, with 20 per cent gene frequency, produces 4 per cent homozygotes and 32 per cent of heterozygotes: its total advantage will be largely determined by the success of the heterozygotes. This may be expressed in yet another way. Every extra contribution that heterozygous individuals make to the gene pool because of their longer life or greater fertility, consists of equal numbers of the two alleles; and adding *equal* numbers to two quantities that are *unequal* makes the difference between them proportionately less. If the rarer of the two genes increases in frequency, as we would expect in this situation, its advantage becomes continually less. For all such situations, in fact, there is a particular gene frequency at which neither allele has a net advantage over the other. Exactly what this balance point is depends on the difference, if any, between the selection coefficients of the two homozygotes. In any case, the gene frequency tends to return to an intermediate point after it has been disturbed in any way (Figure 20). We can imagine the beginning, in any population, of a polymorphism produced by heterosis. If the population initially had only one of the two genes, and then the second appeared by mutation or was introduced from some other population, the new rare gene would at first rapidly increase in frequency, exploiting its advantage of nearly always being present in heterozygotes. Then, as it became common, its advantage would decrease and finally disappear, and it would remain as a constant fraction of the gene pool from that time on. A heterotic advantage of this kind will result in similar gene frequencies in many different populations, regardless of how long ago they first became heterozygous for the locus. Figure 20 shows some calculations of changes in gene frequency due to heterosis. The most successful genotype is the heterozygote Aa: either allele in homozygous form produces a less successful individual, with the aa genotype rating lower than the AA genotype. Three populations are shown, starting with different gene frequencies. As generations go by, the frequencies slowly change: in two cases A increases; in one case A decreases. But in all cases the frequency of A is being drawn toward a level of about 60 per cent—the level at which the advantages of the two alleles are tied. The differences in the original gene frequencies of the various populations disappear as this conver-

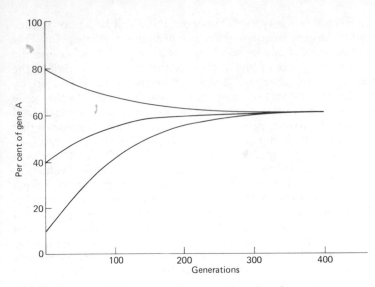

Figure 20 Selection by heterosis: no matter what the starting gene frequencies, all populations change towards the same level. Selection coefficients, in all 3 cases: AA = 1.00, Aa = 1.02, aa = .99.

gence takes place. Many puzzling cases of polymorphisms continuing to exist in widely separated human populations may be explicable in this way.

THE EFFECTS OF ISOLATION

Obviously, any forces that tend to bring about genetic differences between different populations of a species will not be effective unless these populations are separated to some extent. Without separation (not necessarily obvious geographical separation), the whole species would be a single randomly breeding unit. But how much separation is necessary for differences of a racial kind to develop? The breeder of animals generally thinks that total genetic separation of his stock from all others of the species is essential to developing a new breed. But his genetic aims are extremely ambitious when compared to the natural processes by which subspecies or races develop. It is expected of an artificial breed that all individuals in it will be of uniform appearance (in certain characteristics, at least) and so distinct from other breeds that no purebred animal would be mistaken for a member of another breed. Human populations, on the other hand, show much variation *within* populations in the same characteristics that we think of as defining racial differences; and it is only when we deal with populations that originally lived quite far apart that we find it possible to diagnose the race of each individual with any degree of certainty. Furthermore, the animal breeder hopes to develop his breed quickly. There is not much satisfaction in working on a breed that only your great-grandchildren will see in final form. Even if the animal you are breeding has a generation time of one or two years, twenty or thirty of its generations take up quite a bit of a human life. Natural selection does not make such haste, nor does it need to. Because we find in the natural world no fences or cages separating populations, and relatively few natural barriers that are really formidable, this does not preclude the development of quite marked regional differences within a species.

To understand how regional differences develop, we must have a way of defining just what degree of isolation exists between various population groups. In man, as in most of his closer relatives among the primates, *groups* are real. In simpler cultures we may call them *bands* or *tribes.* These are aggregations of individuals, most of whom are related to one another genetically; they recognize that they share certain important interests, usually bound up with a shared territory; and they are more likely than not to marry within their own group. Such affiliations are less strongly felt within the large communities of a modern society; in these there may be many intersecting groups having some of the characteristics we have described, so that the boundaries between them become less clear. (But even a hermit or a sociopath can generally name a group he belongs to, though he may not like his fellow members.) As a result, it is feasible to define patterns of genetic relationship within the human species in terms of (1) basic population units that are random-breeding, or nearly so, within themselves; and (2) amounts of *gene flow* between these units. Such descriptions are the same in form for groups of independent tribes at a culturally simple level as they are for complex communities within, or including the whole of, a modern nation. One way of looking at such a population structure is in terms of the amount of local inbreeding, as opposed to random mating across the board. However, if we take into account the detailed relationships of various units in terms of gene flow, particularly relationships which are the result of geographical position, we begin to understand more about how selection operates in a complex world.

Gene flow is an abstract term for a very personal kind of event. Though some exchange of genes between population units may take place as a result of casual contacts, most of it occurs when an individual actually moves from one group to another; that is, finds a mate, settles down, and raises a family in a group other than that in which he was born. A rough estimate of gene flow can be obtained from a census that tells us how many individuals now permanently residing in a population were born elsewhere. A more accurate estimate takes into account the age of individuals in relation to the age at which people produce the most offspring. On this basis, for instance, a quick estimate of the amount of gene flow *into* the United States at the present time is a little less than 5 per cent per generation from all sources. Gene flow *out*, if it involves individuals who are a random sample of the population, will not affect gene frequencies in the area they leave, though it may make changes elsewhere. Often, of course (this would usually be the case in groups of tribes in a simple culture) gene flow is a more or less mutual exchange. In other cases, such as the United States for over 200 years, gene flow has been very unequal, with many migrants coming in and few going out. This kind of information gives only a very incomplete picture of genetic relations in a complex society. Degrees of genetic isolation exist also between groups within a nation or community, based on race, religion, social class, and national origin, and it would be nearly impossible to express all these relations fully. Under simpler conditions, such as very few people experience in modern times, but which were normal during much of the history and prehistory of man, gene flow between groups was largely based on simple geographical proximity, and can be expressed in a rough way by an ordinary two-dimensional map. We can think of genetic space as something related to physical space, but different from it (Birdsell, 1950). Genetic space would be exactly like physical space if the chances of an individual finding a mate at any given distance from his own birthplace were the same *in any direction*. Even the simplest kind of organization into tribes changes this. An individual is more likely—perhaps much more likely—to find a mate ten miles east of him, if that is within the boundaries of his own tribe, than ten miles west of him, if that is across a tribal boundary. Obviously, too, if a group has more friendly relations with some of its neighbor tribes than with others, mating is more likely to cross some tribal boundaries than others. If we think of a distance in genetic space as expressing the likelihood of gene flow between two points, then two places equally far apart in real space may not be equally far apart in genetic space. Genetic space is a distorted version of real space. It is distorted not only by social groupings, but by geographical features. Barriers to travel, such as mountains, deserts, seas, and great rivers, are also barriers to gene flow, to a degree depending on people's ability and motive to cross them. To peoples of an earlier day, boundaries between ecological zones, though they might be level and easily walked across, were also discouragements to migration. To leave a known kind of territory and go into one where the means of subsistence were different, was too formidable a change to be lightly under-taken. Exploration just to satisfy curiosity, which we see among modern peoples, does not interest people of simple culture. Even the legendary invasions of protohistoric times probably involved rela-tively few individuals. It is likely, therefore, that gene flow between populations during the period when human races were forming was mostly the result of exchange of mates between adjacent tribes. Low population densities prevailed during most of that time, and this would have affected gene flow. If populations were so scattered that uninhabited areas of some size actually separated tribes, this would have resulted in a high degree of isolation. However, some studies of aborigines in Australia, who lived until recent times by hunting and gathering in an area of thin resources, show that gene exchange between tribes actually moves genes across space faster when the land is unproductive, population thinly scattered, and tribal territories large (Birdsell, 1950). More abundant resources, with less necessity for foraging over large areas, can result in less mobility of people, and therefore in less mobility of genes. The villages of the early era of agriculture may therefore have been more inbred than the tribes of the previous hunting era. One thing is sure: we are mistaken if we think of gene flow during most of the history of the human species as being anything like that of the last few centuries, when oceans, previously total barriers to human migration, were crossed by tens of thousands of people. Past patterns of gene flow would have been stable over long periods, and closely parallel to the geography of the world's land masses. It was under such conditions that the basic pattern of distribution of human races must have developed. In these times there would have been extremely little travel in the modern sense. Few individuals would be likely to cross more than one tribal boundary during their lifetime, and gene flow would consist of small but rather constant amounts of migration by individuals who moved once during their lifetime from one population unit to an adjacent one.

The question we are approaching, of course, is that of the *origin* of the racial differences we see at the present time in the human species. It is plausible to suppose—and much information about other species supports this—that a considerable part of these differences have arisen as a result of different selection effects in different environments. But how much genetic difference can be brought about by locally differing selection, if there is continuous gene flow between various population units, and therefore no such thing as complete isolation of populations? Here again, the resources of the computer come to our aid. It is a painstaking but not a difficult task to construct a computer program that will make a simplified model to show us what happens if certain selection differences exist within a group of populations that are continually exchanging genes at a limited but constant rate. A very simple case is shown, diagrammatically, at the left in Figure 21 (population a and its neighbor). Two populations are represented, living under different conditions, so that natural selection is favoring one of two alternative alleles in the first population, and acting against it in the second population. The selection is such that the homozygote of one allele has an advantage of 2 per cent, the homozygote of the other a *dis*advantage of 2 per cent, and the heterozygote is neutral. In the beginning, both populations have the same gene frequencies: 50 per cent of each allele. If these populations were entirely isolated from one another and from all other populations of the same species, they would gradually diverge in gene frequencies so as to become quite different, eventually totally different, in respect to this particular genetic locus. (One example of an isolated population, (e), is represented in Figure 21, for comparison.) However, we have

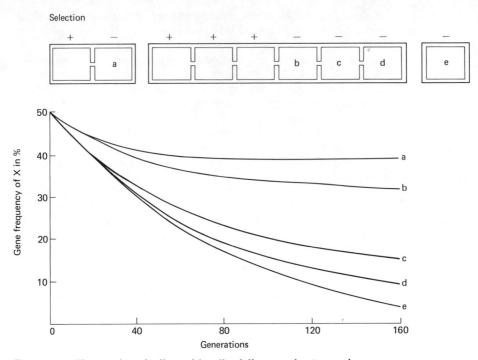

Figure 21 The combined effect of locally different selection and gene flow.

     a: a population negatively selected, adjacent to one positively selected for the same allele, with 2 per cent gene flow.

     b,c,d: three populations negatively selected, part of a chain with three others positively selected, 2 per cent gene flow between adjacent populations.

     e.   a population negatively selected and completely isolated.

     Selection: 2 per cent advantage for one homozygote, 2 per cent *dis*advantage for the other homozygote, heterozygote neutral.

also specified that there is some migration between population *a* and its neighbor, averaging 2 per cent of each population during each generation. We have here a set of two opposing forces. Selection will tend to make gene frequencies in the two populations differ; gene flow will tend to equalize them by mixing the genes of the two populations. The model has been set up so that the net result will be quite symmetrical: the first population will lose one allele just as fast as the second gains it. To simplify the diagram, we have shown what has happened in only one of the populations, that which is losing the allele indicated in the graph.

Following line *a* of the graph, we see selection beginning to change gene frequencies in population *a* from the arbitrary starting point of 50 per cent. The trend at first is rather constant from generation to generation. After about forty generations, the line begins to turn. This is because the *effect* of gene flow between the two groups, as they develop gene frequency differences, does not remain the same, though the *amount* of gene flow remains the same. So long as the groups differ only slightly in gene frequency, the mixing has a minor effect, and selection consistently changes gene frequencies by about one-quarter per cent from one generation to the next. As the difference between the groups becomes greater, however, the gene flow from one group to the other tends to cancel out any further increase of the gene frequency difference. Eventually, in this case at about the seventieth generation, the process becomes a draw. Selection and gene flow cancel out, and the situation stabilizes, with a gene frequency difference that will no longer increase unless some of the underlying conditions change. In this case, the *equilibrium condition* is one in which the difference between the two groups is not very large. Population *a* has gone from 50 to 40 per cent; its counterpart (not shown), from 50 to 60 per cent. Certain changes would obviously affect this result. If the difference in selection between the two areas were greater, *or* if the amount of gene flow between the areas were smaller, the amount of genetic difference finally attained would be greater. Similarly, the amount of difference that would be attained would be less if selection were weaker or if gene flow were greater. It is clear why any attempt to modify the genetic characteristics of a population by deliberate selection will be successful much sooner if the group is entirely isolated, as population *e* in Figure 21.

The situation of two populations with a mutual exchange of genes but with no contact with anybody else, is so simple that it has probably never existed. A more realistic picture would show a number of populations spread over a large area, with gene flow across all of their various boundaries. In this case, any selective factors that were acting would probably be much the same or similar within areas that included several populations. In this situation, many population units would have direct contact only with others that were subject to selection similar to their own. Such a situation is shown in simplified form in the center of Figure 21. Here we have shown six populations, half of them selected in favor of a particular allele, and half of them selected against it. The intensity of selection, and amount of gene flow between adjacent groups, is the same as before. It is clear, however, that in this situation much more striking differences have built up in the same length of time. The populations at the frontier between different selection effects are still so affected by gene flow that they cannot develop very distinctive gene frequencies: *b*, in the six-population chain, is affected not much more strongly than *a* in the first example. But populations *c* and *d*, adjoining others which are selected in the same way as themselves, are relatively protected from the leveling effects of gene flow. The gene frequency levels attained by *c* and *d*, though not as extreme as that of population *e*, which is totally isolated, approach it. The series of genetic barriers, each with a small amount of gene flow, that lie between the populations most distant from one another, are as effective as one barrier with almost no flow at all. Distance itself becomes a formidable barrier because individuals, for the most part, are not traveling far from their places of birth. So long as selection continues to change gene frequencies a little more rapidly than they can be changed back by the averaging effect of gene flow, gene frequency differences between different parts of the area will continue to increase. In a situation like this we would not expect *total* differences between populations to be produced; that is, situations in which one population has only one allele, another population only the other. But this is not what we find in natural racial differences. Development of differences similar to racial differences in man, therefore, requires only *relative* isolation, not complete isolation. The usual condition in man conforms nicely to this model: that is, intermediate gradations exist between populations that are geographically separated and genetically different.

Patterns of change such as this go a long way toward explaining the existence of racial differences in man, and similar differences in other species. However, there are some exceptions to the rule that isolation by distance can limit the distribution of a trait that is favored by selection. So far, we have discussed genes that are increased by selection in one area and decreased by it in another. What if a gene is selectively favored in one area and is quite harmless or neutral in another? It will tend to increase, at the expense of other alleles at the same locus, within the area in which it is favored. Then it will diffuse outward to other areas, not nipped off by adverse selection anywhere else, and thus will gradually spread and increase over a large area. Given enough time, such an allele will extend to the limits of the species, in small but slowly increasing numbers (Figure 22, gene A).

What if a gene is advantageous everywhere, and is perhaps one of the important mutations that give a universal advantage to the whole species, regardless of local environments? Such a mutation acts like an infection. Once it filters into any new area, it proceeds to increase there until it far outnumbers any other genes that may have been introduced from the same neighboring territory, even by the very same migrating individuals. Its destiny is to become universal. For a while it will be commoner in areas near where the mutation occurred, if it occurred only once; but eventually it will be so widespread that it will be difficult to guess where it originated. Such a spread of *progressive* genes can take place effectively even with the relatively small amounts of gene flow that we have seen to be compatible with the development of local racial variations. (See Figure 22, gene B.) This is of considerable interest to students of the evolution of man, who are interested in the question of how many

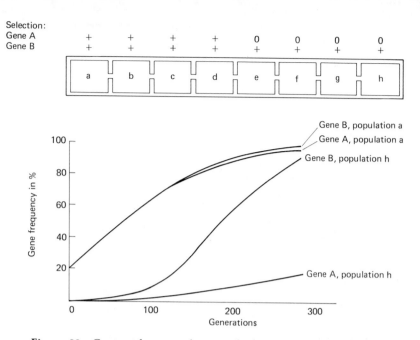

Figure 22 Contrast between the spread of a gene into an area in which it is positively selected, and its spread into an area in which its selection is neutral. Eight populations with 2 per cent gene flow between adjacent ones. Populations a–d start with 20 per cent of both genes and have positive selection for both. Populations e–h start with none of either gene and have positive selection for gene B only. All selection is of blending type, with selection coefficients of homozygotes differing as 1.04 to 1.0.

of the various fossil forms found in various parts of the world actually form part of the direct ancestry of man. At one time we looked for a "cradle of man," a sort of Garden of Eden where the crucial evolutionary changes that led to the human species took place in a small population restricted to a limited area. If an evolutionary process, involving the occurrence and fixation of a number of progressive mutations one after the other, can occur in a species that is widespread in range and includes many partially isolated and racially different populations, our picture of evolution is rather different. For one thing, it makes it easier to believe that each of the large number of mutations required for the change—which has been a very rapid one as compared with many other evolutionary processes that have been studied—could actually have occurred at least once in the species. The possibilities for progressive development would be severely limited if they were confined to the small number of mutations that might occur in any one local population.

GENETIC DRIFT

Isolation of population units can have effects other than that of making the results of local selection more distinct. One of the recurrent problems in the breeding of domestic animals is that small groups of selected individuals, assembled and bred together under artificial conditions, may, quite coincidentally, display characteristics that are undesirable. This may not be apparent until various recombinations of genes have taken place, particularly those which result in the emergence of traits due to recessive alleles. Except in certain cases, this is not due to any true correlation between the traits selected for and the others that appear in the same stock. It is inherent in the process of drawing a small sample from a larger population. If a population is polymorphic for many traits controlled by genes at different loci, any small group of individuals taken from it will have unrepresentative gene frequencies for many of the variable traits. This will be true even if the selection of individuals is entirely at random, with no attempt at selection in favor of any particular variation.

A special situation that can arise under natural conditions, and which must often have occurred in the early history of man, is the colonization of a new area or habitat by a small group of individuals. In the world as we know it today, there are no longer any uninhabited areas to be added to man's range, except those which are almost uninhabitable. But at one time in human prehistory such opportunities could occur. A notable case was the occupation of the Western Hemisphere by man at a relatively late time in the history of the human species. The genetic result that can occur in such a situation is called *founder effect.* The genetic characteristics of a population derived from such a group of pioneers, self-isolated in a new area, will depend on the genes actually carried by its *founders,* not on the gene frequencies of the larger population from which the founders were drawn. The smaller the founder group, the greater is the chance that certain of the less common genes in the larger population are poorly represented or even absent; and that other genes are present in less or more than the average amount. An extreme case would be a new population founded by a single male and female: its characteristics would be as distinct from those of the parent population as are the characteristics of a single family within our own communities. The "family likeness" in ordinary circumstances disappears as the children mate back again into the community. In a founder situation, the family characteristics become the permanent basis of a new population. This may appear to fracture the Hardy-Weinberg law, but in this case one of its conditions has not been met: we are dealing with small numbers, and the law is a statistical one which holds only for large numbers. Like a public opinion poll, it breaks down badly if it is based on only a few households. Thus, in certain circumstances, chance can play a part in producing populations with gene frequencies quite different from any that previously existed. It is important to remember that, just as in the case of changes resulting from selection, there is no reason for gene frequencies in a population produced by this kind of fragmentation to return to the "original" values. Each generation takes a new start from the genetic characteristics of the parent generation just preceding it.

Founder effect is not difficult to understand: we can relate it to a single and unusual historical event. But in a small population the same kind of thing happens over and over again, a process less dramatic but very effective. Think of each generation in any population as drawing a *sample* of genes from the stock offered by its parents. If the population is a large one, large enough for the Hardy-Weinberg law to hold true, this sample will be large enough that chance effects cancel out, and the new gene frequency is not perceptibly different from the previous one. But if a population is small, and depending on how small it is, the sample drawn will be an inaccurate representation of the gene pool from which it was drawn. This is, in effect, a minor kind of founder effect occurring not once, but over and over again in every generation. Under these conditions gene frequencies change erratically, sometimes up, sometimes down; the smaller the population, the greater the amount they are likely to shift. This effect is called *genetic drift*; it produces changes in gene frequency that are not consistent from generation to generation (in contrast to changes due to selection). Neither will the changes be in the same direction or of the same amount in any two populations, even though they have been subjected to the same environment. Figure 23 shows three possible outcomes for an outnumbered allele in populations of small size (25 individuals), over a period of twenty generations. In the course of the erratic fluctuations of frequency, one population has already

Figure 23 Genetic drift: how the numbers of a gene fluctuate in three isolated populations of only 25 individuals each, over a period of 20 generations.

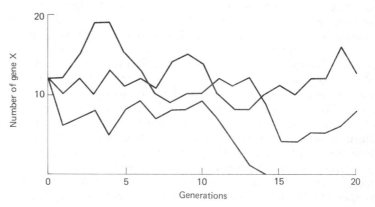

lost the less common allele. If the process continues, the other populations may lose it also. (The rare gene in these cases is in a situation similar to that of the gambler who enters the casino with too small a bank roll: though theoretically he should break even in the long run, bankruptcy may cut his run short.) A characteristic result in these small populations is the complete loss of many of the alleles with which they started. If only two alleles are present at a locus, the loss of one makes the population thenceforth homozygous for the other. Less often, a rare allele will increase markedly. This is particularly noticeable in the case of recessive genes, which throw many more phenotypes when their frequency increases above a minimal level. The effects on the frequency of genes that are nearer the 50 per cent level are just as distinct, though generally less conspicuous. These effects are in no way different from those associated with *inbreeding,* and for good reason: The situation in which genetic drift occurs is an involuntary form of inbreeding, simply the result of physical isolation. Inbreeding in man resulting from social factors, or inbreeding in domestic animals resulting from the desire to develop a "pure line," can produce the same results—with an intensity that is related to the smallness of the group within which mating takes place. Unpredictable changes in gene frequencies, and hence in phenotype, with an increased likelihood of the appearance of undesirable recessive traits, appear in all these situations. Technically, the differences can be described as loss of heterozygosity and reduced polymorphism. Two processes will tend to act against this kind of genetic change. *Stabilizing selection* has already been mentioned. This eliminates individuals who diverge too far from the normal phenotype of the species. For a small population this may be a costly process in terms of deaths and impaired function. This is particularly so for a human population in which poorly functioning individuals are, up to a point at least, supported by the efforts of the able. *Heterosis* also tends to prevent the loss of heterozygosity at certain loci, though genetic drift in a small population may cause the loss of one allele in spite of heterosis, depending on how strongly the two processes are operating in a given case. The ever-present possibility of genetic drift can present us with insoluble mysteries when we attempt to reconstruct the histories of human populations. Because it is a chance process, it introduces an element that makes it impossible to predict the genetic future from the genetic past—except to say that it may be different. For the same reason, genetic drift makes it impossible to infer the genetic past from the present. Two populations that now show genetic differences may have been derived from a common source. We may guess that they came from a common source, and mistakenly attribute their present differences to different selective effects; or we may mistakenly believe that their ancestry was *not* the same, when in fact it was. The possibility that stabilizing selection or heterosis has kept populations more nearly the same in some traits, whereas drift has caused them to diverge in others, further complicates the picture. Genetic drift also means that any population, if it is of small size, or has been at any time in the past, has acquired a genetic uniqueness and can never be duplicated by any other population.

The importance of drift in the development of human racial differences is very difficult to estimate. The period in human pre-history when genetic drift would have been most effective lies very far back, when human population density was very low, and man was probably an endangered species in parts of his range. The weakness of genetic drift as a mechanism for differentiating popu-lations lies in the random nature of the changes it produces. The genetic peculiarities that develop in a single isolated population because of drift may differ from those of even its closest neighbors, so that they are readily washed out by gene flow. In addition, the existence of prohibitions against incest in all peoples, probably from very early times, imposes limits on how small a human popu-lation can be and still maintain genetic isolation. The effects of genetic drift would be most evident in populations peripheral to the general distribution of the species, where gene flow is less likely to obliterate local differences. As we have seen, selection effects may also be more conspicuous in such areas (Figure 21), and can equally well account for their genetic distinctness. But a possible role of genetic drift in developing some of the regional varieties of man cannot be discounted. In cases where population differences seem entirely unadapted to local environmental conditions, it is always a possible explanation.

GENETIC CHANGE IN POLYGENIC SYSTEMS

The computer models we have presented describe genetic change from the point of view of single genetic loci. This serves the proper purpose of a mathematical model, which is to simplify matters. The realities of human inheritance involve multiple genes for many traits. In most cases these genes probably act in an additive manner. That is, if either gene X or gene Y or gene Z makes you tall, any two of them acting together will make you taller; and the combination of X, Y, and Z will make you still taller. The studies of inheritance of body size indicate that this is approximately true. Other gene interactions may not affect observed traits in such a "sensible" way. But some general rules can be made for the effect of selection and of genetic drift on polygenic systems such as described above. The phenotype in these situations is, of course, characteristically varia-ble over a range that includes many intermediate individuals—size characteristics in man being a typical example. What happens if selection favors one end of such a range, acting most strongly on the individuals of extreme phenotype? One of the two alternative al-leles at each of the loci involved will be more often present in a favored genotype—though sometimes it will get stuck in bad company, so to speak—and selection will change gene frequencies at all the loci, though less rapidly at each than it would if a single locus were responsible for all the phenotypic variation. If an intermediate phenotype is the most successful—for instance, near-average body size as opposed to very small or very large—selection for or against any one allele will be inconsistent. If genetic drift also plays a significant role because of isolation and small population size, some of the loci may attain a 100 per cent level of the "small" allele; others may attain a 100 per cent level of the "large" allele; and still other loci may remain heterozygous. In any case, the selection process *does* tend to maintain the population within the phenotypic range that is most successful.

To the student of racial differences and racial history, the greatest significance of polygenic inheritance is that polygenically determined traits, as opposed to traits of more simple inheritance, give us some hint as to whether differences between populations are better explained by different local selection effects or by genetic drift. The characteristic of genetic drift is that it operates in a chance fashion, increasing or decreasing the frequency of a gene impartially and independently of its phenotypic effect. Its action, in fact, will be shown most clearly in traits upon which selection has no impact whatsoever. Selection, however, is tied to the phenotype, and (except where intermediate phenotypes are favored) has a *direction* in any particular environment. An example may be given from human skin color, which is clearly polygenic in its inheritance, though the exact number of the various loci and the magnitude of their effects are not known. Genetic drift, acting on these various different loci, would alter gene frequencies in a random way. In a single population in which drift was acting, it might increase the "dark" alleles at some loci, the "light" alleles at other loci, with a net effect on the phenotype that was neutral or not very great. Only by occasional coincidence would genetic drift alter gene frequencies *in the same phenotypic direction* at many or all of the loci. Selection based on phenotype, however, will do exactly that. It will tend to change all the gene frequencies in a population in such a way as to produce the maximum phenotypic change, and consequently will produce marked phenotypic differences between populations that have been subject to different selective pressures. There has been much argument among human geneticists and anthropologists about the relative value of simple single-gene traits (such as the blood groups) as compared with polygenic traits, as means of evaluating population history. The single-gene traits are much more congenial to the geneticist's methods of analysis. The very thought of *selection* is disquieting if we are attempting, for instance, to infer historical relations between populations on the basis of their gene frequencies at "simple" loci. But if we are specifically interested in the role of natural selection as a factor in the differentiation of human populations, the polygenic traits offer us not only much additional evidence, but some evidence that is uniquely valuable. In the discussion of the variable traits of man that follows, therefore, there will be no discrimination against traits polygenically determined or against those that for any other reason are not clearly understood genetically, provided there is evidence that they are in fact inherited in some manner and to some degree. Particular attention will be given to the ways in which they may be of selective value in some or all the environments in which the human species has lived.

5 Pigmentation

Differences in color are among the most conspicuous of human physical variations. Skin color is often regarded by the layman as virtually synonymous with race, despite the fact that similar skin color is found in populations that are very different in other respects. Probably the most meaningless term ever used in referring to race is *nonwhite,* which lumps together people who, when all traits are taken into account, may differ more from one another than any of them differ from Caucasians. In addition, *nonwhite* is usually interpreted to include populations in Asia that have skin color as light or lighter than some Europeans. To use the term is to perpetuate ignorance. Marked differences in skin color have a great visual impact, and people who have not previously encountered anyone with skin color very different from their own often find it hard to believe. Light-skinned travelers in remote places have had the experience of being spied upon by people to whom extensive clothing was as much a novelty as light skin; they were intensely curious to know whether the strangers were really that color *all over.* The impression given by difference in skin color seems stronger than that produced by differences in hair and eye color perhaps because the coverage is so complete, suggesting a difference in the inner substance. Yet the color is actually limited to a microscopically thin layer of the skin. The intensity of the pigment that produces it can be judged from a single dark hair: it can be completely black with pigment in spite of its very small diameter. The pigment-bearing layer of the skin is in fact about a hundredth of an inch thick, the diameter of a medium-fine hair.

The basic colors of skin, hair, and eyes are produced by the same pigment, *melanin,* an insoluble substance highly resistant to chemical change and fading, which is present in minute granules. In man there are two forms of melanin: *eumelanin,* which produces various shades of brown or black, and *phaeomelanin,* the pigment of red hair. Melanin occurs in these two forms in many mammals and birds. Some species have two distinct color phases, red and black, which appear in individuals otherwise quite the same. The two melanins differ chemically, and form granules of different shape, the black granules being more elongated than the red. Melanin granules are produced by a special type of cell, the *melanocyte,* which has an unusual origin and life history. All of the cells responsible for pigment in the skin, hair, and the visible part of the eye originate, in the embryo, from an area lying close to the midline of the back. (This same tissue also gives rise to parts of the nervous system.) The melanocytes migrate laterally from this area, multiplying as they go, and locate in the various areas where melanin will later be formed.

SKIN COLOR

In the skin, most melanocytes come to rest in the *germinative layer* of the epidermis. This is the deeper of the two principal layers of the epidermis, and consists of live cells that continue to grow and divide throughout the individual's life (Figure 24). Overlying this living layer, and separated from it by a thin transitional zone, is the *stratum corneum,* a layer of dead cells which forms the actual surface of the skin. The epidermis is a very active tissue. The live cells of the deeper layer are continually multiplying and pushing new cells upward. As these cells approach the surface they become infiltrated with a horny substance called *keratin,* and die. In this way the superficial layer of dead cells is continually replenished to compensate for material removed from the surface by friction. As a result of this constant growth process, the thickness of the various layers remains more or less constant, although individual cells are continually being born, growing old, and finally being shed from the surface of the skin in minute dry flakes. The melanocytes, scattered among the living cells in the deepest part of the germinative layer, have the special function of producing pigment. The form of a

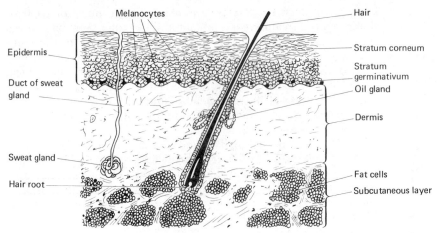

Epidermis

Melanocytes

Hair

Stratum corneum

Duct of sweat gland

Stratum germinativum

Oil gland

Dermis

Sweat gland

Hair root

Fat cells

Subcutaneous layer

A. Cross section of human skin

Figure 24 Cross-section of human skin. (From R. E. Haupt, et al., *Elementary Physiology and Anatomy: A Laboratory Guide.* Courtesy of Macmillan Publishing Co., Inc.)

melanocyte in the skin is reminiscent of nerve cells, which are derived from the same embryonic tissue. Each melanocyte has a number of slender branching arms that reach out between the epidermal cells and transfer to other cells melanin granules that have been formed within the melanocyte. A relatively small number of pigment-forming cells, therefore, produce melanin and distribute it to the numerous cells around and between them. Because new cells are continually formed in the germinative layer, the production of melanin is a continuous process also.

The color of the skin depends principally on the amount of melanin in the epidermis; however, the number of melanocytes is essentially the same for all colors of skin. The difference lies in the amount of melanin produced by each melanocyte, and the way in which the granules are distributed. In a true albino—an individual who has no pigmentation at all—melanocytes are present but never produce melanin. In light-skinned persons the melanocytes produce melanin slowly, and in dark-skinned persons, melanin is produced rapidly and in large quantities. In addition, the melanin granules in lighter skins are clumped into groups, and those in darker skins are separate and more evenly dispersed (Szabo, 1969). In the latter state they absorb light more effectively, thus producing a darker color with the same amount of melanin.

Certain other factors influence skin color. In skins that have little melanin, the color is visibly affected by the blood in the superficial blood vessels. The amount of blood that comes close enough to the skin surface to be visible is controlled by the nervous system and can change, sometimes very quickly. (We will discuss this in Chapter 10.) In this way heat, cold, and emotional conditions can affect

Carotene

the skin's pinkness or lack of it, and physical irritation of various kinds can produce temporary or chronic reddening in exposed areas. The thickness of the *stratum corneum* also affects skin color; the keratin it contains is faintly yellowish, and a thick stratum corneum tends to conceal the color resulting from blood. In addition, *carotene* (not to be confused with keratin), a pigment present in numerous common vegetable foods, adds a yellow tone to the skin if it is abundant in the diet. There appear to be different shades of color in dark skins, varying from a warm or yellowish brown to a cold or grayish brown. For reasons that will be more fully discussed when we consider eye color, the apparent color of a dark pigment like melanin is affected by the thickness and transparency of the material that overlies it. If the overlying tissues are thick or faintly opaque, the surface color appears gray or bluish. Thus, a dark skin that is oily—because oil increases the transparency of the superficial layers—will appear browner in tone, and a dark skin that is dry or scurfy will appear grayer. One type of definitely "bluish" coloring is known to be the result of the presence of melanin at a deeper level than normal. This is the "sacral spot," a gray-blue mark at the base of the spine, the result of melanin in the *dermis*, a deeper layer than the epidermis where most melanin is located. This occurs most commonly in Mongoloid races, but is not unknown in other populations (Comas, 1960). The melanin is the same color as usual; the greater thickness of the overlying tissue is responsible for the different color effect.

Within any one population, average skin color is darker in males than in females. Though this is often accentuated by habitual differences in exposure to the sun, it is a real difference. Male sex hormones apparently increase melanin formation somewhat (Edwards, 1941). Melanin is poorly developed in newborn infants. Babies of light-skinned races are quite red at birth, because the nervous mechanisms that control blood-flow near the surface of the skin are not yet functioning. Newborns of dark-skinned races are a brick red—the combined effect of the "blood" color and an amount of melanin much less than they will have later. After birth, they darken rapidly as more melanin forms. In old age the formation of melanin in the skin appears to be somewhat reduced, though by no means as markedly as in the hair.

Freckling is common in lighter shades of human skin. These spots of darker color sometimes seem to appear in response to exposure to light; however, this may be at least in part illusory, the result of darkening by a tanning effect which makes the freckles more conspicuous. They do appear to come and go to some extent, and it would be interesting if we had some careful records to show whether or not an individual's freckle pattern remains the same from year to year. Freckles are sometimes so numerous that they merge into large irregular patches. The apparent correlation of freckling with hair color is interesting, and will be discussed later.

Anyone of a light-skinned race is aware of the dramatic changes of skin color that can take place as a result of exposure to the sun.

These are the result of only a single component of sunlight, the *ultraviolet* radiation. The total range of solar radiation is more than is apparent to the eye. Visible light consists of various wavelengths that are perceived as different colors, ranging from violet through blue, yellow, and red. Beyond the visible red, and continuous with it in a physical sense, is the *infrared* radiation that is perceived as heat: it may be felt by holding the hand near an object that has been heated, but not to the point of emitting light. Most radiant light sources emit infrared as well. Extending beyond the visible spectrum on the other end is the ultraviolet, the radiation that produces sunburn and tanning. These rays are not present in ordinary artificial light. Sunlight contains a large component of ultraviolet as it comes from the sun, but the ultraviolet is screened out to a greater extent by the atmosphere than is visible light. When the sun is low in the sky, and its light must pass at an angle through the atmosphere, the ultraviolet component is greatly reduced. This means that ultraviolet exposure is much less in the temperate zone than in the tropics, particularly in winter. Consequently skin color is at its lightest in temperate-zone dwellers during the winter, and their skin is nearly the same color in the parts not covered by clothing as in the parts that are. In the spring the exposed skin surfaces tend to darken, especially in an individual who is outdoors much of the time. If exposure to the sun is sudden and intense, sunburn, with its unpleasant symptoms of pain, blistering, and peeling, may result. It is well-known that the skin darkens after a sunburn episode, and having once darkened, is relatively immune to further sunburn for that season. The course of this entire process has been experimentally studied on human subjects, to whom we must express particular thanks, because their volunteer services included allowing small pieces of their skin to be removed for microscopic study. The first forewarning that skin has been exposed to ultraviolet beyond its current tolerance is a reddening that appears several hours after exposure, too late to do anything about it; this reddening reaches a maximum in two days. The color results from excessive blood flow to the affected areas, a reaction to cell damage by the ultraviolet rays. At the same time, the growing cells in the lowest layer of the epidermis begin to throw off new cells at an increased rate, peaking in about three days. As the red color of the skin fades, it becomes apparent that the skin is developing a brown color (tanning). This color effect reaches its maximum in about eight days, and then very slowly fades. With no further exposure to ultraviolet rays, it takes the skin about three months to return to its original color (Daniels, 1964). The first reaction of tanning is that melanin in the skin begins to move toward the surface, from the germinative layer into the stratum corneum. In addition, melanocytes are stimulated to produce melanin more rapidly. At the same time, the stratum corneum increases in thickness (Yoshimura, 1964). The changed color of the tanned skin results primarily from the increase of melanin, partially from the increased thickness of the stratum corneum and the melanin that has moved into it.

These changes in the stratum corneum probably play a considerable part in protection against future sunburn. Occasionally, Negroes with quite dark skin may experience sunburn (Daniels, 1968), showing that the *amount* of melanin does not guarantee against tissue damage: the slight change in its position is important also.

The effectiveness of the tanning response varies among individuals, just as does the amount of melanin present in the unexposed skin. Very pale skins, particularly those of individuals with red hair, respond poorly to light, and these individuals may never develop enough tan to withstand much exposure to the sun. In individuals with brunet or light brown skins, the tanning capacity is generally quite large, so they change color very markedly with the seasons, and show a startling contrast between the normally exposed and unexposed parts of the body surface. In dark skins, the tanning effect is less noticeable, but nevertheless present; it is inconspicuous because the additional melanin in a skin already quite dark is not very obvious to the eye (Weiner, 1964).

Ultraviolet light has significant effects other than producing sunburn. It may produce a long delayed but more serious effect by causing cancer of the skin. The risk of this malignancy is high in lightly pigmented persons who live in areas of high solar radiation, particularly if they are engaged in outdoor occupations. Fair-skinned persons of Northern European ancestry who now live as farmers or ranchers in dry, sunny areas of the western United States, for instance, are particularly vulnerable. Many years of chronic sunburn, resulting from inadequacy of the tanning process, often precede the appearance of the cancer. It has been questioned whether the adaptations of the skin for resisting ultraviolet radiation are important factors in natural selection. Sunburn, after all, is not a fatal disease, and death from skin cancer would not generally occur early enough in life to limit an individual's reproductive performance. But we also know that in some peoples of primitive culture, the older males attempt—with greater or less success—to monopolize the younger women; therefore, increased mortality even in later life might have selective effect. It has been pointed out also that disorders and eruptions of the skin, may decrease an individual's physical attractiveness, so as to affect reproduction.

Another significant effect of ultraviolet is its role in the formation of vitamin D (Loomis, 1967). This vitamin is produced within human skin by the action of ultraviolet radiation on naturally occurring cholesterol. Unless the diet is rich in vitamin D, the amount produced in this way may be essential, especially during childhood. In a northerly climate, where sunlight is limited during the winter and is especially lacking in ultraviolet, and where the body is generally rather fully clothed against cold, this vitamin synthesis will depend on the exposure of a small area of skin to relatively small amounts of ultraviolet. Some northern peoples, such as the Eskimos, have no problem because there is adequate vitamin D in their diet. But if this is not the case, vitamin D must be synthesized. A large amount of melanin in the skin may be the critical factor that makes this synthesis inadequate. In the late nineteenth and early twentieth centuries, when many Europeans and Americans crowded into urban environments darkened by coal smoke, vitamin D deficiency was common. This resulted in impaired bone development in children, called *rickets*, which was followed by permanent deformities of the skeleton. Though the victims usually survived, distortion of the pelvis frequently caused affected women to experience difficult childbirth—which in those days was often fatal. In United States cities it was conspicuous that Negroes were more susceptible to rickets than other races, a fact we now know to be due to their dark skin, which is less able to form vitamin D. It appears, then, that there are at least two counterbalanced selective effects of those adaptations of the skin that screen out ultraviolet radiation. Too much penetration of ultraviolet results in tissue damage, too little results in possible vitamin deficiency (Loomis, 1967). Consequently the skin color that is advantageous in one part of the world is disadvantageous in another.

Ultraviolet radiation is not the only component of sunlight that affects the skin. We are all aware that a dark-colored object exposed to the sun becomes hotter than a light-colored one. This poses a problem for a dark-skinned individual who is exposed to the sun in a climate in which heat is a major environmental problem. Some of the heat felt from sunlight is the result of infrared radiation that warms any skin, regardless of its color. The effect of visible light, however, is different. Visible light is converted into heat when it is absorbed by a pigment such as melanin. A surface that appears light in color is reflecting much of the visible light that reaches it: about 45 per cent in the case of the lightest human skins. A dark surface reflects much less: about 16 per cent in the darkest human skins. The visible light that is not reflected is converted into heat. This additional absorption of light and production of heat in darkskinned individuals exposed to bright sun places an extra load on the physiological mechanisms that keep the body temperature normal in heat (Hamilton, 1973). (The problems of body cooling are particularly serious during exercise, a matter that will be more fully discussed in Chapter 10.) Thus increased melanin in the skin may have some disadvantage as well as advantage where the sun is bright. Another effect of skin melanin has recently been reported (Post, 1975). For reasons that are not clear, skin that contains large amounts of melanin is more severely damaged by freezing. This may be a factor in the racial differences in tolerance to cold, which are also discussed in Chapter 10.

There is another way in which surface color may be adaptive to a particular environment. Many animals are *protectively colored*; that is, their coloring blends into their surroundings in such a way that they may escape the notice of other animals, particularly when they are not moving. Natural selection may bring about striking differences between local populations on this basis, as discussed in Chapter 4. For this reason yellowish or tawny colors are most likely to occur in mammals of arid areas. Here vegetation is sparse, its leafy portions often brown or yellow during much of the year, and the soil is usually light in color. Dark coloring is more likely to be found in warm, humid areas, where vegetation is dense and produces dark shadows (Mayr, 1970). White fur, rare in most parts of the world, is seen in arctic mammals; this color blends with the snow cover that is present at the most critical time of year for survival. The most specialized adaptation is the change in coat color from dark to white that takes place with the change of seasons in some northern species of mammals and birds. Protective coloration seems to be as useful to predators as to their prey, the former taking advantage of it for better stalking their victims. Lions and mice alike exhibit it. Now we might like to think that man is always brave and bold, and does not need to skulk or hide: but even this self-acclaimed noble animal has nothing to lose by remaining unobserved when he so desires. Of course clothing may conceal much of man's skin color but faces and hands are not normally covered; and in some climates any great amount of clothing is intolerable much of the time. So it is not surprising that man sometimes follows rules of protective coloration similar to those of other mammals (Cowles, 1959, 1967). Dark skins are commonly found in the humid, dark-shadowed tropics. Man does not follow the rules well in temperate humid areas, perhaps because there he is usually more fully clothed. But some peoples of dry areas are yellowish in skin color; and the lightest skins are found in northerly latitudes, where man alters his color somewhat with the seasons—though in a different way from other mammals. Selection, of course, may be reversed with changes in environment. Nowadays dark-skinned pedestrians walking by a road at night are endangered because motorists do not readily see them; their protective coloration has become hazardous, and they are advised to wear light clothing as a safety measure.

The existence of a range of skin color between the lightest and the darkest indicates that several independent genetic factors are involved in the activity of skin melanocytes. Attempts to guess how many there are have not been very successful, but it seems clear than there are a number of genes with small but not necessarily equal effects, combining additively to produce the large variety of human skin colors. Studies of families in which both parents are racially mixed show that children are rarely very much lighter or darker than either parent. This agrees with the supposition that numerous genes are involved. The greater the number of independent genes, the less is the chance of any child reverting strongly to the skin color of either original race. Tales abound of dark-skinned infants who give away carefully hidden secrets in the family tree. In most of these cases, one or both of the parents approach the borderline of skin color at which people's judgment of race changes. Other factors—facial features, hair form, and so on—have combined in such a way as to make the child appear racially different from the parents.

Regional differences in skin color must be assessed carefully, because casual observation of peoples who lead outdoor lives, seen in their customary clothing, may lead one to mistake a heavy tan for a naturally dark skin color. In populations of the Old World, however, regional skin color difference are far too great to be confused by this. The differences are quite noticeable even within the so-called whites of Europe. Predominantly fair skins are found in northern Europe, from the Atlantic coast eastward to the steppes of Russia; southward, average skin color gradually becomes darker, being a typical brunet white in the Mediterranean area. We have seen that depigmented skin is an advantage where exposure to ultraviolet radiation is limited. This is especially true in northern Europe. In areas far from the equator, much ultraviolet is filtered out because of the low angle of the sun's rays. The effect is greater if the climate is damp and cloudy, because both clouds and water vapor further reduce the amount of ultraviolet that reaches the earth's surface. In the Eurasian land mass, humidity and rainfall are concentrated on the west side; northern Europe has a minimum of ultraviolet radiation compared with areas equally far north in Asia. Thus the climate of the area where human skin is lightest is exactly that in which reduced pigmentation is advantageous to facilitate the synthesis of vitamin D. In such an environment, of course, the need for pigmentation as protection against excess solar radiation is at a minimum. In the latter part of the Ice Age these damp, cloudy conditions extended further south in Europe, so that the adaptation may have started very long ago. Perhaps the European Neanderthals were the first blonds. It is not surprising that in southern Europe, where the balance of advantage is different because of greater ultraviolet radiation, average skin color is darker.

In North Africa, along the shores of the Mediterranean, skin color does not differ greatly from that in southern Europe; a dark brunet, with good tanning capacity, is typical. In some areas, individuals and groups with darker skin color are found, evidence of a somewhat recent admixture from populations south of the Sahara Desert. Ancient art shows that in Egypt, as long as five thousand years ago, brunet white skin color was normal. Egyptian artists clearly distinguished the color of their own people from that of Negroes, whom they knew well. A heavy tan must have been universal. In Egypt, solar radiation is as high as anywhere in the world and cloudless skies the rule, and the ancient Egyptians wore a minimum of clothing under this brilliant sun; clearly, they tolerated ultraviolet well. South of Egypt and the Sahara, however, we encounter some of the darkest skins in the world. The center of blackness in Africa seems to be the great concave bend of its west coast, and the valley of the Congo River extending inland along the equator. This is a hot region but not a particularly sunny one: rainfall is heavy and much of the land forested. The distribution of skin color in Africa suggests that dark-brunet skin (at least a skin capable of turning this shade with sufficient tanning) is quite adequate for protection against maximum ultraviolet radiation, and that something else has favored the development of really black skins. In West Africa this may very well be the protective coloration effect we have discussed. The distribution of skin color in the rest of Africa is inconsistent, however. Very dark skins extend outward into the drier zones around the rain forest, east into Ethiopia, and into relatively dry South Africa. In some of these areas the extra heating effect of the sun on black skin should be noticeable; it appears not to have had any effect, at least not during the time these dark people have been in these areas. It might be noted that many of them are cattleherders, who no longer have need of the hunter's color camouflage. The Bushmen of southwest Africa, who are an older population in the area, and one still living primarily by hunting, differ from their neighbors by being yellowish-brown in skin color. This is the perfect adaptation for the desert hunter—dark enough to stand the sun, yet inconspicuous against the colors of the desert.

There is a similar gradient of skin color from Europe southeast through the Middle East and India. In the dry and sunny areas of southwest Asia, skin color is brunet, usually heavily tanned; and in India, skin color varies but is very dark in many individuals. India, like Equatorial Africa, has rain-forest areas, arid areas, and intermediate climates as well, in a close mosaic not now particularly correlated with skin color. Here, as in Africa, the critical selective force may have been protective coloration in the rain forest, not particularly disadvantaged in the drier areas, with the effect confused by population movements and by the decreased importance of hunting during the last few thousand years.

In Central and East Asia, the northern peoples are also fairly light-skinned, though their depigmentation is not as extreme as that found in northern Europe. In comparing the climate of Asia with that of Europe, a good general statement is that for the same latitude, Asia is always drier. Thus, in the most northern parts of Asia sunlight is more available than in northern Europe, and the selective effect in favor of light skin color would not be as strong. All these peoples, of course, are Mongoloids, racially quite different from northern Europeans. Some comment is appropriate here on the difference in skin color which, though not very great, has caused these peoples to be referred to as a "yellow" race. Mongoloids tend to have a thicker stratum corneum than Caucasoids. This has two effects: it imparts a slightly yellowish cast to the skin—the color of keratin—and it conceals the blood color that gives a pinkish tone to most lighter Caucasian skins. The amount of melanin in the skin of the Asian Mongoloids is often no more than that of Europeans living at the same latitudes, though a difference in hair and eye color may give an *impression* of a different complexion. The thicker stratum corneum has another effect on the Mongoloid skin: it tends to suppress the fine hair-line wrinkles that are a sign of advancing age in Caucasoids. When a Mongoloid skin does wrinkle, it does so late, and in deeper and coarser wrinkles. This makes it hard for a person from a Caucasoid community to judge the age of a person of Mongoloid race. Recently a promoter in the United States took advantage of this difference by making the claim that the retention of youthful smoothness in the skins of Chinese women resulted from the use of an "ancient remedy" called ginseng oil; this he generously offered to sell for only eight dollars an ounce. There is some southward increase of darker shades of skin in the East Asian Mongoloids, but it is not very marked, even in Burma and Viet Nam, which are at the latitude of India.

In the great offshore islands of Indonesia, skin color is predominantly medium brown; these are the darkest of the Mongoloids. Yet this skin color does not compare with that of central Africa, which, like Indonesia, straddles the equator. The relict Negrito populations of this area are, however, much darker in skin color. Probably in Southeast Asia and Indonesia the Mongoloids have not had time to develop the dark coloration appropriate to the rain forest; and perhaps they have not been under any great pressure to do so because their movement into that area brought agriculture and a relaxation of the need for color camouflage. East of Indonesia is Melanesia, which has a similar tropical climate. The population here is apparently "original," that is, descended from the first major population group that inhabited the area. The Melanesians have skin color comparable to the equatorial Africans, though they seem not to be closely related to them. This, as in Africa, appears to be a color adaptation that has developed over a very long time.

The native Australians present the same paradox as the black-skinned South Africans. They have skin color like their Melanesian relatives nearer the equator, but have moved into a drier habitat where the very dark skin is not obviously adapted in color, though they have remained hunters. It may be of some significance that soil color in Australia is predominantly red, and probably appears rather dark to the color-blind marsupial game animals. Perhaps if this were not the case the Australians might have become somewhat lighter-skinned during their possible twenty thousand or more years in their present home.

The New World differs from the Old by having only a moderate and unclear correlation of skin color with latitude. Many North American Indians fall well within the skin-color range of Europeans—if they live urban, white-collar lives, as many now do. They tan heavily when exposed to the sun, which has given them the reputation of being darker than they really are. It is an irony of popular thinking that a Caucasian who has no lighter skin than an Indian when both are leading indoor lives, and turns as dark as an Indian when exposed to the sun, is thought of as "white" and the Indian is not. Some Central and South American Indians are as dark as Indonesians who live in the same climate and type of environment. As we have pointed out in discussing the Old World, this amount of pigment is more than adequate to cope with the damaging effects of too much ultraviolet. But there is no extreme blond depigmentation in the New World except as a rare mutation, and no real black or near-black. The reason probably is that the American populations, derived from northern Asia, had only limited genetic potentialities for skin color difference, the same that exist in the Asian Mongoloids.

In summary, there seem to be three major selective adaptations of human skin color. The first, effective in latitudes more than 50 degrees from the equator—which means, of the world's inhabited land masses, only in the Northern Hemisphere—is a relatively depigmented skin. This is carried to an extreme in the damp, cloudy north of Europe. The second, effective in those areas where solar radiation, and particularly ultraviolet, is high, is skin pigmented to a brunet stage, with the potentiality of tanning to a light-medium brown. The third major selective adaptation is dark brown or black skin color, which serves as concealing coloration in populations of tropical rain forests. The latter adaptation is primarily important to hunters, and wanes in significance with the advent of herding and agricultural economies. A less important factor is adaptation to desert areas by yellow or light-brown color, again primarily in hunting cultures. This is difficult to evaluate because its effect so often coincides with that of adaptation to high solar radiation. A selective factor probably much less important than any of these is the adverse heat-absorbing quality of very dark skin under high solar radiation. The gradient from fair skin in the far north to black in the tropics is not as simple as it seems: it involves both adaptation to ultraviolet and concealing coloration. It is coincidental that these effects form a gradation of color between tropical Africa and the regions north of it of such a kind that gene exchange between these areas has produced no anomalies of functional adaptation. Some of the irregularities of skin-color distribution in Asia and its offshore islands have probably come about because the color-camouflage adaptations have declined in importance in recent millenia, as hunting became a less essential food technology. It is likely that the genes necessary for true blackness of skin were traded around by small amounts of gene flow between the tropical peoples of the Old World, and subsequently attained high gene frequencies in different areas by independent selection. The rain-forest populations of the New World never obtained these genes, and hence never developed skin as dark as that found in various tropical areas of the Old World.

HAIR COLOR

Hair is an extension of the epidermis and becomes pigmented in a similar way. The hair follicle is a narrow pocket in the epidermis, extended in depth so that the epidermal layers lining it actually push into the deeper layer, the *dermis* (see Figure 21). The lining of the follicle is a continuation of the germinative layer of the epidermis. Within the follicle the cells of the germinative layer behave as elsewhere, continuously producing new cells which eventually become filled with keratin, and then die. However, the structure of the follicle is such that these expendable cells, instead of forming a flat layer, are extruded as a thin filament. Melanocytes, with the same origin and history as described for the skin, are located in the hair follicles, and there produce melanin and transfer it to the cells which form the hair. Hair color in man is complicated by the presence of the two different melanins, brown and red, which together produce a great variety of shades. The darkest human hair is quite black, with large amounts of eumelanin; in such cases the red phaeomelanin, if present, is not visible. However, if the amount of eumelanin is less, the phaeomelanin is visible, resulting in a great number of shades of brown, which vary not only from dark to light, but also in degree of reddish tint. If phaeomelanin predominates, the hair is usually called red; but this term includes many shades, from a color that contains as much eumelanin as a medium-light brown, with a large amount of phaeomelanin in addition, producing a dark but intense red, to a pure light red in which no eumelanin is apparent. If neither melanin is present in appreciable amounts, the hair has a pale straw color, the color of the keratin which forms the body of the hair.

So far as we know, the melanocytes that are present in the hair follicles do not differ from those which supply melanin to the skin (Chase, 1958). However, the activity of a melanocyte is affected by the location in which it finds itself. Hair color may differ from skin color, not only in man but in other animals. It is common for dark hair to grow out of light skin, less common for light hair to grow out of dark skin. Also, hair follicle melanocytes may produce varying amounts of melanin, and varying relative amounts of eumelanin and phaeomelanin, in different parts of the body. This is particularly conspicuous in bearded men, who may have a reddish beard with brown or blond head hair, or a black beard with lighter head hair. Sometimes the mustache and the chin portion of the beard are lighter than the rest of the beard—reminiscent of the lighter ventral color seen in many other mammals.

The study of hair color in man is complicated by age changes. The amount of melanin in the hair may increase with age for a number of years, then decrease abruptly as the hair grays. The light-blond hair of childhood often does not persist into adult years; frequently it darkens to a greater or less degree. The principal change seems to coincide with puberty and is presumed to be influenced by sex hormones. The most dramatic changes occur in males, in whom, sometimes, the hair color change from childhood to adult years is from golden blond to black. In women the change is generally less marked, often going only from blond to medium brown. The timing is very unfortunate: just at the age when the young female begins to appreciate her blond hair, the color begins to turn muddy, and requires artificial assistance to regain its "natural" hue. Red shades of hair are particularly subject to darkening by the later appearance of eumelanin; therefore true reds are rarely permanent. Childhood red hair more often turns to reddish medium brown in females or dark brown or black in males. Sometimes infants are born with dark hair that is soon replaced by lighter hair: this may be the result of a temporary response to sex hormones which reach the fetus by way of the placenta.

"Graying" of the hair with advancing age is the result of abrupt cessation of melanin formation in one hair at a time. The "gray" effect is due to a mixture of pigmented and white hairs; an individual hair is either pigmented or white, or, rarely, pigmented at the end and white at the base, if melanin formation ceased while the hair was growing out. The immediate cause of this pigment loss is not known, but it is probably the result of the death of the hair follicle melanocytes; in any case, they cease to function (Fitzpatrick, 1965).

The genetics of hair color in man, like that of skin color, is complex, as indicated by the great variety of colors. The study of hair color in other mammals has demonstrated such a variety of factors that it offers no encouragement to easy genetic analysis of human hair color (Searle, 1968). The patterning of red and brown shades in many humans has analogues in dogs and horses; in these animals, a variety of alleles governing these patterns are known, but not clearly understood, even though controlled breeding in these animals makes genetic study much easier than in man. Two common types of pattern seem to be shared by men and dogs. The black hair-red beard pattern of man is similar to the black-and-tan pattern seen in terriers, hounds, and some other breeds; and the blond hair-black beard pattern is similar to the fawn-with-black-muzzle of boxers and bulldogs. In men with these color patterns, hairs of different colors may be mingled in a single area, a condition called *brindle* in animals (Henderson, et al., 1974). In these color patterns we see a clear "location effect" on the activity of the melanocytes. The age changes, at least of red hair, may prove to be another manifestation of the versatility of these cells. Graying of the hair is known in other mammals and can be genetically predicted in some, confirming its hereditary nature. The age at which graying begins in man is often similar in members of the same family. White hairs apparently have some social function in other primates. A thick scattering of white hairs on the back of a male gorilla denotes full adulthood, and presumably indicates to other gorillas that he is an individual to be respected. If this was once the function of gray hair in man, it is not working very well at the present time.

Hair color probably shares some of the adaptive effects we have discussed in connection with skin color. Any protective coloration advantage due to skin color would be spoiled by a contrastingly colored head of hair. Because most animals other than primates are colorblind, red hair would be seen by them as another dark shade and would be of no particular significance. The effect of dark color in intercepting solar radiation at the surface and in preventing it from heating deeper layers, would be much more marked for head hair than for skin. Dark hair becomes superficially hot to the touch when exposed to the sun, especially with the sun high overhead, as it is in southern latitudes. Because the hair itself forms a considerable insulating layer, most of this heat is lost to the air instead of being transmitted to the skin. Hair *form* may also be involved here, a matter which will be discussed in another chapter.

The geography of hair color can be told almost solely in terms of

Europe: everywhere else in the world human beings, with few exceptions, have black hair. Hair other than black is mostly limited to northern Europe and areas that have had some population movement or gene flow from northern Europe. In these areas hair color, like skin color all over the world, has infinite gradations; this is indicative of multiple gene action and is therefore very resistant to conventional genetic analysis. Even within the "blond" areas, light hair is by no means the rule in adults. There have been a number of surveys of hair color of school children in various European countries, which give an exaggerated impression of the amount of both blond and red hair. Comparing data from different areas is difficult at best because of the different ways in which blondness or redness can be defined. However, for adults in modern populations, 40 per cent of clearly blond hair (not light brown) and 3 to 4 per cent of definite red hair can be considered high (Martin and Saller, 1956). (The classical reports of "red-haired barbarians" are hard to evaluate because of the difficulty of interpreting color words in dead languages.) Unexpected blond and reddish-blond hair color is sometimes seen in Australia and Melanesia, where it appears to be a local mutation.

EYE COLOR

Variations in human eye color should be of particular interest to those of our readers who are of northern European ancestry, and are accustomed to observe the entire range of human eye color within their own communities or even within their own families. The colored portion of the human eye, the *iris*, is not simply ornamental, but plays an important part in vision. At the center of the iris is the *pupil*, a round dark area, most conspicuous when the iris is light in color, which changes its diameter according to the amount of light to which the eye is momentarily exposed. The pupil is not, as it might appear, a structure; it is an aperture that appears black because it opens into the dark-lined inner chamber of the eye. The changes in size of the pupil serve to maintain the illumination that reaches the retina of the eye at a fairly constant level in spite of extremely large changes in outside illumination. The changes in the pupil are the result of muscular action in the iris, which contains fine muscle fibers that act by reflex in response to light. Some of these fibers are circular, surrounding the pupil, and they close the aperture by their contraction; others extend in a radial direction and serve to enlarge the pupil.

In most mammals, most primates, and the vast majority of human beings, the color of the iris is medium to dark brown. This color is the result of melanin produced by melanocytes present in the iris tissue, which have an origin similar to those found in skin and hair follicles. They differ from the melanocytes we have previ-

ously discussed in that they retain the melanin the)
their own cell substance, and do not have to contin
melanin throughout life. Melanin is also present on the ↓
surface of the iris, which faces toward the interior of the eye aι
retina, and is not directly visible, though sometimes it plays a ↓
in eye color. This posterior pigmented layer of the iris is continuouს
with a pigment layer that completely lines the inner chamber of the
eye, including the retina, and is functionally important. Light reflecting back and forth within the eye would impair distinctness of
vision; thus a pigmented lining is advantageous for the same reason
that the interior of a camera is painted black to prevent reflection.

The lightest color ordinarily seen in the human eye is a pure blue.
This color is not due to any blue pigment, but rather to ordinary
melanin in a particular relation to other layers. If the anterior part of
the iris is lacking in pigment, it becomes hazily translucent. Such a
substance, although in the true sense colorless, tends to turn back
light rays at the blue end of the spectrum but allows yellow and red
wavelengths to go straight on through. Poets sometime liken blue
eyes to the sky. This is a very exact analogy. The blue color of the
sky results from blue wavelengths of light refracted by small parti-
cles in the atmosphere, seen against the black of outer space. Similarly, the blue of the iris results from refraction of blue light by the
unpigmented anterior part of the iris, as seen against the black of
the melanin-rich posterior layer.

There are individual differences in the structure of the iris as well
as in its color. The dark-brown iris has a smooth surface formed of
a continuous layer of cells containing large amounts of melanin.
Behind this layer lies a layer of connective tissue, the *stroma*, containing minute blood vessels, and behind that, the muscles of the
iris (Sommers, 1949; Balcet, 1942). In many human eyes the layer of
pigment cells in front is incomplete. Where it is broken, the connective-tissue layer is exposed and is often seen to be indented by
crypts, spaces filled by the fluid which lies in front of the iris. (See
Figure 25.) These crypts are rounded in outline and their depth may

Figure 25 An eye showing a
cryptose structural pattern of
the iris.

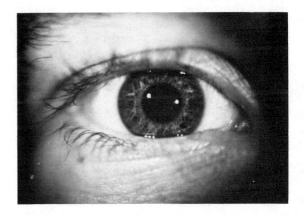

s of the iris. In cryptose eyes, brownish pigmen-
to follow the raised portions of the stroma,
appear blue. Often, however, fiber bundles of
unpigmented and appear as white or gray lines
ckground, thus producing a "pure" light eye

n is sometimes classified into blue and brown.
Close inspection of a few eyes will show that this classification is
very inadequate. Even a rather impressionistic evaluation of eye
color includes ambiguous shades such as green and hazel. A careful
examination of the iris shows that many individuals, in populations
in which light shades of iris color are present, have intermediate
colors—actually mosaics combining light and dark areas. The pattern varies, but some general rules can be made about it. The
contrast in color between different parts of the iris may be very
great; distinct areas of blue or gray are combined with spots of
brown. In other cases the variegation, combining more similar hues
such as green and yellow, or dark green and brown, is not so
obvious. The darker color is generally concentrated toward the
center of the iris, but the pattern is often irregular, with rays of
darker color extending towards the edge.

We have already discussed the reasons for the blue color that is
the basic hue of depigmented eyes. Sometimes this color is modified by diffuse pigment lying anterior to it. Thus, a thin wash of
yellowish pigment in the anterior layers of the iris combines with
the basic blue to produce a green shade. Gray is another modifica-
tion, perhaps due to increased opacity of the iris tissue as well as to
pigment. The discrete color spots of the mixed-color eye range from
yellow through orange to various shades of brown. The total
amount of variation in mixed-color eyes is enormous because of
differences in component colors, in amount of the various colors,
and in the particular pattern formed.

The impression of color by which a person's eyes are usually
described depends on the component shades and their relative
amounts. An eye that contains both blue and brown areas, in a
pattern which is very distinct if looked at closely enough, will be
described as "blue" if the brown markings are limited, "brown" if
they are extensive. If the different colors are more equal in amount,
it may be described by an ambiguous word, like "gray" or "hazel."
It is quite remarkable how few people ever look at anyone else's
eyes (or even their own, in a mirror) closely enough to see what is
really there. The combination of a blue or gray background with
yellow or orange detail color is nearly always referred to as "green."
A truly uniform green is almost nonexistent in nature and can be
safely diagnosed as a tinted contact lens. Some people claim that
their eyes change color from time to time. The eyes that are reported to do this are usually those of mixed colors. The fine mosaic
pattern of various colors picks up and accentuates differences in the
hue of the surrounding light; rearrangement of the color pattern as
the pupil expands and contracts also plays a part in this apparent

color change. We know very little about true change in iris color with age. Newborn infants have a range of eye color from light blue to a dusky violet blue: the latter color seems to presage a change to brown. One genotype has been reported in which brown eye color in childhood changes to a "green" in later life: this seems not to be very common (Dove, 1974).

The inheritance of eye color is certainly not as simple as it is sometimes declared to be in genetics texts, which like to describe "blue" and "brown" as an example of recessive and dominant traits in man. The mere fact that there are so many varieties of iris color other than simple blue and brown shoots down this system. More careful study indicates that the pure, uniform brown shades—the typical eye color of most human populations—are probably dominant over both light and mixed shades. Mixed eye color is more common in women and appears to be due to a sex-linked dominant gene (Brues, 1946a). In addition, there must be a number of modifying factors affecting shades of blue and gray, the amount and pattern of dark markings in mixed eyes, and so forth, that have yet to be identified.

Light eyes are not common anywhere in the world except in a limited area in Europe: this suggests that they confer some sort of advantage under local conditions. Blue or gray eyes do occur sporadically as unusual variants in non-Caucasian races, indicating that, as we might expect, the genetic mutation which produces light eyes has occurred from time to time in many human populations but, once having occurred, has failed to increase and become common in most environments. To some degree, light eye color has a useful camouflage effect for a hunter in a snowy landscape. Animals are intensely aware of one another's eyes, and are alarmed by a fixed gaze. When we consider that the snowy times of year are likely to be the most difficult for subsistence, and that the eyes cannot be concealed by clothing, perhaps light eyes are an advantage to hunters in the far north, though some other arctic predators (and, to be sure, many Arctic people) get along very well without them.

The occurrence of depigmented eyes in other animals, though suggestive, offers no clear conclusions. All the cats, both large and small, have fairly light eyes; the Siamese breed even has typical crypts in some cases. Among primates, light eyes occur sporadically, ranging from yellow and orange to red shades in a number of species, notably among the lemurs. One species of macaque, the "snow-monkey" of Japan, which is the most northerly of the widespread macaque group, has yellow eyes in adults and blue eyes in infants, though its many close relatives farther south are brown-eyed (Anonymous, 1970). Among the dog family, some northern wolves and arctic breeds of dogs, which share the same habitat and also some of their genes, have gray or blue eyes. In some of the primates with conspicuous red or orange eye color we may suspect a social recognition value, because some of the same or related species also have conspicuous body coloring. Aside from this, we can see possible connections of light-colored eyes with predatism, nocturnal habits, and high latitudes.

A psychologist has published data indicating that eye color in man (which he divides into blue and brown), is correlated with behavior patterns: that dark-eyed individuals are most efficient in activities that involve quick, simple reactions, and that light-eyed individuals are most efficient in activities that involve delayed and considered actions (Worthy, 1974). These differences appear in sports performance, and seem not to involve race and its sociological complications. Examples have been adduced showing the same correlation in animal predators.

One indirect social effect of eye color in man is known. Because of the interrelations of nervous control of the iris muscles and some other brain functions, the pupil of the eye may dilate or contract as a result of emotional reactions, quite independently of its normal reaction to light. It has been shown that people are aware of this at an unconscious level, and that it therefore serves as a means of communication by which an individual's emotions are revealed to anyone who is looking at his eyes. However, if the iris of the eye is dark brown, the contrast between iris and pupil is so slight that pupil size is apparent only to very close observation. The light-eyed person, then, telegraphs his emotions from a much greater distance.

There has been much debate about the possibility of correlation between eye color and vision. In albino individuals even the posterior layer of the iris may lack pigment, allowing excess light to flood the interior of the eye and interfere with vision. But the normal blue-to-brown variation of the iris does not affect vision in this way. However, there is a correlation between the color of the iris and the amount of pigment in the retina of the eye. Here, in the actual light-sensitive portion of the eye, there is an opportunity for pigment to affect vision directly. The changing size of the pupil keeps constant the amount of light reaching the retina over a considerable range of differences in the brightness of the field of view. However, it cannot compensate for very dim or very bright illumination. Studies of many animals of different habits have shown that those which are active mostly at night have less pigment in the retina than those which are active in the daytime. The color of the retina in man varies from a light red-orange to a dark brown or gray, and the lighter retina is more likely to be found in an individual with a light iris. The light eye, then, is an indirect indication of a moderate *nocturnal* adaptation. This is consistent with the occurrence of depigmented eyes in northwestern Europe, which has not only the long winter twilight and night of a northern latitude, but an unusually large amount of cloud cover. This contrasts with the drier Asian and American Arctic, where high illumination is the greatest visual problem. Here, the combination of bright sun and snow in the spring, can cause an incapacitating inflammation of the retina called snow-blindness. Light eyes do not occur in the natives of the latter regions. It has not been at all easy, however, to show that eye color or retinal pigment is clearly related to visual acuity (as measured by ability to read an eye chart accurately). Experiments have shown that individuals with light retinas, when confronted with very bright illumination, can see clearly, but complain of acute discomfort from the bright light. A questionnaire revealed that these individuals are the main support of the sunglass industry; people with dark retinas rarely feel the need for sunglasses (Hoffman, 1973).

A question that deserves investigation is whether the thinning out of the iris, which often occurs in lighter colored eyes, may increase the range of contraction and expansion of the pupil and so facilitate extreme accommodation to light. A special adaptation in the domestic cat—the slit-like pupil—makes it possible for this animal to hunt effectively both in full daylight and at very low levels of illumination: the presence of light eyes in other felines, many of whom are both night and day hunters, suggests that depigmentation of the iris may have some advantage in this way of life. Much work remains to be done on the possible adaptive effects of eye color.

CORRELATIONS OF PIGMENTATION

The various colors of skin, hair, and eyes in man, like so many human variables, show a partial correlation; this is harder to explain than a perfect correlation or no correlation. If these variations of color were due to a genetic locus at which one allele resulted in abundant melanin formation at all sites in the body where melanin occurs at all, and another allele inhibited melanin formation at all sites, we would have two "complexions," black and blond, with nothing in between. If we had a number of genetic loci affecting pigment formation by degrees, but with each affecting it equally in skin, in hair, and in eyes, we would have a gradation of phenotypes, each of which would have nicely matched intermediate shades in all three of the pigmented structures. Such effects would indicate completely pleiotropic genes. This perfect correlation obviously does not exist. An exactly opposite situation would be that the genetic factors for skin, eye, and hair were entirely independent. If this were the case, an individual or race with black skin would be no less likely to have blue eyes and fair hair than one with fair skin, and so forth. The truth seems to lie between these two extremes; there appear to be some factors that operate pleiotropically on pigmentation in all three structures and some that operate independently. One thing is certain: we should not expect the explanation to be simple. Many genetic experiments have been done on the pigmentation of laboratory animals, most of which have concentrated on hair color. The many varieties of the common mouse that have been bred under laboratory conditions appear to have about fifty different loci affecting the color of the hair in one way or another, some of which also affect eye color (Searle, 1968). Comparative study indicates that some of the mutations involved in the hair color of mammals are limited to one or a few species. But in a number of instances, similar color variations occur in animals as different as rodents and carnivores. This suggests that there are parts of the biochemical process of formation and distribution of pigment that are very basic, and have been altered by mutation in the same way in different orders of animals.

What was the original pigmentation of man? Because man presumably evolved in tropical regions, our best guess can be made on the basis of man's closest relatives, who live in the tropics, and of those contemporary humans who still live there. The guess would be: dark brown eyes, black hair, and skin color somewhere between medium brown and black. If early man was an open-forest or savanna dweller, as is generally believed, he was more likely medium brown than black in skin color; that is to say, more like a chimpanzee than like a gorilla. It is probable that from some such beginning the many races of man have diverged in pigmentation, more often by decreasing than by increasing it.

In general, light skin is the most widespread of the "light" colors in man. It is not only common in Europe, where it has reached its most extreme form, but in large areas of central and north Asia. In both Asia and Europe, as well as in North Africa, there are many people with skins light brown or lighter who have black hair and dark brown eyes. Statistically speaking, this is the commonest pigmentation pattern of the human species. In some cases these individuals have skins that are almost without pigment, at least when protected from the sun. Because it is clear that skin color is controlled by a number of independent genes, this indicates that during the history of the species a number of mutations conducive to lightening of skin color *without any effect on hair or eye color,* have occurred and become prevalent as the human species moved into the more northern parts of the Old World. We have already discussed the reasons why selection would favor such mutations. Less common, in terms of world population, are individuals combining light eyes with black hair, or even light eyes with black hair and dark skin. In Europe, the blue eye-black hair combination is most common in the northwest, reaching its highest frequency in Ireland, where it is quite characteristic. Light eyes also occur sporadically in black Africa and India, and are not uncommon in some North American Indian tribes, where they are usually described as gray. The individuals who have them also have black hair, as do the rest of the populations to which they belong, and skin color no different from their neighbors. In some cases these light eyes have been attributed to admixture with less pigmented races. But regardless of whether this or independent local mutation is the reason in any particular case, the occurrence of such individuals is evidence of the existence of a gene for light eye color that has no visible effect on skin or hair color. Is this the same mutation in a black-skinned black-haired, blue-eyed African as in a fair-skinned, black-haired, blue-eyed Irishman? It may very well be: the Irishman's light skin is normal for his population and due to an independent lot of genes. It seems most likely that there is a light-eye mutation which has occurred numerous times throughout the world but which has only become prevalent in northern Europe (Brues, 1975). Light hair, as an independent trait not affecting pigmentation of skin or eyes, also occurs. This is most striking among certain tribes of central Australia, where fair hair is very common in children, usually darkening later in males but not always in females; and among the closely related peoples of Melanesia. Popular opinion has always tried to explain this away. In the case of the Australians, it is "explained" by European admixture—though the fair hair is most common in areas least subject to this effect. In the case of the Melanesians, the "explanation" is bleaching—though no folk method of bleaching can do more than brighten a moderately light head of hair. But though this light hair, growing out of black skin, totally affronts popular stereotypes of pigmentation, it is nevertheless genuine. In generally light-skinned populations, fair hair with dark eyes sometimes occurs; in Europe this is most common in the central and eastern areas, east of the greatest concentration of the "Irish" combination. These fair-haired, dark-eyed individuals may be genetically akin to the Australians, sharing the same mutation (Brues, 1975).

There are, then, independent factors for skin, eye, and hair color that may result in a high degree of pigmentation of any one of these without a visible effect on the others. Are these the only genetic factors present? That is, are there *no* pleiotropic genes? If this were the case, the concentration of light eyes and hair in Europe, where the most extreme form of skin depigmentation also occurs, would have to be explained as the coincidental appearance and multiplication of a number of different mutant genes for depigmentation. However, there are indications that there may be a pleiotropic gene (or a set of them) for depigmentation also. We previously mentioned albinism as a trait that expressed itself in a pleiotropic fashion by inhibiting melanin formation everywhere in the body. The classic albino has totally white skin, hair with only the faint yellow color of keratin, and eyes that are pink because of the lack of melanin even in the posterior part of the iris. These individuals have severely impaired vision, especially in bright light, and are totally and permanently susceptible to sunburn. However, many human albinos are not so extreme. They may have blue eyes, some skin pigment—often in the form of freckles—some color in the hair, and their vision may be normal or nearly so. Albinos can occur in any race, and they are far more conspicuous in areas where the normally pigmented individuals are dark. The less extreme albinos, in fact, would not be noticeable except among more heavily pigmented races, because the condition grades imperceptibly into ordinary blondism. Modified albinism appears repeatedly in some American Indian tribes in Panama and New Mexico; another center of such mutants seems to be in New Guinea (Stout, 1946; Woolf,

1965; Walsh, 1963; 1971). It seems, then, that there are pleiotropic depigmentations affecting skin, hair, and eyes simultaneously; that these may include blondism in the ordinary sense, and that some such mutations may have become common in Europe in addition to the independent blue-eye and fair-hair mutations. We still have to explain why several independent and separately acting mutant genes have all thrived in the same area. Only a "protective coloration" hypothesis related to phenotypically light color would explain this, but it might put a severe strain on the hypothesis.

Red hair is also limited in distribution and concentrated in the same areas where blondness is most common. The most obvious selective liability of red hair is its correlated effect on the skin. Redhaired persons are even more susceptible to sunburn than light blond-haired persons. Their skin is often paler than that of ordinary blondes, and though they may have freckles of darker color, they continue to sunburn between the freckles. The freckle phenomenon itself is interesting. We have mentioned that red hair often occurs in symmetrical patterns, with different shades of the red-black series in head hair and beard. This patterning sometimes involves darker and lighter shades of hair, neither of which is red. In other mammals this kind of patterning has been attributed to a specific genetic locus with multiple alleles. As we have previously mentioned, in some animals a condition attributable to this locus, called *brindle*, involves a mingling of different colors of hair on a single part of the body; this is also observed in humans with patterned hair colors. This suggests an interesting analogy to freckling of the skin. Is freckling a "brindle" condition of the skin? In the red hair phenotypes, melanocytes are responding differently in various parts of the body with respect to the amount and kind (red or black) of melanin they produce: melanocytes in one hair follicle may respond differently from those in adjacent follicles, and all may change their response with age. Differential melanocyte response could also explain freckles, and their tendency to disappear in adult years as the skin becomes more uniformly pigmented. In any case, a dysfunctional degree of depigmentation of the skin often accompanies redness of the hair. It appears as if the biochemical switch from eumelanin to phaeomelanin in the hair is expressed, in the skin, as a complete inhibition of melanin formation. Whatever the factors for red hair are, they seem not to affect eye color: red or reddish hair occurs with all the shades of eye color that are combined with nonred hair in the same populations. Selectively, red hair, because of its associated skin color and sunburn susceptibility, would be even more disadvantaged in sunny areas than blondness, so its concentration in northern Europe is easily explained on that basis.

We began by saying that differences in coloring are among the most conspicuous of human physical variations. It is clear that they are also among the most complicated and difficult to explain.

The Face

The features of the face display some of the most conspicuous variation of the human species. A really hard look at our own population may convince us that it includes every possible variation of the parts of the face that is anatomically functional. But each region and race of the world has its specialities in facial features, traits which it shows most frequently and in the most extreme form. Consequently eyes, nose, mouth, and other features, particularly in combination, are a strong indication of the area from which an individual's ancestors came. The great variety of facial features within any single population undoubtedly has an important social function. In any species with a true social structure it is necessary that individuals react to one another, not just as members of the same species, or as members of the same or opposite sex, but as individuals. Individual A treats and is treated by B in a way different from the way he treats and is treated by C or any other member of his group. Without these diversified relationships, A does not have a meaningful social personality. In order to establish relations of this kind, individuals must be readily recognized by others in the community, preferably even at a distance and under poor lighting conditions. Many of the traits we have already discussed contribute to the ease of personal recognition, and to the development of personal relations based on personal recognition. But the face is of special interest because it is a focus of attention during social reactions for still another reason: in man, as in many other mammals, its expressive movements are important in communicating emotional feelings, in addition to (and sometimes in spite of) spoken words. We often overlook facial features in making judgments of race, if pigmentation gives us the principal clue. Caucasians are probably more conscious of the distinctive facial features of East Asians, who do not differ from them greatly in coloring, than they are of the facial features of Africans. It is a curious fact that people are usually poor observers of individual variation within a race other than their own, and see the individual of another race simply as a type. In legal proceedings involving personal identification, this is a real problem: people often have difficulty in identifying an individual who is not of their own race and whom they have seen only once. This imperceptiveness undoubtedly contributes to impersonal and unsatisfactory relations between persons of different races.

In evaluating facial features the anthropologist often makes a distinction between the parts that are determined by the bony structure of the skull and those made up of soft tissue. One reason for this is that he is sometimes called on to identify an unknown skeleton by comparing a skull with photographs of a missing person. Many features of the living face cannot be inferred from the skull; so he concentrates on those parts—forehead, root and bridge of nose, prominence of the cheek, and border of the lower jaw— where the skin surface closely corresponds to the contours of the bone. Again, the anthropologist may be asked to examine the remains of persons many centuries dead, to judge whether they resembled the people now living in the same area, people now living elsewhere, or perhaps no people now living. Such judgments may be valuable in reconstructing the prehistory of human migrations.

NOSES

The nose, a distinctive feature of many faces, is a good example of a structure in which bone and soft tissue combine to produce a highly varied and often irregular outline. We could probably recognize many of our friends by the nose alone, with the rest of the face covered. The upper half of the nose is a bony protuberance covered by a uniform and rather thin layer of tissue; the lower half (the division is readily found by wiggling one's nose with one's fingers) is composed of cartilage and some fatty tissue, covered by a thin layer of skin. The bony portion of the nose is described in two parts: the *root*, which is the portion lying between the eyes, and the *bridge*, which continues down to the junction with the cartilaginous portion. This small area of the skull packs in much information about the racial affiliations of the person to whom it belongs. The extent to which the root of the nose projects forward is remarkably variable (Figure 26). In one extreme, evident in ancient Egyptian and classical Greek art, the root of the nose is so high and straight that it appears to be a continuation of the profile of the forehead. This is hard to find in any modern population, and probably was not very common in the populations whose artists depicted it. (All peoples, including our modern selves, have standards of beauty that do not always correspond to reality.) The other extreme is a nasal root so low that, when one views the face directly from the side, it is possible to look past the nose and see the eyeball on the far side. This is a specialty of the peoples of East Asia, among whom moderately low nasal roots are the rule, although the extreme just described is not common even there. A projecting, sharp-edged nasal root is characteristic of Caucasoids, and is a source of wonder and disadmiration to people of other races. The nasal root of Negroes is generally intermediate in degree of forward projection, but it has distinguishing characteristics of its own. If the nasal root is compared to a roof (put the individual on his back to get the corresponding position), the nasal root of a typical African black forms a smooth curve from side to side, like a quonset hut. The characteristic Mongoloid nasal root resembles a somewhat sagging tent, with a median ridge which is distinct although low; and the typical Caucasian nasal root is an A-frame with the sides rising steeply upward. It is not surprising that the old-fashioned eyeglasses which clamped

Figure 26 Variation in the nasal root; left, a Chinese girl; right, a north European man.

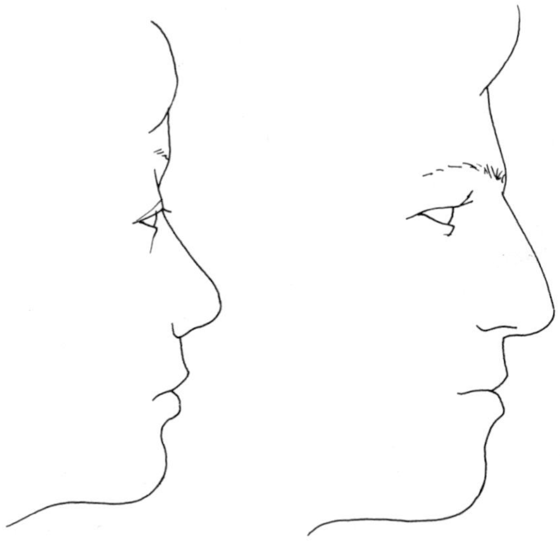

onto the root of the nose were invented in Europe; they could not get a grip on any typical non-Caucasian nose.

The *bridge*, which is the downward continuation of the nasal root, has its own variations. The most modest nasal bridges merely continue the profile of the root, but often the bridge curves forward in a hump, drooping a little at the end. Whether it does this or not—though more often if it does—the bridge may be distinctly wider than the root. When we speak of a person having a "big nose," it usually means that the bridge is both protruding and wide. The lowest part of the nose consists of cartilage and fatty tissue; it includes the *tip*, and the two *wings* or alae, which surround the nostrils. Although these parts of the nose contribute considerably to the appearance of the face, they have been neglected by anthropologists because no one has devised a very good method of measuring their variations. They are probably just as significant genetically as many other features that have been studied in detail. The shape of the nasal tip is roughly spherical and varies greatly in size. A small tip makes the nose appear pointed; a large one makes it appear rounded or blunt in outline, and may look "knobby" from the front. Among Caucasians, a small nasal tip, so placed as to make the profile of the nose appear straight, is generally considered attractive. More often, however, the tip projects forward or droops downward so as to make the nasal profile irregular. The wings of the nose vary in size and flare, and their shape determines the maximum width of the nose, which is often used as a racial criterion. Other variations of the wings of the nose determine how much of the nasal septum can be seen from the side, or the nostrils from the front.

The combinations of root, bridge, and tip variation produce a virtually infinite variety of shapes. Most easily described is the profile of the nose as seen on side view. In the Asian peoples already referred to, who have a low nasal root, the bridge of the nose usually continues the line of the root, and the tip is of modest size, so that the whole nose is low-lying and straight. When the bony part of the nose in Europeans is low-lying (this is commoner in eastern than in western Europe), the tip often seems too large for the nasal skeleton and projects forward, producing a concave or "turned-up" profile. More commonly, in Europeans, the bridge of the nose is prominent, and the cartilaginous portion of the nose not quite equal to it, so that the general profile of the nose is convex. Frequently it has a quadruple curve: concave at the root, convex at the bridge, slightly concave in the upper part of the cartilage, and ending in the convexity of a rounded tip. The most striking nasal development within Caucasoid populations is the large convex nose of the Middle East, often erroneously called "Jewish" by Europeans and Americans. Actually, the center of the area in which this kind of nose occurs is in the mountain regions lying between Israel and India, and the form seen in Jewish populations is a rather watered-down version of it. This form, sometimes called the "Iranian Plateau" nose, is massive in both bone and cartilage, wide as well as protruding, with the heavy tip usually forming a downward curve. This type of nose, at least in modified form, appears occasionally in India, extends north to Armenia, and has infiltrated the peoples of the Mediterranean region, whence its popular association with the Jews. In marginal areas, and especially extending west along the shores of the Mediterranean, we often see noses that are as convex as the Iranian Plateau type, but narrow and thin-tipped; its possessors sometimes describe it as "Roman." The genetic relation between the Roman and Middle Eastern noses is problematic. Both types, as depicted in ancient art, have been present in their respective areas for a long time. Great convex noses similar, or at least facsimiles, of the Middle Eastern type, appear rather inexplicably in New Guinea and adjacent islands, and among some American Indians (Figure 34E); this has led to fanciful speculations about the "lost tribes of Israel."

Another major type of nose is that characteristic of Negroes. We have already mentioned the shape of the root: moderately low, and smoothly rounded (Figure 33C). In its most typical form the nose is also short from top to bottom, and relatively wide across the wings. Its breadth in the lower part corresponds to wide and round nostrils, and is reflected even in the skull, which shows a wide opening at the point where the nasal passages enter the skull. This difference in proportion—less height and greater breadth—reflects the shape of the internal nasal passages that convey air backward through the skull. In order to function properly, it is probably necessary that the narrower nose should have greater height, and vice versa. This, of course, does not explain why different shapes have become common in different parts of the world. Another characteristic of the African nose, though it is seen in other low-bridged noses also, is a tendency for the nostril openings to face forward so that they are visible to a straight-ahead view. Some variations in the lower part of the nose are related to jaw development, which we will discuss later.

There has been much speculation about the different nose forms of different races, and whether they have developed because of particular advantages in particular environments. Perhaps it would be well to consider first why humans have noses of the kind they do, because the human nose is a rather unique structure. Most mammals have the openings of the nostrils, surrounded by a small cartilaginous blob, at the end of a long bony snout. The snout, which contains internally the hollow passages that carry air from the nostrils to the top of the throat, is as long as the jaw and the tooth row that lie below it. In man, the snout is markedly reduced as a result of the much smaller size of the teeth, and the face is therefore small, a modest appendage below the brain instead of a great prow in front of it. In the course of this readjustment, the nasal bones have become greatly reduced in size, and are more nearly vertical than horizontal; and the cartilage surrounding the nostrils has become the projecting nasal tip in man.

It is fortunate that humans are able to perceive their noses as ornamental, because they are not particularly functional. The value of the whole system (here we speak of mammals in general rather than just man) is problematic. The internal nasal passages are subdivided by thin scrolls of bone, which obviously serve no purpose but to increase the surface past which air flows as it is breathed in. It is often said that this arrangement serves to "warm and moisten" the air in order to protect the lungs from stress. But actually there is little evidence that dry or cold air is harmful to the lungs. In days when tuberculosis was prevalent, and no antibiotics were available to combat it, moving to a dry climate, and, when possible, breathing unheated winter air, were recommended as beneficial to those who suffered from this disease. If the "warming" theory was correct, animals living in cold climates would be expected to have longer snouts for greater warming effect. This is not true; in fact, as we will discuss shortly, the reverse is the case. A more likely function of the nasal passage is its use as a dust filter. But in any case, as far as man is concerned, the external nose—the visible, projecting part—contributes only a small fraction to the total warming, moistening, or dust-absorbing area of the lining of the nasal passages. There is another possible consideration. In the upper part of the internal nasal passages lies the special area that contains the receptors of the sense of smell. This area, incidentally, is much smaller in man than in most mammals, a result of the disappearance of the projecting snout; this fact is reflected in the relatively small importance of the sense of smell in man as compared with other senses. An increase in the moistening surface of the nasal interior, if it lies in front of the sensory area for smell, may make the sense of smell function better in a dry atmosphere. A protruding external nose will have this effect.

How does all this fit in with what we know of nose variations in various parts of the world? Perhaps the most easily explained, in ecological terms, is the low-profile nose found in central and eastern Asia. If, as some believe, the racial characteristics of this area were developed in response to the extreme winter cold of Central Asia, the nonprotruding nose is an adaptation similar to that in many other mammals (Coon, et al., 1950). Any protuberance of the body is a hazard in a cold climate, and the narrower or more extended it is, the greater the problems. Noses and ears are among the first parts of the body to get cold because of the large amount of exposed surface and the difficulty of circulating enough warm blood through them to counteract the heat loss. In warm-blooded animals, therefore, species living in cold climates tend to have smaller ears and less projecting snouts than those living in warm climates, a generalization known as Allen's rule (Mayr, 1970). This reduces the loss of body heat and lessens the chance of direct injury to these parts by freezing. Man, of course, can and does cover his ears when the weather is cold. But larger noses in man seem to have been selected against in cold climates, just as the long snout and large ears have been selected against in other mammals. Some of the largest and most projecting human noses, in the New World as well as the Old, seem to center in arid and often dusty areas. Here, the air-filter function and the moistening of air before it passes over the area that serves the sense of smell, may have been selective factors. But some large noses are found in humid tropical areas; pure genetic chance may be at work here. As a general rule, wide noses, with nostrils tending to open somewhat forward rather than directly down, are more prevalent in tropical areas (Weiner, 1954). This is undoubtedly the most efficient nose simply for breathing. There is, in fact, a reflex, involving certain very small muscles, that widens the nostrils and turns them slightly forward during forced breathing. Down-facing nostrils force the air to make a right-angled turn every time it goes in and out, which, if nothing else, is noisy, like a badly designed air-duct system. If no particular climatic hazards are present, perhaps the best nose is one in which the air stream is straightest and interferes least with hearing at times of stress and flight. In this sense, all human noses are inefficient compared with those of other mammals.

The nose, like other parts of the face, changes considerably in shape as well as in size during the growth period. In a newborn infant the bony portion of the root and bridge is quite undeveloped, and the small tip, a lonesome blob of cartilage, is essentially the entire nose. As the bone develops, the root and bridge become larger, jut farther forward, and finally, at about puberty, attain adult proportions. A baby with a pretty nose—that is, one with a little shape and character to the root and bridge—will probably develop rather distinctive features as an adult. These growth changes of the nose tend to be more conspicuous in males, so that the adult female nose is somewhat closer to the infantile type. Consequently, concave (turned-up) noses are more common in women, and convex noses more common in men. This difference is less noticeable in races in which the nasal root is relatively low-lying. Another type of change occurs in the nose from mature years into old age. This is a slow increase in size of the cartilaginous part of the nose, which continues after most body growth has stopped. This change is so slow that it is not noticed in a person one sees regularly. But if we compare the face of an older person with pictures taken in early adulthood, we often see a startling difference. Some of the facial changes are superficial—development of wrinkles and loss of firmness of the soft tissues. But the change in the nose—its tip wider, blunter, and tending to droop downward so as to produce a more convex profile—accounts for much of the change in appearance.

EYES

The most striking variation of the eye, the color of the iris, has been discussed in Chapter 5. However, there are variations in the shape of the lids and other tissues around the eye that are sometimes distinctive, though they have nothing to do with the function of the eye itself. It is a cliché that "Orientals have slanted eyes." This is an inaccurate description of a phenomenon that involves several different elements; and by the time we have finished discussing it, we will have touched on almost everything that can be said about variations in the region of the eye.

The most unique feature of the Oriental eye is a delicate fold of skin at the inner corner, just by the root of the nose, that curves downward and toward the midline. This is called the *Mongoloid fold* because of its typical racial occurrence (Figure 27). In an eye that lacks this fold, there may be seen at the inner corner of the eye a small pale bump; this marks the point at which the tears that bathe the eye drain downward into the nasal passages (unless they are temporarily increased so as to overflow the lid). In an eye that has the Mongoloid fold, this little bump is concealed. In the peoples in which this fold occurs, we often observe, also, that the whole upper eyelid appears rather plump. The skin of the eyelid is extremely thin, but like skin in most parts of the body, it has a more or less developed fat layer lying just below it. In a few individuals the upper eyelid is virtually devoid of fat. In this case, the lid lies quite flat against the eyeball, following its contours. However, if the lid contains a fair to large amount of fat, it puffs forward and a fatty fold tends to sag down and come to rest on top of the eyelashes.

Why does the Oriental eye appear slanted? In part, it is an optical illusion; when the Mongoloid fold is present, the lower end of the fold appears to be the inner corner of the eye, whereas when it is not present, we see the true corner of the eye, which lies somewhat higher. The concealment of the true corner also makes the eyes appear farther apart, even though the working parts of the eye are

Figure 27   The Mongoloid eye fold: *above,* Chinese man; *below,* north European girl.

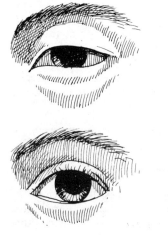
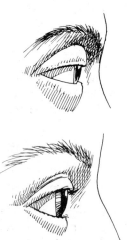

spaced the same as in other individuals. However, still another variation is involved. If the part of the cheek bone that lies at the outer side of the eye is prominent, the outer corner of the eye may be somewhat elevated, enhancing the slanted appearance. Now, although the classic Oriental eye combines three features—the eyefold, the fatty lid, and the upward trend of the lateral corner of the eye, these features do not seem to be inherently related. Many Caucasians have fat eyelids which bulge down against the lashes, but have no trace of the median eyefold. Many Asians with the well-developed Mongoloid eyefold do not have a particularly fat eyelid, or any elevation of the lateral corner of the eye. So it appears that these three features are coincidental, though when combined they produce a striking effect. The truly racial characteristic seems to be the median fold, which is found with surprising unanimity among Chinese, Japanese, and many related peoples. What causes it? It appears to be related to the low-lying nasal bridge which we have previously discussed. Though the mechanics are obscure, it seems difficult for the fold to coexist with a well-developed, forward-projecting nasal root. In populations in which the eyefold is present in some individuals but not in others, it seems to correlate with nasal root development. Thus among some American Indians it is reasonably common in females but not in males, and among Caucasians a trace of the eyefold may be present in an infant, but rapidly disappear as the nasal root begins to develop its adult form. Any useful function of the fold is difficult to see. However, the whole effect may be related to two cold-weather adaptations: the nonprotruding nose, which we have already discussed, and the fat deposits of the eyelid, which are part of a general development of protective fat on the face.

EARS

The external ear in man is a sorry, immobile remnant of what is a large and very active structure in most mammals. We have all seen how expressive the ear is in a cat or dog. Raised and turned forward, it indicates attention and interest, because in this position it most efficiently picks up sound and reflects it into the inner ear. Laid flat toward the back of the head, it indicates fear and expected attack and its position is adapted to decrease the chance of injury to itself. In highly social wild animals, such as wolves, the nuances of ear movement and position are a means of emotional expression which facilitates the social adjustments of members of the pack to one another. Many small muscles are involved in the mobility of the ears of these animals. In man, the ear itself is reduced in size, and the muscles are largely nonfunctional. Ear-wiggling in man is only an amusement, and many persons never acquire control over the ear muscles. A comparison of your own ear with the family dog's will show that the convoluted portion right around the earhole is the least changed. The typically human characteristic of the ear is the reduced size of the large, relatively flat portion called the *helix,* which ends in a point in most mammals. This portion in man is rounded and the edge is more or less rolled upon itself. The rolled edge varies from a narrow rim turned at a right angle to the plane of the helix, to a band almost a quarter of an inch wide, folded flat against it (Figure 28, especially A and E). The amount of rolling is usually not the same all the way around the helix border. A point or nodule may be present on the rim somewhat back of the top of the helix; this is called *Darwin's point,* because Charles Darwin surmised that it represented the pointed tip of the original

A

B

Figure 28   An assortment of ears. Soldered lobe, A and B; attached lobe, C and D; free lobe, E and F. Marked rolling of helix, A; slight rolling, E. Darwin's point, B and D.

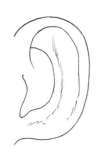

C

E

D

F

mammalian ear (Figure 28, B and D). A detail unique to the human ear is the lobe, a soft tab of tissue at the lower end. Most of the ear is made up of cartilage, like that of the soft part of the nose. The lobe has no cartilage, and consists only of fibrous and fatty tissue; its function is obscure, except that many primitive and some civilized folk have used it to hang ornaments on.

The external ear in man has only a minor function. Its forward-facing concave surface serves to some extent to reflect and focus sounds coming from in front toward the ear hole, and thus aids hearing in that direction. Moving the ear with one's hand will show how this works: the ear pulled forward makes sounds from the front seem louder. Presumably, individuals with protruding ears, though they are not aware of it, hear sounds from this direction more clearly than the rest of us. A cupped hand held behind the ear further increases the effect, of course, so that this habitual gesture is indicative of hearing impairment. Man has nothing like the wonderful "directional-hearing aid" represented by the swivel-ears of the donkey. Because the human ear has completely lost its expressive function, people rarely pay much attention to one another's ears. It would probably be generally conceded that the human ear is indifferent in appearance at best, and ugly at worst, and only the most deluded lover could admire one. Perhaps ignoring ears is a form of politeness. But the variation of its many details is enormous, and one never need be bored in a crowd if he likes to observe ears. Many years ago, the French anthropologist, Bertillon, developed a system for recording the variations of the human ear, and trained a generation of gendarmes to examine ears instead of faces, for spotting wanted criminals on the streets. Ear observation has fallen somewhat into disuse for police purposes. But if you are ever accosted by a masked robber, remember his ear. You might be able to identify him by it later.

As befits a largely useless organ, the human ear varies greatly in size and proportions. The most variable part is the lobe. The lobe varies in both size and shape and in its degree of attachment at its forward edge. The *free* lobe is attached only to the ear, not to the side of the face in front of and below the ear (Figure 28, E and F). The *attached* lobe blends into the back of the cheek (Figure 28, C and D); the *soldered* lobe is an extreme version of the attached form (Figure 28, A and B). In a very general way, lobe attachment correlates with lobe size: the very largest lobes are free ones, and a soldered lobe may be almost nonexistent—the despair of a young lady who wants to wear earrings. But lobe size varies independently of attachment, to a considerable degree.

Certain combinations of ear details are characteristic of the major races. In Negroes the ear often combines small size, a small, free lobe, and a well-rolled border of the helix; it rarely protrudes from the head (Figure 28C). Mongoloid races are more likely to have attached or soldered lobes and a protruding helix. Caucasians have extremely varied ears, and they have some of the largest free ear lobes, with the exception of Australian aboriginals. The ear shares with the nose not only its cartilaginous character, but its tendency to keep on growing with advancing age. Big ears with fat lobes are most common in the elderly.

MOUTH AND LIPS

The mouth and lips in man are quite different from those of other mammals, as a result of the reduction in size of the teeth and the disappearance of a projecting muzzle—changes we discussed in connection with the characteristics of the nose. A dog can lay a bone crossways over his back teeth and crack it without stretching his mouth; man cannot. As the muzzle disappeared, the mouth became small, adapted to admit food in dainty morsels, or at least not in prodigious ones. At the same time, the sides of the mouth became more fully closed, producing a more effective resonating chamber for the production of vowel sounds. The lips also took on new functions related to speech. No other mammal has lips in the human sense. The closed mouth of other mammals reveals only hair-covered skin. The pink, hairless zone, which is the transition between typical skin and the mucous membrane which lines the mouth, is turned under and concealed. Only in man is a pink *membranous lip* exposed. The degree to which this area is turned outward—called *lip eversion*—varies greatly in different individuals. In some, the membranous lip is almost concealed, except for a thin rim around the mouth opening, and so the mouth looks very little different from that of our relatives among the apes. In others, the membranous lip rolls backward in almost a 90-degree arc. Though the human condition presumably is related to greater mobility of the lips in speech, there is no evidence that people with the "rat-trap" mouth are less articulate than those with the "rosebud" mouth! Surrounding the mouth opening in the deeper tissues lies the *orbicularis oris,* the circular muscle with which one "puckers up." This muscle and the connective tissue within which it lies form the *integumental* lip, which varies considerably in thickness. An individual with a very thick integumental lip and little eversion may even have a slight convexity in profile above the mouth, where most individuals are more or less concave. A thick integumental lip, however, may also be accompanied by strong lip eversion. In general, the integumental lip is thinner and the membranous lip more everted in females than in males. Lip variation is so subject to individual variation that it is hard to make any generalizations about race, except to say that the most striking cases of a thick integumental lip combined with strong lip eversion are seen in Negroes, and the most striking cases of *non*eversion are seen in Caucasoids and Australoids. Otherwise the mouth and lips are pretty much an individual matter. Another characteristic of the lip seen in Negroes is the *lip seam,* a thin raised ridge at the juncture of integumental and membranous lip (Figure 55A).

THE FACIAL MUSCLES

The facial features of man cannot be discussed without a consideration of the facial musculature that directly underlies them. These muscles are small and delicate, and unlike most muscles of the body are not attached primarily to bones. The facial muscles lie close to the surface in fine sheets or bands, sometimes attached to bone at one end and to the deep layers of the skin at the other, or attached at both ends to the skin. They are the remnant of a much more extensive muscle sheet that lies close to the surface in other mammals—including that by which a horse twitches a fly off his flank. This muscle group in man is almost limited to the face, though it includes some muscles in the scalp, the muscles that move the ear, and one thin sheet which extends down the front of the neck as far as the clavicle. Interestingly, they are all supplied by a single nerve with widespread branches. The major present function of the facial musculature in man, to produce changes of facial expression, is very important. This is not unique to man; other social mammals use the facial muscles to communicate emotions and attitudes. (The highly developed ear musculature, part of the same system, plays an important part in some of them.) In man, this old form of communication has not degenerated, but actually has become more subtle, and still expresses feelings in addition to words—and sometimes in spite of them. Much communication by facial expression is involuntary, but many people learn more or less successfully to misrepresent their emotions by control of the facial muscles. Success in the acting profession depends largely on this ability.

The facial-muscle system is extremely complicated, and many small muscle units, some consisting of only a few bundles of muscle fibers, have been described by anatomists. The muscles are imbedded in connective tissue that corresponds to the superficial fat layer of the rest of the body, but is denser and more fibrous. These muscles are of no clinical importance, except when large areas of them are paralyzed by nerve injury. They are very difficult to dissect, and consequently, although thousands of human bodies have been dissected by generations of students, careful studies of the facial muscles are very few. We have already mentioned the orbicularis oris muscle that surrounds the mouth in a circular form. From this circular muscle other muscles radiate out, like spokes of a wheel, and serve to draw the lips back and to pull the corners of the mouth up, to the side, or down. Other muscles move the cartilages of the nose, the skin around the eyes, and wrinkle the forehead or move the eyebrows. Contraction of a facial muscle often results in the formation of a crease in the skin which overlies it. These creases come and go as the muscles act, but they eventually become permanent lines over muscles that an individual contracts frequently. These lines in the face of an older person indicate the muscles most used, and therefore indicate habitual facial expressions and, indirectly, emotional disposition. Because of the difficulty of studying the facial muscles, we have little information about individual variations, let alone their inheritance. Some variations are quite distinct, especially those which produce dimples. A dimple is the result of a small bundle of muscle fibers that attaches to the skin from below and produces a depression when it contracts. These, like other contours of the face which are the result of muscle action, are generally symmetrical, as are the facial muscles themselves. This symmetry is a fair indication of an genetic basis; but it is still difficult to judge to what extent facial expression is the result of the anatomy of the muscles, and to what extent of habits of using them. Muscle *tonus*—that is, habitual partial contraction of parts of the facial musculature—alters the appearance of the features, and is so much a part of the face that people sometimes have difficulty identifying the face of a dead person, even someone they have known fairly well. These muscle contraction patterns may be learned by unconscious imitation of one's associates. The fashionable or accepted facial expressions of a culture may be so distinct that they become recognition marks for nationalities, and could be mistaken for racial characteristics. A generation ago it was not considered difficult to recognize Jews by their facial features; at present it does not seem that easy. The change seems to be a matter of expression. Certain of the facial muscles pull the wings of the nose slightly up and backward, accentuating any downward curvature of the nasal tip, and at the same time curling the upper lip slightly. Anyone can learn to contract these muscles and produce the expression—which now seems to have gone out of style among the people who at one time frequently showed it. Other styles in facial expression, or the lack of it, may come and go in various groups, undoubtedly sometimes serving the purpose of voluntary group identification.

Some studies, which call for further confirmation, indicate that there are anatomical differences between races in the structure of the facial musculature (Loth, 1931). In at least some individuals of Mongoloid race, the musculature around the mouth appears to be less divided into separate parts than is usual in Caucasoids. The principal difference lies in the development of the distinct muscle bundles that radiate out from the corners of the mouth and serve to pull them up, down, or laterally. Functionally, this would indicate less flexibility of expression in the lower part of the face. Is this anatomical difference the basis of the common complaints, by Caucasoids, that Asians are "inscrutable," that is, that their thoughts, like those of a good poker player, are difficult to read in their faces? This has been interpreted as indicating a difference in emotional reactions. Perhaps there are simple anatomical differences which can make facial expression in one race difficult to interpret for those who have lived among people with somewhat different facial musculature.

The Skull

Most people find the sight of a human skull or skeleton unnerving, and many cannot bear to touch one. In some periods of the past this feeling was exploited in the interests of moral improvement, and the skeleton or the skull was displayed or illustrated as a reminder of human mortality and the necessity of being prepared for the day of judgment. The anthropologist has more positive feelings about skeletal remains. The skull or skeleton may be the only source of information about the biology of populations now long dead. In order to interpret the features of the bones of an extinct population it is necessary to compare them with similar remains of more modern populations, whose known relatives can be examined in life. Some features that can be seen in the living are more clearly seen in the bare bones; and some features of the bone may not be observable in the living subject at all, or only by X-ray. Thus the skull often becomes an object of study in itself, and collections of skulls are carefully preserved by museums so that we may answer the questions: Have there always been races of man? Were they similar to those of today? Did they live where they now do? We have already discussed those facial features that are simply "not there" in the skull: the soft parts of the eyelids, the lower part of the nose, the mouth, and lips. Even in these areas the structure of the underlying bone sets some limits on the contours of the living face. There is no reason to believe that bony structure is any more or any less under genetic control than are surface features. The anatomist speaks of the skin and tissues close to it as "superficial," in contrast to "deep" structures. But we should not be misled by supposing that parts of the body near the surface are "superficial" in the figurative sense—that is, transitory or insignificant. All parts of the body develop simultaneously, and their structure is determined in the same way. Soft-part variation is largely genetic, as can be seen in the remarkable similarities of facial features in identical twins; and bones are not entirely unaffected by nongenetic forces. So there is no special or profound significance to variations of the skeleton; but they confirm and add to the total information by which we judge the genetic relations of human populations.

The region of the root and bridge of the nose is one in which the surface contours and the underlying bone correspond very closely, so that most of what we can say about the variations of this region of the skull have already been discussed. The high, narrow nasal root of the Caucasian, the low, rounded one of the Negroid, and the low, slightly ridged one of the Asian Mongoloid are as distinctive in the skull as in the living face, and become particularly important if race is to be judged without the help of the perishable parts. The nasal opening in the skull is much larger than in the living; with the soft parts absent, it extends above to the point of juncture of the bony and cartilaginous portions of the living nose. The width of the bony nasal aperture correlates to a fair degree with the width measured across the broadest part of the wings of the nose; both dimensions are related to the position of the nostrils. So, for purposes of comparison between living and ancient populations, we may consider the nasal breadth of the skull, which is generally greater in African blacks and Melanesians, and less in Caucasoids and many Mongoloids—to correspond roughly to visible nose breadth as seen in the living. The region above the nasal root is also interesting. A little disguised by facial muscles, still more so by the varying shape and bushiness of the eyebrows, the bony contours of the lower part of the forehead are not clearly seen in the living face. But it is obvious that in some individuals there is a horizontal ridge of bone, sometimes very prominent, which underlies the eyebrows and often extends right across above the root of the nose (Figures 29, 33D). This projection in the midline sometimes makes the root of the nose appear to be depressed even though it stands clearly forward from the plane of the eyes. The effect may be described as "beetling brow" or "deep-set eyes." This *brow-ridge* is one of the features of the skull that is better developed in males and is therefore used in judging the sex of a skull. When it is strongly developed, it makes the forehead appear sloping, even though the shape

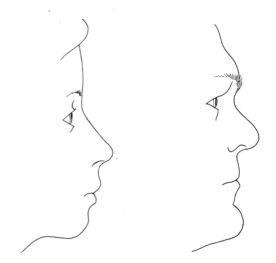

Figure 29 Extremes in browridge development: *left,* browridges absent; *right,* browridges very large.

of the inside of the skull is quite ordinary. The space inside the brow-ridge, that is, between the forehead in front and the brain behind, is often filled by a large frontal sinus, the function of which, as everyone knows, is to harbor infections. Thus, though the brow-ridge gives an impression of ruggedness, it may not be an asset to health. This heavy, bony brow is generally well developed in early prehistoric man, and this, together with its development, in males especially, has suggested that it serves as a reinforcement of the skull against the heavy pull of the jaw muscles in individuals with large jaws and teeth. This does not accord exactly with its distribution in modern man. Heavy brow-ridges are characteristic of Melanesians and Australians, who do indeed have large dental equipment. Brow-ridges are relatively slight, however, in Negroids and Mongoloids, who have moderately large teeth but often fairly conspicuous in Caucasoids, who generally have the smallest teeth and jaws among living races. To some extent the brow-ridges may augment the function of the eyebrows by serving as a built-in eyeshade against bright overhead light; again, this does not explain its racial variations. In one unusual variant of this portion of the face, the brow projects forward far over the eyes, then, instead of receding backward again to form a sloping forehead, rises straight up in a rounded dome. This is sometimes seen in native Australians, who are said to have "primitive" faces, though this forehead contour in no way resembles the brow-ridges of fossil man. For what it is worth, Charles Darwin also had this kind of a forehead.

Some things that are easy to see are hard to describe, and even harder to measure—an example of this is the characteristic of the Mongoloid face that we describe as "flatness" or "prominent cheek bones" (Oschinsky, 1962). To understand the essential feature of this shape, imagine a horizontal outline of the face just below the eye. The most forward point is the bridge of the nose. The sides of the nose slope back to a somewhat indefinite point where nose joins cheek. The cheek then faces more or less forward. At the side of the face the outline curves again, from the front to the sides of the cheek, and then back to the side of the head just in front of the ear. The cheek contour, as seen in such an outline, would vary between two extremes: one in which the cheeks curve smoothly back in a streamline contour, and another in which the cheeks extend flatly to the side, then turn back at nearly a right angle. This effect is seen in the skull as well as in the face, and somewhat more clearly, because there are varying amounts of fat in the living cheek that disguise the bony contour. In the skull, it is clear that in the second type of face the surface of the cheek bone below and in front of the eye faces so definitely forward that it is hardly visible in a side view, and that the lateral border of the orbit lies nearly as far forward as the medial border. This is the essential characteristic of the "flat" Mongoloid face (Figures 30, 34A and C). When this face shape is combined with a low nasal root and a low-lying nasal bridge and tip, the effect is very distinctive. The greatest contrast to this is the facial contour seen in many Caucasoids, in which the bony part of the nose projects forward and the cheekbones recede (Figures 30, 33A). Frequently a person of Mongoloid race can be identified from behind and a little to the side, with none of the face visible except the prominent cheek, which is seen to best advantage at this angle. Other major races are intermediate between these extremes.

The shape of the lower part of the face is controlled by the development of the jaws, which in turn is controlled by the size of

Figure 30 The "flatness" of the Mongoloid face: *left,* Chinese girl; *right,* north European girl.

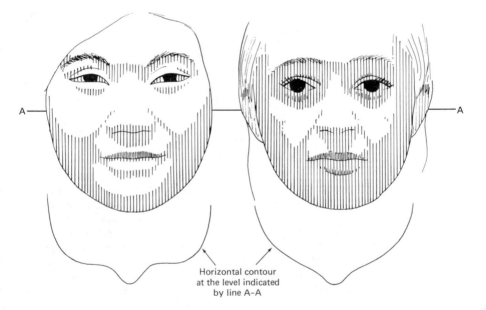

Horizontal contour
at the level indicated
by line A–A

the teeth. The most marked change in the face during the course of the evolution of the human species is, as we have already discussed, a reduction in size of the teeth, with a corresponding radical change in face proportions. The peculiar forward projection of the human nose is the result of the upper teeth having, so to speak, retreated from under it; and the projection of the human chin, also unique among animals, is the result of the lower teeth having receded from above it. Evolution has not proceeded altogether smoothly in this region—a fact from which orthodontists profit. The decline and fall of the teeth and their supporting bony structures has proceeded furthest in European Caucasoids and their far-flung descendants. The jaw structure is sometimes more reduced than the teeth themselves, resulting in difficulties of tooth eruption and alignment. The variations in development of the teeth result in racial differences in the profile of the middle and lower part of the face. A set of teeth which is large compared to the facial skeleton projects forward and produces the effect the anthropologists calls *prognathism:* literally, "forward jaw" (Figure 31, 33E). The mouth and lips, of course, are pushed forward also. The shape of the lower part of the nose is altered by this push from behind. The projection (tip of nose forward from lip) is reduced, making the nose appear flat; and the nostrils, which are usually narrower than they are deep in a nonprognathous person, become round or even wider than deep. This difference is best seen by looking at the face from somewhat below. An associated change is often observed in the skull, when prognathism is marked: the lower border of the nasal aperture ceases to have a sharp edge, as the angle between the floor of the nasal passage and the facial surface becomes less acute (Figure 33E, F). Various ways have been devised for measuring prognathism. It can be defined by relating the position of the most forward part of the upper jaw to a reference point at the nasal root; but because the forward projection of the nasal root is itself a racial variable, it is not clear what this really measures. "Prognathism" in a Mongoloid skull may mean merely that the nasal root is flat. Also, a face that is long from top to bottom may accommodate a large set of teeth

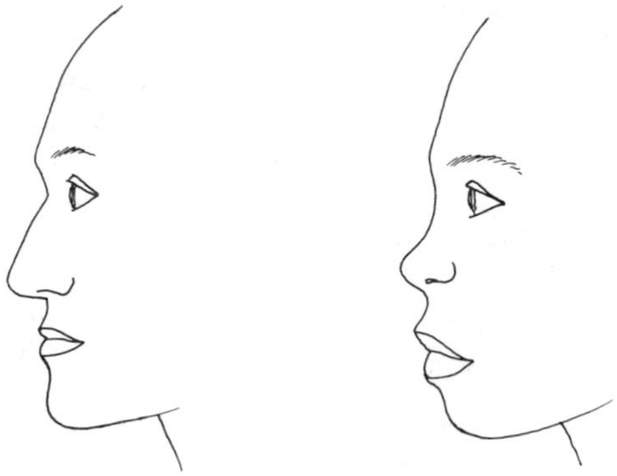

Figure 31 Prognathism: *left,* European without prognathism; *right,* African with moderate prognathism.

without being visibly angled forward. The effects of prognathism on the lower part of the face are inconsistent. In general, the projection of a large tooth row makes the chin less prominent. In "classic" examples, the facial profile between the nose and the chin would be, in a prognathous person, convex, and in an extremely nonprognathous person, concave. But a strongly developed jaw may produce a good chin in spite of prognathism, and there is another type of receding chin in which the dentition is average or small and the jaw abnormally small for the size of the teeth. Other misfits of teeth and jaws may result in overbite or underbite—that is, the upper teeth projecting in front of the lower, or vice versa. It is interesting that the dentist's standard of normal bite, that is, a slight overbite, is not appropriate to noncivilized peoples, whose teeth often meet edge-to-edge. It is customary to attribute reduction in tooth size and its associated facial changes in man, and particularly modern civilized man, to a decreased need for a large dentition as a result of dietary changes. But it is unlikely that dietary differences alone are the cause of the racial difference. European populations showed reduced prognathism long before they enjoyed a soft modern diet. There is probably a constant advantage to reduction of jaw size, which has operated throughout human evolution, in that the extra off-center weight of a protrusive jaw impedes rapid turning of the head (Brues, 1966). In animals with true muzzles, the forward projection definitely interferes with vision downward into the area where man manipulates and makes things with his hands—another possible reason for the facial changes that took place in the evolution of man. Actually, though few people are aware of it, the facial features affect the visual field to some extent in all of us (McCullough, 1970). Careful mapping of the field of vision shows that heavy brow-ridges and prominent cheeks limit vision above and to the side (Figure 32). A prominent nose cuts a little out of the field of view of each eye, limiting the area within which the vision of the two eyes overlap and depth judgment is possible; hence, a maximum field of binocular vision is made possible by the low-lying Mongoloid nose. The degree of prognathism found in man, however, rarely limits vision below: the eyelid and upper cheek are usually limiting factors.

The characteristics of the lower part of the face are essentially those of the lower jaw. This, the only "moving part" of the skull, has to be rather standardized in its basic shape, and it is surprising that it manages to show as much variation as it does. There is a marked sex difference. The major sex differences in the shape of the skull are that the male has (a) a larger face in proportion to the rest of the head and (b) a larger lower face and lower jaw in proportion to the upper part of the face. These sex differences are quite consistent in different races. The larger size of the male face is not noticeable until late childhood and adolescence, when the permanent teeth erupt. The face grows and changes its proportions in both sexes at this time, to accommodate the new and larger set of teeth, but the change is greatest in males. As a result, girls often

Figure 32 Two different views of the world. Visual fields of the individuals of Figure 29: without brow-ridges (*above*) and with large brow-ridges (*below*). After McCullough 1970.

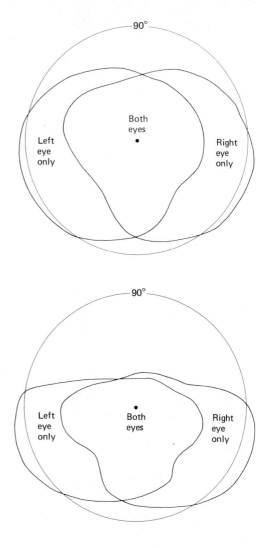

begin to look like their mothers during childhood, but boys rarely look very much like their fathers until they have gone through the facial growth of adolescence. In addition to the basic sex difference in face proportions, there is a greater thickness of bone and greater development of various protuberances and ridges in male skulls. Among the sex markers of the male skull are heavier brow-ridges, larger mastoids (the bony bumps below the ear, which are felt rather than seen in the living), and a more prominent protuberance of the chin. Males generally show a greater thickness of bone in the lower jaw, both in breadth and in depth (that is, distance from the gum line to the lower border). The back corner of the jaw, just below the molars, is disproportionately wide in males, partly as a result of stronger muscle attachments. The total size of the face—

and this is partly but not entirely the result of jaw development—is a racial characteristic as well as a sexual one. Faces that are large, particularly in the breadth of the upper part, are found in Asiatic Mongoloids, though not in all of them. Faces that are very large in both length and breadth, above and below, are characteristic of many American Indian populations (Figure 34F).

THE BRAIN-CASE OR NEUROCRANIUM

The anatomist divides the skull into the *facial skeleton,* which we have already discussed, and the *neurocranium,* which is nontechnical language is called the *brain-case.* The facial skeleton is relatively fragile, and comprises all the portions of the skull associated with the eyes, the nose, and the mouth. The brain-case is rather sturdy and thick-walled, except for a few areas on the sides and bottom that are covered by muscle. It is further strengthened by its vaulted shape, well-designed to house the complicated control mechanism of the animal body. There has been endless speculation about the possible relations of the size and shape of the skull to the functions of the brain within it. The total size of the brain is a striking difference between man and his primate relatives, as well as between primates in general and most other mammals, and this correlates well with the differences in complexity of behavior which they show. In the fossil record, the brain size (as judged by the capacity of the neurocranium) is the basis for assumptions as to how far various ancestors of man have changed from the mental capacities of the present-day primates in the direction of the present human species. How closely the adequacy of brain function correlates with brain size within the more limited range found in modern man has, however, been a matter of dispute, which will be discussed more fully in Chapter 12.

The question of the effect of brain shape, rather than size, in relation to its function was the basis of *phrenology,* an ambitious pseudoscience of a century ago. Phrenology attempted to localize such abstract aspects of behavior as pride, affection, and contentiousness in thumbnail-sized spots on the surface of the brain; it further claimed that pressure arising from overdevelopment of these virtues or vices would result in bumps on the surface of the skull. Supposedly, the skilled practitioner, by running his hands over someone's head, could evaluate his character. Then, as now, people could be fascinated by being told things about themselves that were unexpected, and quite possibly untrue. Phrenology was a spinoff from the very earliest studies of localization of brain function. The scientific study of brain localization has developed along rather different lines, showing that the organization of brain functions, though quite meaningful, corresponds not at all to the mental and moral categories of phrenology. (See also Chapter 12 and

Figure 44.) The brain, in any case, does not develop bumps from exercise, and cannot produce bumps on the skull, because in the living condition the brain is almost fluid in consistency.

We will be misled about the relation of brain and skull size if we think only in terms of the adult brain and its very solid and rigid bony container. In infancy and childhood, when the brain is growing rapidly, the skull bones are thin and not solidly joined to one another. During early infancy the skull can be deformed by external pressure, either inadvertently or by design. The results become permanent and some of them are among the most remarkable of man's cosmetic efforts upon his body. These cranial deformations appear to have no effect upon an individual's mental or social functions. In these cases the skull bulges out at the points where it is not pressed upon, so that the total internal capacity remains the same. It seems unlikely, therefore, that individual variations in shape of the skull affect the brain, or that brain growth affects the skull, except to determine its final size. The dimensions of the floor of the neurocranium are probably determined independently of anything affecting the brain. The vault of the skull grows so long as the growing brain exerts a slight general pressure. If the skull base is large, the brain may be quite large without bulging upward and outward very markedly; this was the case with our unfairly criticised forbear, Neanderthal man, who had a very large brain in spite of a most unintellectual profile. If the skull base is small, and the brain medium or large in size, the vault bulges upward and outward. These general principles, however, cannot account for all the variations in skull contour and profile. Early anthropologists laid great stress on the *cranial index*—a measure of the ratio between the maximum breadth of the skull and its maximum length from front to back. This shows much variation: the breadth varies from 75 to 90 per cent of the length in averages of populations; from 60 to 100 per cent in extreme individual cases. The cranial index was of particular interest to European anthropologists because it showed a wide range of variation in European populations, and appeared useful in assessing relationships and prehistoric migrations within that area. However, generalizations about other races can be made: that the cranial index is high in most Mongoloids, low in most races other than Mongoloid or Caucasoid. It is interesting that quite recently an analysis of racial differences in the skull (made by computer techniques, thus avoiding any preconceptions of about what measurements would be significant) showed that skull breadth was indeed a racial characteristic of prime importance (Howells, 1973). It also showed some things that had escaped the notice of early workers. Not the breadth at the widest point, which may be well above the ears, but the breadth between the ear-holes was most significant. Also, the breadth itself, regardless of its ratio to the skull length, was the important factor. Secondarily, the computer analysis showed that the massive face of the Mongoloids was related to the broad skull, and correlated with it between individuals as well as between populations.

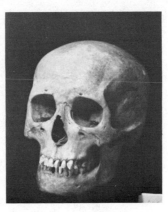

Figure 33 (a–f)
Skulls from the
collection of the
U.S. National Museum.

(a) a Bohemian of the Neolithic period.

(b) a Lapp.

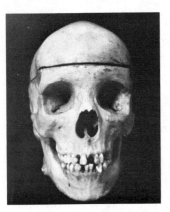

(c) a Negro from Africa.

(d) an Australian aboriginal,
province of Victoria.

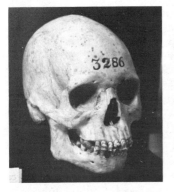

(e) a Melanesian from New
Britain.

(f) a Philippine Negrito.

Figure 34 (a–f)
Skulls from the
collection of the
U.S. National Museum.

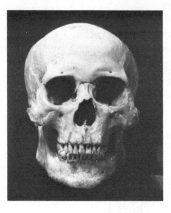

(a) a Mongol.

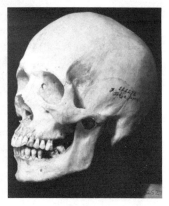

(b) a Japanese.

(c) an Alaskan Eskimo.

(d) a California Indian.

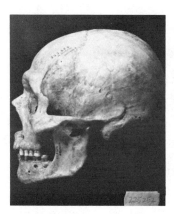

(e) a North Dakota Indian.

(f) a New Mexican Indian.

Teeth

The whole story of cranial differences, let alone the history of the study, is a book in itself. The computer project referred to in the last paragraph used over fifty measurements of the skull (including the face) of seventeen populations. (The lower jaw was not included because it is often missing in museum collections.) This represents only a selection from the numerous measurements that have been devised by one anthropologist or another for the human cranium. We still do not know why some skulls are flat in the back and some protruding, why some are rounded across the top and some peaked, or the reasons for a hundred other individual shapes. The genetics of these variations is undoubtedly appallingly complicated. The population differences, however, are definite and consistent. When the computer was asked to sort out the sixteen-hundred-odd skulls of the study into the seventeen populations, on the basis of measurements, it did so with an accuracy of 92 per cent. This of course was helped by the fact that the seventeen populations had been chosen to be well-spaced out across the map of the world, with intermediate areas eliminated—a procedure which makes racial distinctions appear clearer. Still, it was considered an error if a skull was assigned to the *wrong* population within the *right* major race. This compares very favorably with the zoologist's definition of a subspecies, which requires that 80 per cent of all specimens are capable of being correctly assigned to their population. Clearly, the variations of the skull represent a vast body of information about regional variations in gene frequencies, though we are as yet unable to interpret it in conventional genetic terms. Measurements of the same kind have been utilized in a slightly different way to calculate the "betting odds" that an unknown skull is that of one race rather than another. Mathematical formulae can be devised to make such assessment automatically, without reliance on the skill or experience of the observer (Giles and Elliott, 1962).

TEETH

Teeth have been of great value to students of evolution because they are the most durable part of the animal skeleton, often surviving when all else has been destroyed. Many fossils have been described and named from teeth and jaw fragments alone. The number of teeth and their shapes are very specific for each species, and are generally closely adapted to diet. The durability of teeth in the fossil record may be surprising news to modern man, who finds that his own teeth are likely to be "here today and gone tomorrow," in spite of very considerable dental bills. But teeth in the living mouth are in a hazardous situation, surrounded as they are by a warm, fluid medium which fosters various destructive bacteria. The frequent decay and loss of teeth in humans contrasts unfavorably with the experience in most other mammals, and the experience of people of highly civilized habits and diet seems to be worse than that of their fellow men who live closer to nature. This raises interesting questions: are there genuine individual, race, or species differences in the *durability* of the teeth, or are the apparent differences caused by diet or other environmental factors? We must also consider the effect of the increased lifespan of man as compared to that of most other mammals. It may well be that the useful life of teeth composed and constructed according to the plan that has worked for other mammals falls short of the limits of human life, because human life has been greatly extended. In the elephant, another very long-lived mammal, the molar teeth erupt one at a time; when one wears out, another replaces it. The stretched-out sequence of human molars, with the third (the wisdom tooth) appearing as much as twelve to sixteen years after the first, may represent a start in this direction. Man may have inherited teeth with an obsolescence factor which natural selection has not yet modified to match his extended lifespan. Correspondingly, in any population that has a relatively low life-expectancy, general dental condition may *appear* to be better because fewer people outlive their teeth. There are other cultural factors acting also. One of the hazards to tooth survival is the presence of small folds in the enamel between the cusps, which are a starting point for decay; in modern humans their former locations are often marked by fillings. In a less fastidious way of life, when grain and other vegetable foods were inadequately cleaned and meat was butchered on the ground for lack of tables, there was enough grit in the diet to sand down these irregularities in the enamel before decay started in them. Dirt in the diet may be carried too far, however. This is particularly obvious among some Indians in North America, who ground corn on slabs of sandstone. The amount of grit that became incorporated into the cornmeal was so great that it often wore teeth down all the way to the pulp cavity when individuals were still in their thirties and forties. Teeth sometimes survived this, but were frequently lost in a very painful way. Those communities that used grinding stones of hard volcanic rock did not have these problems. But sandstone was more easily shaped, and, as in the case of some modern technological advances, the cheaper way proved to involve some unrecognized hazards.

There are definite individual variations that affect tooth survival. Some persons, for reasons not known, seem to be immune to dental decay. This may be the result of an immunological condition rather than of structural characteristics of the teeth. A trait of rare occurrence but clear inheritance is defective enamel which results in general tooth disintegration a few years after eruption. Certainly some individuals are prone to excessive dental decay although they appear to have diet and hygiene similar to other individuals whose teeth remain sound (Bordoni, 1973). The sifting out of the various genetic and environmental causes of dental problems is not going to be easy, and many people will have many toothaches before we know the answers.

We have already referred to the size of the teeth as related to prognathism. Tooth size is easily measured; it is less easy to relate it to head or to body size. The breadth and length of a molar tooth, in the horizontal plane, can be combined to give a measure of the total chewing surface; the length (front to back) alone may be combined for molars and premolars to give a total length of the cheek teeth. A very obvious difference affecting total tooth function is the failure of one or more of the third molars (wisdom teeth) to be formed at all, a condition found in about 20 per cent of modern humans (Brothwell, 1963). These differences are not combined in a consistent way. Australians and Melanesians have large molars, rarely lack any of them, and sometimes have a fourth molar—a rare occurrence in any other race (Birdsell, 1950; Dahlberg, 1951). At the other extreme, Caucasians have relatively small teeth, and about 20 per cent absence of one or more third molars. Mongoloids have a high incidence of third-molar absence, but the teeth they do have are large. Negroes have relatively small molars, but nearly always have a full set of them. In some of these cases, obviously, molar size and molar number compensate, rather than varying together in response to some "need" for chewing capacity. In general these data correlate with the facial profile. Australians and Melanesians are the most prognathous (though we associate the condition with Negroes because they are the prognathous people we most often see), and Caucasians the least prognathous of modern races.

One tooth variation definitely associated with race is the *shovel incisor*. This is a front tooth of distinctive shape, which ordinarily escapes notice because only the back side of the tooth is affected. In these teeth there are strong vertical ridges on either side, making the back surface concave like that of a scoop or shovel. Figure 35 shows a moderate "shoveling," not the most extreme form that occurs. There are also various degrees of lesser shoveling, grading imperceptibly into a flat surface. Moderate to marked shovel incisors are almost universal in Mongoloid races, including Asian Mongoloids, Eskimos, and American Indians (Dahlberg, 1951, 1963; Carbonell, 1963). In the other major races very few individuals have even a slight development of the trait. In view of the rather incomplete genetic separation of Mongoloid and Caucasoid populations in Eurasia, the clarity of this difference is rather remarkable. The shovel incisor is as clear a racial marker as numerous traits often considered to be of primary racial significance. The shovel incisor is a more massive tooth than a flat-surfaced one, and when it is worn down by rough diet, it presents a larger surface, perhaps a

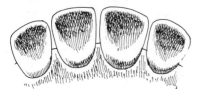

Figure 35 The "shovel incisor": from casts of the upper front teeth, viewed from the back side.

more useful one. But it is hardly possible to explain the distribution of the trait by selection: diet in Asia and Europe is not, nor has it been, very different. Another conspicuous variation involving the incisor teeth is the condition popularly called "buck teeth," in which the upper incisors are angled slightly forward. This condition is occasional in European Caucasoids, now usually corrected by the orthodontist in anyone who can afford it, and seems to be commoner in Chinese and Japanese, though not in more rugged-faced Mongoloids (Figure 34B). This may be an accommodation to teeth slightly too large for the jaw; yet in Europeans a disharmony of this kind more commonly results in rotation or overlapping of the teeth. The lateral incisor is usually smaller than the central one, and may be peg-like or absent. After the third molar, it is the tooth most likely to disappear from the human dentition (Brothwell, 1963). A reduced or missing lateral incisor is common in many races (5 to 10 per cent) though quite uncommon in Negroids (Dahlberg, 1951).

Another tooth variation associated primarily with a single race is Carabelli's cusp, a small extra projection on the inner side of a molar tooth (Lasker and Lee, 1957). This has many variations, from a tiny irregularity to a clearly defined cusp, and in its more marked manifestations is virtually limited to Caucasoids. This cusp does not form part of the chewing surface and has no obvious value. Its limited regional distribution makes a good case for genetic drift. Other variations of cusp patterns of the teeth are interesting to specialists, but we will pass them over.

THE SUTURES OF THE SKULL

We have previously mentioned that during the growth period the bones of the skull vault are not solidly joined together. At birth these bones are thin, curved plates of bone connected by a tough membrane which allows a degree of movement between them; they do move somewhat, in fact, during birth. At the top of the head in a newborn baby there is a "soft spot," the point where four of these bony plates meet, leaving a considerable area protected by membrane only (Figure 36). In front of this spot are the two halves of the *frontal* bone, behind it the right and left *parietals*. A few inches farther back, the parietals diverge to leave room for the *occipital* bone, a triangle with base down, which forms the back of the cranial vault. As these various bony components increase in size, the strips of membrane joining them become narrower, and at the age of five or six years the two halves of the frontal bone normally fuse into a single unit. Narrow lines of separation called *sutures*, which may become quite wavy or jagged, continue to separate the remaining bone components. Growth of the skull vault takes place by the deposition of new bone along these lines. The separate bones do not fuse together solidly until adult life, when the brain has

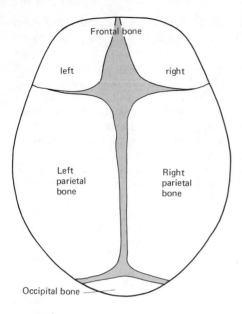

Figure 36 Top view of the human skull at birth, showing soft areas (shaded).

attained its full size. Though it is necessary that lines of separation should exist during the growth period, there is no particular reason, except evolutionary tradition, why these sutures should be exactly where they are, and there is in fact some variation in the suture patterns.

A fairly common occurrence is the failure of the two halves of the frontal bone to fuse with one another. This leaves a *metopic* suture running down the middle of the forehead. This condition occurs at a frequency of around 10 per cent in Europeans, is about half as common in some Asiatic Mongoloids, and quite rare in other races (Martin and Saller, 1956). In medieval European illustrations it is frequently shown, not because it was more common then than now,

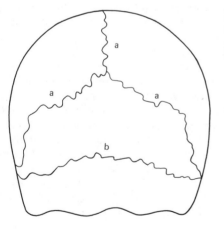

Figure 37 A skull viewed from behind, showing normal sutures (a) and the extra suture (b) that forms on Inca bone.

but because, together with the other more normal sutures, it formed a cross, which appealed to a symbol-obsessed age. Another fairly frequent suture variation is a separation of the occipital into upper and lower parts by an extra horizontal suture (Figure 37). Such a suture, not always at the same level, is most common in American Indians, with the maximum, 30 per cent, recorded in Peru, which is why the extra bone formed is called the *Inca bone.* This variation appears sporadically in Africa and Melanesia, but is generally rare in Europe (Martin and Saller, 1956). The rather late closing of the sutures of the skull, first on the inside of the vault and later on the outside (completely obliterating any indication of their previous location), is useful in estimating an individual's age at death (Krogman, 1962). This is helpful in identification problems, and for assessing life expectancy and health conditions in prehistoric populations.

8 Skin, Hair and Fat

FINGERPRINTS

Human fingerprints, or *dermatoglyphics,* as they are technically called, are well-known for having so much individual variation that even a fragmentary impression left behind at the scene of a crime is suffi-cient to establish who was there. The *dermal ridges* that form the fingerprint pattern have a very practical purpose, that of increasing the friction between the skin and objects which are grasped or rested upon, and are characteristic of toes and feet as well as of palms and fingers, not only in man but in other primates. The monkeys whose tails are used for grasping even have such ridges on the skin of the tail. But though the presence of these ridges serves a purpose, their exact pattern is not important, no doubt the reason why it varies so much. The matching of two prints is easily demon-strated—no other kind of evidence has survived legal challenges so successfully—but it is less easy to measure the degree of similarity of two nonidentical prints or sets of prints. A start can be made from the kind of classification that has been developed in order to match an unknown print in a collection containing thousands of records. The first sorting of such a collection is into three basic pattern types: arches, loops, and whorls (see Figure 38). Further description, for purposes of filing, involves such traits as whether a pattern slopes to right or left. Geneticists and anthropologists, however, have been most concerned with the general *complexity* of fingerprint patterns, not with their smaller details. There is a natural sequence from the arch—which is the simplest pattern and the one commonly found in most primates—to the loop, which is interme- diate in complexity, and finally to the whorl, which is the most complex. The sum of an individual's fingerprint complexity, or an average of the fingerprint complexity of a population, may be expressed in percentages of the three kinds of prints. Normally we use all ten fingers of every individual. A representative sample of European Caucasoids will have about 5 per cent arches, 65 per cent loops, and 30 per cent whorls. Such percentage figures are hard to use in comparing populations, so a single number expressing com- plexity may be used, the most common being an index derived by counting every arch as zero, every loop as one, and every whorl as two. Applied to the population just cited, this would give an "aver- age" of 12.5 (six and a half loops per person, plus (2 × 3) whorls). Another method of rating fingerprints, the *ridge count*, is sometimes used. In general, individuals and populations with high pattern indices have high ridge counts also.

Genetic studies of fingerprints have shown that they are largely determined by heredity (Newman, 1930). The fingerprints of iden- tical twins are much alike, even to the type of pattern occurring on a particular finger, though they are never so much alike as to cause any confusion in personal identification. Comparison of fingerprints between other relatives shows, as might be expected, a partial similarity. A summary of such data gives an estimate of heritability of fingerprint patterns of about .90. This means that although the general pattern is genetically determined, some chance factors affect the precise way in which the ridges develop. As in the case of other traits with wide possibilities for variation, there is no convincing way to explain fingerprint variation in terms of one or a few sets of

Figure 38 Fingerprint patterns: whorl, arch, loop.

alleles. It has been found that a number of the disturbances of chromosome numbers that result in developmental defects have specific effects on fingerprints also, indicating that factors influencing the fingerprint pattern are distributed among a number of chromosomes.

Like other individual variations, fingerprint patterns show statistical differences between different races and populations (Rife, 1953). The most widely published data are pattern indices such as those just described. Lowest indices (that is, the simplest patterns) are found among the small Pygmies and Bushmen of Africa, who may have 10 per cent or more arches; their indices are less than 10. Somewhat more complex patterns characterize Europeans and most Africans (12–13). Peoples of Asia and the New World tend to higher indices (about 15), and the most complex patterns of all are found in the Australian aboriginals, with indices as high as 17, that is, they have more whorls than loops. A classification of races based on fingerprints alone would combine populations which were very different in other traits.

SKIN GLANDS AND SECRETIONS

The surface of the skin is abundantly, though invisibly, equipped with glands. The *sebaceous glands* are associated with hair follicles and secrete an oily secretion into the follicle. They are present and active, however, in those parts of the body where hairs are very short, as well as where hairs grow long and conspicuous. The amount of secretion varies with the individual and tends to decrease with age, causing the hair and skin to become drier. Women are particularly aware of these differences and changes. Racial differences in these glands, if any, are not known. *Sweat glands* are quite independent of hairs, and in fact occur abundantly on the dermal ridges of the fingers. They produce a watery secretion only, which we will discuss in Chapter 10 because of its physiological importance in heat adaptation. However, a distinct type of gland, producing some oily matter as well as a watery secretion, is present in certain areas of the body, most noticeably in the axilla, and is notoriously associated with "body odor." Variation in the odor associated with the axillary glands is a contentious subject and we have little objective information about it. Man's sense of smell is the poorest of all mammals, and we have only a vestigial vocabulary to describe odors; also, the identification of odors has been entirely bypassed by the modern explosion of laboratory technology. Consequently there is virtually no *science* of odor, the subject is still in the realm of folklore. We do know that the odor associated with the axillary glands seems to develop, largely at least, after bacteria on the skin break down the oily secretion. Antibacterial agents applied to the skin will prevent the formation of marked odor although the glands continue to function. When bacteria are not active the odor is usually faint and not disagreeable. Undoubtedly some components of body odor are present in the secretion as it is produced and others develop secondarily. Hormonal changes, such as during menstruation, affect the odor, and probably other metabolic products, and even dietary substances, may be secreted by these glands when present in the bloodstream. There is a marked racial difference in the development of these axillary sweat glands. They are usually poorly or not at all developed in Mongoloid peoples, but are well-developed in the other major races. In Japan, odorous sweat is considered to be an unfortunate abnormality, and if Caucasians are not aware of this opinion, it is because of good manners (Baker, 1974). The domestic water buffalo of Southeast Asia have a notorious dislike for the scent of Caucasians. It is likely that the unfamiliar odor produced by the axillary glands is what they detect and resent. All individuals with well-developed axillary glands smell if they are not regularly washed, though many persons claim that unwashed persons of different races smell differently—and that everybody else smells worse than themselves. There appears to be a correlated effect between the development of the axillary glands and the function of the glands that produce wax in the external opening of the ear. Individuals and races with poorly developed axillary glands have earwax that is dry in texture, and persons with well-developed axillary glands have moist earwax. This has been extensively studied in Japan, where dry earwax is the rule (Adachi, 1937; Matsunaga, 1962). The inheritance seems to be simple, with the "wet" trait dominant. Dry earwax has been found to be predominant in American Indians as well as in Asian Mongoloids (Petrakis, 1967), and the wet type is virtually universal in Caucasians and Negroids. This somewhat obscure trait is therefore strongly differentiated by race. It is apparently also an example of a pleiotropic effect. Two different types of skin glands of distinctive function are affected by the same gene in distinctive ways.

HAIR

Human hair, unlike that of most animals, is patchy and concentrated in impractical areas. None of the primates from which the human species has descended, appears to have lived in a climate that required a pelt of the kind that protects from cold. Many of our modern primate relatives have sparse and stringy coats. Some primates, however, have distinct and showy color patterns, involving skin as well as hair, so it may well be that one of the important functions of hair in man is, as many generations of humans appear to have believed, an ornamental one.

Human hair covering is more complete than it appears. Large numbers of hairs, called *vellus* hairs, which are very short and fine, faintly pigmented, and virtually invisible, are abundant in apparently hairless parts of the body. *Terminal* hairs, which are much coarser and more visible, replace vellus hairs to a greater or less extent according to age, sex, and part of the body. Terminal hairs appear in the scalp and eyebrows at an early age, sometimes before and sometimes shortly after birth. A major period of transformation of vellus to terminal hair is at puberty, when axillary and pubic hair appear in both sexes. At this time general body hair and facial hair, which vary greatly in amount according to sex and race, and between individuals, become conspicuous also.

Human hair covering, even in the most hirsute males, is hardly sufficient to afford much protection against cold, except on the head, and it is reasonable to suppose that the development of clothing has been correlated with the reduction of body hair in man, whether as cause or effect. Head hair affords some protection against heat and sunburn in a particularly exposed area, because it protects not only the top of the head but, if uncut, the back of the neck. The eyebrows serve the special function of shading the eyes from strong overhead light; it is interesting that they are likely to be dark in color even in individuals with depigmented head hair, indicating that this shading function is of some importance. There are a number of side effects of the presence or absence of abundant body hair. In many primates other than man the mother of a young infant is able to move freely because the infant, by clinging to her body hair, relieves her of the necessity of carrying it. The human infant still has the ability to grasp tightly with its hands, but has nothing to hold on to. Alternatives which human culture has developed are artificial carrying devices, protected places where the infant can be laid down, or simply the acceptance of the mother's being impeded in carrying out her work. On the other hand, reduction of body hair deprives certain biting parasites of their comfortable refuges (Olson, 1966). Lice, for instance, require hairs on which to lay their eggs, with the exception of the body louse, which is so adapted to human habits that it lays its eggs on clothing. Hit-and-run biters like mosquitoes, of course, find a naked skin all the more convenient. Many mammals spend much time grooming their fur, and among primates this often is a mutual process with much social significance. (In man, the talking animal, trivial conversation performs this social function.) The function and significance of the beard, and of axillary and pubic hair, have been much debated. It is not simply that the mammalian hair covering has been retained in these areas. Most mammals have shorter hair on the face than on other parts of the body, and the hair in their axillary and pubic regions is sparser than most of the coat. It has been suggested that the patchy effect of these special hairy adornments in the naked male has a visual impact which enhances threat and thus promotes the safety of their possessor. Beards, particularly large and bushy ones, can certainly make one who grew up in a beardless era feel ill at ease! There is a curious paradox here: nature has provided humankind with a complicated set of facial muscles by which emotions, attitudes, and social intentions can be communicated, and then provided the adult male with facial hair that conceals his expressions. (Perhaps there is a friendly expression behind that beard, but how is one to know?) It is certainly true, however, that the beard and the greater amount of body hair, particularly on the front of the body, are distinct sex markers, and by signaling sex at a great distance may serve as social facilitators. The pattern of beard growth is also one of the numerous variations in man that can serve as a personal identity marker; and the addition of art to nature in this regard produces phenomena the study of which falls within the field of the psychiatrist rather than the anthropologist.

One of the most conspicuous variables of human hair is its curvature, which varies from entirely straight to wooly, a range paralleled in mammals only by the wild sheep and their domestic relatives. The curvature of human hair is most easily seen if a short piece of the hair is allowed to rest on a flat surface so that it forms a circle or part of a circle. The diameter of the circle that indicates its curvature can be measured. The most tightly curled hair, that usually referred to as wooly or frizzly, may form a circle only one sixteenth of an inch in diameter (Day, 1932). The curvature of the hair is not always continuous or uniform (Hrdy, 1973). It may change in direction in such a way that if a hair is laid on a flat surface, part of the curl may lie flat, and part may curve up and away from the surface. Also, the curvature may change, so that some parts of a single hair are more strongly curved than others. Both of these effects are sometimes called "kinks," though the term *kinky* has been so freely used for any tightly curved hair that it is no longer clear in its meaning. Hair that is uniformly curved can be trained into smooth waves by combing; hair that is kinky, in either sense of the word, is very resistant to this kind of grooming. The degree of curvature of the hair varies with sex: in all races in which curved hair occurs at all, more strongly curved hair appears to be more frequent in males. In some cases, the hair may turn curly at puberty, in formerly straight-haired boys. Beards seem to be curly more often than head hair, and more likely to have curvature that changes in direction and degree within a single hair. Because hair form has a strong correlation with regional ancestry, it has been used as a secondary or even primary classifier of race (Haddon, 1925). The most tightly curled forms are found in Africa and are as characteristic of Negroid races as skin color. The most extreme hair curvature occurs in the African Bushmen, and is sometimes called "peppercorn hair." This odd designation refers to the fact that the very tightly curved head hairs tend to roll themselves up into balls or knots formed of a number of adjacent hairs, and the effect resembles peppercorns attached to the scalp. Other Negroids have wooly or very tightly curled hair. Strong hair curvature is also found in Melanesians: they differ from Africans, however, in having hair with characteristically very irregular curvature, therefore their resemblance to Africans in hair form is more apparent than real. Caucasian hair form varies from curly to straight, and Mongoloids have hair which, with few exceptions, is quite straight. The large continuous range of hair form indicates that a number of genetic loci must be involved. Individuals of mixed descent, part Caucasian and part Negro, have intermediate hair form with much individual variation (Day, 1932). This is what we would expect if a number of genetic factors had a more or less additive effect. The function of curly or wooly hair is debatable. An equal amount of wooly hair has greater insulating value than straight hair, because of trapped air spaces. This suggests that it would be advantageous in cold climates—precisely the environment in which it does not occur. However, by being present on the head only, it would not add much to general body insulation, but could be important for protection against solar heat, particularly when the sun is directly overhead, as it is in tropical areas. This would give it some selective advantage in the regions where it obviously occurs. Against this is the fact that many wooly-haired individuals living in tropical Africa customarily shave the head. Moreover, the peppercorn hair of the Bushmen has carried curvature to the point where it serves no insulating function.

The texture of the hair, whether coarse or fine, also varies individually and with race. A majority of Europeans have hair as straight as typical Mongoloids, but European straight hair is characteristically fine in texture, and Mongoloid hair is coarse. These head hairs of Mongoloids, including both Asian Mongoloids and American Indians, not only have a greater diameter, but greater development of an irregularly hollow core, the *medulla*, which adds somewhat to the insulating properties of the hair (Brown, 1942). The total bulk of Mongoloid head hair, as seen if it is gathered into braids, is often impressive. Such hair bends less readily than the relatively limp Caucasian hair, and often will not lie flat on the head where it is parted. Men in whom this stiffness of the hair is marked, as often occurs in Asians and American Indians, have to make a choice between cutting the hair quite short and letting it stick straight up, or growing it long enough so that it lies flat of its own weight. Any intermediate length defies control.

Another variation in head hair is the length to which it grows. Human hair is so frequently cut to some socially approved length that we have only glimpses of its potentiality. Many people, in fact, are surprised to hear that humans, like cats and dogs, may be long-, medium-, or short-haired by nature. Every normal head of hair has a length it will not exceed, no matter how long it is left uncut. A few instances have been recorded of human head hair that seemed to grow indefinitely; this, like the 12-foot tail feathers of certain fancy Oriental roosters, seems to be a rare mutation. Normally, each single hair grows for a certain length of time until it reaches its destined length, then ceases to grow for awhile, and finally drops out, to be succeeded by a new hair growing from the same follicle. Man differs from many other mammals in that there is no obvious seasonal cycle of growth or period of mass sheeding of hair. Careful study has shown that humans in the North Temperate Zone shed more hairs in November than in any other month, perhaps a vestige of shedding in preparation for growing a new winter coat (Oren-treich, 1969). Most people do not notice this—though it would be interesting to know if there is a seasonal peak in sale of prepara-tions supposed to be good for "falling hair." In general, however, the shedding and regrowth of hairs in humans is a more or less continuous process. The result of this is that the length of the uncut head of hair remains the same indefinitely, though there is a con-tinual turnover of individual hairs, each growing to its proper length before stopping growth and later being shed. The lower edge of an untrimmed head of hair "feathers off" because all hairs do not attain the same length. The rate of growth of head hairs is about one-half inch per month, the life of an individual hair probably anywhere from two to six years.

Data on true head hair length is difficult to obtain because of the rarity with which human beings leave their hair alone. It is clear from drawings of eighteenth-century men who let their hair grow, and from observations of modern college students, that head hair in Caucasian males usually does not attain much more than shoulder length. In Caucasian females, however, it often reaches to the waist or below. Thus there is a natural basis for the custom among many peoples of allowing the hair to grow longer in females than in males. Evidence from a short period in China when men grew their hair long, and from some American Indians, indicates that in these Mongoloid populations head hair not infrequently attains waist length in males. Mongoloid females often can grow hair that reaches well below the waist; in fact one may sometimes correctly guess their race from behind, simply by the very long straight black hair. Women of India also may have hair that is very long by European standards. Maximum hair length in wooly-haired popu-lations is hard to evaluate because of the shortening—as much as one-half or two-thirds of the length—resulting from the close cur-vature. There is also, of course, much individual variation in the length of the head hair. A hundred years ago the length of the hair in American females was a matter of much emulation. It was a source of rare pride to have hair long enough to sit on, but we have no records of how many women could do it, or what spinal contor-tions some of them went through to persuade themselves that they could. Now, when long hair is again fashionable among young women, it is usually trimmed a little when it gets ragged at the lower edge, and the anthropologist seeking hard data on hair length is still thwarted.

The amount and distribution of body hair is not a characteristic that the layman usually thinks of as racial. Nevertheless there are, in addition to the obvious sex differences in body hair, some marked racial differences. These differences even override the sex differences so that women of some races are hairier than the men of other races. Most comparative observations have been made on males because they exhibit a wider range of variation. Although there are some individual differences in detailed pattern, particu-larly apparent in the beard, there is a general relation of pattern and quantity, with certain parts of the body more prone to be hairy than others. Pubic and axillary hair are always present in adults. The most glabrous human males have only a few scattered beard hairs, mostly on the chin and upper lip, and less body hair than the average Caucasian female. The next most hairy have a respectable beard but little body hair. With increasing hair development, the beard extends upward on the cheeks, the scalp hair begins to extend down on the back of the neck and the beard on the front; hair appears on the arms and legs, particularly the distal segments, and on the chest; and the pubic hair extends upward on the abdomen and finally forms a continuous mat up the front of the trunk. In the most extreme cases hair appears on the back, and, in fact, covers nearly the whole body except the palms of the hands and soles of the feet. In races that exhibit extreme hairiness among men, the amount of beard and body hair in women, though not as great as in men, appears quite remarkable to those not accustomed to it, though it is accepted and duly admired by their own people.

Among the more widely distributed races, Caucasoids are distinguished by the greatest hairiness, Mongoloids by the least. The Ainu of Japan and the Australoids are the most hirsute of humans. Among Caucasoids, the greatest development of body hair and beard is in the Near and Middle East and in the eastern part of the Mediterranean region. The function of these differences is puzzling. The distribution of greatest hairiness among Caucasoids certainly does not suggest even a vestigial function of hair as protection against cold; in the Near East, heat is a greater problem. An explanation has been offered for the extreme condition of hairlessness where even the beard is virtually absent. In extreme cold the beard may become encrusted with frozen vapor from the breath and thereby become a nuisance (Coon, et al., 1950). That this may be a selective factor is suggested by the fact that a very scanty beard is characteristic of Central Asian peoples who experience the extreme inland winter cold of northern Asia. Here again, as in the case of hair length, cultural practises limit observation. A very sparse beard does little for one's looks and consequently it is often removed, sometimes by the painful process of pulling it out one hair at a time. Thus, some nonhairy races may not be as smooth-faced as they appear. A clean-shaven face has been in style off and on since Roman times, even among heavily bearded populations, and even when beards are "in," we do not know whether the clean-shaven males are simply those who have found they cannot produce a very impressive beard. Careful study has revealed a further difference in beard growth between Caucasoids and Mongoloids. A comparison of men of both races and of different ages showed that the thickness of the beard, that is, the number of hairs per square inch, reached its maximum at the age of 35 in Caucasoids and not until 65 in Mongoloids (Hamilton, 1958). This undoubtedly explains the different symbolic value attached to the beard in Western versus Oriental cultures. Westerners think of the beard as the symbol of masculine vigor and the badge of the warrior; in the Orient the beard, scanty as it is, has been regarded as the symbol of elderly wisdom and the ornament of the philosopher. Apparently there is a physical basis for this difference in semantics.

Another peculiarity of many humans is the loss of head hair with age, in a pattern involving the top of the head and usually also the forehead. This hereditary condition, which even commercial experts no longer claim to cure, is called "male pattern baldness" because of its virtual limitation to the male sex. It is one of the few human variables that appears to have a fairly simple pattern of inheritance, although this has been obscured by its relation to sex. Apparently the genetic condition can occur in either sex, but is unlikely to express itself in the absence of the male sex hormone. This has sometimes led bald males to comfort themselves with the thought that baldness indicates special virility. However, if a man inherits the proper genes, only a modest amount of male hormone is necessary to make the hair vanish. Baldness is quite rare in some human races, rather common in others. In general, populations with high baldness rates are those with large amounts of body hair—Caucasians and particularly Near Eastern races; populations with slight body hair and beard—Asian Mongoloids and American Indians—almost never become bald. However, there seems to be no particular correlation between the two conditions in individual cases. Body hair, with its varying amounts and areas of development on the body, is obviously not inherited in as simple a fashion as baldness. It is interesting that a minor amount of retreat of terminal hair at the forehead is normal at the time of puberty, converting the rounded hairline of the child to the squared-off forehead of the adult. This process is most marked in males, and pattern baldness seems to be an extension of it.

Much more research could be done on human hair. Not only its color, as discussed in a previous chapter, but its abundance, distribution, and even curliness are subject not only to racial differences, but sex differences and age changes. All of these factors will have to be sorted out if we are to understand the genetics of hair.

FAT AND ITS FUNCTIONS

Directly below the skin lies a layer of tissue that goes by more than one anatomical name, but which we will call the *subcutaneous fat*. This layer contains connective-tissue fibers intermingled with special cells called *fat cells*. These cells are capable of storing fat, by which they may become so distended that the protoplasmic part of the cell appears tiny by comparison. It is largely by the increase or decrease of the amount of fat in these cells that body size changes with an increase or decrease of food intake. Fatty tissue is not limited to the subcutaneous layer; there is a considerable amount of fat within the abdominal cavity, and it is found in and between muscles and in various other places. But the subcutaneous fat affects body appearance most conspicuously.

The fat layer has two quite unrelated functions: it serves as insulation to prevent the loss of body heat to the environment, and it acts as a reserve of energy that can be drawn on at times when food is scarce. The insulating function is more complicated. In discussing pigmentation in relation to solar radiation, we were concerned with heat coming to the body from outside. In addition, a constant component of the body heat is that generated by the body's own metabolism. This varies widely according to degree of activity. It is of critical importance that a warm-blooded animal maintain a constant body temperature through great variations not only in outside temperature but in amount of metabolic heating. If muscular activity, producing much internal heating, and/or warm sun were always combined with cool air temperature, we would feel good all the time. And if darkness and rest were always accompanied by warm covers, that would be good too. But often muscular work has to be done in the heat of the sun, and (more often for our ancestors than ourselves) sleep takes place under chilling conditions. The problems are solved in man partly by clothing, which probably became a necessity as soon as the ancestors of modern man moved far away from their original tropical habitat. But older mechanisms are still in existence and operating very efficiently.

Clothing has a great advantage as insulation because it can be taken on and off as conditions change. An anatomical form of insulation obviously cannot do quite this. In mammals and birds, body insulation may be increased or decreased by fluffing up or flattening the fur or feathers. Man still has the muscles that erect the hairs in conditions of cold, and they still work (if we look at the bases of the body hairs in a chilled individual, we see the raised openings of the follicles which are called "goose-pimples"), but with the rather scanty hair covering of man, no real insulating advantage results. The well-developed subcutaneous fat in man serves, in another and more complicated way, the function of insulation that can be turned on and off. (It is interesting that the closest anatomical parallel to the subcutaneous fat of man is found in man's good friend the domestic hog, who is also a relatively hairless inhabitant of the Temperate Zone.) When the surface of the skin is warm, and the outside air is cold, heat is continually lost from the body through the interface between the two. In order to retard heat loss, it is necessary to keep the skin cool while the active body tissues, including the muscles, remain at normal body temperature. The generally uniform temperature of the internal parts of the body is maintained by rapid circulation of the blood, which in addition to transporting nutrients and the waste materials of metabolism, picks up heat where it is generated, particularly in actively contracting muscles, and gives it out to cooler tissues, particularly at the skin surface and the atmospheric contact areas within the lung. Heat loss through the lung cannot be reduced, because for other reasons it is necessary that warm blood must continually circulate close to the internal surface of the air-filled lung. But the amount of blood circulating through the skin can be controlled by contraction or dilation of the small arteries that supply the dermis and the lower layers of the epidermis.

The physiological mechanism that diverts blood to or away from the skin, as circumstances require, will be discussed in more detail later. But it is clear that the effectiveness of such a system will depend on the existence of an insulating layer between the deeper heat-generating tissues and the body surface. If the fat layer is of moderate thickness, it insulates the body when blood flow is withdrawn from the skin. Of course, when blood flows freely in the skin, heat is lost from it and the fat layer is effectively bypassed as insulation. An extremely thin fat layer—in some individuals it is virtually reduced to the connective-tissue component—does not serve the insulating function at all; and a very thick fat layer cannot be fully bypassed because the fat surrounds and covers the superficial veins. This interference with cutaneous heat loss explains the characteristic sweaty misery of obese persons in very hot weather. Thus the thickness of the fat layer interacts with other more complicated factors to affect the individual's ability to cope with extremes of temperature. Leanness is best for heat, fatness for cold.

The second major function of fat is that of storing energy for future use. Fats and oils, as every dieter knows, contain more calories of energy per unit weight than any other component of animal or plant tissue. They are used throughout the animal kingdom as energy reserves. The storage of energy within one's own body is not important to prosperous peoples with adequate means of storing food outside the body, but it was quite important to our ancestors, and still is to some of our contemporaries. In cultures that depend on hunting and fishing under primitive conditions, food supplies may be intermittent or seasonal, and feasts may be separated by days or weeks of famine. Methods of preserving food are inefficient, and it is easier to eat all you can when it is fresh. The development of agriculture as a primary means of subsistence did not change this situation greatly, except insofar as some agricultural products are easier to preserve for future use than meat and fish. Still, in some parts of the world, it is normal for rations to be scanty at some seasons of the year and abundant at others. Man survives these annual cycles, just as other animals do, by storing energy— that is, getting fat—in the seasons when food is readily available, and using up the stored fat in the seasons when it is not. There has been a lot of acrimonious debate about whether or not the tendency to put on too much weight has a genetic component. One school of thought has held that overweight is strictly the result of bad habits, flabby willpower, and moral frailty. Others have held that there are genuine individual differences in the ease with which "normal" weight can be maintained. One problem in measuring man's fatness is that it is not easy from outward inspection to determine how much of a person's body bulk is muscle and how much is fat. A fair estimate can be made from careful inspection of the body contours, because a well-developed fat layer tends to conceal the finer detail of bone and muscle shape. However, a more accurate evaluation of the subcutaneous fat can be made by actually measuring its thickness at various locations on the body. Neither method takes into account fat deposits deeper in the body, however. The best evidence for a genetic component in body-fat accumulation has come from hog breeders. The amount of fat in a hog has been of considerable economic importance for a long time. Before vegetable fats were as extensively used for food purposes as they are now, lard—purified hog fat—was a culinary staple. At that time the ideal hog was virtually cylindrical with fat. When the demand for lard decreased, the lard hog was replaced by a pork-chop hog, which had a muscular carcass with only a moderate amount of fat. These changes were not brought about by dietary alteration but by genetic selection. Carefully controlled recent tests have shown that it is possible, within a few generations, to develop from one stock two different strains of hogs that will differ in the relative amounts of muscle and fat tissue they produce when consuming exactly the same diet (Hetzer, 1967). There is no guesswork here; the hog can be cut up and the amounts of fat and muscle exactly determined. Because there is no reason to believe that man is different in this respect, it seems certain that, although diet obviously can alter weight, there are real individual differences in the amount of fat stored with similar availability of food. Like so many variable traits of man, fatness is apparently the combined result of genetic and environmental factors. Incidentally, the frequent increase of fat with age is not confined to man: beef is usually fatter than veal, and a stewing hen fatter than a broiler.

The subcutaneous fat is not of equal thickness all over the body. Its irregularities are most conspicuous when the individual fat cells are engorged with fat as a result of abundant diet. The pattern of fat distribution varies with sex. The female breast, though it contains a certain amount of glandular tissue, owes most of its size and shape to deposits of fat: the breast is in fact a development within the subcutaneous fat layer. Females are also prone to greater fat deposits around the hips, and in general have a thicker fat layer all over the body than do males in the same state of nutrition. In contrast, males usually show greater fat deposits around the waist, and on the abdomen and back of the neck, though fat males often have a noticeable bulge in the same region as the breast in the female. In both sexes fat is generally less conspicuous toward the ends of the limbs than on the trunk and parts of the limbs closest to the trunk. This probably has a mechanical explanation: excess weight on the more rapidly moving parts of the body would impede freedom of motion. In addition to sex differences, there are obvious individual differences in fat deposition. Some individuals, for instance, tend to develop fat on the front of the neck—a "double chin"—whereas others may become considerably overweight without accumulating fat in this area. Other personal specialties are potbellies, fat buttocks and ham-like upper arms. The basis for these variations in body-fat distribution is not really known. The nature of the fatty tissue suggests that the number of fat cells in the subcutaneous layer may differ from one part of the body to another and from one individual to another, and that the characteristic individual patterns of fat accumulation may be due to equal enlargement with fat of cells that are unequally distributed. The microscopic studies that would be necessary to determine this have not been made. Genetic studies would also be of great interest. Some racial differences in fat deposition have been noted. The large and globular female breast that is common among well-nourished and overnourished Caucasians, and that has been regarded as ornamental by them at various periods in history, is a racial specialty not shared with all the world. The breast is less fatty and flatter in most women of Mongoloid races, and is often long and conical, with a large nipple, in African women (Martin and Saller, 1956). The large breast is not an indication of a superior ability to nourish an infant; the essential glandular tissue that serves this purpose is only a small part of the breast and is entirely adequate in many women who are flat-chested by contemporary Western standards. It has been suggested that the conspicuous breast has developed as a result of sexual selection; that is, because it served as an attractant which caused its possessors to have more offspring. One fanciful theory even supposes that there is special charm (and selective advantage) to a bosom so massive that it mimics the buttocks. However, the evidence from art is that, during most of human history, aesthetic tastes were much more realistic, accepting the average female figure as it really was. This undoubtedly promoted the happiness of both sexes. It is even likely that admiration for the large breast did not originate primarily as a sexual symbol. It is known that in some cultures female obesity in general has been admired as an indication of family prosperity and hence as an economic status symbol for the male. The cult of the overgrown breast may actually be a spinoff of this phenomenon. Unfortunately, the contemporary Western female is expected to have fat breasts and be thin everywhere else—an anatomical anomaly.

The most remarkable racial specialty in fat distribution is *steatopygia*, a condition in which there is a marked accumulation of fat over the female buttocks, even when the fat layer of the rest of the body is slight or moderate. In extreme cases the upper surface of the buttock is so large and horizontal that a two-year-old can stand comfortably on it, with his arms around his mother's neck, looking over her shoulder (Coon, 1965, Plate 65). Steatopygia is commonly found in the African Bushmen and in the Negritos of the Indo-Malayan area, who are both of very short stature but who do not otherwise appear to be closely related to one another.

Both of the functional aspects of body fat—cold protection and energy storage—may have had selective effects in special areas. General body leanness seems to be commoner in people of tropical areas. Among young American males, all at a similar level of physical fitness under military training, the subcutaneous fat layer averages considerably less in Negroes than in Whites (Newman, 1956). Within the United States the fatness of individuals of the same racial stock tends to be less in the South than in the North (Newman, 1955). However, nutritional differences are hard to control. Despite the fabled lushness of the tropical environment, human populations of tropical areas are often overcrowded and undernourished as compared with Temperate Zone populations. A direct effect of cold weather in stimulating appetite and thus encouraging weight gain may be a factor also; the tendency to respond in this way to cold may itself be something which natural selection has brought about. A possible effect of selection is the well-developed superficial fat of the face in the peoples of central Asia. This, as we have already described it, extends to the eyelid and forms one of the characteristic features of the Mongoloid face (Coon, et al., 1950). Because man was originally a tropical animal, and did not move into cold climates until some form of clothing had been invented, it is reasonable to suppose that an adaptation to cold in the form of fatty insulation would have become most marked in the face, which usually remains exposed, and especially around the eyes, which cannot be covered. The second function of fat, as energy storage, may be important in many environments. When food supplies are intermittent, it is essential that fat be put on readily when surplus food is available. Any genetic differences in the tendency to gain weight readily would be a selective advantage at such times. The selective situation, however, is quite different between primitive and civilized environments. The ability to accumulate fat in times of abundance may be very desirable, even life-saving at times, for individuals subject to the feast-and-famine conditions of a life close to nature; but in a culture where famine never comes it leads to obesity and its associated health hazards. The continual weight problems of so many people in our civilized surroundings are probably the heritage of an earlier day when the ability to gain weight readily was an asset rather than a hazard. The sex difference in amount of stored fat in the body may be related to the extra energy needs of pregnancy. In a primitive culture with periods of low food availability, the combination of famine with pregnancy would be a particular risk to the female, and selection for adequate fat storage in women would be most important. Continuing weight gain during pregnancy, if adequate food is available, would also be advantageous to both mother and child by providing reserves for the production of milk. This pregnancy weight gain also seems to be built into the human system, though it may be undesirable under civilized conditions. The two functions of body fat may combine to explain steatopygia. It seems to occur only in tropical areas, and is most conspicuous in the desert-dwelling Bushmen of Africa. It has been suggested that the concentration of fat storage in a limited area of the body is an effective compromise between the necessity of storing energy and that of losing body heat through a relatively fat-free body surface. If this is true, the strategy is the same as that of another famous desert-dweller, the camel, who stores fat in his hump (not water, as is sometimes said) and leaves the rest of his angular body free to radiate heat to the air without the impediment of a layer of subcutaneous fat.

Fatness is sometimes discussed as a component of *body build*, a general descriptive term that also involves skeletal proportions and muscle development. In this connection, we will say more about it in the next chapter.

9 Body Size and Shape

Variation in body size is marked both within and between populations. The tallest and the shortest of the same sex within a population may differ by more than a foot in stature, and there is no overlap in individual stature between the shortest and the tallest peoples of the world. Males of the same population are consistently taller than females; women's stature is generally somewhere between 92 and 95 per cent of that of their brothers, the sex difference being proportionately greater in taller races. Stature has emotional connotations (Feldman, 1975). In childhood we "look up to" the adult or older child who is of greater strength and authority, and take pride in every inch we add to our own stature. As adults we may speak of "looking down on" someone we hold in low esteem, even though they are physically as tall or taller than ourselves. There seems to be an unconscious bias toward putting taller individuals into positions of leadership: in the majority of United States presidential elections, the taller candidate has won. It has been shown that under controlled conditions (job applicants being interviewed by persons who have not previously known them) taller individuals are offered better salaries. The short person, particularly the short man, feels cheated. One result is that most people honestly believe themselves to be taller than they actually are. They take the highest figure possible for their correct height, usually a figure arrived at when they were measured with their heads tilted slightly back. The wise physical anthropologist, measuring height austerely with the head precisely level, will take this into consideration when the subject asks how tall he is. For any American male under six feet in height, it is appropriate to add from one-half to one and one-half inches—the larger figure, of course, for the shorter individuals. This will please everybody and make the anthropologist's work easier.

THE MULTIPLE CAUSES OF SIZE VARIATION

Although modern peoples have an emotional bias in favor of large body size, it is not necessarily a biological advantage. Nature has produced cats as well as lions, sparrows as well as eagles, and usually the smaller species is more numerous and successful: very large body size has often been the precursor of extinction. The individual with a large body not only requires more food to carry him through the growth period, but will have a greater calorie requirement all the rest of his life. In a primitive economy or under crowded conditions, the large body may be an expensive luxury. Only if it increases foodgetting ability enough to more than compensate for its greater food requirements, will it be an asset. This is probably the case when subsistence involves hunting large game (though the pygmies of Africa kill elephants by a combination of quickness and nerve) and when it involves control of large domestic animals. In agricultural labor, on the other hand, a big body probably does not have enough extra productivity to do more than balance out its extra food requirements, if that. A genetic potential for large body size may be particularly hazardous during childhood in regions where food runs short, because the same ration that is adequate for a naturally small child may leave a large one chronically hungry. Small size as well as large size, therefore, may be a successful adaptation, depending on circumstances (Frisancho, 1973). It is not unlikely that body-size differences between populations in many cases represent the workings of natural selection over many centuries of particular subsistence strategies. The situation is complicated by the possibility of direct environmental effects on body size: that is, modifications of the expected genetic size attainment, due to diet or other factors acting during the individual's own growth period. The various causes that may enter into the determination of stature have proved inordinately difficult to unravel. It does not mean much if we find that populations of generally small body size are consuming less food, on the average, than populations that are large-bodied. Small people, like small breeds of any species, will not eat as much even if they have access to unlimited food. Figures for total food consumption of whole populations are likely to be unreliable anyway. Most are based on the amount of food purchased and make no allowance for wastage. In prosperous countries like the United States food may be thrown away if not eaten at the first meal, and fats used for cooking or excess fat on meat may be discarded. The fats are the most calorific part of the food; that, of course, is why diet-conscious people throw fats away. Recent studies have indicated that the normal calorie intake of Americans may be as much as 15 per cent less than previously believed (Abraham, 1974). In poorer countries, food waste is negligible. Studies of twins have not been helpful in evaluating the effect of diet on body size. Identical twins are less alike in stature than we would expect from study of other traits. Twinning is an abnormal condition in humans, and results in crowding and competition of fetuses and placentas within the uterus, so that one twin may get a very bad start on body growth. Some studies have been made comparing the stature of people of known foreign extraction in the United States with that of populations in the countries from which they came. Many questions have been raised about these data, which generally show the American-born to be larger (Hulse, 1968). Immigration itself can be a selective process. Larger individuals, probably because of the greater self-confidence they develop, seem more prone to undertake the adventure of moving to a new land. Also, migration to a new country tends to break up local inbreeding patterns that may have existed in the old country, so that a subtle genetic difference may exist between the migrants and the stay-at-homes. United States army recruits during the Civil War included many foreign-born men, because this was just after a period of massive immigration. The stature of many of these men was recorded and can be compared with data obtained during World War II (Baxter, 1875; Brues, 1946). The American-born drafted men measured at the later period were asked to state, as well as they could, their ancestry in terms of national extraction. Thus we can compare those of the latter group who claimed to have ancestry from only one nation, with the sample of the actual immigrants who were their forebears eighty years before (see Table 6). In general there was a stature increase of one and one-half inches. The Scandinavians, who were the tallest as immigrants, were still the tallest; the French and Mediterraneans remained the shortest. The tallest stocks had increased stature the most, thus widening the gap. There was clearly a change caused by the new environment, but there were some irrepressible genetic differences as well.

The problem is compounded by the fact that in developed Western countries there has been an increase in stature with successive generations during the last hundred years, irrespective of migration (Tanner, 1968). Some of the data indicative of this are well-controlled genetically, consisting of comparisons between parents and

TABLE 6 STATURE TRENDS OVER 80 YEARS
IN AMERICAN WHITE MALES

National Extraction	1860's Foreign Born	1940's Native Born, of Unmixed Ancestry
British	66.6 inches	68.5 inches
Irish	66.8	68.1
Scandinavian	67.2	69.0
Germanic	66.4	67.8
Slavic	66.4*	67.9
Russian	66.4*	67.3
French	66.3	66.6
Mediterranean	65.9	66.5

*Poorly represented in the early data.

From Baxter, 1875, and Brues, 1946.

children based on measurements taken at the same ages (Bowles, 1932). Even here a complication arises. There is evidence that the age of puberty has not been constant throughout history; that puberty occurs at a younger age now than it did a century ago, probably at as young an age as it ever has (Daw, 1970). It happens that growth in stature is closely tied to the same developmental timetable as puberty, so that individuals who mature early also complete their growth early. The records that indicate the increase of body size from generation to generation are mostly based on individuals of an equal and rather young age—military recruits in Europe, called up at age eighteen, and college students in the United States of about the same age. However, an American physician was able to say, one hundred years ago, that young men did not attain their full stature until they were twenty-five (Baxter, 1875). At the present time, with a generally accelerated process of development, full stature is attained some years before this by most individuals. At least some of the apparent change between generations, then, may be the result of comparing individuals who were still growing a century ago with ones who are full grown at the present time—though their actual ages at the time of measurement were the same.

Whatever real difference there is—and there undoubtedly is a difference—can be explained in a variety of ways. We can play a game of itemizing all the environmental differences between American life today and a century ago, and take our pick of which of these differences we attribute the change to. The most popular theory seems to be "improvement in diet." This is rather ironic, because nutritionists continue to tell us that modern American diet is terrible and that the diet of our teenagers, at the most critical stage in their growth process, is the worst of all. The significant factor might be simply total calories, it might be protein, it might be the excessive amounts of calcium ingested in the form of milk and milk products. If we assume, as many people do, that "big" is "good," it is natural to attribute large size to other things we conventionally consider "good," such as protein and milk. But this is not scientific proof. Another possibly important factor is the virtual elimination of a number of diseases such as measles and mumps, which almost every child contracted once during his childhood until about 1930, when artificial immunizations were developed. For all we now know, the sedentary habits of modern youngsters—who ride everywhere instead of walking as their ancestors did—may increase stature by relieving the growing leg bones of their weight-bearing function. Other theories are welcome—any number may play this game!

The question of environmental effects on growth and size attainment has become an unpleasant one, for the reason that population differences in body size, combined with the emotional prejudice in favor of largeness, has sometimes entered, at least unconsciously, into racial and ethnic prejudices. It has not been involved in relations between whites and blacks in the United States because American blacks, like many of their relatives in Africa, grow tall even without any visible environmental or dietary advantage. But there still seems to be some political virtue in asserting that population differences in size potential do not exist.

Some idea of genetic differences in body size may be obtained from family studies. An aspect of particulate inheritance that is often not thought of is that differences *within* the family are often the best evidence of the workings of genetic factors. Recombination of genes produces differences between offspring of the same parents. These differences are less than, but in a definite ratio to, differences between unrelated individuals within the population from which the parents were drawn. Diet and other environmental factors, however, are as closely standardized within the family as they can ever be. Nevertheless, we find a wide range of body size among full brothers and sisters raised together, with maximum differences of about six inches between full brothers or between full sisters, and comparable differences between siblings of opposite sex, when the normal sex difference is taken into account. Differences between unrelated individuals drawn from the same general community are greater, as we have already mentioned, being as much as twelve inches in many cases. Obviously there can be a wide range of body size independent of environmental background. It is in fact essentially impossible to increase the growth and final stature of naturally short individuals. It has been attempted by the best pediatric experts, on the nondeprived children of those who can afford the best pediatric experts, and has not worked. Some cases in which specific hormonal problems exist can be helped; but ordinary healthy shortness is so far "incurable."

Actually the only test for nutritional effects on population averages in body size will be the experimental one of altering nutrition. Comparisons of size between different social classes within a population that is racially homogenous may not give us the answer, because large body size may be a factor in the attainment of social position. It would be unfortunate to hold out to shorter races a false hope of becoming giants by way of diet. In fact, with the threat of global food shortages looming over the world, it would be more desirable to find ways of shrinking genetically tall people. The large body, like the large automobile, will not be an asset in time of energy shortage.

The inheritance of body size characteristics is obviously not going to be explained by any simple genetic scheme. Body size in experimental animals was the first physical trait used as an example of multifactorial inheritance, and we cited it in Chapter 4 as an example of the normal curve distribution that is indicative of polygenic inheritance. Such traits can be rated only in terms of total heritability. There have been numerous studies of the heritability of various body measurements, with results that vary somewhat in accordance with the disturbing factors that always plague heritability estimates. But, it is safe to generalize that in almost all cases, stature, or any other body measurement that is not too difficult to take accurately, and which represents a permanent skeletal dimension (i.e., not subject to short-term effects of nutrition) will have a heritability of about .8, indicating a four to one predominance of genetic factors over environmental ones (Osborne and DeGeorge, 1959; Cavalli-Sforza and Bodmer, 1971). Weight, because of its nutritional components, has a low heritability; and other measurements in which the thickness of the fat layer plays a part have relatively low heritabilities also.

PROPORTIONS OF THE BODY

Body *proportions* also vary from individual to individual and between races as well. The shape of the body may be considerably affected by the amount of accumulated fat and its distribution. We have discussed this in a previous chapter. But even if fat were negligible, all people would not be the same shape. The two major shape variations are referred to as *linear* and *lateral* build. Linear build may be described as slender, but in a special way, because the term does not refer to lack of fat. True linearity is the result of narrowness of the rib cage and of the bony pelvis, as compared to stature. Because the position of the shoulder blade is determined by the width of the chest, such a person usually has narrow shoulders also. In a person of lateral build the proportions are reversed: shoulder, chest, and hips are wide in comparison to stature. A person of marked lateral build may be overweight by the standard height-weight charts even if he has almost no fat on his body at all. Also, a person with a basically linear build may fall within the proper bracket in the height-weight standards even if he has an excessive covering of fat. Published weight standards sometimes include allowances for light, medium, and heavy build; these are probably more often used as an apology for one's weight deviations than in the way they were intended—that is, to allow for genuine linearity or laterality of build. True build differences should be evaluated independent of fatness. In fact, though muscle development generally correlates rather well with skeletal development, excessive muscle development due to heavy usage should not be mistaken for laterality, nor should a wasting of muscle caused by severe undernutrition be mistaken for linearity. Unfortunately the data accessible to the anthropologist most often include only the easily taken measures of height and weight, with no useful data on build or fatness.

An interesting study on body-build differences has been conducted in Africa, where tribes sometimes show genetic differences from one another as great or greater than those between nations in other parts of the world. Two neighboring tribes differed from one another rather noticeably in both stature and build, one averaging tall and slender and the other short and stocky (Hiernaux, 1964). In making the comparison, the possible effect of different diet had to be considered. Here we see some of the difficulties of judging nutrition by its effect on growth and size. If we were to judge nutrition by ratio of weight to height, we would suspect that the tribe of more linear build was nutritionally deprived; if we judged nutrition by height alone, we would suspect the shorter tribe to be nutritionally deprived. Clearly, neither height or weight, nor both together, are adequate to judge nutritional status unless we know an individual's genetic background—which in this case was clearly different for the two tribes. A method generally used at the present time by physicians to judge whether development is proceeding normally in children is to see whether their height and weight maintain a constant relation to the average for children of their age (Wetzel, 1948). This accepts the fact that some children are small for their age and will be small adults, that some are large for their age and will be large adults, and that these differences should give rise to medical concern only if their stature or build shows a deviation from their own previously established growth pattern. If a "standard" is to be used, at least it should be adjusted to the known body size of a particular child's parents, in order to give a realistic expectation of what that child's present and eventual body size should be. Similarly, genetic differences in size and build may characterize populations, and must be taken into account. Clinical standards for growth and development have been based primarily on Caucasian populations in North America and Europe, simply because that is where the research workers are. This should be regarded as a makeshift; ideally, standards of this kind should be developed specifically for each population in which they are to be used (Garn, 1965).

Another important variation in body shape is the ratio of limb length to trunk length. The usual way of evaluating this is by measuring the "sitting height" from the surface of a table on which the subject is sitting, and comparing it with ordinary standing height. In normal individuals sitting height varies from 49 to 55 per cent of standing height; the ratio averages slightly higher in females. If two people differ markedly in this proportion they may find that one of them is taller standing and the other taller sitting down. In general, the relative sitting height is greater in short individuals than in tall ones, indicating that variation in stature results to a greater extent from differences in leg length than from differences in trunk length. Arm length usually correlates with leg length, though not perfectly. Another variation that affects body appearance rather markedly is the ratio of breadth of shoulder to breadth of hip. This ratio is notable for its large sex difference. The ratio of hip breadth to shoulder breadth in Caucasians is about 81 per cent in females, 75 per cent in males, producing a characteristically very different shape to the trunk, even if more distinctive fleshy appurtenances are disregarded. (See Table 3.) Individual variations are also very great, and so there is considerable overlap between the sexes in this ratio. The wider hips of the female are a functional adaptation to childbearing; the narrower hips of the male probably increase efficiency in walking and running and, in the absence of other necessity, have developed by selection for this advantage. There are also racial differences in the shoulder-hip ratio, which we will discuss later.

GROWTH, SIZE, AND SHAPE

Variations in proportions cannot be understood apart from the growth process by which they come about. In the development of the embryo the limbs do not appear at all until the general outline of the rest of the body has been roughed out; and at the time of birth the arms and legs are still poorly developed compared with the head and trunk. Throughout childhood the trunk continues to grow faster than the head, and the limbs faster than the trunk, so that the heavy-headed, short-limbed infant gradually approaches adult proportions. In the early months of life a great part of the skeleton is not yet mineralized and consists of soft tissue, mostly cartilage. All during the growth period the soft tissue models are being converted into bone by the appearance and gradual increase in size of bony centers within them, which eventually replace the original models and assume their shape. The long bones of the arm and leg show a characteristic pattern of ossification. A single, long ossified portion forms the shaft of the bone, and one or more separate centers of ossification at each end represent the enlarged portions of the ends of the adult bone. The end portions, or *epiphyses*, finally fuse with the shaft to make the long bone a single unit.

This last process in bone formation is a very critical one. After the epiphyses have fused with the shaft the bone can no longer increase in length. Up to this time the bone has grown by the addition of new material to the ends of the shaft. The final fusion puts an end to this process, and thus ends also the increase in length of the arms and legs, and, for practical purposes, increase in stature. (A small amount may be added to stature afterward by growth of the vertebrae.) The fusion of the epiphyses is only one of a series of closely coordinated events that occur around the time of puberty. As in everything else, there is individual variation in the exact age at which these events occur, but an individual whose skeletal development, including the fusion of epiphyses, occurs early will also go through the physiological changes of puberty earlier than the average. Thus two children of the same age may be the same size throughout childhood, yet one—the earlier maturing of the two—will be shorter as an adult because his growth in height stops sooner. It is at this point that stature predictions based on body size during childhood may fail, unless they have been corrected for bone-maturity status as determined by X-ray. The early-maturing individual will have relatively shorter legs, because the extra growth of the late-maturing individual will be more in the legs than in the trunk; also, his leg and arm muscles will appear thicker because they have not been stretched out by the elongation of the limbs. Thus a whole pattern of body proportion may be changed by a difference in the timetable of development. To some degree the sex differences in body size and proportion appear to result from a difference in timing. The extra height of the male is partly due to growth taking place between the earlier time of female puberty and the later time of male puberty: and, as expected, the difference is greater in leg length, resulting in the characteristically longer leg proportions of the male. (There is a common misconception that women have relatively longer legs than men. This is because the greater fullness of the hips makes the waist higher. When the leg is measured to the hip joint, this apparent difference is reversed. In popular calendar art, the length of the female leg is sometimes exaggerated by as much as 15 per cent.)

Adult stature, which seems a simple enough thing to measure, thus clearly involves at least two sets of causal factors: those affecting growth rate, and those affecting the onset of puberty, the latter limiting the length of time during which growth continues. Nutrition can affect both rate and duration of growth, with contradictory effects on stature. In undernourished individuals growth rates may be reduced, but puberty is likely to be delayed also. The time of sexual maturation seems rather sensitive to environmental stresses. In populations that are fairly uniform genetically, sexual maturity has been found to occur a few months earlier in upper-class children than in lower-class ones (Lee, 1963). We have already mentioned that the apparent changes in stature from generation to generation may be somewhat illusory if based on young individuals, because relatively short stature until the late teens may be made up by an extended growth period. There is a kind of compensation, then, for environmental factors inimical to rapid growth: longer continuation of growth tends to equalize final stature. How complete this compensation is depends on specific circumstances.

A particularly interesting difference between populations involves the rate of development during the first years of life. It has been observed among Negroes, both in Africa and in the United States, that the eruption of teeth and ossification of the skeleton take place earlier than in the white "standard" populations on which most studies have been based (Massé and Hunt, 1963; Tanner, 1966). This difference disappears or is reversed at about the age of four. Some studies of native peoples in Central America have shown the same trend (Garn, 1965). The age at which the infant starts to walk is also earlier. Early walking is not, as might be thought, related to the development of the limb skeleton, but is the result of earlier maturation of conducting fibers in the nervous system. If the differences were in the opposite direction, they would easily be explained away as being the result of environmental disadvantage. Is this a long-term selective adaptation which makes it possible to accomplish some critical growth while the infant is still on mother's milk, not yet weaned to the protein-deficient diet these populations have chronically suffered from? We really do not know.

Obviously there are many ways of looking at body shape; we have only discussed a few of them. It is hardly necessary to say that two individuals who rate the same in linearity, have the same sitting height index, and the same shoulder-hip index can be different in other details of body shape. Though we ordinarily recognize people by their faces, no doubt we could do as well by inspection of the rest of the body—perhaps nudists *do* recognize their friends in that way! Various attempts have been made to reduce this variation to a simple scheme of classification. A system proposed in 1921 divided body build into three main types. The first, *asthenic* (which literally means weak) was characterized by marked linearity. The second, *athletic*, was lateral in build and heavily muscled; it was also pictured as broad in shoulder rather than hip, though this is not necessarily correlated with muscularity. The third type, *pyknic*, is heavy-set, but in a different way—fat rather than muscular (Kretschmer, 1921). (The term *pyknic* comes from a Greek word meaning *thick* and has nothing to do with tastes in style of dining!) These descriptive types were used in the study of correlations between body build and disease susceptibility or psychological characteristics.

A more refined system, using different terms, was developed a few years later. This system is still often referred to at the present time. Body build was described not in terms of types, but of *components* (Sheldon, et al., 1940). The fat component of body build is called *endomorphy*; the muscular component, *mesomorphy*, and the linear component, *ectomorphy* (see Figure 39). In this system, each component is rated on a scale from 1 to 7, and ratings of the three components (in order) form an abbreviated code, called a *somatotype*,

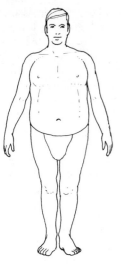
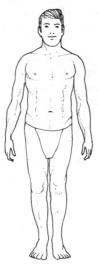

Extreme
endomorphy

Extreme
mesomorphy

Extreme
ectomorphy

Figure 39 Somatotype.

for an individual's general body build. For instance, a "4–6–1" is a very heavy-set person (minimum ectomorphy) with very heavy musculature (high mesomorphy) and a little more than average fat (above-average endomorphy). A "2–4–5" has little fat, good musculature, and is relatively slender. This system packs a lot of descriptive information in a small space, and evokes a clear image of a body shape. Looked at critically, it appears to rate some rather different things as if they were equivalent. Endomorphy corresponds rather closely to the development of the subcutaneous fat layer; a constant problem of somatotype rating is how to allow for age and nutritional changes in fat accumulation. Ectomorphy reflects the elongation of the long bones, which, as we have already mentioned, is the result of an interaction between growth rates and age of sexual maturity. Mesomorphy is essentially muscle bulk; yet, as we have already suggested, the same amount of muscle may appear bulkier if the bones of the limbs do not grow very long.

Thus, though this system provides neat descriptions, it does not look so neat when we examine it with a view to understanding the underlying causes of body-build differences. Sex inevitably affects it; endomorphy will be higher, mesomorphy lower, in females than in males. It also presents difficulties in measurement; in fact, it was originally designed to be done by visual inspection only. Numerous people have worked on more objective ways of rating these components or aspects of body build. An approximation of ectomorphy can be obtained from a comparison of height and weight. The most commonly used formula divides the height in inches by the cube root of the weight in pounds. (The cube root of weight is used to compensate for the fact that the volume of two objects of the same shape is proportional to the *cube* of their linear dimensions.) This leaves the really sticky question of how to measure fat-versus-muscle in an objective way (Brozek, 1963). The fat layer may be measured with fair accuracy by pinching it up into a fold (this is possible because it is very loosely attached to the underlying tissues) and measuring the thickness of the fold. Because the fat is compressible, this must be done with care. However, even if this measurement is made on the same part of the body in every individual, it may not adequately reflect the total amount of fat on different bodies. An estimate of fat content of the body may also be made by determining the specific gravity of the body; fat is lighter than other body tissues, therefore a fat body is lighter in relation to its volume. Unfortunately, determining the volume of the body accurately involves immersing it completely in a tank of water, which is a messy process at best. Also, the very lightest ingredient of a human body is one that may change from hour to hour—the gas in the digestive tract—and this throws the calculations off. All in all, this approach is not popular. Estimates of muscle bulk have been made by measuring metabolic products of muscle tissue excreted in the urine (Tanner, 1964). The whole subject of body build and composition has become a very complicated one, even without consideration of conspicuous phenotypic differences such as shoulder-hip proportions, which do not correlate well with generalized components.

RACIAL DIFFERENCES IN SIZE AND SHAPE

Average statures of populations over the world differ considerably, more than can be accounted for by contemporary environmental differences, so stature can be considered to be in some degree a racial characteristic. By coincidence, the two major racial stocks now present in the United States, Caucasian and Negro, are nearly the same in stature, though so different in other conspicuous characteristics. Both are quite tall people as compared with most of the world. Early accounts of travelers and adventurers in unfamiliar places have given rise to stories of tribes of "giants"—who usually have not appeared so impressive on later examination. The apprehension of an explorer facing possibly hostile natives undoubtedly makes them look bigger. Of course the body size of the informants has to be taken into account: Spanish and Portuguese, themselves of moderate height, found more "giants" than did Englishmen or Scots. Racial differences in stature are probably partly responsible for the mistaken idea that people mature earlier in the tropics. Travelers were impressed with "mere girls" carrying infants. In some cases, of course, they may have been older sisters rather than mothers; but undoubtedly they were often young women of diminutive size whom the big-bodied strangers could not believe to be fully grown. In general, stature tends to vary on a rather local basis, so it is easier to point out differences *within* major races than to make generalizations on a continental scale. It may surprise some people to hear that there is probably no population in the world in which an honest sample of adult males averages as much as six feet tall. Our conceptions of other people's height, as well as of our own, are inflated. A fairly recent sample of 18-year-old men in the United States averaged a little under 5 feet 9 inches, with less than two-tenths of an inch difference between whites and blacks (Karpinos, 1961). This is about an inch taller than during World War I, at which time, also, the two races averaged the same in height. A comparable sample of American women would be about five inches less, a height which is normal for *males* in many parts of the world. Because it is tedious to continually cite figures, we will take 5 feet 4 inches to 5 feet 6 inches as a standard of "medium" height for males, and discuss world stature variation by reference to this.

As we would expect, stature comparable to that of modern Americans is found in Europe and Africa in those regions from which the ancestors of these Americans came. Stature in northern and northwestern Europe is consistently above medium, with highest figures from the Scots, who have been noted for tall stature since Tacitus wrote about them in the first century A.D. In central and southern Europe stature falls in the medium range. The most aberrant of Europeans in stature are the most northerly, the Lapps, who average about 5 feet. In a limited area of Africa, we find the only populations distinctly taller than present-day Americans, the Nilotic Negroes of the southern Sudan. Carefully measured samples of these people have averaged as much as 5 feet 11 inches (all these figures are for males). Other black Africans, in an area extending down through East Africa to the southern tip of the continent, are still tall by world standards, but are no taller than their present relatives in the United States. In the West African area, from which most of the direct ancestors of American Negroes came, stature is somewhat lower. As in the case of their white neighbors, American Blacks now exceed in height even their rather tall ancestors. Africa has the shortest people in the world as well as the tallest: the pygmy groups of central Africa have statures below 5 feet, as low in one case as 4 feet 8 inches, and the Bushmen are in the same range.

Populations of Asia fall generally in the medium range: this applies to the Caucasian populations of western Asia as well as to the Mongoloids of East Asia. In both there is a general trend toward somewhat taller stature in more northern areas: this is apparent in both India and China. Some populations in Pakistan and the Iranian plateau region, probably some also in North China, would average in the category we have called tall, that is, more than 5 feet 6 inches. In Southeast Asia and Indonesia we encounter some very short groups, 5 feet or less, some of whom are true Negritoes, others of puzzling affinities. Australoids, both in Melanesia and Australia, are medium in height. Polynesians and New World populations range from medium to moderately tall. The taller include some in North America, notably the more northerly Indian tribes of the United States, and some in South America, especially far south in that continent (though the Patagonians are not, as once rumored, really giants). In the rest of the Western Hemisphere, including the southwestern United States and Mexico, stature is medium. A complete account of world stature variations would be very complex. Everywhere that populations retain the older pattern of tribal divisions, stature is likely to be one of the visible differences between adjacent tribes. Most striking are the differences between true pygmies and their full-sized neighbors, in several places in the Old World. The evidence is that these groups of people with contrasting body size have existed side by side for a long time. Very small stature evidently acts as an effective survival strategy in certain environments, and may also result in genetic isolation. This is an intimation of one of the ways in which species differences may arise, though this has not occurred and is not likely to occur in the case of man.

There are some more or less consistent differences in body proportions between the three major races. Negroids are inclined to linear build, in fact, they include the most linear of all populations, and are particularly narrow in the hips. They seem in general to have a thinner fat layer, though obese Negroes do exist. They also have a low sitting-height index, that is, a relatively short trunk and long legs. Arms as well as legs are long also, in accordance with the general growth pattern previously described (Herskovitz, 1930). (Some people have tried to claim that one race is more "ape-like" than another in body proportions. But apes have *long* arms and *short* legs—a combination that does not correspond to any racial variation in man.) Mongoloids, both in Asia and America, tend toward the other extreme: lateral build and long trunk with short limbs. This contrast between Negroid and Mongoloid does not appear to be simply the correlated difference of tall versus short. A study of American-born Japanese, who had grown considerably taller than their immigrant parents, showed that their trunk–leg ratio was not changed as a result: they still had legs relatively short as compared to the trunk (Greulich, 1957). In these variations of proportions Caucasians are intermediate between the two other major races. A distinctive feature of body shape in Negroes is the combination of wide shoulders and narrow hips (Herskovitz, 1930; DeGaray, 1974). Some African populations differ as much from Caucasians in the ratio of hip to shoulder as do males from females of the same race, and in the same direction. This means that the trunk proportions of Negro females are close to those of white males. This curious overlap is apparent even in the bony pelvis. In cases where an unknown skeleton has to be judged for sex, there is a risk, if race is not taken into account, of judging a female Negro pelvis as male. This creates a dilemma for anyone who likes to think that the characteristics of whites, and of males, are superior to those of their opposite numbers. One cannot have it both ways, at least insofar as body proportions are concerned. Fashion illustrators should take note of this racial difference. In the attempt to "integrate" their art work without going to the trouble of redrawing it, they often paint in dark skins on sketches made from white models. This results in totally inappropriate facial features for their supposed blacks, of course, and also errs in depicting full hips and narrow shoulders, which would be most unusual in a well-built black girl. The usual proportions of blacks are an asset in the modeling business, because wide shoulders make clothes look good on either sex. Racial differences in proportion are particularly evident when the body is in motion, so movement patterns may be indicative of race as well as of sex to the practised eye.

Some studies of races have used somatotype ratings. Caucasian populations tend to rate "average" in all three somatotype components, which indicates nothing more than that the rating scale was originally standardized on a Caucasian population. In a group of Nilotic Negroes, linear build was found to be so extreme that the scale for ectomorphy had to be extended, adding scores of 8 and 9 to the original 1-to-7 scale (Roberts, 1963). These people were very low in both fat and muscularity (endomorphy and mesomorphy). A less extreme Negro group did not show this high linearity, and was much more muscular. Both, however, rated low in fat. Strongly contrasted with the Nilotics were a sample of Japanese, in which almost none rated more than 2 in ectomorphy (Kraus, 1951). They made up the difference in muscle rather than in fat. This confirms the generalization of Negro linearity and Mongoloid laterality.

BODY BUILD AND SELECTION

Body proportions are related to coping with climatic stress, quite aside from the component of stockiness which is due to body fat. The amount of heat generated within the body by metabolism and muscle action is roughly proportional to the weight of the body, but the ease with which heat is lost to the environment depends on the area of body surface. Increased size alone, with shape remaining exactly the same, decreases the ratio of body surface to body volume. In many warm-blooded animals, populations that inhabit colder climates are likely to be larger than similar species living in hot areas—a relation called Bergmann's rule (Mayr, 1970). In an elongated animal decreased body circumference in relation to length also changes the surface-volume relationship and facilitates heat loss. Thus, a more compact build is also an adaptation to cold. Extended or narrow appendages such as big ears, long nose, and slender limbs are a liability in an animal who has to contend with cold, but an advantage in a hot climate. In some cases—elephants for instance—the principal function of the external ear seems to be as a radiator to shed body heat. The perfect body shape for cold weather would be a perfect sphere with no appendages! But the relation of body shape to climate does not work out very well for man. The development of clothing has partially solved the problems of preventing heat loss in cold climates, though of course clothing cannot help when it is necessary to *lose* heat more efficiently. In some areas, such as Europe, North America, and India, there seems to be a trend toward larger body size farther north (Newman and Munro, 1955). Yet in Arctic Europe and North America, the trend is sharply reversed by the short-statured Lapps and Eskimos. The linear build of the Nilotic Negroes is certainly adapted to a hot climate; but other peoples living under equal or worse heat stress do not resemble them. These variations, then, do not appear to be a major selective force in the human species.

Another correlate of body build, seen in many animals, is the relation of build, particularly linear form and length of limb, to speed of movement. The mechanical effect is a rather simple one. Most muscles exert their pull on a bone close to the joint, and the bone forms a long lever arm which effects a useful movement some distance beyond the muscle attachment. The longer the moving limb segment, the faster the end will move, given the same amount of muscle contraction. In animals whose principal defense is flight, such as deer and antelope, elongation of the legs to increase running speed is very marked. In man, of course, a new major class of actions, involving use of the hand, has been developed. Here again, long limb segments are conducive to speed of motion. There is however, a corresponding disadvantage to the long arm: as speed is increased by elongation of segments, the maximum pulling force that can be exerted by the hand is decreased because of a less favorable leverage. Thus, few people are distinguished both as sprinters and weight-lifters. It is interesting that the two principal weapons used by hunting peoples for thousands of years, the spear and the bow, demand different types of arm leverage. The range and effectiveness of a spear depend on the speed with which it is moving when it leaves the hand, and therefore on the maximum velocity the hand itself has attained at that moment. The range and effectiveness of a bow depend on the stored energy of the drawn bow, which is proportional to the pounds of pull the arm can exert on the bowstring. Obviously, people of linear build and long limbs will operate more efficiently with a spear, and people with lateral build and short limbs, with a bow. The bow is a more recent invention, yet it was known throughout most of the world when it was finally superceded by firearms. However, it is interesting that in sub-Saharan Africa, though the bow was known as a children's toy, or for special purposes such as fishing, these long-armed people still clung to the hand-thrown spear as a principal weapon. They even scorned the throwing-stick, an accessory to the spear or javelin, which artificially extended the arm so as to attain greater initial speed of the projectile, although at some sacrifice of accuracy. Apparently the efficiency of different types of body build for the use of these essential cultural artifacts has affected the choice of weapon when both were known. More importantly, it may be that the adaptation of lateral build to the use of the bow, which is essentially the better weapon, may have selectively altered average body build in those areas in which it has long been in use (Brues, 1959).

For many centuries there has been a belief that variations in body build correlate with temperament, and it is easy to cite quotations from Hippocrates and Shakespeare on the subject. This belief once kept company with such theories as that character could be read from the shape of the facial features, or mental ability from the bumps of the cranium. The belief in correlation of body build and temperament has been more durable than its companions, which suggests that there are some real physiological correlates. The matter of social functions of personality difference belongs in another chapter, and in any case the question of whether temperament is hereditary or not should be considered independently of whether it correlates with bodily characteristics. The qualities of temperament that were suggested as being associated with somatotype components were easy-going good nature (viscerotonia) with fat; vigor and aggressiveness (somatotonia) with muscularity; and (perhaps by default) nervousness and intellectual intensity (cerebrotonia) with linearity (Sheldon, et al., 1942; see also Chapter 12). If these relations really exist, and they probably do, though not as clearly as some people have claimed, the cause and effect relations are obscure. A relaxed disposition is undoubtedly more conducive to weight gain than a nervous one—though in our modern weight-conscious culture, a fat person is often irritable because he is on a diet. A love of physical activity may result in actual increase of muscle bulk through exercise, but on the other hand, a reasonably good set of muscles may lead to physical activity for the simple reason that people like to do what they are good at.

The most interesting light shed on this subject has to do with the relation between body build and age of sexual maturity. It has already been mentioned that early maturity, other things being equal, results in shorter limbs, therefore shorter stature and relatively more lateral build. Because there is a great deal of individual difference in the timetable of maturation, this means that individuals of differing build are likely to have had somewhat different social experiences at the critical period of puberty (Tanner, 1964). Our present educational system is closely tied to chronological age: individuals born in the same year are constantly associated throughout childhood. And because physiological and chronological age correspond rather imperfectly, there is a period—about the sixth to tenth grade—when within the closely associated school unit there are individuals of quite different stages of maturity: some are physiologically adult, some are still children. At this time the early-maturing males are more assertive and competitive; they have the enhanced muscularity that males acquire at puberty, and so place the late-maturing at a social disadvantage (Tanner, 1964). For a short period the early maturers have things their own way; then their companions catch up hormonally and psychologically and they find themselves back in the ranks again. Even worse, they discover, after this period of easy leadership, that many of their classmates, who have continued to grow all this time, are taller than themselves, and they spend the rest of their lives as the "short guys" in the crowd. Ironically, this does not happen in a simpler society in which years are not recorded and counted so carefully. There, a child who approaches puberty is taken out of the company of children and initiated into the company of men at the exact time when it is appropriate for him, regardless of chronological age, and the experiences of all are essentially the same. This is only one of many ways in which social experiences, expectations, and disappointments may differ according to one's physical characteristics, and result in different responses and attitudes. Any correlations we seem to find between build and temperament need not indicate a mysteriously predetermined relation between the two.

BODY BUILD IN OCCUPATIONS AND SPORTS

Body size and build have been shown, not surprisingly, to influence choice of occupation in a developed society. In a primitive society there was little choice of occupation, in fact there often were only two jobs, the man's job and the woman's job, both involving what we moderns consider rather heavy work. In later times, life became easier for a person not endowed with physical power, as various specialized careers, beginning with that of the medicine man and now including a horde of sedentary jobs, opened up in a more complex society. However, after many centuries of transition in which different occupations required different amounts of physical strength, we are again approaching a kind of uniformity; instead of *all* jobs requiring muscle, *none* do. Task after task ceases to be a matter of pulling, shoving, or lifting, and is reduced to manipulation of controls. This makes it increasingly hard for individuals with fine large bodies to pretend that their anatomical equipment serves any practical purpose. One of the last of the "he-man" occupations was truck driving. But, having succumbed to the comfort of power steering and power brakes, truck drivers now find themselves competing with women. Correlations have been found between body size and build and choice of crime in those who attempt to short cut the social path to prosperity (Hooton, 1939). Robbery is the large man's crime, forgery the small man's. Presumably, the 90-pound weakling learns early in life that if he is to prosper, it must be by guile and not by force.

One of the ways in which civilization finds occupation for fine bodies is in the field of sports. There are some obvious and some not-so-obvious ways in which body size and proportions affect aptitudes for various athletic activities. A study of participants in the 1968 Olympic games showed that the most striking characteristic of athletes as a group, compared with nonathletes of their own race and sex, was a high score in mesomorphy and a low score in endomorphy (De Garay, 1974). This excess of muscle and lack of fat probably represents two things: first, a self-selection by which individuals with certain body characteristics find athletics more rewarding; and second, an accentuation of these characteristics by intensive exercise. The contrast between nonathlete and athlete in degree of mesomorphy was less marked in women, who did not, even among the athletes, show such marked muscularity. The women athletes, however, differed markedly from the comparison group of their own sex by having a low shoulder-hip index, about halfway, in fact, between nonathlete males and females. The normally wide female pelvis is apparently not adapted to physical activities of the kind that males have incorporated into their recreations. In this respect, then, the female athletes are a selected group of women. Other variations of body proportion may be specifically advantageous for particular sports. An extreme case of specific bodily adaptation is seen in basketball, where the combined height and arm length of the player, determining how nearly he can reach to the basket, is a major factor in his scoring ability. Where specific physical proportions are useful in a particular sport, it is not surprising that different races and nationalities have shown special aptitudes for them. The importance of total upward arm reach in basketball has resulted in the recruiting of many American Negroes to this sport, because they are particularly likely to combine tall stature with long arms. Football and its immediate progenitor, rugby, are the specialties of large people: most of the world is not interested in playing these games. The original ancestor of football, soccer, is a game of agility rather than weight and is the most international of present-day sports, being a favorite among many small-bodied races.

We have already discussed the role of long limb segments in speed of motion. This gives a natural advantage in running speed to individuals with relatively long legs. It is not surprising, therefore, that many Negroes have made outstanding speed records, and that they compete in disproportionate numbers in Olympic track events (Smith, 1964; De Garay, 1974). Olympic-level competition, of course, draws only individuals who have already demonstrated outstanding competitive ability in particular sports. An interesting contrast becomes apparent, however, when we examine records for long-distance races as opposed to shorter sprints. Winning a short race is a matter of making the feet move as fast as possible. The muscles can operate in part on stored oxygen, independent of the supply coming through the bloodstream, and thus can, up to a certain limit, operate "on credit" as far as energy is concerned. This is possible through adaptations going back to our remote vertebrate ancestors, who often had need (as we have not) to save their lives by dashing from predators. But in a long run, the physiological logistics become more complicated. To operate muscles for a long time on a pay-as-you-go basis, the liver must supply stored fuel, the lungs must supply oxygen—lots of it—and the heart must keep both fuel and oxygen moving rapidly to the muscles. The fine art of running consists of pacing your speed so that the muscles do not outrun their supply lines until you reach the finish line. For this reason the marathon runner does not at any time approach the maximum speed of which he is capable. The longer the race, the less important is the length of leg, which produces speed, and the more important the body's powerplant. Thus we find that in long-distance racing, long legs are not essential; it is more important to have a large trunk allowing lots of room for the essential viscera—lungs, heart, and liver. Individuals of Mongoloid race tend to replace Negroids as contenders in these long-distance events.

A special case of physical adaptation is seen in swimming. Humans, unlike other mammals, cannot conveniently raise their noses above the surface of the water unless they lie on their backs—a possible but not a good position for swimming. Part of a swimmer's muscular effort must be devoted to getting his breathing apparatus above water at least intermittently. The specific gravity of the body becomes important here. If the body is relatively bouyant and floats high, less effort is required for breathing. In most sports fat is solely a handicap: it adds weight which must be moved around, and adds nothing to strength or speed. But the fat in a swimming body does not have to be supported, and because it makes the body float high, its extra bulk does not add greatly to water resistance. Thus it is actually an asset rather than a detriment to the swimmer. The comparatively high fat content of the female body, which is generally a disadvantage in sports activities, is not a serious handicap in swimming. Negroes are not outstanding as swimmers: their low fat ratios and poor buoyancy are perhaps responsible (Newman, 1956; Baker and Newman, 1957; Smith, 1964). In the Olympic rosters they are almost unrepresented in swimming events. In contrast, the Mongoloid races produce good swimmers.

The ultimate score, when all kinds of sport activities are included, is probably a draw. In the 1964 Olympics the final run-off for the decathlon, which includes several events of different types, including both 100-meter and 1,500-meter races, was between a Japanese and an American Negro, showing that the intent of the decathlon—to measure all-round athletic ability—was properly served, and evened the advantages between these two contrasting races (Smith, 1964).

10 Physiology

RESPONSE TO HEAT AND COLD

Many of the variable traits of man discussed in previous chapters are those that could be observed, as they often are in animals other than man, in nonliving "specimens." But some very important traits are functional and can only be studied "in action." These traits are often of first concern to the physiologist, the physician, or the nutritionist, but are only beginning to be studied by anthropologists. Many of them involve practical matters that we need to do something about. The earliest studies of such characteristics usually aim to establish norms of body response, on the assumption that all people are more or less alike, and on that basis to rough out treatments, cures, or requirements for good health. The anthropologist asks more than this. He does not believe that the responses of any species to its surroundings have been established by supernatural foresight; he believes they have developed by the workings of natural selection on populations in which there was some individual variability in response patterns. We have little choice but to assume that if individual variability has existed in the past, it still does. Because the human species has occupied a vast range of different environments, more so than any other living mammalian species, differences in norms of response may have developed in different populations. So it is not sufficient to find an average datum for the population that happens to be most easily available to the investigator, and to assume that this is normal for the whole species. Knowledge of any real differences in physiological functions between individuals and groups will be required if we are to promote human health and comfort more effectively throughout the world. But information of this kind is not easy to obtain. Accurate data can come only from experiment, and experimental subjects must be persuaded to take part. Some populations are difficult to get to or may be reluctant to be studied. In the absence of experimental data, we sometimes rely on indirect information, which may be confused by a number of disturbing factors.

Adjustment to the environment may be made either by *adaptation* or by *adaptability*. By an adaptation we mean a characteristic for which an individual is genetically programmed and which he will have regardless of the environment in which he lives. He may have this characteristic because his ancestors have long been subject to selection in this same environment. The disadvantage of an adaptation is that the individual is stuck with it if he moves to an environment different from that of his ancestors. Adaptability is the capacity to respond in a particular way, when needed, to a temporary external condition. Adaptability itself may have a genetic basis and be better developed in some individuals than in others; thus, it also may be affected by natural selection. A good example of the two contrasting ways of adjusting to the environment is seen in skin pigmentation. Pigment serves as a protection against solar radiation. As a result of this, genetic differences in skin color have arisen in response to different environments, with natural selection favoring increased skin pigment where solar radiation is high. This is an adaptation. But most individuals of light or medium skin color also have a capacity for tanning, so that their skin becomes darker in direct response to the sun, and thus acquires extra protection during the season when it is most needed. This tanning capacity is a form of adaptability. When adaptability is very great, adaptation is less necessary. As in the case of skin color, nature often provides two mechanisms that partly, but not entirely duplicate one another. Adaptability is the most flexible form of response; it can adjust to changing seasons, from hour to hour, or even momentarily, as in the case of adjustment to temperature. But adaptability has its limits, so that both ways of coping with the environment are useful. The anthropologist, then, is concerned with both adaptations and adaptability, and particularly with whether the limits of adaptability are the same in different populations.

Changes of external temperature are conspicuous environmental problems for many animals. The Temperate Zone, despite its name, is notorious for its climatic extremes. In most of the United States, including some of its most thickly inhabited parts, the temperature range within a single year is usually more than 100 degrees F. In warm-blooded animals the normal body temperature is only 8 or 10 degrees below that at which protoplasm is destroyed, with fatal results. And except in certain unusual cases, a drop in temperature this far *below* normal presages death also. Generally birds and mammals, including man, manage to maintain the internal body temperature constant within a degree or two. This represents a continually adjusted balance between the internal production of heat by tissue metabolism and muscular activity, and loss of heat to the external environment. If heat needs to be conserved, insulation by fur, feathers, or clothes can do part of the job. We have already discussed the fat layer below the skin, so variable in humans, and the body shape itself, and how they influence heat retention or heat loss. But physiological mechanisms play an important role. Though the fat layer cannot be taken on and off like clothing, its insulating action can be alternately utilized and bypassed by changes in the pattern of blood circulation. This is a good example of physiological *adaptability*.

The smaller arteries that carry the blood supply to various parts of the body have within their walls small amounts of muscle tissue which can increase or decrease the diameter of the artery and thus control the flow of blood. This muscle, like other muscle of the body, is controlled by the nervous system. In this case it is activated by the *autonomic* portion of the nervous system, which operates on a reflex basis, independently of consciousness or will. This solves an obvious problem for reactions which must go on automatically, even during sleep. When the body surface is exposed to heat or cold, the muscles in the arterial walls react appropriately so as to vary the amount of blood flow to the skin from very large to almost none. If the skin has little pigment, this change is quite visible. Increased blood flow, the normal response to heat, reddens the skin; decreased blood flow makes it appear pale. Functionally, the importance of this process is that blood flowing near the surface of the skin loses heat to the environment, if the outside temperature is less than that of the body, as it usually is. If blood flow to the skin is reduced, the skin itself feels cold, but little heat is lost at the surface. The function of the arterial muscles is like that of the thermostat in the cooling system of an automobile engine, which closes down circulation to the radiator when the engine needs to warm up, and opens it up when excess heat must be eliminated.

In a cool or cold environment a contradictory situation exists. Then heat loss from the body surface is likely to be greater than the amount produced by normal metabolism and muscular action. Because the body cannot tolerate a net loss of heat for very long, blood is withdrawn from the skin in order to lessen heat loss. If this does not correct the condition, metabolism must be increased or extra heat generated by voluntary muscular action or by shivering. These responses use up energy. This may not be of importance to an overfed civilized individual who can spare a few calories for this purpose, but to our less pampered ancestors it was a serious matter. The extra dietary calories required to make up the loss of heat might be hard to come by, especially in the middle of winter. Thus, lowering the temperature of the exposed skin to the greatest degree possible is an important way of conserving energy. So long as the temperature to which the skin is exposed is above freezing, this is a satisfactory strategy. But if the outside temperature goes below freezing, too complete a withdrawal of circulating blood from the exposed parts of the body is hazardous. Actual freezing of the tissues, particularly of the hands and feet, may occur, and if this is severe, tissue destruction and mutilation may result. Therefore, the best strategy for moderate cold—maximum cooling of the skin—is dangerous in very intense cold.

Corresponding to these different situations, there are two contrasted types of physiological adjustment to cold: insulative, which avoids heat loss by cooling of the skin, and metabolic, which concedes a heat loss in order to keep a safe amount of heat at the body surface, and makes up the difference by increasing metabolism (Hammel, 1964). The two strategies are not exclusive in a single individual: careful monitoring of skin temperature shows that when hands or feet are exposed to cold, the skin temperature may drop initially, but then rise again intermittently by as much as 20 degrees, at intervals of twenty minutes or a half hour (Yoshimura, 1964). These warming cycles protect against tissue damage, but of course cause some energy loss. The hands and feet are particularly susceptible to cold damage because of their large surface in relation to volume, their small amount of heat-generating muscle, and their distance from the main bulk of the body. In a clothed man in cold weather, the hands in particular are likely to be poorly protected— too bulky a glove may not be tolerable because it impedes dexterity. The circulatory system of these parts is particularly adapted to effecting this protective increase in blood flow (Horvath, 1964). As a result, the hand that is "white with cold" may later turn "red with cold," or may even appear bluish if deoxygenated blood accumulates.

There has been considerable study of the physiological response to cold in different populations. The data are sometimes hard to summarize because different physiologists have been partial to different methods of evaluating it. Usually the procedure is to test, under identical conditions of cold stress, some individuals from a selected population side by side with members of the research party, who are generally of northern European ancestry. A distinctive type of cold adjustment has been found in the Australian aborigines, who are the world's champions of the insulative response (Hicks, 1964). These natives are accustomed to live without clothing in a cool temperate climate which may have night temperatures approaching the freezing point during the winter. They sleep in the open without cover, and in apparent comfort despite extremely low skin temperatures. The skin-warming response does not occur and the metabolism does not increase (Hammel, 1959). This is an extremely good strategy for conserving energy and involves no risk because the temperatures to which they are exposed are not low enough to cause tissue damage.

A similar response has been found in Bushmen of South Africa, who live under similar conditions. It had long been known that American Negroes were more susceptible to frostbite (freezing damage to tissues) than American whites, and this was recognized as a problem in military operations under conditions of exposure to cold. It has been found that the skin-warming response is often inadequate in Negroes, accounting for the greater danger of freezing (Rennie, 1957). Eskimos, by contrast, maintain high skin temperatures in the extremities and compensate by raised metabolism—an optimum response to subzero cold with its high risk of tissue damage. Some other New World groups have been tested: Arctic Indians, high-altitude dwellers of South America, and Indians of the cold southern tip of South America. All of these show a metabolic type of cold resistance, prodigal of calories but maintaining high skin temperatures (Hammel, 1964).

From these data we can reconstruct an outline of the evolution of cold-resistance in man. We know that the human species originated somewhere in the Old World tropics. In this area severe cold would never occur, and the only cold stress would be moderate chilling at night during part of the year. The insulative response would be well-adapted to this environment. Those populations still living in various parts of the Old World tropics and subtropics, both north and south of the equator, were never exposed to conditions to which this type of cold response was not adequate. Populations that moved southward did not go far: the habitable parts of the Southern Hemisphere do not extend beyond the middle of the Temperate Zone. The Australians in their present habitat are exposed to as cold a climate as anyone in the Southern Hemisphere of the Old World. They may have increased the effectiveness of the original insulative cold response, but had no need for any other type of response. The spread of man to the Northern Hemisphere, however, brought him into areas of truly severe cold. Here, presumably during the Pleistocene, the metabolic cold response was developed. It would have been a necessity in most of Europe, and particularly in northern Asia, which has cold more severe than any part of Europe. We see the metabolic cold response in perfected form in the Eskimos, with their warm hands and virtual immunity to frostbite. The rest of the picture is consistent with what we would expect from the fact that the New World was populated from Asia by way of the Arctic: American Indians all the way to the southern tip of South America have an Arctic type of cold response, inherited from their Asian ancestors.

The physiological response to heat has not been as crucial a matter as the response to cold, because heat, except in the absence of water, is rarely a threat to life. It is generally alleged that races of tropical, or originally tropical, habitat "stand heat better," but enduring heat is often a psychological rather than a physiological matter. The most common and best accommodation to environmental heat is to convince oneself that nothing strenuous needs to be done, at least not before sundown. The problems of heat are closely related to the level of muscular activity. An individual sitting quietly can radiate his metabolic heat by way of the skin at an external temperature as high as 85 degrees F (Yoshimura, 1964). If he is producing extra heat by exercising, or if the external temperature increases above 85 degrees, the efficiency of heat loss can be increased by increasing the cutaneous blood flow. This alone, however, is adequate for only moderate heat stress. The auxiliary mechanism of sweating, also under the control of the autonomic nervous system, is the next resource called on. The evaporation of water actually uses up heat, so that when the skin is moistened by sweat, heat loss at the surface takes place as freely as if the outside air temperature were much lower than it is—and that is just how it feels. The process is most effective if blood flow to the skin is ample also. Unfortunately, humidity of the outside air reduces evaporation, which finally ceases altogether when humidity is 100 per cent. Thus perspiration does the most good in dry heat, when it evaporates quickly and is hardly noticed; and the least good in moist heat, when it lies sticky on the body or drips off. For this reason dry heat causes relatively little distress so long as adequate water is available to replace that lost as sweat.

There have been attempts to find racial and regional differences in sweating capacity, but the results are ambiguous. First, the sweating potential of all humans is prodigious. One quart an hour is possible as a more or less sustained rate; even greater amounts may be produced for short periods under severe stress (Ladell, 1964). Furthermore, sweating is greatly affected by practise. Days or weeks of exposure to heat increase the flow, bring more sweat glands into action, and reduce the salt content (Hensel, 1964a). Consequently, there may be differences in the efficiency of sweating between residents of the tropics and newcomers that have nothing to do with genetic difference and will disappear after the newcomers have become acclimatized. Some differences have been found in the total number of sweat glands, but this does not seem to be consistently related to climate (Yoshimura, 1964). It appears that the sweating mechanism is about equally capable in all races. Perhaps this is not surprising, for though there are places in the world where severe cold never occurs, there are few where there is not sometimes enough heat to require considerable sweating, at least during heavy exercise. There does, however, seem to be some difference in overall heat tolerance, and some truth in the idea that Negroes function better in moist heat, which is the stressful kind of heat. We have already alluded to the disadvantage of very dark skin in intense solar radiation, when heat absorbed by melanin actually increases the heat load. But in the forests of West Africa it is hot, damp shade that produces the greatest stress. A good objective test of heat tolerance is the internal temperature of the body, taken by the usual clinical methods. The better the physiological adaptation to heat, the more stable the internal temperature will be. In a poorly acclimatized person the body temperature rises under the combined stress of heat, humidity, and exercise; and if this rise is great, it is a forewarning of collapse. Under similar conditions of heat stress, with all subjects well-acclimatized, Negroes maintain a more stable internal temperature than Caucasians and are less subject to heat stroke. It is not clear how this is done, because skin temperature and amount of sweating seem to be about the same in the two races (Riggs, 1964). Apparently there are some racial differences in heat tolerance that have been successfully selected for in the tropical West African climate.

It might appear that heat stress, unless very severe, would affect only comfort and would not be a major selective factor. However, its biological significance may be more than this. Statistics from several areas, including the southern United States, show that seasonal variations in temperature are reflected very clearly in birth rates. The rate of conception during the middle of a very hot summer may be as much as 30 per cent lower than in the same area a few months later (Chang, 1963). Whether this difference is the result of lessened sexual activity or of reduced fertility is not known; however, it indicates that acclimatization to heat may have a genuine selective effect.

ALTITUDE ACCLIMATIZATION

Altitude differences do not affect the lives of as many people as temperature differences, but have received much interested attention from physiologists. The effect of altitude on the animal body (aside from cold, which often accompanies altitude) is the result of the reduced availability of oxygen when atmospheric pressure is lowered. The vast majority of the human species lives at altitudes less than 5,000 feet, at which level the availability of oxygen is about 83 per cent of that at sea level. Most individuals can go from sea level to 5,000 feet without noticing the difference, except perhaps when climbing stairs, and so forth, and they usually become acclimatized after a few weeks. At 10,000 feet, oxygen availability is about 70 per cent of that at sea level; at 15,000 feet, about 58 per cent. At these altitudes the symptoms of oxygen shortage become more marked, more individuals notice adverse effects, and it takes longer to adjust.

All the effects of altitude on the body and its functions appear to be the result of a reduction in the supply of oxygen available to the tissues. Artificial correction of the condition can be made in two ways. Increase of pressure within a closed space, as in a pressurized aircraft cabin, completely neutralizes the effect of altitude. Another method, used by climbers of very high mountains, is to add oxygen to the air that enters the lungs. The amount of oxygen taken up by the blood can be restored partially or completely to normal by increasing the amount of oxygen in the air, though the air pressure remains low. But in the absence of any such artificial aids, body functions are restored to normal, or partially so, by various physiological changes. First, pulmonary ventilation—that is, the amount of air breathed in and out of the lungs in a given period of time—increases. This may be as much as 40 per cent greater for the same body weight in a person acclimatized to high altitude. Second, the number of red blood corpuscles, which carry oxygen from the lung to other parts of the body, increases. A less obvious change is an increase in the number of small capillary blood vessels, not only in the lung but in muscles and brain (Hurtado, 1964). All these changes increase the efficiency with which oxygen gets from the atmospheric air to the body tissues that need it. These are not the only changes that take place, but they are the most important ones. Any healthy individual will begin to show these changes when exposed to high-altitude conditions. One may wonder why, when so few human beings over past generations have been exposed to high altitude, this adaptability is so universal. It is probably because it is useful under conditions other than altitude. These mechanisms are called into play whenever the supply of oxygen to the tissues is inadequate, whether by reason of anemia, impaired lung function, or increased physical activity; therefore they are, selectively speaking, universal advantages. It is hard to be certain, therefore, to what extent the ability of native populations to function well in high altitude is the result of prolonged exposure, and to what extent the result of genetic differences. One anatomical difference that has been noted in high-altitude native populations is a wide and deep chest, which facilitates the extra pulmonary ventilation that is one of their adjustments (Hock, 1970). It is not certain that chest size may not become larger as a result of consistent deep breathing in the growing individual (Frisancho, 1975). However, there are genetic factors in chest size, as in other body-size traits, indicating that this would also be subject to selection. In addition, most of the permanent populations living above 10,000 feet are of Mongoloid races, which already have relatively large trunks and chests.

An example of genetic adaptation is seen in domestic cattle. In mountain areas of the western United States, cattle are sometimes taken to high mountain pastures for the summer months. Some animals suffer pulmonary failure as a result of the altitude change (so-called *brisket disease*). Not all animals of a herd are affected, however, and it has been found possible by breeding from resistant animals to produce herds that are unaffected by the altitude change (Anonymous, 1969). The same condition, rare but occasionally fatal, has been reported to be hereditary in man (Fred, 1962). This is an interesting example of the potentialities for selection in relation to an environmental hazard.

The most serious problem of altitude, for a resident population, is the effect on reproduction. This was early noted by the Spanish in Peru. At the time of the Conquest, they were immediately drawn to the large native cities and the mines, all above 10,000 feet, and attempted to settle there. Reproduction proved to be very difficult and it became customary to send Spanish women to a lower altitude during pregnancy (Baker, 1966). Recent study has shown that in altitudes around 10,000 feet in the United States, among populations recently derived from low-altitude ones, miscarriage and prematurity are common, and birth weights are low (Grahn and Kratchman, 1963). It is clear that though adults may adjust more or less to the effects of altitude, the developing fetus, receiving its oxygen secondhand, is suffering. Yet native populations at this and greater heights are obviously reproducing adequately, or they would not be there. These populations undoubtedly arrived at their present homes by a gradual uphill migration extending over many generations, during which time natural selection would have rapidly eliminated the genes of those whose reproduction was most adversely affected by altitude. Adequate reproduction in these circumstances apparently requires more than the adaptability adequate for ordinary physical activity.

As in the case of temperature stress, it appears that altitude stress is countered by two kinds of mechanism: adaptability, which gives all humans means of coping with it, and specific genetic adaptations, which are developed in a population by selection. The total effect is so great that the high-altitude residents of the Andes region have been called Andean Man (Monge, 1948)—a special strain of man capable of pushing the physiological accommodation to low oxygen supplies to its ultimate limit. Andean Man is provided with an appropriate body build, a capacity to maintain physical and mental activity even with low internal oxygen levels, and furthermore, enjoys the indispensable assistance of Andean Woman, with her unique ability to produce healthy offspring under physiologically desperate circumstances.

RESISTANCE TO INFECTIOUS DISEASE

Many of the diseases from which man suffers have always been related to environment and geographical area, and some are known to have spread from one region to another at specific times. A whole class of unpleasant conditions are called *tropical diseases* because they first came to the attention of European physicians at the time when Temperate Zone peoples and their medical scientists began to move into the tropical areas of the world. In other cases, very severe and sudden onslaughts of plagues or pestilences have been traceable to specific outside areas in which the diseases had been previously known. This regional distribution of diseases has caused some races to be more exposed to certain diseases and to suffer more from them. (It has also resulted in some nasty recriminations about who caught what from whom.) But diseases due to parasites, microbes, and viruses will move in on anyone who is susceptible. There are other conditions, called "diseases," that are of a quite different nature—genetic problems that have arisen by mutation. Some of these "diseases" are for one reason or another more common in some populations than in others. But here we are concerned with what are usually called the infectious diseases. Populations that have been more exposed to certain of these diseases over long periods of time have a degree of resistance to them. Thus one race may communicate to another a disease which it has learned to live with, but which affects the other quite seriously. The picture is complicated by the capacity of disease organisms themselves to undergo mutation and evolve. Sometimes this evolution can be very rapid, as shown by the regular appearance of new strains of flu. When almost everyone has had the old strain and is immune to it, the spread of the disease comes to a standstill; but when a mutation occurs that bypasses the previously acquired immunity, the new strain quickly and totally replaces the old one—natural selection on a grand scale—and another epidemic ensues. There is another kind of mutation, one that may be successful in the case of a very serious disease. It is not in the best interest of a disease organism to kill the patient too quickly; the longer the patient drags around infecting others, the more the disease spreads and thrives. Consequently, mutations of a disease which moderate its severity may be selected for, altering its course and symptoms. The effect of such mutations is an unpredictable change of a disease from a virulent to a mild form, often noted within the space of a few years (Motulsky, 1960). These changes make it extremely difficult to identify diseases of the past, which may seem different from anything we know at the present time. Add to this the problems of diagnosing a disease from the bones of a patient who died a few thousand years ago, or from an account written by a physician of another age, whose concepts of disease were different from ours, and there is much room left for disagreement about the history of disease. There have been many heated arguments about these matters, and what we say here will not be agreed upon by everybody.

Sometimes useful inferences about disease history can be based on population resistance. Individual resistance to disease is fairly well understood. The most dramatic form is immunity, which develops after a disease has been contracted. The body has the ability to produce antibodies which neutralize the effect of the invading virus or organism, thus bringing the infection to a halt. The immunity produced is usually permanent and prevents the individual from contracting the same disease again. Until very recently, it was considered normal for every individual to acquire immunity to a number of these diseases the hard way; now artificial immunization bypasses this unpleasant process, and the "childhood" diseases rarely occur. Infants do not contract these diseases during the first few months of life, even when the virus is abroad in epidemic form. This because of the transmission of antibodies through the placenta, a process by which the infant acquires the antibodies, and thus the immunities, of the mother. These congenitally acquired immunities gradually wear off, though they may mitigate the severity of the disease when it is later contracted. This is as close as anything we know to "inheritance of acquired traits," though it is not true genetic inheritance.

Another factor in population resistance to disease is largely an unknown. If there are genetic differences that cause certain individuals to suffer less severely from a disease, this provides an opportunity for the action of natural selection of a rather strong kind (Motulsky, 1960). Any genes that operate in this way, unless they have some other recognizable effect, will be difficult to identify because the contraction of a disease and the severity of its course are subject to so many accidental circumstances. It has been possible in certain cases to estimate the heritability of disease resistance. Most striking, however, is the effect of a newly introduced disease on populations who have not been previously exposed to it. In these circumstances, the virulence and mortality rate of a disease are often appalling, and in some cases have virtually exterminated populations (Burnet, 1962). A disease that is relatively mild in one population may be deadly in another—another complication that makes it difficult to evaluate historical records of epidemics. After a period of time, which ranges from quite short in the case of rapidly spreading diseases to much longer in the case of slow-acting diseases such as tuberculosis, the newly exposed population—at least the descendants of the survivors—can fight the infection quite as well as populations that have been subject to it for a long time. The best known modern examples of this sequence took place with the introduction of a variety of European diseases to North America after the year 1500. The reduction in numbers and power of the Indian population during this period was largely the result of these diseases rather than of political and military action, though history books rarely mention it. Attempts to deliberately infect Indian groups are reported; so are sincere attempts to prevent them from being infected. But, given the lack of any real medical treatment for the diseases at that time, nothing could have changed the course of events, except temporarily. The Pilgrim Fathers praised God for having conveniently removed most of the Indians from the area they proposed to colonize. Actually, the Indians were killed by epidemics spreading north from the earlier white settlements in Virginia. Similar tragedies occurred in the islands of Polynesia and Melanesia, where "mild" European diseases such as measles caused devastating epidemics with very high mortality (Burnet, 1962). In such cases the death rate is often increased by a state of panic that disrupts all care of the ill.

Epidemics were regarded for many centuries with superstitious fear and were often attributed to divine vengeance. But modern epidemiologists have reduced the explanation to some very simple laws. So long as each victim, on the average, transmits the disease to more than one other person, the disease increases, potentially to a disaster level. If the average transmission drops to less than one, the disease slowly dies out. If the incubation time and the course of the disease are measured in days, and the transmission rate is high, the spread is very dramatic. If the disease is chronic and the spread of the infection slow, the whole process lasts much longer. An important factor in determining the transmission rate is the number of susceptible individuals in the population. The very dreadful epidemics we have just described occurred when the susceptibility of the population was 100 per cent. The epidemic subsides as the susceptibles either die, or recover and are consequently immune. Other factors that facilitate the spread of the disease include such circumstances as the presence of animals or insects that carry or transmit the infection. Most important, from the anthropological point of view, is the density of the population, which increases the mutual exposure of people to one another. For this reason the role of infectious diseases in man's history has probably become increasingly more important as the human species has become more abundant (Black, 1975).

TUBERCULOSIS

Tuberculosis has been known in the Old World for many centuries. It was described in classical times in the Mediterranean region, and left its mark on skeletons earlier than that, in Egypt (Wells, 1964). But it apparently did not reach epidemic proportions until medieval and later times. Contrary to popular belief, it is not a very infectious disease, and would not have survived if its clinical course had not been protracted; tuberculosis victims have years rather than days to expose others to infection. It is essentially a disease of high population density and urbanization, conditions in which each individual comes into constant and frequent contact with others in the community. External factors sometimes cited as conducing to tuberculous infection are overwork, lack of fresh air and hygiene. These things are, of course, all aspects of poverty. From the point of view of the transmission of tuberculosis, another aspect of poverty, crowded living, is probably the most important, as shown by the greater prevalence of the disease among the urban poor as compared with the rural poor.

We know more about the inheritance of susceptibility to tuberculosis than about that of susceptibility to other diseases. It has been shown that it is quite common for both of identical twins who have been raised together to contract tuberculosis. Nonidentical twins raised in as close proximity to one another are likely to differ, one contracting the disease and the other not. There is also a surprisingly low rate of infection in spouses of tuberculous patients.

The heritability is estimated, on the basis of this data, to be about 60 per cent (Cavalli-Sforza and Bodmer, 1971). Apparently there are important genetic factors that make some persons susceptible and others resistant, and resistant individuals may remain healthy even after prolonged exposure. This accords with the long-known fact that large numbers of individuals have minor tuberculous infections and acquire immunity without ever showing clinical signs of the disease.

The history of tuberculosis in various racial groups confirms the importance of genetic factors. In Europe its prevalence seems to have peaked at the time of the Industrial Revolution, when many country folk migrated into crowded urban environments. From that time on there was a leveling off, because of the elimination of genetic susceptibility. At that time it became noticeable that the races of Africa and North America were distinctly more susceptible than those of European descent; evidently the disease had been little known among them previously (Burnet, 1962). It took about a hundred years for Negroes, both in Africa and in the United States, and for American Indians, to acquire the genetic immunity of the European races. At the present time their susceptibility to tuberculosis, for a similar environment, appears to be no more than equal to that of whites. This parallels the stories of epidemics such as smallpox, except that it is played out in extremely slow motion, as a result of the protracted course and low transmissibility of tuberculosis. It is of interest that susceptibility to tuberculosis among various European peoples differed during the late nineteenth and early twentieth centuries. In rather similar and very crowded urban conditions in the United States (in the very same housing, in some cases, now occupied by urban minorities), the Irish, mostly of recent rural origin, appeared more susceptible than average, and the Jews less so (Motulsky, 1960). Because of restrictions on land-holding in Europe, the Jews had been more intensively urbanized than other Europeans, and as a result seem to have undergone natural selection for tuberculosis resistance somewhat earlier. Not all the credit for the marked reduction of the disease goes to modern medicine. The tuberculosis epidemic was undoubtedly approaching its natural decline by 1900.

An interesting factor in tuberculosis susceptibility, and probably part of its hereditary component, is anatomical. The pulmonary form of the disease, the most common and most serious form, has a preference for individuals with relatively high and narrow chests. The infection usually gets its foothold in the apical lobe of the lung, which is constricted in persons of linear build. This relation has often been confused because of the failure to distinguish between skeletal linear build and nutritional thinness, or between healthy nutritional thinness and beginning emaciation resulting from tuberculosis prior to its diagnosis. A narrow chest is therefore a liability in environments where tuberculosis is likely to be acquired. This may have been a significant selective factor in the last few millenia, in areas that developed dense populations during that period.

SYPHILIS

The early history of syphilis is somewhat doubtful (Wells, 1964). It seems likely that it originated in the New World and later spread to the Old World, unlike other presently world-wide diseases. In the sixteenth century it spread over Europe in a very virulent form, transmitted at first so readily that it bypassed the conventional route of infection. In a land already beset with many deadly diseases, for which there was no adequate therapy, it was regarded as particularly nasty, probably because it cast a shadow over the brighter interludes in a dreary life. It was a matter of much recrimination among nations and was characteristically named after the unpopular neighbor nation from whom you thought you got it. This controversial character still remains and colors the argument about which hemisphere first suffered it. It has been positively identified by one pathologist or another in ancient bones from both Egypt and Peru, though it is most unlikely that both are right. Perhaps the best evidence for its New World origin is that it did not become epidemic among American Indians in the same way as other diseases known to be of Old World origin, but *did* behave like a new disease in Europe. In the nineteenth century it was especially prevalent among American Negroes, suggesting that it had not reached Africa from Europe before 1800 and that they were first exposed to it on this continent, with the usual reaction to a new disease. The susceptibility of the races now appears to be about equalized.

MALARIA

Probably the most serious of all human diseases, in terms of total death and disability, is malaria. It is one of a family of diseases, varieties of which affect many mammals and birds; it is carried from one victim to another by mosquitoes. It has always been most prevalent in areas of warm or hot climates, where its vectors are continuously active throughout the year. The immune reaction to the malaria parasite is incomplete, and though the disease is usually contracted during childhood in malarial areas, adults may be reinfected. Malaria is of interest from the point of view of genetics because it has created a strong pressure for selective change, and is responsible for some rather remarkable genetic adaptations. The best known of these is the *sickle-cell gene*. This mutation became known as the cause of a very severe and generally fatal anemia in children, which occurred principally in Africa, among Negroes of the tropical belt extending from West Africa across to Madagascar. It acts by producing an abnormality of the hemoglobin in the red blood cells. The gene is a recessive one which produces the anemia when in the homozygous state. In certain areas the gene frequency is as high as 20 per cent. This results in only a 4 per cent incidence of the anemia itself. However, the gene, though recessive, is almost completely lethal. For a lethal allele to attain a frequency of 20 per cent in any population is very remarkable, and for it to have spread in substantial amounts over a large area seemed incredible. Study of the gene was facilitated by the fact that its heterozygous carriers could be identified. In individuals suffering from sickle-cell anemia, the red blood cells spontaneously shrivel up from their normal round shape into a crescent—hence the name *sickle cell*. In the heterozygotes, who often will be parents or siblings of a sickle-cell victim, the red blood cells can be made to assume the sickle shape after a drop of blood has been removed from the body. The condition in heterozygotes is called *sickle-cell trait,* to distinguish it from the anemia of the homozygote. Study of heterozygotes solved the mystery of how the gene had become so common in this one area. The heterozygotes suffer less severely from malaria than persons who lack the sickle-cell gene altogether (Allison, 1954). This results in a situation of heterosis (see pages 70–72). A survival advantage to the heterozygotes—which, it should be noted, would only exist in an area where malaria was prevalent—counteracts the lethal disadvantage of the homozygotes to just the degree necessary to maintain the gene at its high level. The death of one out of twenty-five infants is the price paid for the improved health of one out of three of the survivors.

The sickle-cell allele has been found in Arabia, India, and parts of southern Europe, as well as Africa (Barnicot, 1964). Its local differences in frequency tell a complicated story. The prevalence of malaria in any area will affect the selective balance. The more prevalent the disease, the greater will be the advantage of the heterozygote, and the more common the allele will become. (The homozygote has zero survival value everywhere.) It is believed that in West Africa the threat of malaria has increased during the last centuries because of increased agriculture, which disturbs drainage and provides more breeding places for mosquitoes (Livingstone, 1955). Thus the gene frequency in some areas may not yet have come into balance with the recent selective pressure. The concentration of the allele in and close to Africa, though malaria is present throughout the Old World tropics, indicates that the mutation occurred in Africa but has not yet spread to many areas where it would multiply if it were once introduced. Its spread would follow the pattern of spread of an advantageous gene (pages 78–79). The control of malaria by reduction of mosquito breeding has now altered selection pressures again, this time in the direction of *decreasing* the frequency of the sickle-cell gene. In the United States the frequency of the gene varies in different areas. In the coastal regions of South Carolina, where the Negro population is relatively unmixed, and where malaria has remained a common disease, the frequency is about the same as in West Africa. In other parts of the United States, because of the combined effect of greater racial admixture and less exposure to malaria, it has dropped to about half that amount (Pollitzer, 1958). In an entirely malaria-free environment, it should eventually disappear.

Another mutation, similar to sickle cell but not the same, is found around the shores of the Mediterranean Sea, as well as in Asia Minor, India, and some parts of Indonesia. This mutation produces in homozygotes another severe childhood anemia called *thalassemia*, which is also the result of an abnormal hemoglobin. Evidence of its relation to malaria resistance is not conclusive, but its distribution suggests that it acts similarly to sickle cell. Another trait affecting the red blood cells is G6PD (*glucose-6-phosphate dehydrogenase*) deficiency (Motulsky, 1960). This is a sex-linked trait that results in abnormal responses to certain foods and drugs, and it appears, also, to confer some protection against malaria. This gene is found in the Old World tropics, from Africa to Melanesia. In New Guinea it is limited to coastal tribes and does not extend into the highlands, where malaria is not a problem.

YELLOW FEVER

The malaria-infested jungles of West Africa are the home of another major tropical disease, *yellow fever*. This also is insect-borne, by a different genus of mosquito from malaria. The spread of these two diseases is interesting. We know that yellow fever was brought to the New World by Negro slaves from West Africa (Burnet, 1962); it later spread widely in both Central and South America, even to the United States at one time. There is some evidence that human malaria also may not have been present in the New World until Europeans breached its bacteriological isolation (Dunn, 1965; Wood, 1975). Yellow fever, and possibly malaria, became hazards to the Indian populations of the tropics, just as European diseases threatened them in North America. The Negroes themselves were relatively immune. In the case of yellow fever, it is uncertain how much of this genetic immunity resulted from generations of exposure, and how much from childhood immunization—for children usually take the disease well and acquire a lifelong immunity (Burnet, 1962). In West Africa few Europeans stayed around long enough to find out if the next generation would be resistant to it. Yellow fever and malaria together effectually prevented European settlement in the tropical lowlands of Africa, leaving European influence limited to economic and political control. This contrasts strikingly with the history of European settlement in North America, where, with their own diseases as powerful weapons, Europeans displaced and outnumbered the original inhabitants. Indian populations in the New World tropics had to contend with yellow fever, but profited by the discouragement of Europeans. Even now, in Central and South America, Negro populations seem to be concentrated in the lowlands, where the insect-borne diseases thrive, and

Indian and European-derived populations in the highlands. A secondhand feedback from malaria may be involved here. The sickle-cell trait of the heterozygote, which ordinarily causes no problems, may, under conditions of severe physical stress combined with altitude, result in blood cell destruction—even to the point of fatality. Thus a side effect of malaria resistance may have discouraged the movement of Negro populations to higher altitudes.

NUTRITION

Nutrition, of all matters biological, is of the greatest interest to the general population. This has been a problem of the science: its findings are no sooner made than they are popularized and often distorted. In addition, bits of nutritional theory are likely to be seized upon by segments of the food industry for promotional purposes, sometimes before they are soundly proved. Two assumptions underlie popular nutrition theory: first, that nutritional requirements, although correlated with age and to some degree with sex, are free of other individual variation and are therefore the same for all populations in the world; and second, that the nutrients customarily consumed by a well-to-do family of northern European or American white extraction can be taken as a universal standard for all mankind. Early nutritionists were unhappy to be reminded of peoples who ate very differently from their "standard people" and yet remained quite healthy. For instance, it was once claimed that carbohydrates should be about 50 per cent of the diet, though people such as the Eskimos lived for centuries with virtually no carbohydrates. Professional nutritionists now view these "requirements" more realistically. Although recognizing variation in individual requirements, they nevertheless still recommend, to be on the safe side, quantities of certain nutrients that represent not normal need but amounts sufficient to take care of those individuals who for some reason have greater than average need, up to an undefined statistical limit. Nutrition has also been enlisted in arguments for the alleviation of poverty, with a bias toward exaggerating nutritional needs. Although the redistribution of wealth is a perfectly legitimate moral and political issue, it is unfortunate if nutritional information has been misrepresented because of it. Of interest to the anthropologist are the true ranges of individual requirements for various nutrients as well as any population differences that may have arisen as local adaptations to dietary resources.

Modern nutritionists avoid overly specific recommendations of dietary components, and usually give only minimum requirements for essential elements such as protein and certain vitamins and minerals. Protein has received much attention because its sources tend to be limited in some environments, and because it is generally the most expensive item of the diet in a market economy. In hunting cultures, and in prosperous classes in industrial societies, protein supplies are more than ample and are often consumed in excess of real need. As a result, much protein is burned as fuel, a process comparable to heating a house by burning beefsteaks in the furnace—adequate, but expensive. Many of man's wild relatives among the primates subsist largely on vegetable products, and have minimal protein intake, by human standards. But because early man was primarily a hunter, it was not until after the development of agriculture that protein was likely to be a limiting or deficient element in human diet. Agriculture, after small and slow beginnings, became culturally significant in the Near East about 5000 B.C. and spread slowly over the cultivable portions of the Old World. The availability of protein to an agricultural people depends on the use of domestic animals, first as food, later as milk-producers; on the continued availability of game animals, which decreases with increased community size and population density; and on the kinds of crops grown. The use of animal food can be estimated by archaeologists from the number of animal bones found in ancient garbage heaps. Plant protein sources can be estimated from the type of crop. Legumes—beans, peas, and so on—have enough protein to compensate for its lack in other vegetable products; these were cultivated in both the Old and the New World. The Temperate Zone cereal crops, primarily wheat, contain enough protein that individuals depending on them heavily as a food source are unlikely to run short of it. Rice, the staple cereal of Asia and its offshore islands, is marginal as a protein source; so is maize, the cereal crop of the New World. The greatest risk of protein deficiency is in the deep tropics. Here soils are generally poor in nitrogen, a necessary component of protein, and the common vegetable crops of these areas, in both hemispheres, are root crops that are extremely low in protein. Clearly, the "standard man" of the nutritionist, a northwestern European, though he is not as carnivorous as his hunting ancestors, has enjoyed a high protein intake in the last few thousand years as compared with many populations of the world. This is because of the late arrival of agriculture in his homeland, his considerable dependence on domestic animals, and the use of wheat as a staple grain. This raises questions about European man's suitability as a standard for estimation of protein requirements, and brings us up against an almost complete lack of nutritional studies on other populations. If there is any genetic leeway in dietary requirements, it is likely that some peoples have been *selected* for an ability to thrive on less protein than Western man. We do have some information from the other extreme of dietary variation: tropical root-crop agriculture in New Guinea, where it has a long history. The protein intake of some natives in this area has been estimated at 33 grams per day, approximately half of the conventional "minimum daily requirement." These natives are wiry and muscular, and have great physical stamina though growth and maturation seem slow

(MacPherson, 1966; Malcolm, 1970). Much more information is needed on diet and dietary requirements of various populations before we can begin to plan intelligently for the world's food needs.

Another interesting apparent difference in dietary requirements is found in regard to niacin. The lack of this vitamin causes *pellagra,* a serious deficiency disease. This condition is common in populations that have come to rely largely on maize for food. This includes some in Europe and Africa, and whites and Negroes living in the New World. But Indians in the New World, many of whom, especially in Central America, are very dependent on maize, appear to be nearly immune to pellagra (Roe, 1974). The explanation may lie in the history of the crop. Maize was domesticated in Central America about 3000 B.C., and has been intensively used there since then. It was introduced to other parts of the world only after 1500 A.D., though its use spread rapidly, especially in Africa. The people who are likely to suffer from pellagra on a maize diet, then, are ones who have been using it for only about one tenth as long as those who are not pellagra-prone. Though there is no definite information about differences in niacin requirements, the presumptive evidence is strong that where populations have relied on maize as a staple food for a long time, natural selection has taken a hand by promoting genetic variations that make it possible to tolerate lower niacin intake. Man is notorious among animals for having adapted to a greater number of different environments and to more different dietary opportunities than any other mammal. These dietary differences and changes are potentially very powerful selective forces. We need to know a great deal more about individual dietary requirements, and the extent to which they are hereditary; and more about how selection may have played a role in the remarkable dietary versatility of the human species.

LACTOSE INTOLERANCE

In Chapter 4 we mentioned briefly, as an example of an enzyme, *lactase,* a substance present in the digestive tract of some but not all individuals. Lactase converts *lactose,* the sugar present in milk, to a form that can be absorbed into the body. (The ending, *ase,* in biochemical language, refers to an enzyme that acts upon the substance designated by the root of the word.) An individual who lacks lactase cannot digest milk sugar, which then ferments in the intestine and produces a distressing gassy indigestion. This condition is known as *lactose intolerance.* The lactose represents about one-fourth of the caloric value of the milk. All infant mammals have lactase and can fully digest milk during the period when they are dependent on it for food. Later, they lose their ability. This is true even in most cats, who never seem to learn that this tasty substance, which they enjoyed in their kittenhood, now disagrees with them. The production of lactase in adult life is an abnormal condition for mammals in general, but has become quite common in some human populations—so much so that the absence of adult lactase was rare in the populations nutritionists first studied. Thus the abnormal came to be thought of as the normal. Racial differences came rather forcefully to the attention of dieticians of the United States Army, who have the responsibility of feeding both white and Negro soldiers in large numbers, as well as smaller numbers of other racial backgrounds. In the United States, the drinking of milk has come to be regarded as almost a religious duty; whether this is related to the cult of the female breast (see Chapter 8) is unknown. In any case, current nutritional practise demanded that Army dieticians attempt to make all their customers drink milk. A high percentage of Negro soldiers, and a few whites, found this abdominally distressing. Subsequent investigation has shown that, with a few exceptions, the ability to digest lactose is limited to Caucasians of European origin (McCraken, 1971). It is interesting that many other peoples of the world have found ways of using milk without the lactose. Lactose readily breaks down into lactic acid if milk is kept in a warm place. This familiar process is known as "souring." After this has occurred, the milk no longer contains lactose and can be consumed by a lactose-intolerant person without ill effects. The other nutrients of the milk, protein and fat, are unaffected, so that the soured milk still has most of its original caloric value. Buttermilk, clabber, yoghurt, and cheese are all milk products from which the lactose has been removed. The most interesting way of obtaining lactose-free milk has been developed in northern Asia, where the lactose is fermented into alcohol. The resulting beverage is called *koumiss*, and those who have sampled it say it tastes terrible but is very exhilarating. Canning or drying of milk retains all its lactose. One of the first impulses of well-intentioned Americans, on hearing of famine anywhere in the world, is to send quantities of dried milk. Unfortunately, in most cases, this strange commodity is politely sampled, and then, after its effects are felt, it is thrown away as unfit for human consumption. It could be used by *infants* in any population, but the adults who try it out do not know this. So, though milk is utilized for food in some form by many peoples, its use by individuals of all ages, in the simple and obvious form, as it comes from the animal, is limited to certain populations. It can hardly be doubted that the adult ability to digest lactose is a selective advantage, especially where dependence on agriculture has reduced the protein level of the diet. This suggests that it was originally, in man as in other mammals, an unusual condition, and became common only after milk became available as a food. This leaves some questions unanswered. Did there have to be a population with a considerable number of lactose-tolerant individuals (as a result of mutation and genetic drift) to *originate* the arts of the dairyman? Possibly not: the simplest method of removing lactose from milk—souring—takes place so quickly in the unpasteurized, unrefrigerated article that far more human effort has been devoted to preventing it than to producing it. The use of fresh milk as opposed to soured milk or cheese may have developed after the use of domestic animals (which originated in the Near East) was introduced to cooler climates where milk could be kept fresh for an appreciable length of time. At any rate, lactose tolerance is still regionally limited and has become a major racial trait.

It is hardly possible to leave the subject of milk consumption without some comment on the "calcium requirements" generally accepted in the United States. These standards set a minimum of 800 milligrams per day for most persons, an amount which can hardly be obtained without the use of milk. This amount of calcium is supposedly necessary, among other things, to maintain the mineralization of the skeleton. The bones of American Negroes, however, are distinctly heavier and better mineralized than those of American Caucasians (Baker and Angel, 1965), and this in spite of the fact that the consumption of milk is limited in Negroes by lactose intolerance. Surveys of the amount of calcium available in the food supplies of India and Japan show that it is less than half of the United States "requirement" (Wilson, et al., 1965). These, of course, are populations with very low milk use—in the case of Japan, less than 7 per cent of the United States amount. This might suggest some racial differences in calcium requirement. However, the official recommendation for calcium intake in the United States exceeds by 60 per cent that recommended in Canada, with essentially the same racial composition in the two nations. It seems most likely that the United States standard for calcium intake is grossly inflated, and is based not on established need but on customary consumption.

DIABETES

In Chapter 4 we referred to insulin as another example of an enzyme. Insulin acts a little later in the cycle of food absorption than lactase, serving to convert various sugars, after they have been taken into the bloodstream, into forms that can be utilized by the cells. Insulin is produced by the pancreas, a large glandular structure associated with the digestive tract, but the insulin it produces is secreted into the blood rather than into the intestine. Diabetes results when insulin is deficient, and its various symptoms result from the accumulation in the blood of sugar which cannot be utilized by the cells, and which cannot be converted into usable forms because of the lack of insulin.

Diabetes now can be treated by the administration of insulin, but was once an incurable and generally fatal disease. It can be mitigated by reducing carbohydrates in the diet, thus lowering the amount of sugar that accumulates in the blood. The disease is a good example of a condition that is hereditary but not congenital, and in which an interaction of heredity and environment is involved. The condition develops at different ages in different individuals; the most serious cases appear during childhood, but most cases appear later in life. The liability to develop the disease has a definite hereditary component, but its development in a particular individual is not certain: a person may be susceptible but not develop it, or only late and in a mild form. One of the factors that increases the chance of diabetes developing is an overload of carbohydrates in the diet. Like other digestive glands, the pancreas increases its output of the enzyme in direct response to the intake of the foods on which it acts, and it appears that failure of insulin production may eventually result from overwork of the cells involved. The genetic predisposition to diabetes is common enough to have roused considerable curiosity as to how it has managed to survive the effects of natural selection. A clue may lie in the frequency with which obesity precedes the onset of the disease in civilized, well-fed people. If the tendency to accumulate fat easily is truly correlated with the predisposition to diabetes, the genes responsible for it may have been positively selected in the days when rapid accumulation of fat in good times provided an energy reserve that could be drawn upon in hungry times (Neel, 1962). Man's cultural progress has made food supplies more stable, but it has also changed their nature. Prior to the invention of agriculture, and its introduction at various times to different parts of the world, the amount of carbohydrate in human diet would not often have been very great. Though hunting in simple cultures is generally supplemented by the gathering of wild vegetable products, these are usually limited in amount. Thus carbohydrate overload, the environmental component of diabetes risk, would be almost unknown. In this situation the genetic predisposition to diabetes would not be a hazard. Such a change from advantage to disadvantage of the same trait may explain the prevalence of diabetes in modern societies. A trait that was once positively selected for has now become a risk, and there has not been time for the selective process to reverse itself. If this is the case, we would expect diabetes to be a more serious problem in people who have more recently made the transition from the low-carbohydrate diet of a hunting culture to the high-carbohydrate diet of an agricultural economy. This is borne out by a high incidence of diabetes in American Indians (Judkins, 1974). We usually think of populations "closer to nature" as being relatively free from defects or illnesses of a hereditary kind. The diabetes problem in Indians therefore seems anomalous. But in this case we may see a population newly confronted with an environmental hazard of civilization—excess carbohydrate—which it has yet to adapt to. Was there a time, shortly after the beginnings of agriculture, when the populations of the Old World suffered, even more than now, from a strange, deadly disease we now call diabetes? Very likely so.

Another condition we will include with nutrition-related diseases is alcoholism. This is a complex condition which interests sociologists and psychiatrists, some of whom claim to have the sole answer to it. But genetic studies on twins and other relatives, including many in adoption situations, show that heredity also plays a role (Mc Clearn and De Fries, 1973). These findings, like all findings on the subject, are greatly confused by difficulties and disagreements in *defining* alcoholism. But there seems to be no disagreement that the chronic excessive use of alcohol, for both physiological and sociological reasons, decreases reproduction (Van Thiel, 1974). If this is so, any genetic factors predisposing to the abuse of alcohol would be strongly selected against in the presence of the external agent. Now alcohol is essentially a by-product of agriculture, which cannot be produced in any but small quantities by people who do not have ample sources of carbohydrates. In the Old World, grain-based fermented beverages were probably manufactured very soon after the cultivation of cereals in the Near East, and later, wines were produced extensively in southern Europe. Beverages higher in alcoholic content than ale did not become generally available in Europe north of the grape-growing areas until distilled spirits began to be produced from grain about 1500 A.D. (Tannehill, 1973). In general, the areas in Europe where alcohol has been longer in use appear to produce fewer alcoholics. This has been interpreted as the result of a cultural adjustment to alcohol, though it certainly can be interpreted genetically also. The most acute problems, however, have emerged in populations where alcohol was unknown until recently, and where the first exposure was to distilled beverages. The inability of many of their people to cope with alcohol has been a source of concern and embarrassment to responsible American Indians for many decades; American Prohibition, in fact, began in the 1840's when the autonomous nations of Indian Territory enacted laws against the manufacture and importation of liquor (Foreman, 1934). These tribes had been quite innocent of alcohol prior to the arrival of Europeans: in the New World, the only alcoholic beverages previously produced were rather mild fermented drinks made in the major agricultural areas south of the present U.S. border. The problem of alcoholism among them appears, then, to be parallel to that of diabetes. Genotypes that are unable to tolerate alcohol have not until recently been selected against, because the environmental hazard has only recently been introduced. In populations that have been exposed to alcohol for a longer time, the vulnerable genotypes have been partially eliminated by natural selection. The analogy may be extended even further: alcohol and excess carbohydrate can be compared to the virus of smallpox; when introduced by a relatively immune population, they put a susceptible population in jeopardy. It is of interest, especially in view of the emphasis that has sometimes been placed on alcoholism as a psychological reaction to powerlessness, that American Negroes appear to respond to alcohol no better and no worse than their Caucasian neighbors. Their ancestors have been agriculturalists and have known alcohol for a very long time. Unfortunately, there is no easy remedy to offer to people who are late starters in a process of natural selection.

FERTILITY

The essential and direct path to biological success is the production of offspring. Everything else upon which natural selection acts is involved only indirectly, to the extent that its effect on survival or longevity increases or decreases the number of offspring produced. But it appears that essential fertility (or *fecundity*, as demographers prefer to call it) is not subject to much individual genetic variation. The heritability of fecundity has proved to be low not only in the human species, but in domestic animals (Falconer, 1960). This is probably because fertility is so highly selected for that it causes all populations to approach a maximum level, leaving little room for individual variation. Genes for relative infertility are in effect lethal ones, and have remained rare. In ancient times when droughts, disasters, and plagues could nearly exterminate tribes and nations, the ability to "be fruitful and multiply" was essential if a population was to restore its numbers before its territory was taken over by someone else. At other times fertility might exceed resources, and many peoples of primitive culture solved this problem by abortion and infanticide.

One obvious element in fertility is the length of the reproductive span in the female. This is definitely subject to environmental influences. Higher nutrition levels result in earlier sexual maturity. The early puberty in modern Temperate-Zone industrialized nations as compared with tropical and underdeveloped countries, and even as compared with their own ancestors of a few centuries ago, is probably the result of higher caloric intake. There is even a direct correlation between fatness and age at puberty on an individual basis (Frisch, 1974). The highest age of puberty recorded in peoples now living is among Melanesians living by tropical root-crop agriculture, with low protein intake (Malcolm, 1973). Dietary composition as well as quantity may be involved. Undernutrition, however, seems to have little effect on human fertility once the sexual cycle has been established; if it did, some of the serious imbalances between population increase and world food supply would not have arisen. In this respect modern man is less well adapted than most other animals. High fertility may in fact be encouraged by artificially stabilized food supplies. Man's domestic dog and cat also have abnormally high fertility, breeding twice or three times a year as compared with once a year in their wild relatives—a rate that

would be counterproductive under wild conditions because of ex-
haustion of the mother. Excessive fertility in present-day man, by
not being immediately counterproductive, has become dangerously
so in the long run.

One specific reproductive adaptation has already been mentioned: the ability of populations living at high altitudes to reproduce successfully on limited oxygen. The possible effect of heat
acclimatization on reproduction has also been mentioned.

A very specific reproductive characteristic that shows definite
racial differences, though it is not very significant for total reproductive efficiency, is the rate of occurrence of twins. There has long
been a general knowledge that twins "run in families," and this
phenomenon has been investigated by geneticists for some time.
There are two kinds of twinning, caused in quite different ways.
Identical twins are produced by the splitting, at an early stage, of a
single fertilized egg. Such twins are identical genetically and are
always of the same sex. *Fraternal* twins result from the release of two
eggs from the ovary, and their subsequent fertilization by two
sperm cells. As with any two siblings taken at random, they are just
as likely to be of the opposite sex as of the same sex. Genetic
studies have shown that the hereditary factor involved in production of twins is a characteristic of the mother, and shows itself only
in the frequency of fraternal twins (Wyshak and White, 1965).
Statistically, this means that repeated occurrence of twins in a
family, where it involves identical twins, or where it seems to come
from the father's side of the family, is no more often than would be
expected by chance. The hereditary component in twinning, then, is
simply the liability of a woman to release two eggs from the ovaries
simultaneously. The heredity of twinning has been difficult to
demonstrate because even a woman who is "twin-prone" produces
twins only occasionally. Numerous studies of the frequency of
twins have been made on a regional or racial basis, using statistical
data. In such studies it is not possible to evaluate the status—
identical or fraternal—of same-sex twins. However, the relative
frequency of the two types in a population can be estimated from
data on twin pairs identified simply as same- or different-sex.
Because fraternal twins are same- or different-sex in about equal
numbers, the total number of fraternal twins is estimated as twice
the number of different-sex twins. Such estimates show that identical twinning is equally common in all populations studied, with no
indications of either genetic or environmental effect. But the genetic
factors that affect *fraternal* twinning differ in different populations.
The lowest rates are in Asiatic Mongoloids (1 out of 400 pregnan-
cies in Japan); medium rates in Caucasoids (1 out of 135 in United
States whites); and the highest in Negroes (1 out of 25 in Nigeria)
(Morton, 1967). It is difficult to see any great selective effect here:
even the highest rates would only contribute an extra 4 per cent to
total birth rates. An unknown factor in the distribution of twinning
is the effect of cultural attitudes and practices. Twins are sometimes
regarded with fear and suspicion in primitive cultures. The reasons

given are various: that twins are an evil omen, are evidence of adultery, are guilty of prenatal incest (if of opposite sex) or, quite practically, that the mother cannot raise both infants successfully. As a result, some peoples have made a practice of killing one or both twins at birth, and it is likely that if we were able to trace this custom far enough back in time, we might find it among the ancestors of modern populations that have completely forgotten it. Therefore, there may have been selection against the genetic factors for multiple ovulation, stronger in some parts of the world than in others. Whatever the reasons, the frequency of twinning is definitely known to be a racial trait at the present time.

11 Blood Groups and Other Biochemical Traits

So far we have discussed many visible traits by which human individuals and populations differ from one another. We have had to concede that though these traits are certainly inherited, as shown by their recurrence in families and consistency in races, their inheritance is not of a simple nature and so cannot be fitted into classic patterns of experimental genetics. This is not surprising in the case of variations in shape and size of parts of the body. These differences result from growth processes extending over long periods of time, which involve chain reactions of many enzymes produced by many different genes. Other traits can be described as more "simply determined"; meaning that their phenotypic variations appear to be due primarily to one or a few genes. This usually means that the end result we observe is only a step or two removed from the gene itself, and bears a simple relation to it. In these cases we can recognize the presence of the gene more or less directly by detecting in the body some biochemical substance—a large organic molecule—which is produced only when that particular gene is present.

Examples of genes that can be detected in this way are those responsible for the A–B–O and the M–N blood groups, and it was for this reason that we used these traits as examples of Mendelian inheritance in man. As a result of the positive identification and clear inheritance of such traits, they may also be used for legal purposes in cases where the genetic relationship of individuals is in doubt. Biochemical variation of this sort is not a special characteristic of man. There are laboratories that do blood grouping of cattle and horses to resolve questions of disputed paternity—no small matter to the purchaser of an expensive and supposedly pedigreed animal.

THE DETECTION OF BIOCHEMICAL VARIATIONS

There are numerous ways, some involving obscure laboratory procedures, by which biochemical differences between individuals can be discovered. Specifically, what we wish to detect in body cells (often blood cells, which are the most easily and painlessly detached from the owner), in the blood serum, or sometimes in the urine, is a substance that is present in some individuals but not in others. The number of these "optional" components of the human body is surprisingly large, and the list is continually being added to as new techniques are developed and applied. When such a substance is identified, it can then be studied in family groups to determine whether, and how, its presence is inherited. Most of these variations are genetic, and the alleles involved show clear dominant-recessive relationships. As in the case of most individual genetic variations, differences in the incidence of these biochemical traits are often correlated with region and race.

One type of procedure for identifying specific biochemical substances is *chromatography*. This technique takes advantage of the fact that the large and complicated molecules we are looking for differ from one another in the rate at which they seep through an absorbing medium when in solution. The simplest method consists of placing a mixed solution of various organic molecules on the edge of a piece of filter paper, and later determining how far the various substances have traveled in a given length of time. By using different solvents, different absorbing media, and sometimes by the application of electric currents across the field in which the solution is moving (*electrophoresis*), many different molecules can be recognized by their patterns of movement. In this way, the presence or absence of certain substances in different individuals or different species can be detected, even though the substances involved are not chemically identified.

Another major way of finding biochemical variants in man is by the study of what are called *immune reactions*. In Chapter 10 we discussed the historical significance of the various infectious diseases from which no individual suffers more than once. After contracting and recovering from such a disease, the individual is from that time on *immune* to it. This immunity is the result of a substance present in the body, particularly in the blood, which has the property of attaching itself to the characteristic molecules of the harmful virus or organism, rendering them ineffective. This is a very specific relation. We term the foreign substance that induced the reaction an *antigen,* and the substance produced in response to it an *antibody.* Antibodies can be transferred from one person to another, or can be induced by means short of contracting the disease: this is the basis of the artificial immunizations commonly used at the present time. Many organic substances not normally present in the body may act as antigens and result in the formation of antibodies which respond only to their own antigens. Sometimes this type of reaction occurs unnecessarily and with disagreeable results, as in the case of the response called *allergy.* An allergy is a reaction to a foreign protein, apparent only after a first exposure to it, which may later produce distressing and even dangerous symptoms. This is an exaggerated form of the immune response, and occurs in some individuals even though the foreign substance involved is really quite harmless and produces no reaction in most people. An interesting example of response to foreign protein occurs when the attempt is made to transplant body tissue from one individual to another. Such operations, which may be quite simple surgically, are subject to eventual failure because after a period of time the transplanted tissue or organ is "rejected" by the body in which it is placed, and dies. This is the result of a multiple immune response to components that are present in the transplanted tissue but are foreign to the recipient. The genetic nature of these differences is dramatically shown by the one exception to this rule: if the individuals are identical twins, tissue may be transplanted from one twin to the other as easily and with as much success as from one part of an individual's body to another part of it. The completely identical genetic "information" that the twins receive when their mother's single fertilized ovum split into two parts results in identical chemical components in their tissues, so there are no biochemical differences to cause an immune response.

The very specific nature of the relation between antigen and antibody makes it possible to identify antigens even though we do not know their chemical structure. It is only necessary to know that certain individuals (which may be experimental animals) are sensitized to a particular antigen, and then see whether they react to a sample of an unknown substance. A small amount of the sensitized individual's blood may be adequate to make the test.

THE BLOOD GROUPS

The idea of blood transfusion as a supportive measure in illness is not new. In the seventeenth century transfusion was being attempted, often with fatal results. This was discouraging even by seventeenth century standards of medical practise, and the procedure was soon abandoned. The explanation of the sometime-success and sometime-failure of blood transfusion between humans was discovered at the turn of the century (Landsteiner, 1900) and resulted in the demonstration of what we now know as the A–B–O blood groups. The reason why this blood-group system was the first of many to be discovered is a simple one. For reasons not fully known, persons who do not have the A antigen always have an antibody to this antigen, and persons who do not have the B antigen always have an antibody to it. In other cases of immune reactions, an individual must be exposed to an antigen once in order to develop an immune reaction to it. In the case of allergy, there is no reaction at the time of the first exposure to the antigen, only in subsequent exposure. In the case of tissue transplants, rejection occurs only after a delay of days or weeks. But in the case of the antigens of the A–B–O blood-group system, individuals who lack one or both of the antigens will react against them immediately, on first exposure. The actual process that occurs when incompatible bloods are mixed involves an antigen present on the surface of the red blood cells of the donated blood and an antibody present in the serum of the recipient. The antibody in the serum alters the surface properties of the introduced red blood cells so that they clump together in clots that are capable of blocking small blood vessels— with the well-known serious and sometimes fatal results. (The antibody in the serum of the transfused blood is usually diluted beyond the point of having the same effect on the recipient's red blood cells.) Blood groups are tested by using solutions containing known antibodies: the reactions of an individual's blood cells to these solutions identify him as belonging to either A, B, O, or AB blood group. This makes it possible to know in advance which individuals cannot safely receive transfusion from a particular donor. This has made it possible for blood transfusion to become common and lifesaving medical technique. At the same time it provides a classic demonstration of the laws of Mendelian inheritance in man, as related in Chapter 4.

Understanding the A–B–O blood-group system opened the way to the discovery of other blood groups, which had to be studied indirectly, because they involved antigens whose corresponding antibodies had to be produced by experimental means; they were not, as were the anti-A and anti-B antibodies of the A–B–O system, present naturally in individuals who lacked the corresponding antigens. The following is the basic procedure for studying these antigens: Inject red blood cells of a human individual into an experimental animal (often a rabbit); the animal will develop antibodies to any antigens present in these blood cells. Take blood serum from this sensitized animal and remove from it, by an absorption process, any other expected antibodies (such as anti-A or anti-B). Then test the serum of this animal against blood cells of other humans. It may be found that the individual against whose blood cells the experimental animal was sensitized has some antigen in his blood which is present in some humans but not in others. If this is the case, a new blood group has been discovered. A newly discovered antigen may prove to be so rare that it is called a "private" antigen: that is, it is found only in members of a single family—an example of a very rare mutation. Or it may prove to be shared by a number of people in a population, or even to be present in individuals in many parts of the world. An example of the latter class, with a wide distribution of both alleles, is the M–N blood-group system.

One of the best known of human blood groups, because of its medical aspects, is the *Rh-system*. This blood-group system was discovered in a slightly unusual way: not by comparison of humans with one another, but by comparison with another species. "Rh" is an abbreviation for *Rhesus*, the name of a species of monkey often used for experimental work. Injection of red blood cells of Rhesus monkeys into rabbits showed that there was a particular antigen present in the cells of all Rhesus, to which the rabbits developed an antibody. Subsequently it was shown that in a human population (in New York City, where the study was conducted) approximately 85 per cent of the human population carried this same antigen, but the other 15 per cent did not. The antigen was universal for the monkey species, but was variable for humans. Later work showed that this Rh antigen was of particular clinical importance in man. The reproductive mechanism in mammals rather effectively separates the bloodstreams of the mother and the developing young: if this were not the case, all kinds of immunological reactions might take place between mother and fetus in cases where the child inherited from the father some antigen not present in the mother. But the separation of maternal and fetal blood may sometimes break down, if not during pregnancy, at the time of birth. Thus a mother who lacks the Rh antigen (we call such a person Rh-Negative) may develop antibodies to Rh antigen carried on fetal blood cells. This can occur when a mother is Rh-negative and the child Rh-positive. These anti-Rh antibodies may have a serious effect if the same mother bears another Rh-positive child. At that time, the antibodies seep through the placenta and damage the red blood cells of the fetus, which will be born suffering from a dangerous form of anemia. The same condition may result even in an Rh-negative woman's first child, if she has inadvertently been transfused with Rh-positive blood at some time in the past and has thus become sensitized to the Rh antigen. Care is taken now to avoid Rh-positive transfusion of Rh-negative females; and when an Rh-negative mother is carrying the child of an Rh-positive father, physicians are prepared to take action at birth if the child suffers the Rh-induced anemia. It is of interest that later the same sort of reaction was found to occur as a result of incompatibility between mother and child in the A–B–O blood-group system. In this case the effect is more severe, killing the fetus at a very early stage, often before the pregnancy is even diagnosed. For this reason the A–B–O blood-group incompatibility effect remained unknown for a long time, and was detected only by the observation that certain combinations of parent genotypes failed to produce the expected number of certain blood types in their living children (Waterhouse, 1947; Matsunaga, 1956).

THE A–B–O BLOOD GROUPS AND RACE

To the anthropologist, the most interesting aspect of the blood groups and other biochemical traits is their geographical distribution. Because the simple inheritance of these traits makes it possible to calculate gene frequencies of a population from statistics of its phenotypes, we can infer with some assurance, in the case of a population of mixed ancestry, what proportions of the "parent" races combined to form it. To do this on the basis of skin color, or body size, or any other trait that is inherited in a complex way, with unknown dominance or recessiveness, involves a great deal of guesswork. At one time it was believed that blood groups were entirely unaffected by natural selection, and therefore might reveal very ancient genetic relations between populations, which had become obscured because selection in different environments had affected the frequencies of the more visible traits. Now, we are not at all sure that blood groups are necessarily less affected by natural selection than other variations of man. In fact many hypotheses based on selection have been proposed for explaining the geographical patterns of blood-group distribution. Still, however, blood-group frequencies are a valuable objective test of the genetic relations of different populations.

There are several reasons why the A–B–O blood groups are better known than any other in terms of their distribution over the world. Of course, they were the first discovered, and there has been more time for information about them to accumulate. Also, their importance in transfusion has resulted in widespread blood-typing of individuals who enter hospitals or are inducted into armed forces, and these data have been assembled and filed away. As a result, more information about the A–B–O blood groups all over the world is available than about any other genetic trait.

The fact that there were geographical differences in the frequencies of the A–B–O genes was first discovered during World War I, about twenty years after the blood groups were recognized (Hirszfeld, 1919). It was then observed that the percentage of B and AB phenotypes was higher in central and eastern Europe than in western Europe, indicating that the B gene was more common in those areas. This was the beginning of our realization that the A–B–O blood groups were not simply individual genetic variations within populations, but were correlated with geographical area and race, just as many visible traits were known to be. As we might expect, the differences in blood-group gene frequencies are not entirely erratic, and rarely show abrupt differences over short distances; but,

Figure 40 A–B–O blood groups of the Eastern Hemisphere.

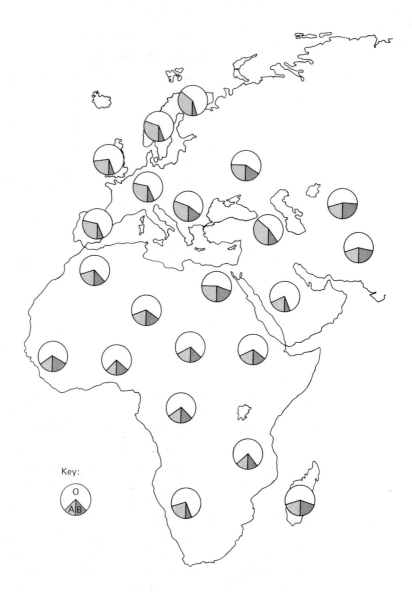

Key:

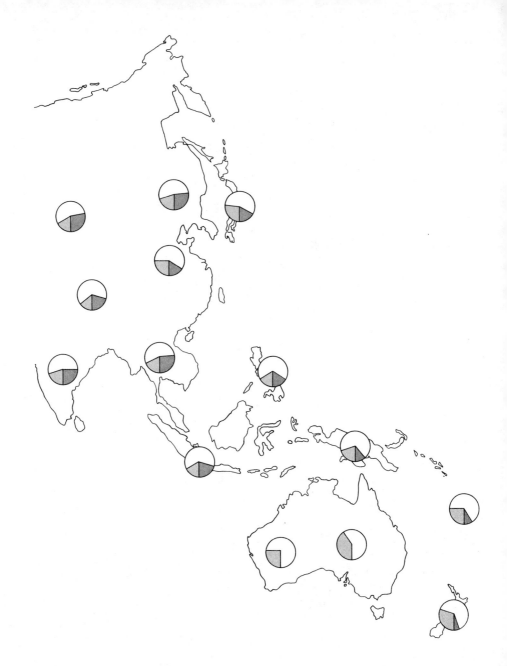

Figure 41 A–B–O blood groups of the Western Hemisphere.

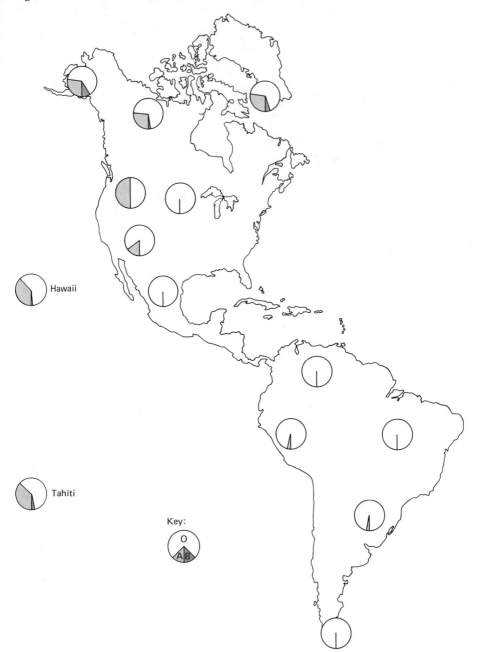

Hawaii

Tahiti

Key:

O
A B

as in the case of other racial traits, they tend in most cases to vary rather gradually with distance—a reflection of the imperfect isolation of most populations from their neighbors. The A–B–O blood-group data, of which we now have so much for so many parts of the globe, lend themselves to the construction of maps, such as Figures 40 and 41. Such maps must be viewed with some reservations. More detailed maps of gene frequencies would show ups and downs that reflect the individualities of small population groups. In some regions, a population which occupies a single area may be divisible into separate communities which, for religious or other reasons, remain genetically separate though they are geographically superimposed, and may differ in blood-group frequencies. But, though we should always remember that the real situation is more complicated, these generalized maps of gene distribution are very informative. The fifty "spots" in Figures 40 and 41 show typical A–B–O frequencies for rather broad areas, and are abstracted from hundreds of separate studies (Mourant, 1958). In constructing this map, we ignore the massive population movements of the last four centuries, and represent world populations as they were distributed before that time: thus, for instance, North America shows Indians only, disregarding the large numbers of other races that live there today.

The total range of frequency is not the same for the two alleles. The O allelle is never less than 40 per cent and in some populations reaches 100 per cent. A, the next most common allele, ranges from zero to about 55 per cent, and B ranges from zero to 30 per cent. In Europe, the frequency of the A allele is about 25–30 per cent, with some local variation. It would appear less uniform if more detail were included in the map. Outside of Europe the A allele reaches equally high frequencies in some areas of East Asia, in Australia, among Polynesians in the Pacific, along the coasts of Arctic North America and Greenland (these are Eskimos), and attains its world peak of 50 per cent in certain western American Indians near the United States-Canada border.

When we examine the distribution of the B gene, we see that the higher frequency in eastern as compared with western Europe is only part of a trend that extends into Asia. The B allele is in excess of 20 per cent in parts of Asia, and is at least relatively high throughout the Continent: China, Japan, and Indonesia have between 15 and 20 per cent. In Africa the frequency of B is between 10 and 20 per cent, higher than in western Europe, but not as high as in Asia. A moderate amount of the B gene is found in the Eskimos of North America, most noticeable in those closest to Asia; but B appears to have been extremely rare, if not entirely absent, among other native peoples of the New World. The B gene has also reached Micronesia and Melanesia and, though this does not appear in Figure 40, is found in some Australian aborigines in the northernmost part of the continent. In Polynesia, B is present but is quite rare. Here, as it occasionally appears in the New World, it may be because of recent admixture. Workers interested in the

anthropological distribution of the blood groups have tried to eliminate individuals of recently mixed ancestry from their records but
this is very difficult to do *completely.*

The O allele, of course, is high wherever A and B are uncommon.
It virtually monopolizes South America and the southern part of
North America because of the absence of B and the rarity of A.
Correspondingly, it is at its lowest frequency in Asia and Eastern
Europe, where the sum of A and B is highest.

In addition to the three basic genes, there is a distinction between
two forms of the A allele, which are designated A_1 and A_2. The A_2
antigen shows somewhat weaker reactions and may be overlooked
in careless laboratory typing. The A_2 variant is commonest in
Europe, reaching its highest frequency in the Lapps, and in Africa.
In the rest of the world A_1 predominates. This adds still another
geographic detail to the A–B–O system.

This distribution pattern is somewhat systematic, at least in the
Old World. The B allele gives the impression of having radiated out
from a center in Asia, reaching Europe and Africa in moderate
amounts but not touching Australia or the Western Hemisphere
except marginally. A is more generally distributed, though it is not
present in many areas of the Americas; and it appears to bear a
somewhat negative relation to B in that the highest frequencies of A
are where B is absent, and increasing amounts of B seem to limit the
frequency of A. If we thought that the A–B–O blood-group system
took precedence over all other traits as a criterion of race, we might
hypothesise three original races, an O race, an A race, and a B race,
which we probably would assume to have originated in that order.
We would say that the O race first spread over the whole world,
including the Americas; that the A race came next and spread over
most of the world, mixing with the O race; and that the B race
originated last, in Asia, and is in the process of spreading out from
there. (If we consider A_1 and A_2 separately, this is not so simple.)
This kind of explanation was fairly popular fifty years ago, when
hypothetical ancient populations were moved all over the world like
pieces on a chessboard, to "explain" trait distribution. A paradox of
such an explanation is that the hypothetical A, B, and O races
would be remarkably heterogeneous in many other respects. The
O–A peoples of North America and the similar O–A native Australians are radically different from one another in many other ways.
Some nearly exact matches of O, A, and B frequencies can be made
between certain European and African populations, who differ so
much in other features that they could never be mistaken for one
another. The high-B "race" of Asia, though it appears to be an
entity geographically, actually includes, in addition to the predominant Mongoloid populations of the continent, others in western
Asia and India, as well as the Ainu in Japan, who are markedly
non-Mongoloid in physical type. Furthermore, the pure O populations of the New World share many traits with the Asian Mongoloids, who have the world's lowest frequency of O. To try to divide
the human species into its basic races by means of the A–B–O
blood groups is no more satisfactory than to try, as many unin-

formed persons do, to divide them by shade of skin color alone. Far from explaining everything, the blood groups have merely added another dimension of difference.

THE GEOGRAPHY OF M–N AND RH

Another blood-group system on which extensive data have been collected is M–N. It too presents us with a simple system in which single alleles can be recognized and exact gene frequencies compared between different populations. The picture is a little easier to draw than in the case of the A–B–O blood groups, because there are only two alleles. In every human population that has been studied, both M and N are found, but in varying proportions. M is more common over-all, and its frequency varies from 30 to 95 per cent of the total. The greatest concentration of the allele M is found in North America, where the majority of tribes have from 75 to 95 per cent M. South America also shows a high frequency of M as compared with the Old World, though not as high as that of North America. Most of Europe, Africa, and Asia range from 45 to 65 per cent M, with a few places in Europe and Asia where it is as high as 75 per cent; and there is an area in West Africa where it is less than 45 per cent. Lowest of all the world are the Australian aborigines, with frequencies of M generally below 30 per cent. We noted that North American Indians and native Australians seemed quite similar in the A–B–O system, both lacking B and having varying amounts of A and O. In the M–N system they stand poles apart, at the extremes of human variation. This reminds us again that there are far too many kinds of people in the world for them to be "sorted out" by any one trait. Recently it has been found that another pair of alleles, called S and s, are so closely linked to M and N that they can be considered part of the same system. When these genes are better known in terms of world distribution, they will add further to our knowledge of the M–N locus.

Another extensively studied blood-group system is Rh. At first Rh seemed very simple: there was an Rh-positive and an Rh-negative allele, and the reactions between their phenotypes produced the well-known and rather serious complications of pregnancy we have already described. Further study has shown that the Rh system is more complicated than this. The Rh locus appears to consist of at least three positions very close together on the chromosome, so that they rarely become separated by crossing-over. The result is the existence of eight "complex genes," which are the various combinations of three "positive" and three "negative" alleles. The three closely linked loci have been designated, C, D, and E. Each locus has two alternatives: C or c; D or d; and E or e. The combinations, which as we have said are so closely linked as to be for all purposes permanent, are CDE, CDe, CdE, cDE, Cde, cDe, cdE, and cde. (Incidentally, the original Rh-positive element of clinical importance is D.) Obviously, testing for all the alleles involved is complex. The greatest difficulty lies in the fact that testing for the various antigens present does not tell us the linked combinations the individual has in his two chromosomes. The sum of a *CDE* combination and a *cde* combination cannot be distinguished from the sum of a *CdE* linkage group and a *cDe*. Both give an antigenic formula CcDdEe which, because of dominance, tests simply CDE. What is actually present in an individual's chromosomes must be inferred from the study of other members of his family. The procedures for estimating the frequency of the gene combinations in populations are also complex and involve multiple calculations based, if possible, on large samples of each population.

The world distribution of the various Rh combinations involving C–c, D–d and E–e alleles becomes complicated, even though four of the possible eight combinations are quite rare (see Figure 42). Incidentally, the stability of the linkage groups is shown by the fact that most of the d alleles in the world are in the combination cde, even though many of the chromosomes containing this combination are in populations in which the C and E alleles are quite common, and would have become recombined with d if crossing-over occurred often. World-wide, the most common of the Rh variants is CDe, with frequencies clustering around 50 per cent in European populations, and running somewhat higher—up to 75 and 80 per cent in Asia and Melanesia. In the New World it is usually less than 50 per cent but is still considerable. Only in Africa is this variant rare, with frequencies 10 per cent or less. The typically African Rh combination is cDe, which varies from 60 to 90 per cent among various populations south of the Sahara. The next most common of the chromosomal combinations is cDE, which shows the highest frequencies, running up to slightly over 50 per cent, in certain American Indians. Other world frequencies are 20 per cent or less; in general, higher in Australia and Asia, lower in Europe, and lowest in Africa. The three we have just discussed, cDe, cdE, and cDE, are the principal "Rh-positive" combinations, because D is the allele involved in the clinical Rh effects. The fourth Rh-positive, CDE, is exceedingly rare, with a world maximum of 4 per cent in North America.

The Rh-negative are all those combinations that contain d instead of D. By far the most common of these is cde, which ranges from about 20 to 50 per cent in Europeans, up to 20 per cent in some Africans, and up to 10 per cent in some American Indians. It is virtually absent elsewhere. The combination Cde has been found in up to 13 per cent in Australia, 7 per cent in South Africa, and is very rare or absent elsewhere. The other Rh-negatives are the rarest of all: cdE in a small fraction of some American Indians; CdE in only a handful of people anywhere in the world.

All populations of the world are polymorphic for the Rh system; that is, they have more than one of the eight possible combinations. Most have 15 per cent or more of at least two, which will produce a minimum of about 30 per cent heterozygous individuals. The near-

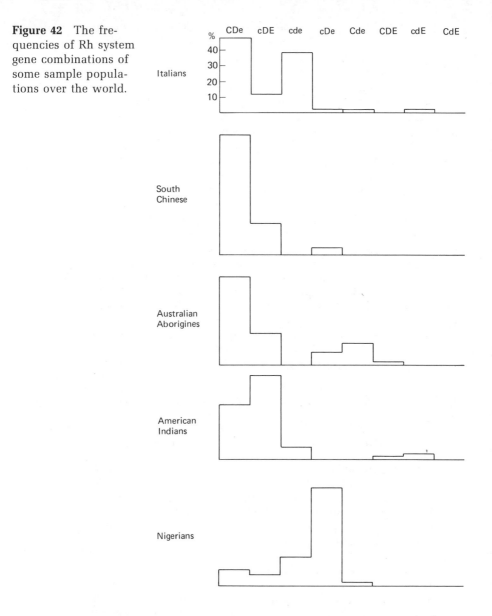

Figure 42 The frequencies of Rh system gene combinations of some sample populations over the world.

est approach to uniformity is among the African Bushmen who are about 90 per cent cDe, and among some Melanesians, who are 80 per cent CDe. Significantly, these are both groups in which genetic drift may have reduced variation. Most populations, however, are considerably more polymorphic than this, and most of the Rh combinations are found at least occasionally in many parts of the world. Consequently, the knowledge of an individual's Rh type does not usually tell us with any certainty what population he comes from, though the statistics of Rh frequencies for an adequate sample may identify the racial affinities of a *population* fairly well. Figure 42 shows some of the characteristic patterns of Rh frequency that have been found in racially different parts of the world.

The three blood-group systems just described are the ones now best known. For medical reasons, A–B–O and Rh blood typing will continue to be done on innumerable individuals. Some other blood groups are of minor clinical importance. But in addition there are many blood-group genes that are of anthropological interest simply because they occur with different frequency in different populations. Some are found in limited areas and therefore do not give us much information about the genetic relationships of various peoples. A typical example is *Diego,* named after the family in which it was first found. The rarer, dominant, allele at this locus is found in about 40 per cent of certain South American Indian tribes. It occurs in smaller amounts in some Central and North American populations, and is present also in small amounts in Koreans and Japanese. The discontinuous distribution suggests that the mutation may have occurred twice, in Asia and in the New World. Such variants will continue to be discovered and will contribute to our knowledge of the genetic relationships of human populations. But if this is not to turn into a catalogue of blood groups in man, we must stop. The general problems of how these polymorphisms have come about, and why they have persisted, can be discussed in terms of these three major blood-group systems.

BLOOD GROUPS AND SELECTION

It is interesting that polymorphism in all three blood-group systems occurs in primates other than man. The substances are not absolutely the same, nor are they always present in the blood cells. But A and B antigens are found in recognizable form in the tissues of the great apes, as are substances very like human M and N, and at least two of the Rh variants (Wiener and Gordon, 1960; Moor-Jankowski, et.al., 1964). Strangely, O, the most common of the A–B–O alleles in man, is found among apes only in the chimpanzee, at a frequency of about 15 per cent. It appears that these polymorphisms are in fact older than man himself or other modern species, and go back at least to the time when there were common ancestors for all the higher primates. The explanation of this situation is not made any easier by our knowledge that, in both the A–B–O and Rh systems, a difference in blood-group phenotype between mother and child may result in the child's death as a fetus or newborn. The incompatibility situations that have these disastrous results involve a mother of recessive phenotype and an offspring of dominant phenotype. The *genotype* of the affected child will always be heterozygous, because he must have received a recessive gene from the mother in addition to a dominant one from the father. Incompatibility is thus the enemy of heterozygotes: only these genotypes are at risk. This can have very interesting consequences. No problems arise, of course, in a population that is not polymorphic for these alleles. In the case of the Rh system, a relatively high incidence of the recessive element d must be present before incompatibility becomes at all frequent. And the incompatibility effect itself will tend to *eliminate* polymorphism in time. According to the Hardy-Weinberg law, gene frequencies go on forever the same, unless something intervenes. The disturbing factor may be mutation, aberration as the result of chance factors, or selection disadvantaging one or more genotypes. In the case of incompatibility effects, the disadvantage seems to be rather impartial: one each of two alleles is lost simultaneously every time a heterozygous fetus or newborn perishes. But suppose we have a population with 80 per cent Rh-positive and 20 per cent Rh-negative (for this purpose we need consider only the D element of the Rh combination). Removing alleles in pairs, one positive and one negative, every once in a while, may be impartial in a sense, but it obviously will affect the less common gene more seriously in proportion to its numbers. Eventually d will be eliminated entirely by this process of "impartial" attrition, leaving D as the sole survivor. Because this happens over a number of generations, the lost offspring will have been replaced, and the population will continue to thrive—no longer polymorphic and having no further problems with incompatibility.

If the population had been predominantly Rh-negative to start with, D would have been eliminated instead of d. A polymorphism that produces incompatibility effects is therefore inherently unstable, and always tends toward the elimination of the rarer gene. We would not expect such a polymorphism to last for very long, certainly not since the early days of primate evolution; neither would we expect it to be a common condition existing in many populations at the present time.

Another question: how can a population *become* polymorphic in the first place if polymorphism causes incompatibility? It is at best a slow process for a new allele to establish itself in substantial numbers in a population, unless it has positive selection going for it; it is impossible when the allele is automatically selected out simply because of its minority status. In the case of Rh, this would be equally true for d introduced by mutation or gene flow into an Rh-positive population, or for D introduced into an Rh-negative population. In either instance the attainment of a condition in which both alleles were present in substantial numbers would be a case of "you can't get there from here." It is often suggested that polymorphism in such a situation is the result of a relatively recent meeting and mixture of two races, one of which was all Rh-positive and one all Rh-negative. But this merely pushes the problem further into the past. In order to give rise to two such races, the species must have previously been polymorphic; or else one race must have changed at some time in the past—in the way we have shown to be so unlikely. (It might be noted again that the creation of *ad hoc* races to explain all the polymorphisms of man soon adds up to more "races" than there are places to put them.)

In Chapter 4 we discussed heterosis, and the way in which selective advantage of heterozygous individuals can effectively maintain a stable polymorphism in spite of various temporary conditions in which one allele is reduced in frequency. The effect of incompatibility in systems such as Rh and A–B–O is just the reverse of this: a mathematical simulation shows that the gene frequency changes brought about by incompatibility compare with those produced by heterosis in a way resembling a film run backwards—gene frequencies are seen to flee polymorphism instead of seeking it (compare Figure 20, p. 72). A possible explanation of the persistence of the polymorphic condition in the blood-group systems is that, in addition to the incompatibility effects, there are physiological advantages to the heterozygous genotypes, which are sufficient to counteract incompatibility with a slightly stronger heterosis. This appears to be the most likely explanation of the way in which polymorphism has developed and been maintained in the blood-group systems. By assuming heterozygote advantage for the A–B–O system, with relative disadvantage of the AA and BB homozygotes particularly, in addition to incompatibility effects, it is even possible to account for limitation of world variation in blood-group frequencies, i.e., the lack of populations with the sum of A and B genes greater than 60 per cent (Brues, 1954, 1963).

Various speculations and investigations have centered on possible correlations of the alleles of the A–B–O system with traits of known selective importance. The almost universal practise of noting blood groups on hospital records has made it possible to relate blood group to the incidence of certain diseases (Buckwalter, 1957). Among the relations that have stood the test of repeated studies in different populations are a higher incidence of stomach cancer and pernicious anemia in persons of blood group A; and a higher incidence of gastric and duodenal ulcer in those of group O. These relations are difficult to interpret in anthropological terms. They could account for regional differences in blood-group frequencies only if the external precipitating causes that make such genetic predispositions hazardous were of varying degrees of importance in different areas and situations. It must also be remembered that the selective effect of any of these diseases will vary with the usual age of incidence—whether or not they cause deaths which cut short the active reproductive period.

It has been suggested that the A–B–O blood-group system is related to susceptibility to smallpox and plague. These two diseases have certainly been of high selective importance at various times in human history, killing many individuals of all ages. There is some clinical evidence that individuals of blood group A are more likely to contract smallpox and suffer more severely from it (Vogel, 1965, 1966). Similarly, blood group O has been thought to predispose individuals to infection with the bacillus of bubonic plague (Otten, 1967). Recently it has been shown that individuals of blood type O are more attractive to mosquitoes and are more frequently bitten than A or B individuals (Wood et al., 1972). The significance of this or other biochemical variants as insect attractants or repellents may be very important, because many diseases—malaria, typhus, yellow fever, plague, to name only a few—are transmitted by the bites of various insects. Another suggestion has been made: that blood groups are correlated with adaptability to different diets; particularly, that the B allele is associated with the ability to thrive on the high-carbohydrate intake resulting from the introduction of agriculture. (Kelso and Armelagus, 1963). A constant difficulty in evaluating the selective effects of the blood-group alleles is that all our statistics are based on phenotype, and combine OA with AA, and OB with BB. If the most significant selective differences are those between homozygotes and heterozygotes, this may entirely conceal the true selective effects.

Population differences in readily diagnosed and widely studied traits have been used in various ways to estimate genetic relationships between populations. A rather ambitious attempt is shown in Figure 43, which depicts the apparent degree of genetic relationship between fifteen populations chosen so as to represent the entire world, as based on the three major blood-group systems we have discussed, plus Diego and one other locus (Cavalli-Sforza and Edwards, 1963). Analysis of this kind assumes that the ancestors of the various groups separated at specific times in the past and had no further contact with one another, and that genetic differentiation is

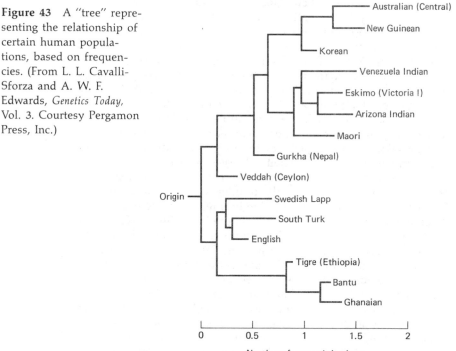

Figure 43 A "tree" representing the relationship of certain human populations, based on frequencies. (From L. L. Cavalli-Sforza and A. W. F. Edwards, *Genetics Today*, Vol. 3. Courtesy Pergamon Press, Inc.)

the result of genetic drift occurring after these separations. Such an analysis has been widely used to evaluate the phylogenetic relations of species, genera, and larger classes of organisms. In the case of a single interbreeding species, there are some complications, because the genetic isolation of its various units is reversible. A separation of populations a long time ago, followed by a later meeting and gene flow, may produce the same results as a single, more recent, separation. Furthermore, if selection is acting on any of the genetic loci used for the analysis, the effects of different environments may mimic the effect of a long separation; whereas residence under similar conditions may retard the development of genetic differences and make the time of separation appear to have been relatively short. The idea, once widely held, that the blood groups are not subject to selection, has become so suspect that we should build theories on it only with great caution.

OTHER BIOCHEMICAL TRAITS

Though blood groups are the best known of biochemical polymorphisms, there are many others. In fact all genetic traits have a biochemical basis, though we are inclined to think of as "biochemical" only those traits having no other correlated effect of which we are aware. Variation in hemoglobins, for instance, which we discussed as related to susceptibility to malaria, could be discussed as biochemistry; so could the basis of variation in pigmentation. But there are other traits that seem to be purely biochemical. Certain protein components of the blood serum, the haptoglobins and transferrins, are individually variable in ways that are genetically determined, and their variants are differently distributed among racial groups. There are also variants of the proteins that act as enzymes, many of which are compatible with healthy existence though they may differ in minor aspects of their function. Other enzyme variants cannot perform the function of the normal substance and are the cause of genetic diseases which, while they may differ in frequency among between different populations, tend to be rare and are therefore not usually of interest to the anthropologist. One substance secreted in the urine in quite different amounts by different individuals has been studied both in families and in population groups. Individuals with a high excretion rate of this substance, called BAIB, are rare in American Caucasians; but they are a majority in some American Indian populations, and in Micronesians, the figure is almost 90 per cent (Blumberg, 1961; Barnicot, 1964). This excretion is probably secondary to a difference in enzyme activity. Interesting indirect evidence of biochemical variation is seen in the ability of animals with a well-developed sense of smell to distinguish individual humans, or even objects they have touched, by odor differences. Man, with a sense of smell exceedingly underdeveloped as compared with other mammals, is quite unable to do this. We employ complicated laboratory techniques and expensive apparatus, in projects sometimes supported by large grants of money, to detect biochemical differences that a dog could sense from a single sniff of air. The subtle differences of scent which the dog, particularly the trained tracking hound, can recognize, like the unidentified genetic differences that threaten the survival of an organ transplant, are indications that our studies so far have only scratched the surface of a great lode of biochemical differences between the members of our species.

It will be interesting to see how these differences are distributed between individual variation and inequalities of racial occurrence. A number of normally successful heart transplants have been between individuals of different racial extraction. Apparently the individual biochemical differences that lead to transplant failure are so numerous that a racial difference adds little or nothing to the possibility of failure.

12

The Nervous System and Behavior

THE SENSE ORGANS

Travelers to remote parts of the world have often told anecdotes attesting to the miraculously sharp eyesight of native peoples. Whether the tales are true is hard to evaluate, but most of them can probably be explained in other ways. In a real-life situation—as opposed to the optometrist's office—it is almost impossible to separate pure *seeing* from interpretation. The native hunter who tracks game by nearly imperceptible signs has learned to do so by lifelong, intensely motivated observation. Such skills are acquired, and reside not in the eye but in the brain. The normal visual acuity, called 20/20 (which means simply, seeing at a distance of 20 feet what you are supposed to see at a distance of 20 feet) is close to the maximum resolving capacity of the human eye as determined by its physical components. It is true, however, that the various deficiencies of vision for which so many civilized people wear glasses are rarer in people who are, or have been until recently, living closer to nature and often dependent on hunting for a major part of their subsistence. Reliable data are not available for most populations of primitive culture. However, we can make an indirect comparison from visual tests given to men drafted for the United States Army, including large samples of both Caucasians and Negroes (Karpinos, 1960). Though the ancestors of both groups have known agriculture for many centuries, its impact on environment and subsistence has been less in Africa. Temperate zone soils generally hold their fertility well, so that large areas can be cleared and kept under more or less continuous cultivation: a pattern that has been apparent in Europe for many centuries. Tropical soils, in contrast, deteriorate rapidly under cultivation, and as a result the land use pattern consists of clearing small plots, cultivation of them for a few years, and abandonment of them as fertility fails. Thus the tropical settlement in rain forest areas remains surrounded by much natural or regenerating forest which provides wildlife habitat. In addition, many of the cultivated crops of tropical areas are seriously deficient in protein, making the proceeds of hunting more important to nutrition. Perhaps also the greater abundance of poisonous snakes in tropical areas has been a substantial hazard to persons with less than perfect eyesight. The United States data show that the percentage of Negroes with less than 20/20 vision, and particularly the percentage with visual defects sufficient to require correction with glasses, is significantly less than is found in whites of the same age group. Since there is a considerable proportion of white ancestry in the American Negro, any genetic factors involved have been somewhat diluted, and the difference is, if anything, less than would be found if a *pure* Negro group had been studied. The difference is in the direction we would expect to find if natural selection were acting, with different degrees of rigorousness, in different environments. Any environmental or cultural change that makes errors of vision more tolerable will produce *relaxed selection;* that is, a situation in which mutations which produce visual defects will have a greater chance of genetic survival. It is interesting that even now the commonest visual problem for which glasses are worn is *presbyopia,* an impairment of near vision with advancing age, which does not affect vision of distant objects. This would not be a serious problem in a hunting culture. Thus the species has been able to tolerate this as a universal age change.

One easily recognized visual defect is *myopia* or nearsightedness. The myopic individual has difficulty recognizing objects at a distance because he cannot focus clearly on them. Many cases of myopia have been studied in family pedigrees and shown to be inherited: more than one genetic locus carries mutations for this condition (McKusick, 1968). Myopia is rare among North American Indians, Australian aborigines, and African Negroes, and commoner among Europeans and Asians. This is in accord with the supposition that it is selected against where hunting still contributes significantly to subsistence, and has increased where this selection is relaxed. Comparative data have confirmed the popular observation that it is commoner among Asian Mongoloids than among Europeans (Mann, 1966). Myopia, unlike some other visual defects, has compensations. The nearsighted individual, because of his ability to focus very close to the eye, can see small details that an individual with normal vision cannot see without a magnifying glass. In fact, when the myopic person wishes to examine objects closely he *removes* his corrective glasses. Before lenses came into general use, this ability was a matter of some awe, and the myopic individual was spoken of as having "strong eyes." An increasing incidence of myopia, appearing under civilized conditions, may not be merely the result of relaxation of selection against it. There may have been some favorable selection because of the advantage of the "strong-eyed" individual in certain occupations. Was the development of intricate craftsmanship and a finely detailed writing system in China the cause or the result of a high frequency of myopia? This would be a hard question to answer. In any case, the present-day availability of magnifying lenses has deprived the myopic individual of his one-time monopoly on the ability to see very fine detail.

Color-blindness is another visual anomaly that has apparently increased under conditions of civilization. There are several varieties of color-blindness, but all seem to be recessive sex-linked traits which appear almost exclusively in males. The seriousness of the handicap of a color-blind person is arguable. Some people may compensate very well for the defect; some may be unaware of it for a long time; and sometimes it is hard to convince someone who is color-blind that he sees things differently from anyone else. Most nonhuman mammals, including hunting carnivores, are color-blind. The case for disadvantage of the color blind person, and natural selection against the genes that cause it, is therefore not so clear as in the case of myopia. However, the differences in occurrence are generally parallel. Color-blindness is most common (about 8 per cent of males) in northwestern Europe and in India, is nearly as common in China, and is rare in most other parts of the world (Barnicot, 1964; Mann, 1966). Perhaps it is less a defect than myopia, but is more rigorously selected against in hunting cultures because of its preponderant occurrence in males.

Some data are available on differences in hearing between different populations. Hearing is slowly damaged by environmental noise, therefore we would expect individuals in uncivilized surroundings to retain hearing to a greater degree with advancing age. One study on an African population still living under natural conditions has confirmed this expectation. The Africans had better hearing than Americans, the greatest differences being in the older groups, and for sensitivity to higher tones (Post, 1964). This suggests that the "normal age changes" of hearing in a civilized community are mainly the result of environmental damage. However, another study of differences between white and Negro populations shows that even within the United States, regardless of rural or urban residence, the age-related hearing loss for high tones is less in Negroes (Roberts and Bayliss, 1967). Thus there appears to be a genetic difference between the races in susceptibility to hearing loss, which, as in the case of visual defects, may be attributable to a relaxation of selection for sensory acuity under conditions of civilization.

Taste and smell have not been much studied even in terms of individual variation. The only taste ability that has been widely investigated is sensitivity to a substance called *phenylthiocarbamide,* mercifully abbreviated to PTC. This tastes intensely bitter to some individuals and is quite tasteless to others; a few individuals are ambivalent about it. The fairly clear distinction between "taster" and "nontaster" has made it possible to classify tasting as a dominant trait. The recessive nontaster condition is very common in northwestern Europe, about 35 per cent, indicating a frequency of the recessive allele of 60 per cent. It is fairly frequent in other parts of Europe and Asia, and in India, and crops up in some other populations—among Eskimos and in natives of Melanesia and Australia (Ashley Montagu, 1960). The rest of the world has little or none of the nontaster phenotype. The trait may have some relation to goiter; both PTC and some naturally occurring substances related to it seem to aggravate the disease. Thus, for populations who may encounter these substances, it may be an advantage to find them distasteful. One racial difference in sensitivity to odors has been reported. Some African populations seem to be deficient in the ability to smell *hydrocyanic acid,* a highly poisonous substance found in certain plants (Allison, 1953). Many animals appear to avoid poisonous substances in their environment, presumably guided by taste and smell; natural selection would act quite powerfully to maintain an aversion to dangerous substances that a population might encounter in its natural environment. Man, for the most part, must be taught to avoid toxic materials; young children will eat or drink almost anything, often with tragic results. But some of man's perceptions of bad taste or bad smell may have developed by natural selection as protective mechanisms against toxic substances in the environment.

BEHAVIOR DIFFERENCES

Less easy to study than the sense organs is the apparatus that interprets sensation and proceeds from perception to action. Here we enter a field that is not only difficult to study, but exceedingly controversial from the point of view of both genetics and anthropology. Early contacts between different races often appear to have aroused more wonder and amazement about different ways of life than about differences in physical appearance. For practical purposes it makes little difference whether we merely observe that an individual *acts* differently from ourselves, or conclude that he *is* different. An uncritical observation of the coincidence of physical and cultural differences leads to the natural, but naïve, judgment that both are the result of innate genetic qualities that will cause the same people to continue to behave differently in the future. This feeling that people are different *by nature,* in ways that affect their behavior, is a part of many beliefs about race. Now, we have said at length that there are genetic differences among populations (though they have to be carefully defined), but that anything that is not heritable cannot be truly *racial.* Is there, in fact, anything heritable about differences in behavior in man? This is not an easy question to answer, even when it is asked about individual differences within a single population; and it becomes inordinately difficult when one compares different populations.

In the past, judgments on these matters were made with cheerful abandon. The literature of European explorations of the world since 1500 is full of comments expressing respect or disdain for native populations, often based on their technology and economic development. Cities and great markets made favorable impressions on earlier travelers, from Marco Polo in China to Cortez in Mexico. Even the simpler cultures did not look bad to Europeans at that time. After all, prior to 1800, firearms were only questionably better than a good bow and arrow in skilled hands; industrial development in Europe was in its infancy, and was not very meaningful to the explorer on his sailing ship; and sanitation as we know it was nonexistent even for the best families. In this period Europeans did not find it difficult to perceive intelligence and good character in people of simple culture. But during the last two centuries there has been an increasing tendency to judge native peoples unfavorably, on the basis of their technology, which lagged far behind during this period of accelerated technological advances in Europe. It was easy to attribute the difference to innate faults of intelligence or character. The initial expectation, that these people would adopt European culture immediately and completely, was disappointed in most cases. And it was felt as an affront that imitation, that sincerest form of flattery, was not forthcoming. To many this appeared to indicate that the native mind was obtuse. Of course, when people from different cultures first encounter one another, whether one or both cultures are simple or complex, adverse moral judgements are made. Even the most broad-minded modern anthropologist is likely to look less than favorably on, for instance, human sacrifice. And at one time some of the most worthy and moral of peoples were viewed with shuddering disapproval because of the nineteenth-century European's abhorrence of nakedness. The judgments that were made, translating characteristics of cultures into terms of personal quality, ranged from stupidity and laziness through licentiousness and cruelty. The opinions of the natives about their European visitors are not recorded, but they were no doubt equally devastating. Even the languages of newly encountered peoples were downgraded, on the grounds that they were simple and lacked abstractions. Later study has shown that many of these languages are complicated, and sometimes inordinately difficult to learn. It was only the version used when talking to ignorant strangers that was simple!

It is not surprising that there has been a reaction against this rather free tossing around of derogatory comments. Cultural anthropologists of more recent years have adhered to a "doctrine of psychic unity," which assumes that psychological differences between different populations do not exist, or at least that they should not be invoked to explain differences in culture. The recent explanation of cultural differences has accordingly been limited to history, environment, and chance. There is at present considerable opposition to even admitting that there are genetic factors involved in psychological differences between individuals within a single population. This opposition has several roots. Part of it is a survival of the theological dualism of body and soul, which has been understood by many in modern times as meaning independence of body and mind—though *mind* and *soul* are not exactly synonymous. Thus, though most people will concede that the body is subject to genetic variation, that the brain is part of the body, and that the mind is a function of the brain, many are reluctant to admit the implication that mental functions may be subject to genetic variation. This creates a paradox in evolutionary theory. We have pointed out that natural selection cannot operate on any trait that is not subject to heritable individual variation. The most striking feature of the evolution of man is a progressive increase in the size of the brain, which now surpasses that of any other animal of the same body size. We explain this by assuming that during human evolution the most important survival factor for this creature, relatively weak in bodily defenses, was complex behavior mediated by a large brain. If complexity of behavior is not at all related to brain size, then the anatomical changes of evolution are not explained. But more importantly, if complexity of behavior has not been both heritable and subject to individual variation during the evolution of man, there is no explanation (except a supernatural one) for the progressive change that has made man behaviorally complex beyond all other species.

If we believe that there is no longer any heritable variation in man's behavioral complexity, we are assuming that the polymorphism that once existed has been used up by selection, and that modern man is therefore incapable of changing, either for better or for worse, in his most important characteristic, until further mutations occur. This would be a situation so different from the polymorphism we see in other human traits as to be somewhat implausible. But the reasons for this point of view include some that are political or ideological, and some even religious in tone—and they are strongly felt. Differences in mental potentiality are thought to be contradictory to the assertion that "all men are equal," or to be inconsistent with a benign concept of the universe. To some, the denial of individual behavioral differences seems essential, regardless of evidence pro or con, as a first line of defense against any assertion of racial differences. A common argument against the existence of genetic factors that influence human behavior is that "all human behavior is learned." But of course, in order to be human and learn a human culture one has to have a human father and a human mother from whom to inherit the human *ability* to learn. We sometimes forget that the most basic part of our inheritance is that which makes us a member of our species. However, given the fact that it is a distinguishing feature of the human species to have a phenomenal ability to modify behavior by learning, one may still ask: Are there genetic differences that make it possible for some individuals to learn more readily than others, or to learn *certain kinds* of things more readily than others learn them? We refer to individual differences of this kind by the terms *intelligence, aptitude, talent,* and so forth. Whether these differences are inherited or are determined solely by chance and instruction is an absorbing question. To understand the question—let alone answer it—we must look critically at the anatomical basis for behavior, which is the central nervous system, primarily the brain. It is here that we expect to find the bodily substrate of behavior, not only for the features shared by all members of the species, but for those features which are individually distinctive.

BRAIN SIZE AND STRUCTURE

Ever since it was understood that the brain was the part of the body in which the functions of thought and memory were located, there has been interest in the possible relation of characteristics of the brain to individual differences in intellectual performance. Before much was known about the internal structure of the brain, this interest focused on the most obvious attribute of a brain, its size. It was rather fashionable at one time to remove and measure the brains of deceased notables, and there are numerous miscellaneous records of this kind from the nineteenth century. This information is quite worthless. The brain is a watery organ, and both its weight and its volume are affected by age and health conditions, as well as by the action of any preservatives that may have been applied to it after death. The best measure of the size of an individual's brain is an indirect one; the volume of the interior of the cranial cavity. This space does not contain much except the brain itself; there are some thin covering membranes, blood vessels, and a little free fluid, none of which contributes much to the total volume of the cranial contents. Because the skull is not subject to shrinkage either before or after death, its capacity reflects quite accurately the size of the living brain. By taking advantage of this fact, brain size can be closely estimated for those individuals, recent, prehistoric, or even fossil, whose skulls have come to rest in anthropological collections. Even measurements of the outside of the skull correlate fairly well with the volume of the interior, though skull thickness and shape characteristics may cause some discrepancies. Measurements of the outside of the head may also be used for an approximate estimation of the brain size—the only method applicable to living individuals.

In any case, size alone is a rather crude measure of a structure as complex as the brain. Part of the brain consists of more or less direct connections to sense organs and to the muscles of the body, and this portion is larger or smaller depending simply on body size. A tremendous amount of study and speculation has been stimulated by the problem of how to interpret the brain size of animals and men, both fossil and modern (Von Bonin, 1937). It seems clear, on the basis of data from modern animals of various degrees of behavioral complexity, that one component of total brain size is involved in the elementary activities of monitoring sensations and operating the muscular system, and that another component is greater or less according to the "intelligence" of the animal. Complicated formulae have been devised for estimating how much of an animal's brain represents the minimum necessary for a given body size, and how much of it is "extra," available for the organizational functions we call intelligence (Jerison, 1963.) Comparison of related species of animals has also shown that brain size tends to be larger in long-lived animals of any given body size. This suggests that some of the "extra" is devoted to memory, for which a short-lived animal obviously has less need (Brues and Sacher, 1965). In living species the internal structure of the brain also tells us something about the division of these various functions. Part of the brain consists of simple conducting fibers, connecting brain and body or various parts of the brain and serving as a means of communication between them. Other portions—the so called gray matter—contain cells which serve the functions of organization and decision. The most significant mass of gray matter in the brain is the cerebral cortex, a layer about one-eighth of an inch thick covering the two major hemispheres of the brain. This is the place where sensory information is consciously organized and integrated with memory, and where the initiation of voluntary activity takes place. In animals with large brains, the cortex is thrown into folds; in man these are separated by grooves about one-half inch apart and of varying depth. This folding, which increases the area of the cortex considerably, takes place during the rapid growth of the brain in the last three months of fetal life. The pattern formed has some constant features but is highly individualistic in detail. Different portions of the cerebral cortex are involved in specific elements of mental function, none of which turns out to be comparable to the virtues and vices that phrenology described (Figure 44).

Most of our knowledge about these relationships has been derived from clinical cases in which the specific mental or behavioral problems of persons with brain injuries have been correlated with the exact location and nature of the injury as verified by postmortem examination. Thus we know that certain parts of the cortex

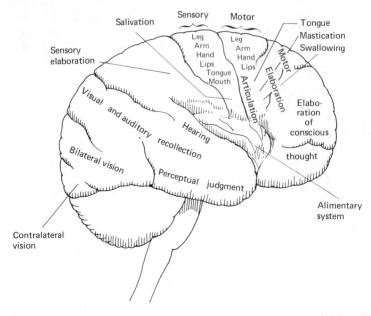

Figure 44 Functional areas of the cerebral cortex. (W. Penfield and T. Rasmussen, *The Cerebral Cortex of Man.* Courtesy of Macmillan Publishing Co., Inc.)

deal with information coming in via various senses; sight and hearing, for instance, are represented quite far apart in the cerebral cortex. Other areas are involved with the organization of sensory information in general. Still others deal with the initiation of activity and various forms of control of activity, ranging from the simplest momentary responses to the most involved social behavior. At one time it was customary to designate a single area for the uniquely human function of speech. There is an area of the cortex that controls the specific muscular movements involved in speaking, and it lies close to the areas controlling other actions of the head and face. However, the understanding of spoken words is localized in a portion of the area for hearing, the understanding of written words in a portion of the area for vision, and the complete speech function involves interconnections between these as well as some other parts of the brain (Luria, 1966).

The functional specialization of the cortex is reflected in differences in its microscopic structure. All parts of the cortex have a layered structure containing nerve cells and conducting fibers of various sizes, which can be seen in properly prepared microscopic sections. The thickness and arrangement of the various layers, and the types of cells found in them, vary according to the specific functions of the parts of the cortex, the most complex microscopic structure being in the portions concerned with vision. Most of these specialized areas, incidentally, are not indicated by any surface markings on the brain. Unfortunately, the tedious nature of this kind of microscopic study of the brain has limited it so far to study of the basic patterns of human brains in general. There are undoubtedly individual differences in the amounts of various types of cortical structure, which may some day tell us something about individual differences in aptitude and personality.

Comparison of individuals and populations has been largely limited to the simplest measure of the brain—its size—as determined from cranial-capacity measurements of museum specimens. Unfortunately the technique of measurement is subject to some error, which introduces doubt into comparisons. A very general average cranial capacity for "modern man," which is generally cited for comparison with fossil forms, is 1,400 to 1,500 cubic centimeters, corresponding to a brain weight of three pounds or a little more. There is much individual variation, with differences as much as 900 cubic centimeters between individuals of the same sex in the same population. In most cases not more than a third of the individuals in a single population would have cranial capacities more than 100 cc. above or below the average (Hooton, 1930). It is apparent that between one human and another, as between different species of animal, the size of the brain correlates with the size of the body (Von Bonin, 1937). In most populations the average cranial capacity for females is about 150 cubic centimeters less than for males, a difference comparable to the difference in body weight, though not as marked. The comparison between different populations and races is made difficult by the fact that although we have data on cranial capacity for "dead" populations, accurate information on body size is available only on living populations—who may or not be similar to them. Some of this comparative data was once welcomed by Europeans, especially the data indicating that northwestern Europeans had the largest brains in the world; of course, as we have seen, they also have larger bodies than almost anyone else. Cranial-capacity averages for various populations show that there are considerable differences *within* major races. This is similar to the variation in stature we find within these major groups, and is probably in large measure because of it. In Europe there are some populations with cranial capacities (for males) at or near the 1,500 cubic centimeter mark, as well as others averaging 10 per cent or more short of this. This is equally true for black Africa, Polynesia, and North America, where there are also some large people as well as smaller ones. It appears that wherever male stature is 5 foot 8 or over, cranial capacities approach 1,500 cubic centimeters. Populations that are generally shorter and lighter in weight have smaller average capacities, with the exception of some Asiatic Mongoloids and Eskimos, who have near-maximum cranial capacities in spite of small body size (Martin and Saller, 1956).

The best check on racial differences comes from the United States, where skeletons of white and (mixed) Negro populations are available, and where body size differences are known to be small. A study in which all measurements of cranial capacity were done by the same hands (an important point) showed a difference between the races of about 3 per cent in favor of whites, considerably less than the sex difference (Simmons, 1942).

Attempts were made very early to find relationships between brain size and intellectual capacity. This work relied by necessity on external head measurements as an indication of brain size. An early study was made on a large sample of school children in England, where racial differences of even small degree are not a complication (Pearson, 1906). The correlation of head size and intelligence was very low (.1), too small to be of any practical predictive value. Other estimates of the correlation range up to .3 (Van Valen, 1974). Some studies have been made on the area or volume of the cerebral cortex, another likely possibility for correlation with brain function; but these studies have not been conclusive. It appears that if there is any simple anatomical clue to brain function, we have not found it yet.

Much attention has been given recently to the possible effects of nutrition on the development of the brain, and measurement of the head circumference has been used to evaluate undernutrition in children. Actually, in man as well as in other animals, the size of the brain is less affected by nutritional deficits than the size of other parts of the body (Widdowson, 1966). In undernourished experimental animals and human children, the brain maintains its growth relatively well, resulting in a head disproportionately large for the body and a brain–body weight ratio higher than normal. Of course this does not prove that there are not injurious effects on the brain, but it does make external head size appear to be a poor measure of them.

INTELLIGENCE, APTITUDE, AND PERSONALITY

Even though "all human behavior is learned," there appear to be differences among individuals that enable some to learn new kinds of behavior more easily than others; and learning some kinds of behavior seems to be easier for some individuals than others. (We are using the term *behavior* here in a very broad sense, including such activities as reading a book, solving a problem, or taking a test.) The ability to learn certain kinds of things more easily than others can learn them is called an aptitude: some kinds of aptitude are conventionally called talents or "gifts." Aptitudes may range from those that are distinctive of a species (as the power of speech is distinctive of the human species), to those that show great individual variation. There is no clear distinction, however; verbal ability, for instance, which is a matter of *degree* in the power of speech, is an individual variable that is often measured as an aptitude. The more general term, used for an ability to learn that seems to augment all or a number of specific aptitudes, is *intelligence*.

Aptitude and intelligence are not easy to define or to measure. Their manifestations are greatly affected by external influences—or at least should be, because the purpose of our educational institutions is to influence them. Thus, there is much controversy about the existence and importance of genetic factors in these abilities, as well as about whether they exhibit significant differences between populations.

One of the oldest and best known of aptitude tests is the Binet test and its family of descendants, from which the familiar "intelligence quotient" or I.Q. is derived. Undoubtedly, many people who are familiar with the abbreviation I.Q. do not know what the letters stand for. It is termed a *quotient* because it represents the ratio of an individual's score to the expected average of individuals of his own age. Indirectly, it can be applied to adults. It is typical of a class of tests that purports to give a single general rating of mental ability, by which each individual may be placed higher or lower along a single scale. It is well to look at the meaning of the term *intelligence* as it is used in a broader perspective, to compare one species of animal with another. A basic definition of intelligence would be "the ability to adapt to situations that are varied and changing, by a learning process involving the central nervous system." Actually, the Binet test was an adaptation of ordinary school tests, with changes designed to make it somewhat more general in its nature. Its present-day descendants still draw to a great extent on the mental skills that are developed, in various degrees, as part of the conventional educational process. It therefore tests a mixed batch of aptitudes indirectly, by measuring the individual's progress in their development under specific conditions. Two major questions arise. First, is there in fact a single variable—intelligence, learning ability, or adaptability, whatever we wish to call it—that is being measured, or are we simply compiling the sum of various abilities of a more specific nature in which individuals differ? The general measure of I.Q. may have a practical value, for instance in assigning students to graded classes, where it is important that the sum total of the demands made on an individual's abilities should not be more than he can cope with. In such a situation it is acceptable—in fact inevitable—that one individual may have more difficulty with one task, another with another; but the system works if all can cope with the total situation. Such a test may be thought of as measuring a general factor in intelligence, which is independent of and in addition to various special aptitudes. But psychologists still disagree on whether such a "general factor" really exists or is an illusion created by the testing process.

A second major question about I.Q. testing arises because of the assumption that the individuals graded have been under "similar conditions." To the extent that tests are the result of an interaction of ability and experience, they cannot measure ability in the abstract. If we make comparisons within a group of children who have been exposed to a very similar environment, we assume that the differences in their progress are largely determined by differences in individual aptitude. If children have attended the same schools for a number of years, a considerable part of their relevant experience is known to have been the same; if their home backgrounds are also essentially similar, their total environment is reasonably standardized. However, if the home backgrounds of the children tested differ greatly, their total experience is not the same. This is the universal weakness of all aptitude tests. No matter how ingeniously they are devised, their results are never entirely independent of environmental background, and to that degree do not accurately represent "native ability." The magnitude of the environmental effects are endlessly debatable and controversial.

In addition to tests that purport to measure general intelligence, many tests of special aptitudes have been devised. The general and the special tests may contain the same or similar items, variously combined or sorted out. Special tests endeavor to assemble items that are similar in some specific way: they have names such as Associative Memory, Perceptual Speed, Verbal Reasoning, Numerical Ability, Mechanical Reasoning, and so on (Vandenberg, 1967). If such a test is well-designed, the items assigned to a single test should tend to be successfully completed by the same individuals; indicating that all the items zero in on a single mental characteristic that is more strongly developed in some individuals than in others. A well designed set of special aptitude tests should show a high degree of independence of scores—meaning that a single individual will rate high in one test, low in another. This defines his individual strengths and weaknesses; the combination is sometimes called a *profile.*

Tests have also been devised for *personality variables*—the traits by which a person is characterized as introverted, intuitive, impulsive, and so forth. Some of these traits are in a border zone of the mind, where intellectual function becomes involved with emotional response. It is interesting that some personality variables can be detected in very young infants. Adaptability, attention span, persistence, and physical-activity level show individual differences in the first few months of life; and these can be traced, in changing manifestations, into later years (Birns, 1969; Thomas, 1970). One ambitious system for classifying personality was developed in connection with the somatotype system of classifying body build, which we discussed in Chapter 9. In this system personality, like body build, is evaluated in terms of three components rated on a 1 to 7 scale (Sheldon and Stevens, 1942). The first component, supposedly correlated with endomorphy, is *viscerotonia.* It connotes love of comfort, easy sociability, and a physical disposition the layman would call laziness. The second component, supposedly correlated with mesomorphy, is *somatotonia.* This connotes assertiveness and love of physical activity. The third component, supposedly correlated with ectomorphy, is *cerebrotonia.* This connotes introversion, irritability, and an interest in mental rather than physical activity. This system shares the difficulties of the system of classifying body build with which it was presented. The full variety of human personality cannot be described by three variables, even in infinite gradations of quantity, any more than body build can be described by three variables. Furthermore the supposed correlation of the attributes of temperament with the components of body build was based on extensive personal interviews during which the visible body shape was a constant background to the interviewer's evaluation of personality. There have also been objections to the assumption that physical and personality traits are correlated at all, because this implies genetic, or at least physical, determination of personality. However, the existence of genetic components in personality, as in any other set of traits, should be determined by objective study rather than by a general acceptance or nonacceptance of the importance of environment or of free will in determining human behavior.

THE HERITABILITY OF MENTAL TRAITS

All the tests we have described may be used in practical ways for the benefit of the individual as he exists right now. They may indicate that more educational effort should be expended to counteract a personal weakness in some important aptitude. In other cases, the tests may indicate that it is worthwhile to develop some strong individual aptitude that is of vocational value. Whether the individual's aptitudes and personality traits are in any way hereditary is a question quite independent of whether individual differences *exist* at any particular age. The question of heritability of intelligence or other mental traits is particularly difficult because of the known weakness of testing methods—that they measure achievement based on aptitude rather than aptitude itself. This is not a unique problem, because traits such as body size incorporate environmental as well as genetic effects. But it is particularly hard to isolate the effect of genetic factors in behavioral traits because nearly all children are raised by their own parents. Thus, the children who profit by the social and economic advantages their parents have been able to achieve are also the recipients of any genetic factors that facilitated this achievement. Furthermore, they profit from the attention and informal instruction of educated and perceptive adults, beginning at birth. To penetrate the confusing effect of environmental factors that may correlate with genetic advantage, special attention has been given to those comparatively few children who are raised by persons other than their natural parents. In a previous chapter we discussed the use of this method of genetic study, and some of its shortcomings. *Heritability*, the measure generally used for summarizing studies of this kind, measures the importance of genetic causes, as compared with *all* causes for the variation of a trait. The total variation of the trait will be the sum of the variation due to genetic, environmental, accidental, or unspeci-

fied causes and their various interactions. This method of calculation makes the genetic component appear more important when the
other factors, which are largely environmental, are less varied.

The most complete studies of the heritability of mental traits
have used the results of I.Q. tests, with all their faults, because these
tests are still the most widely used at the present time. To understand these studies we must bear in mind the amount of variation
that exists in a single population. Any such test must be standardized by trying it out on a large sample of individuals to find the
"normal" performance level of children of various ages. When this
has been done, a raw test grade can be converted into a "mental
age." The I.Q. is then derived by comparing the mental age of an
individual with his actual age: it represents his mental age taken as
a per cent of his chronological age. To take the simplest case, a
ten-year-old with a mental age of nine has an I.Q. of 90, one with a
mental age of eleven has an I.Q. of 110. The usual distribution of
grades is such that about 50 per cent of all children in a sample will
have I.Q.'s between 90 and 110, the rest being symmetrically distributed, one-fourth below 90 and one-fourth above 110. The distribution can be further defined: two-thirds fall between 85 and 115,
with one-sixth below 85 and another one-sixth above 115. For
ten-year-olds, this would mean one-sixth with a mental age below
eight and a half, and one-sixth with a mental age above eleven and a
half. The form of this distribution is similar to that we see in other
quantitative measures of populations, such as stature, as shown in
Figure 16, p. 42, and is typical of traits that are affected by a
number of independent causes.

A summary of some family data is given in Table 7. It is expressed in terms of the average amount of difference between the
two individuals of a pair whose genetic and environmental likeness
or difference is as described (Erlenmeyer and Jarvik, 1964). (If these
differences seem large in proportion to the variability of a whole
population, it is because the difference between two individuals is
often greater than the difference of either one from the average.)
Table 7 shows a number of interesting things. The first line represents the amount of difference we can expect to find between two
individuals who have nothing in common, either genetically or in
their environment, except that they are members of the same population living in the same community. The second line shows that the
average I.Q. difference is slightly less if two unrelated individuals
are raised in the same family, and are exposed to the same home
environment. The third and fourth lines give the I.Q. comparisons
of full brothers and sisters. Remember that full brothers and sisters
will, on the average, share half of their genes. Each drew two, at
random, from the four genes the parents had to offer at any particular genetic locus. Thus, they are more similar genetically than two
individuals drawn at random from the population. Their greater
likeness in I.Q. therefore reflects the effect of genetic factors. The
last two lines show the I.Q. differences of identical twins. They have
all genes in common and have the closest similarity of all in I.Q. In
the case of both ordinary brothers and sisters and identical twins,

TABLE 7	AVERAGE DIFFERENCES IN I.Q. SCORES BETWEEN RELATED AND UNRELATED INDIVIDUALS	
Unrelated persons raised in different families		17 points
Unrelated persons raised in the same family		15 points
Brothers or sisters raised in different families		13 points
Brothers or sisters raised in the same family		12 points
Identical twins raised in different families		8 points
Identical twins raised in the same family		6 points

Recalculated from data of Erlenmeier-Kimling and Jarvik, 1964. The correlation coefficients of the original paper have been converted into expected pair differences on the assumption that the standard deviations of all populations are approximately 15 units.

the similarity in I.Q. is somewhat greater if they are raised in the same family. But the effect of the home environment is less conspicuous than that of the genetic relation. One figure is particularly interesting: the 12-point average difference between one child and another of the same parents, even when they have been raised in the same home. This indicates the amount of variation in I.Q. that parents may expect to encounter within their own families. And at the end, we see a 6-point difference between identical twins, even when reared together. This is the minimum that remains when genetic make-up is the same and when the environment is the same—or as nearly the same as it can be. It represents the effects of chance, inaccuracies of the testing process, and various unidentifiable factors. The heritability of the I.Q. has been estimated from such data to be about .8. This means that within the populations studied, about 80 per cent of the factors that cause individuals to differ from one another in I.Q. are genetic, the remaining 20 per cent are environmental.

Like all heritability estimates, this one is specific for the populations studied. What it says, in fact, is that the genetic diversity of these populations, in whatever factors influence children's test scores, is considerably greater than the environmental diversity. The samples on which these studies are based are admittedly not random ones. Genetic studies of this kind require cooperation from the families concerned which tends to limit them to a segment of the total population that is moderately well-educated and of at least fair economic status. So the environmental backgrounds of the children tested do not differ in major ways. In most of these families the development of mental skills is valued, so the encouragement of this kind of activity in the children is early and consistent. Some studies of economically depressed families have shown lower heritability. It is unlikely that these different populations are more uniform genetically than the ones previously tested. Nongenetic factors may be more variable. For instance, attitudes toward education are less consistent, and the encouragement of reading and other extracurricular adjuncts to education is erratic and accidental. Certainly, if all social and economic classes of a complex society were equally represented in a research sample, the increase of environmental variation would have the effect of reducing the estimate of heritability, as obtained by the usual methods. It would not reduce or eliminate the obvious effects of genetic likeness or difference, as shown by the greater divergence in I.Q. of unrelated persons as compared with natural brothers or sisters, or of the latter as compared with identical twins, when all are raised in the same households. It would simply *increase* the differences that appear when they are raised separately.

The study of the inheritance of specific aptitudes is potentially more interesting than that of "general" factors, such as intelligence. Any trait containing more than one genetic component is discouraging for genetic analysis because the different components are independently inherited. Specific aptitudes may reveal more discrete and clear-cut heritabilities. Experiments on learning in various animals have tended to be concerned with specific problem-solving abilities rather than with "intelligence." It is a measure of the close ties between traditional intelligence-testing and education that we do not try to give I.Q. scores to animals. Because they do not go to school, we need no rating on a single quantitative scale in order to assign them to classrooms. In addition, the tests for special aptitudes—handling numbers, using words, and so forth—suggest a possible relation to the specialization of the cerebral cortex; and this may some day lead us to an understanding of the anatomical basis of mental abilities. Unfortunately, less work has been done so far on the inheritance of special aptitudes than on the inheritance of general intelligence. Of course, the same cautions hold: a special aptitude, just as much as a general one, cannot be tested in the abstract, though skillful test design may eliminate the more obvious practice effects. Furthermore, even if an aptitude is a consistent characteristic of an individual and meaningful for predicting vocational success, it may not be shared by persons related to him; that is to say, it may be a genuine *individual* variation, but not *hereditary*. Among the abilities that seem to be testable, reasonably independent of one another, and genetically determined to a significant degree, are those described as number and verbal abilities, visualization of space, and word fluency (Vandenberg, 1962, 1967, 1968a). These are the special abilities most closely alike in identical twins, even when they have been adopted into different families. Hopefully, in the near future we will begin to acquire a fuller understanding of the hereditary components of special abilities.

A negative aspect of aptitude difference is seen in *specific learning disabilities* (these are sometimes called *brain damage*, but this is a poor term because there is no evidence that anything originally present has been altered.) These are excessively low points in an individual's aptitude profile that interfere with his functioning in specific learning situations. The most researched of these disabilities is *dyslexia* or difficulty in reading (Klasen, 1972). This has attracted the most attention because it interferes with an activity deeply entrenched in conventional educational systems. There appears to be a definite genetic factor involved in dyslexia. Other individual problems, such as incorrigible misspelling in otherwise quite literate individuals, or tone-deafness, which makes a person unable to reproduce a tune, are less serious, but their explanations may be interesting. These problems may be associated with individual differences of an anatomical kind involving the cerebral hemispheres.

Our knowledge of the heritability of personality traits also suffers from restricted use of the tests—they are used almost entirely by research psychologists rather than educators. But we do have evidence that shyness and introversion have a significant genetic component, as shown by a high correlation in twins. Another significantly heritable factor is described as *Achievement Need* (Vandenberg, 1968b). This is an interesting example of the complexity of the problem of inheritance of aptitudes. A personality trait may have a strong effect on motivation and may thus become a factor in the expression of other testable aptitudes. Ambition, competitiveness, and persistence, insofar as they are heritable, may be part of the heritable component of the performances by which we measure intelligence.

POPULATION DIFFERENCES IN BEHAVIORAL TRAITS

Because we still need to know much more about the inheritance of behavioral traits in man, parallel evidence from other species is instructive. Behavior is as important an adaptation as physical structure in many higher animals, and consequently is at least as subject to natural selection. Different species living in the same environment are as different in their behavior as in their physical characteristics (Nagel, 1973). This is not to say that these differences are rigidly determined by heredity. Normal adult behavior in animals, just as in man, is the product of the interaction of hereditary potentialities with a "normal" environment. In primates, for instance, even reproductive behavior and care of infants may be completely ineffective if an individual has not had normal environment and experience, including the opportunity to observe the activities of others of his species (Mason, 1968). Man differs principally from other animals in that he is *more* influenced by a cultural and social environment that is the product of his fellow men. But this difference is a relative one; the interaction of heredity and environment is essential to normal development in all mammals.

An intermediate case between the marked species differences of behavior in nature and the less striking heritable differences of behavior in man is seen in the genetically determined differences in aptitude and temperament which have been artificially developed in various breeds of the domestic dog. These differences are partly intentional: that is, temperament and aptitude have been among the traits considered when selecting parent animals for the development of certain breeds. In other cases, the behavioral differences have been produced not by direct selection, but by genetic drift resulting from the inbred condition of the breeding stock. In any case, breeds have come to differ not only in their emotional disposition, but in the ease with which they adapt to various situations and can be trained to perform specialized activities, such as hunting and herding. Experiments under controlled conditions have verified that there are significant differences between breeds in behavioral responses (Fuller, 1967). These differences, like the physical differences that have been brought about by selective breeding, are so great among some breeds of dogs that they are almost pathological. If the dog were a natural species, not distorted by human fancy into so many varieties, some of them grotesque, we would undoubtedly find that dogs would be more uniform not only in body size, shape, color, and so on, but in temperament and aptitudes as well.

One of the most controversial aspects of aptitude-testing in man has been the investigation of differences between population groups that are distinguished by sociological, cultural, or racial characteristics. (Note that of these three categories only the last implies any genetic component.) We have already mentioned the generalizations that were so freely made in the past, some of which attributed virtually all of the current cultural and technological status of various peoples of the world to their innate qualities. Any generalization of this kind must be made cautiously. If it is assumed to have a genetic basis when in fact it does not, this leads to a false expectation that the difference is a permanent one. Aside from this, even if the generalization is statistically justified, and even if it has a genetic basis, *individuals* may be quite wrongly judged, whether to their advantage or disadvantage, by any opinions held about the *average* of the group to which they belong.

The most obvious classification of human beings, and the one that has accumulated the largest number of beliefs about innate behavioral differences, is sex. Since earliest times, human beings have had a superstitious awe of sex and have encrusted it with legend and custom. It may help us to penetrate this encrustation if we look at some of man's relatives. Man appears to share with many of his fellow mammals a proclivity of the male toward interpersonal combativeness. In other primates, as well as man, this is most obvious just after adolescence: later on, after trauma, comes prudence. The prickliness of the male primate's disposition can be shown experimentally to be due to sex hormones, like other secondary sex characteristics (Washburn and Hamburg, 1968). (This is hardly a new discovery: about 5,000 years ago the early herdsmen of the Near East had found that castration gentled the disposition of male domestic animals.) Thus there appears to be a physical basis for some differences in temperament between the sexes. How great they really are, if the accretions of custom are removed, and whether they are functional or dysfunctional in a contemporary society, remains debatable. Sex differences in aptitudes are hard to determine, because the development of an aptitude in one sex or another may have already been affected by occupational traditions before the age at which it is tested. There does not appear to be any sex difference in the results of I.Q. tests. In more specific tests, however, differences appear; the most consistent one, in the test routines commonly used at the present time, is a lower rating of females on *quantitative* tests (McClearn and DeFries, 1973). It is hard to know to what extent this *becomes* true because it is popularly supposed to be so (giving both teachers and students an excuse for relaxed efforts). This margin of uncertainty is typical of those we encounter in explaining other group differences in specific aptitudes. One quite clear-cut difference is the greater frequency of dyslexia in males (Klasen, 1972). The problem of dyslexia is a complex one, involving the idea of direction in space (the written word) versus order in time (the spoken word); and there may be some valid inverse relation between dealing successfully with the reversible relations of numbers and the nonreversible relations of words.

The most marked group differences revealed by the analysis of I.Q. data are those between different occupational classes in a single community. One study of this kind was done in England, where racial differences of even a minor kind do not complicate the picture as they do in the United States. Average I.Q. scores for unskilled laborers were 15 points lower than average, for clerical workers they were 15 points above. A small sample of the "professional" class scored even higher. The children of these families differed similarly in I.Q., but by about half as much (Burt, 1961). The use of I.Q. for adults is questionable because individuals with different amounts of education and different work experiences are not comparable even to the degree that children in the same classroom are. However, individuals who undertake different occupations usually have a history of different school success and different childhood I.Q. If there is anything functional with which I.Q. correlates, it is adaptation to the conventional categories of occupation. Thus, the I.Q. differences between adults in different occupational classes probably represent real differences in aptitude in the direction indicated, but exaggerate them. The children's scores, of course, are obviously subject to the recognized effects of differences in home environment. Such a study illustrates the problems involved in the use of simple statistical data, and shows why the special cases of adopted children have been so important in the study of heritability of behavior.

This study also illustrates a paradox of *social mobility*, the democratic principle by which an individual is free to rise in the social scale (or to sink, which we do not usually mention), according to his own abilities. The foregoing data indicate that this has worked. Individuals with special kinds of abilities *have* moved into higher economic classes, and insofar as these abilities are inherited, their children will have genetic as well as environmental advantages that will be reflected in the I.Q. Obviously, numerous accidental factors affect social success; and children may exceed or fall short of their parents' abilities as a result of genetic recombination, among other factors. Nevertheless, the result of such a process, if carried out for long enough, would be the creation of a society at least somewhat stratified for native abilities (Holden, 1973). This is perhaps an embarrassing prospect in a democracy; the workings of social mobility would have created a society in which it no longer commonly occurred. But even a moderate heritability of the factors that favor social and economic success will make some degree of stratification inevitable.

In recent years it has been suggested that nutrition in childhood can affect the mental development of individuals and populations. Like many theories involving nutrition, this one has entrenched itself in popular belief with remarkable speed. We have already mentioned nutrition in connection with brain size, which does not appear to be greatly affected by diet. Brain function and brain size are not strongly correlated in any case, and size is obviously of secondary concern. Researchers in the field, however, do not consider that the relation of brain function to nutrition is clearly demonstrated (Magoun, 1966). Some of the evidence is very indirect, based on the mere coincidence of nutritional and behavioral differences among large populations. More specific studies have been done on acutely undernourished children, mostly in undeveloped countries. The children who have come under closest examination have been in such poor condition that they were hospitalized for long periods, and undoubtedly would not have survived at all without this prolonged care. These children have often tested poorly after physical recovery. However, there are many complicating factors. These cases are drawn from an economic class in which test performance is not good even under "normal" conditions. In addition, they have been physically inactive for long periods, sometimes simply staring at a hospital ceiling. Therefore it is hard to evaluate whether their problems are the result of organic damage to the nervous system or are simply the sum of various interferences with the learning process (Cravioto, 1966).

There is one adequate study on the long-term effects of undernutrition on mental function, which cuts across all social classes. There was a six-month period of severe famine in Holland during the German occupation of World War II, when calorie and protein supplies to certain areas were reduced to one-third of normal during a six-month period. Adult weight loss was 25 per cent of body weight in many cases, and birth weights of infants also dropped. Because the most rapid physical growth of the brain is during the latter part of the fetal period, particular interest attached to any long-term effects on the mental performance of children born at the end of this period. Local birth records made it easy to identify these individuals, who were examined at the age of 19. No effect on their mental test scores could be detected (Stein, et al., 1972). So it is unrealistic to hope that food supplements alone will automatically raise low test scores in problem communities. It is more likely that the elements of the environment that affect mental function are primarily those that stimulate the brain by way of the sense organs—including, of course, education, both informal and formal.

The most contentious comparisons of average I.Q. scores are those made between racial groups. Most of this data has been collected in the United States, where white and Negro populations provide large available samples of school children for the psychologist. Such studies have been published over a period of many years. The results have been fairly consistent in showing average I.Q. scores of Negro children somewhere between 10 and 20 points lower than those for white children, though this figure varies from place to place (Shuey, 1966). Figure 45 shows a typical distribution of scores, indicating a mean difference of 13 points; it also shows the amount of overlap between the two populations (Baughman and Dahlstrom, 1968). Such innocent-looking graphs have recently become heated political issues. In the popular mind, the I.Q., though not very well understood, has come to be equated with superiority and inferiority (replacing, to be sure, worse things, such as noble birth or large muscular equipment). Because the I.Q. is essentially based on school achievement, and because the various aptitudes developed in the school system are supposed to be related to future work situations, I.Q. ratings are usually taken as predictive of future occupational and economic status. Thus the I.Q. becomes enmeshed in all the emotions associated with social position; its attainment and retention, and the desires of people of good social status to pass this advantage on to their children. These emotions

Figure 45 Race differences in I.Q. scores. Children from segregated schools in a single county in North Carolina, 1961–1966. (Adapted from Baughman and Dahlstrom, 1968.)

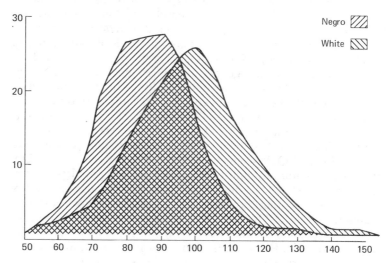

Population Differences in Behavioral Traits

lend a great deal of poignancy to any personal disappointments or social dissension in which I.Q. scores are concerned. But a glance at Figure 45 will remind us that even in a classical situation, that is, where tests are made within a group of individuals who have similar social backgrounds, the scores show a wide range, with members of the same racial group differing as much as 100 points. The first moral to be drawn is that anyone who expects all members of his own race to be equally smart is having problems with reality. In fact, as we have already mentioned, children of the same family may differ markedly from each other and from one or both of the parents.

Figure 45 does not tell us *why* the two curves do not coincide; that is a question we will come to shortly. But it does tell us some important things, strictly on its face value. Although the curves do not coincide, they overlap a great deal. If we had 100 individuals of each race, with I.Q. scores distributed as indicated by these figures, 65 individuals of the "superior" group could be exactly paired off in score with another 65 individuals of the "inferior" group. Another way of putting this is that one third of the individuals in the low-average group are actually above the combined average of the two groups, and vice versa. In the past, differences in *averages* have been used as justification for limiting educational or occupational choices on the basis of race. Any bias of this kind causes individuals from the low end of the curve of "good" races to undertake jobs that could be performed better by members of another race; or to take up the time and effort of educators that could more profitably be expended on these other individuals. This is a hard fact for many people to accept, particularly if members of their own family rate low on the scale. But it is clear that if *averages* guide our decisions in these matters, we will do many things that are not appropriate to the abilities of *individuals* (Thoday, 1973; Loehlin et al., 1975).

The foregoing comments, of course, are based on scores of individuals and groups as they are measured at the present time, and by a particular testing method. If we emphasize the *present time*, we become involved in the argument of heredity versus environment. If the average differences in scores are the result of a difference in *nature* between the populations—that is, if the differences in behavior and performance are genetically determined, they can be expected to remain the same indefinitely into the future. If the differences are the result of environment, they are temporary differences, and can sooner or later be made to disappear. Emotional reactions to these two theories are, for obvious reasons, very different.

This brings us back to the question of the heritability of whatever is tested by the I.Q. It seems well-established that variation in I.Q. scores within culturally and sociologically uniform populations may be as much as 80 per cent due to genetic causes. Because heritability is a ratio representing the proportion of genetic to environmental causes, this indicates that within such groups the pertinent features of the environment are fairly constant, and genetic factors are the principal variable. However, this does not prove anything for purposes of comparing groups. Quite irrespective of what is going on *within* any group, the difference *between* two groups could be entirely environmental, entirely genetic, or due to interactions between environmental and genetic factors. An 80 per cent heritability within a single population tells us only that genetic effects on the I.Q. do exist: it is entirely consistent with the possibility that the differences *between* two populations may be entirely due to environment. Much breath has been wasted on the attempt to infer the causes of interpopulation differences from within-population heritability. This argument rests only on analogy. Others have countered in any way possible, sometimes with the contention that genetic effects on the I.Q. do not exist at all—a hard argument to maintain, in view of the intensive studies done on twins and relatives. The debate will be nicely settled when populations of the two races are living under conditions exactly the same in all respects; at that point, no one will care any more. The first solid experimental data will be those from adoptions of infants into families of another race; such adoptions have only very recently become common enough to promise usable information.

Another line of argument claims that present-day testing methods are unfair. Of those using this argument, the "environmentalist" faction points out the difficulties caused by home backgrounds which represent different cultures and value systems. We have defined intelligence as *adaptability,* and therefore one might expect that any intelligent child, at the age of six, could adapt himself wholeheartedly for a few hours a day to a school system with a set of expectations and rewards different from any he has encountered before. But there is a paradox in human intelligence. The long lifespan of man and his complex culture have made it useful for the human young to learn certain attitudes and motivation patterns very early in life, and to retain them very tenaciously. As a result, the adaptation to school can be quite difficult, except for those who have been preconditioned to it. Another point, more recently made, is that we must recognize that there are different kinds of intelligence; and that the kind of intelligence promoted and tested by educators is a *special* kind, not necessarily the only kind, nor is it necessarily the kind for which natural selection has operated during most of man's evolution. (This argument, of course, concedes genetic differences.)

There is a more fundamental question underlying the argument. Does the I.Q. really predict success in contemporary society? If it does not, it is time we admit it and cease telling young people that education is designed for their personal economic profit. However, if the I.Q. does correlate with economic success to any reasonable degree, it does not help those who score low to tell them that what they have is another kind of intelligence, which differs by not commanding as high a price in the modern labor market. If, however, there are meaningful differences in the *shape* of the aptitude profile in different populations, this information could be used constructively. It would be very interesting and educationally useful to know more about *specific* aptitudes of various populations. The various identified components of individual aptitude—verbal, quantitative, lexic, mechanical—are probably, like other individually variable traits, unevenly distributed among population groups. In addition to studies of specific aptitudes by race, we need comparative information about groups other than American Caucasian and Negro. Surveying most of the literature on I.Q. and race, one might think that those were the only races that existed. Taking human behavior simply as an exercise in natural selection, one would expect the general aptitudes, i.e., intelligence, in the sense of adaptability, to be the most universally useful and the most likely to increase in all areas and populations; by contrast, the more specific aptitudes would be the most likely to advance at various rates and in various ways in different regions or under different cultural circumstances.

Our understanding of differences in *personality* is greatly complicated by cultural background. It is possible to define "typical," "ideal," and "deviant" personalities in all cultures; and when we compare greatly different cultures of the world, we find that the "ideal" personality of one culture may be the "deviant" personality of another culture. There is, nevertheless, a great variety of personality types in all communities and cultures. Personal individuality is as marked among the stone-age survivors of the Australian deserts as among ourselves (Hart, 1954). It is obvious that wherever we go, hardly anyone has a *typical* personality, and perhaps no one is quite ideal by any standard. Although cultures attempt to shape personalities, they have indifferent success because of the intractable variability in the raw material. In social animals such as man, the group profits from individual differences in behavior traits. A community where all individuals are equally bold, equally cautious, or even equally middle-of-the-road has less flexibility of response to either a threatening or a potentially advantageous situation than a community where there is a mix of personalities. The continued existence of polymorphism of personality is undoubtedly the result of the positive contribution it makes to community success. However, genetic variation in personality also creates an opportunity for *directional selection* to operate, if environment, means of subsistence, or the social system itself introduces a bias in favor of certain options of behavior.

Is the personality that makes for the greatest success as a hunter the same as the personality of the most prosperous village farmer? Is the personality that was best adapted to life in an Old World autocracy of 4000 B.C. the one that will achieve optimum success and happiness in a modern technological democracy? Are the personality norms of a population that has been selectively adapted to agricultural life for several thousand years likely to produce the same version of modern society as those of a population that until recently depended for its subsistence on hunting in a sparsely settled environment? The answers to these questions are relevant to an important question of the modern world: Is there a single kind of society or form of government that is best *for all nations?* Most social scientists prefer to ignore these questions at the present time. There is still an aversive reaction against the old assumption that a people's culture is the product of their biological race. Also, if the social scientist admits the possibility that biological influences, even slight ones, may affect cultural characteristics, he concedes that his test tube is contaminated and raises questions about the precision of his analysis. Therefore the question, "Can differences in culture be explained entirely in terms of history, environment, and chance?" is a controversial one. (Incidentally, this is different from the question of whether they can be explained *largely* in those terms.) Of course, some questions about personality are being swept under the rug for fear that the answers might prove to be "racist." The possibilities, however, are interesting and deserve study. A comparatively slight bias in frequencies of contrasting personality types in a population could, over a long period of time, greatly influence the development of its social institutions; similarly, a slight bias in aptitudes could affect its technology. More importantly, if certain personality types are more amply rewarded in a culture, if this reward is reflected in reproductive performance, and if the personality type is at all heritable, the culture may proliferate the type of personality it rewards. This leads us to ask whether changes in traditional cultures—which at the present time are usually accommodations to an economically dominant culture—involve more than temporary distress. Different peoples do have different traditions and different values, which they cherish. This may cause problems in intergroup relations, but the different traditions may represent an optimum adjustment to personality characteristics that are not easily or painlessly altered. In the nineteenth century, most Westerners took it for granted that Western technology, political institutions, domestic animals, food crops, religion, and even clothing (however inappropriate to the local climate) constituted a package deal that not only could, but should, be exported to the whole world, and that anyone who did not find it congenial and flourish in its framework was somehow deficient. In the United States, this sentiment often dominated policy toward the American Indian, and, at the rate of about once a generation, this alternated with a belief that the Indians should retain their community identity and value system. Most American Indians have leaned toward nonassimilation. It is interesting that many minority populations, even those who have suffered severe prejudice because of their minority status, do believe that they have distinctive and valuable characteristics, which are uniquely their own. At the present time, problems arise because these genetic or cultural traits (it hardly matters which, for practical purposes) conflict with economic success in the larger culture in which they are willy-nilly involved. But this is a practical problem, one that requires concessions in action but not necessarily a compromise of values, and it should be solved on that basis. People have the right to form their own communities and cherish their own values, short of damaging others. Just as surely, they are entitled to support themselves comfortably within a common economic system. For a long time these partially closed communities will probably continue to exist, based on shared cultural traditions, and as a result preserving the complex of physical traits we call race.

13

The Geography
of Human Races

Human races are basically geographical phenomena. We arrive at
the concept of race by observing that physical traits, the invisible as
well as the visible, differ in a systematic way in correlation with
geographical area. Of course, human populations have not always
stayed in one place. Some population movements are reliably recorded in written history; some were only recorded from tradition,
long after the event. In some parts of the world, written history is
only a very recent development. Everywhere, the records become
dubious and tinged with legend as we go further into the past, until
historical records in even the vaguest sense cease to exist. When
pre-literate people tell us that their ancestors came from the north,
we consider the information for what it may be worth. When they
tell us that their ancestors came up from the underworld through a
hole in the ground, we are on our own. Fortunately the archaeolo-
gist, and the physical anthropologist working with him, can infer,
from skeletons and other traces of man, something about races of
the past. Were racial differences greater or less in the past than at

present? Which races have remained in the same area? Which have moved or spread? In the far past, did certain of the modern races exist at all? If not, when and from what ancestors did they develop? Unfortunately, the more remote the period we are studying, the less adequate the material we have to guide us. Skulls and skeletons may be few, fragmentary, and, at best, may represent local groups which, in their time, may have been more inbred and unlike their neighbors than are most populations of the present. New material may be found in the future, and it may shoot down our best theories. We may never know all the answers, but it is interesting to try to find them.

At this point we should review what we know about the ways in which populations may come to differ from one another genetically. Natural selection should be foremost in our minds. Acting slowly, almost imperceptibly within the short length of time we are able to observe directly, over a long period natural selection may change gene frequencies so that populations that originated as mere fragments of a single tribe come to differ in many ways, some of them perhaps conspicuous to the eye. Changes of this kind can be observed going on at the present time in many species, and as we have said before, it would require supernatural intervention to prevent these changes from occurring. Selection may cause populations to diverge genetically in many ways when they are subject to different external environmental conditions. Some of these may be obvious, or at least explicable; some may be obscure and so far unsuspected. There are forms of selection that are self-stabilizing. There seems to be something that keeps the A and B blood-group genes from becoming too common in any population; and if this is the case, there are limits to how much populations can diverge in gene frequencies at this locus. A great unknown is the effect of selection of the basis of gene combinations. Does the appearance of a new gene in a population create a situation in which other genes already present, and to all appearances independent of it, become selectively favored or disfavored in a new and different way? The possibility of gene flow is constantly present. In historical perspective, we think of it as *race mixture*. In modern times, under our very eyes, so to speak, we can see populations altered genetically by mixing with other populations, and observe truly new races arising by the blending of different stocks. Such changes must have occurred often in the past, though rarely as spectacularly as in the last few centuries. Although this may seem like a simple reversal of the process of differentiation in isolation, when two populations that were once of similar ancestry merge again, one or both may have changed enough that the result of the combination is distinctly different from the original ancestral population.

The possibility of genetic drift must always be considered. We can become involved in a detailed comparison of gene frequencies, using several decimal places, and forget that *no* population, even if it were totally isolated and subject to no perceptible selective pressures, would remain the same indefinitely. The clear ascertainability of biochemical traits such as the blood groups, from which gene frequencies can be directly calculated, may give us a false impression of historical exactness. But we do not know how these traits are affected by natural selection, and to assume that they are not so affected is at best an act of faith. And blood-group traits are as subject to genetic drift as anything else. The gene frequency changes due to genetic drift are random and unpredictable: they introduce an out-of-focus quality to our picture of the future of any population. Unfortunately, their effect is the same when we attempt to infer the past from the present. Because of drift, our assumptions about past gene frequencies of any population are increasingly less certain, the further back we look. *There is no mathematical cure for this uncertainty.* But it is the speculator's friend. Whatever our interpretation of racial history, genetic drift accounts for the loose ends. This is particularly true if we are dealing with populations of marginal size; and the further back in history we go, the more likely it is that we will find the populations of the time, though they may be ancestral to great races of the present, to have been tribes of only a few members.

A major question in the reconstruction of the racial past is, "How much population movement has there been?" On the basis of events of the last few centuries, migrations and invasions may seem to be likely ways to account for the distribution of racial traits; complicated theories have been devised to account for racial differences within various areas by "waves of migration." In this kind of scenario, new races are brought "on stage" whenever archaeology indicates that a change of culture has occurred, or when a slightly different physical trait in one part of a territory must be explained. Unfortunately, there is not enough room backstage for all these invaders to wait for their cues: in fact there *is* no backstage, since the whole world has to be accounted for in one drama. Therefore, migration theories should be used cautiously. Furthermore, there must be a reason for a population movement and the reasons are limited. There is nearly always a good reason *not* to migrate to a new area: there are people already there, and they will give you a rough time. Drought and famine are sometimes given as reasons for population movements; actually, starving people are less able than well-fed people to brave the territorial defense of their neighbors. In unique cases, such as the first peopling of the New World, the land was unoccupied. But once an area is settled, it resists overrunning by any new population, unless the new population has a technology that enables it to maintain a larger population in the area than is already supported by the simpler means of subsistence. Even then the "invasion" is likely to be slow, perhaps better called an "infiltration." Prehistoric migrants did not have supply lines in their rear to make rapid advances possible. Thus there are a number of limits on successful population movement, which are even more stringent if the migration is even remotely to resemble a *replacement* of population. Even in the period since 1500 A.D., when Europeans spread over the world with some political premeditation, they only replaced native populations where the natives were unable to cope with European diseases. These sudden onslaughts of disease, as we have discussed, resulted from the crossing of great oceans—a modern phenomenon.

Some invasions celebrated in legend probably consisted of a few brigands who bullied the natives but left only a minor genetic trace. If their offspring retained some social dominance, they may have become the custodians of tradition, and made it appear that the genetic change was quite significant, when in fact it was not. There may also be misconceptions about the genetic effect of transitory contacts in historic times. Such contacts are sometimes invoked to explain traits such as blue eyes or blonde hair in areas where popular stereotypes hold that they should not occur. The genetic power attributed to some of these contacts falls strictly in the realm of sex fantasy. If we take the number of male visitors as a fraction of the total adult male population of the tribe, and take the length of their stay as a fraction of the total generation length (about twenty years in most populations), and multiply these fractions by one another, we can compute expected genetic impact of a short and casual visit—usually less than 1 per cent in the case of early explorers. The effects of more permanent residence can be evaluated accordingly. We are probably correct in assuming that in many prehistoric population movements the net result in the "invaded" territory was a population at least 50 per cent genetically derived from the original natives. The most effective population changes have probably resulted when agricultural peoples entered a territory occupied by peoples of a hunting and gathering culture. If the groups remain distinct culturally, and stay out of each other's way, the agricultural people may, by simple increase of numbers, come to predominate. If genetic blending takes place later, they will dominate the racial characteristics of the area. But if genetic mixture takes place early, or if the original population quickly adopts the new technology, the eventual genetic blend will be much more heavily weighted by the first inhabitants.

When we find two populations who are alike in many traits, though not in all, and who live in geographically contiguous areas, we naturally assume that they have been part of a single breeding unit in the past, and may still be to some degree. We will therefore class these peoples as members of one race, but make a distinction of *subrace,* in view of their minor differences. This kind of reasoning is less convincing when geographical continuity of residence is interrupted, and when the genetic similarity is less conspicuous. In this case, we base our judgment of genetic relatedness on the plausibility, in historical and geographical terms, of former membership in a single breeding population, and on our assessment of the "importance" of traits the populations share as opposed to those they do not share. We can automatically discount, to a proper degree, traits that are known to be subject to immediate environmental effects on the living individual. Any trait is suspected of being subject to strong *selection* in relation to environmental differences will not be considered very reliable for tracing genetic relationships far in the past, because strong selection may have produced significant local changes. Another reason for doubting the usefulness of a trait for tracing ancestral relations may be that the phenotype, as we commonly identify it, includes two or more conditions that are not genetically the same. We do not know, for instance, whether the very dark skin that occurs in some widely separated and otherwise different peoples of the world is caused by the same genes at the same loci. We do know that what we call frizzly hair is not all the same when examined closely, and that different types occur in different populations. Considerable stress has been laid on the fact that blood groups and biochemical traits may be shown to be the same, that is, due to the same molecular configurations in the same chromosomes, wherever they occur. But if these or any other verified genetic traits have arisen by mutation more than once in the human species, their identity, for purposes of demonstrating genetic relationships, may not be meaningful. Nor is the unusualness of a trait necessarily a sign of importance for evaluating common ancestry. In the past, attempts have been made to assume genetic continuity for a number of Asian and African populations which are remarkable for very short stature. In this case, however, even if the genetic and physiological nature of the shortness were the same in all cases, which is not proved, the possibility of independent mutation and selection remains. One solution to the problem of evaluating the importance of different traits in assessing relationship simply to use as many traits as possible and assume that all are equally important, or at least that ratings of similarity or difference made on this basis are approximately correct. This may lead us to underrate relationship, however, where there has been intense selection or exaggerated drift due to small population size.

A common kind of hypothesis used to explain differences between populations that are somewhat alike and not too far apart geographically, is that one or both has absorbed to some degree the genes of some other population or populations. The "other population" may be an obvious neighbor. Or it may be a population still existing somewhere in an unmixed condition (or assumed to be unmixed); that we suspect was once more widespread than at present, and has been incorporated as a minor element in populations no longer visibly very much like it. Sometimes the submerged element that accounts for population differences is a hypothetical one, invented for the specific purpose of accounting for them. All such speculations are complicated by our ignorance of exactly what the phenotypic results may be when different varieties of man become mixed. Most modern racial mixtures that have been studied are reasonably intermediate in phenotype between the parent races, though mixed populations often have exaggerated individual variability. Therefore, when we speculate about mixtures in the past, we cannot be certain what the ultimate results would have been, particularly if natural selection has had a long time to act upon the variable population that resulted.

By way of example, we might imagine how we would interpret the present population of North America if all historical records were obliterated. It would not be difficult to see a strong genetic likeness between a major element in North America and various populations of Europe, and between a minor element and populations of West Africa. The fact that these populations were separated geographically in the Old World but not in the New, would indicate that the direction of movement was *to* rather than *from* North America. More detailed study would indicate that there had been some mixture of these two stocks, with most of the intermediate individuals remaining a part of the population of predominantly African ancestry. A third, very much smaller element, would be found in its most distinct form in isolated communities in the Western states. This element would not correspond as closely to any population outside the Western Hemisphere as did the first two; consequently, we would suspect that these people were fragments of an older population which had become outnumbered. A closer look would show us that this racial element had apparently contributed a considerable amount to other populations in certain areas, particularly the Southwestern states and Mexico. Thus we would identify, roughly, the White, Negro, and American Indian elements in North America, and reconstruct their histories and relations. This is the same kind of reasoning we use in the many cases in which historical records are *really* lacking. It might work well in a case as simple as this, but how well would it explain North America five hundred, let alone a thousand years from now?

EAST ASIA

A glance at the map of the world shows that the great land masses of the world are concentrated in what is conventionally called the Eastern Hemisphere (including Africa, Europe, Asia, and Australia), and lie largely north of the equator. In the Northern Hemisphere, great expanses of land extend continuously from the Temperate Zone up to the Arctic; in the Southern Hemisphere the Temperate Zone is mostly ocean, and includes only relatively small land areas. The Antarctic, unlike the Arctic, can be approached only by sea. Long before ocean travel was possible, the human species had spread throughout the northern land masses; South America, Africa, and Australia were dead ends. Man began in the Old World. Remains of his earliest forebears and their kin, some as old as two million years, are being found in great variety in Africa. Later, forms more like modern man appeared in Asia. Later still, the developing species moved into Europe. Man came to the Americas almost yesterday, by the time scale of human occupation of the rest of the world. The lineage began in the tropics and only slowly adapted to the colder parts of the world, but in the end has been most successful, and has established the largest populations, in the border tropics and Temperate Zone. During the last million years, world climate was generally colder than at present, and large areas of the northern continents were intermittently unsuitable for the life our ancestors led. In this same period, there often was a more temperate and moister climate in some of the now hot and arid areas which lie 25 to 30 degrees north of the equator. Thus, there was a wide band of land across southern Asia, from China to Arabia, that was favorable to evolving man; there he lived and developed the various styles of stone tools which we find as evidence of his occupation.

Sinanthropus, a local race of the early species of man, *Homo erectus*, lived in China. Some of his physical traits, notably *shovel incisors* and the *Inca bone*, have led scholars to believe that there is a true genetic continuity between Sinanthropus and the modern Mongoloids. As we have shown in Chapter 4, it is entirely possible for some genes to have remained characteristic of local areas, even while different populations traded, shared, and developed progressive evolutionary traits. Human populations of East Asia, then, may well have been a distinct race a half a million years ago, with some of the same traits as their successors who remain in the same area. However this may be, Southeast Asia, now the home of the Mongoloid races, has probably been a home for man as long as man has existed. The present Mongoloid domain includes all of Asia, as far west as Burma and Tibet in the south, and Turkestan and western Siberia in the north. (The northern part of this western boundary of the Mongoloids is not as clear, racially speaking, as the southern part.) The outlying islands, from Japan south to Indonesia, are also included, as are the more remote island groups of Micronesia and Polynesia.

This huge area obviously includes a great variety of climate. Most people understand that as one goes north the climate gets colder. This does not by any means distinguish all the aspects of climate that are important to man for either his comfort or his subsistence. The amount of precipitation, the season of the year when it comes, and the degree of contrast between winter and summer temperatures are important factors, somewhat correlated to one another; which depend on more than simple north or south latitude. The oceans of the world supply water that reaches the land by being vaporized, carried inland by winds, and then precipitated out again. Large amounts of rainfall can occur in land areas which lie near the ocean, the amount depending on how often the winds blow inland. The location of mountains, which may stop the inland flow of atmospheric moisture, is also important. Large bodies of water also act as temperature stabilizers. Water, including the water contained in moist soil, has a higher capacity to store heat than does dry soil or rock. This modifies climates by decreasing the contrast between winter and summer temperatures in areas near bodies of water, again most strongly where the prevailing winds are inland. The geographer therefore makes a distinction between *oceanic* and *continental* climates: the oceanic climate is moist, with only a moderate difference between summer and winter temperatures; the continental climate is dry, with large seasonal differences in temperature. As the names indicate, oceanic climates are near oceans and continental climates are in the centers of continents. In the temperate parts of the Northern Hemisphere, where prevailing wind currents are from west to east, oceanic climates extend farther inland on the west sides of continents, if mountains do not stand in the way. Also, because of wind direction, the climate of the eastern side of a land mass is more like the continental climate west of it, with greater contrast of summer and winter temperatures and greater variation of rainfall with the seasons. Eurasia, because of its huge size and different distribution of mountains, cannot be compared exactly with North America; but some comparisons can be made which illustrate for the North American reader the variations of climate in Asia. China, Manchuria, Korea, and Japan resemble the central and eastern United States. Evidence of this similarity is the recent exchange of crops: maize, the native American cereal grain, successfully introduced to China, and the soybean to the United States. Cultivated crops are very sensitive to climate. The bulge of southern China extends farther south than any part of the United States, and continues on into Southeast Asia, forming a land continuity into the true tropics. (A comparable situation in the New World would exist if Florida were joined by land to Cuba and Venezuela.) Southeast Asia, the Philippines, and other Indonesian Islands, are truly tropical: hot all year around and with ample rainfall. West of China lies the high plateau of Tibet, with a cold, dry climate that is matched, in North America, only by a few high areas in the western mountains. Northeast of China is Mongolia, with a classic continental climate: dry and with great extremes of temperature. Siberia is like northern Canada, a land of endless coniferous forests and severe winters, where dryness is not a problem as in warmer continental climates, only because of slow evaporation in the colder temperatures. The most northern part of Siberia is treeless tundra.

THE MONGOLOIDS

All of the area we have described is occupied by variants of the Mongoloid race. The people of Mongolia, and their Siberian neighbors, the Buriats, are the type specimens (to use the zoologist's phrase) of the Mongoloid race. The Mongolians and Buriats show in marked form the classic Mongoloid combination of flat face, low-lying nose, and broad cheeks, and a head very broad between the ears (Figure 46A). They have a well-developed layer of fat over the face, especially the cheek, with a fatty eyelid and the typical Mongoloid eyefold. The forehead is rounded, with only slight brow-ridges. The skin is light, though not as light as that of some Europeans, the eyes dark brown, the hair black. The hair is coarse

Figure 46(a) A group of Siberian students. (From *Within the Circle*, by E. Stefansson, courtesy Scribners.)

Figure 46(b) *Left.* A young woman of the Tuchia nation, a minority population in southwest China. (*China Reconstructs.*)

Figure 46(c) *Right.* A man from T'angshan, North China. (*China Reconstructs.*)

Figure 46(d) King Jigme Wangchuk of Bhutan. (Wide World Photos.)

in texture, grows long in both sexes, and seems little subject to graying or baldness. Beard and body hair are slight or absent. In build they are short, especially in the legs, and have a long and massive trunk. It has been suggested that many of these traits are adaptive to the extremely severe winter cold of their area: compact body shape, nonprojecting nose, the coarse hair with its good insulating properties, the fat-padded face, the lack of beard to accumulate frost from the breath. Most of these traits, however, occur with fair consistency in Mongoloids of tropical areas also. It seems puzzling that adaptation to a type of climate in which human numbers must always have been small could have influenced so large an area. Some of these traits may have facilitated the expansion of Mongoloids into cold areas, rather than having developed after they moved there. Certainly their adaptation to cold, and their massive trunk with its large lung capacity, enabled close relatives of the Mongols to move into the high plateau of Tibet, with its thin air and bitterly cold climate. More obscure traits of the Mongoloid peoples are shovel incisors and the extra skull suture which produces the *Inca bone.*

There are several variants of this classic Mongoloid pattern—a major race is entitled to numerous varieties, all equally authentic. One polymorphism in face shape is rather conspicuous. We usually picture the classic Mongoloid as having a face broad in its lower part as well as across the cheeks. However, the lower part of the face is much more variable than the upper. Not uncommonly the cheeks, though broad just below the eyes, are hollowed out lower down and converge toward a narrow chin region, with or without a flaring of the back corners of the lower jaw (Figure 46A). The very broad head of the classic Mongoloids—Mongols and Buriats—is also exaggerated even for Mongoloids. The majority of Mongoloids are *mesocephalic,* that is, more broad-headed than most other people—except for some Europeans—but not extreme. In blood group, the Mongoloids are the "group B" people, showing the highest frequency of this antigen. However, B is common in Asia among non-Mongoloid people also, which may indicate selective effects that obscure its meaning as an indication of relationship.

The Chinese, particularly the southern Chinese, because of their large numbers, have been the best known of the Mongoloids in modern times, and our ideas of the "typical" characteristics of the race have been strongly influenced by these representatives we know best. The Chinese are very similar to the Mongols who gave the race its name, and often have the same very flat and broad face—which is most distinctively Mongoloid in that it is the most different from other races. But the Chinese, as one would expect of any nation so large, vary in physical appearance according to region. The southern Chinese often have a face with a smoothly rounded outline (Figure 46B). Northern Chinese incline to a more angular face, and have a longer head with heavier brow-ridges (Figure 46C). This latter variant appears also in northern and northeastern Siberia, where it has been described as an older or "undifferentiated" type of Mongoloid. Both variants are found in also in Tibet and Turkestan.

It is difficult to evaluate the extent to which Caucasoid strains may have infiltrated East Asia during the last few millenia. The area north of Tibet and west of Mongolia, including southern Siberia and eastern Turkestan, has been occupied for a long time by peoples who were rather mobile but not very numerous—the population per square mile over much of this area can even now be counted on the fingers of one hand. One contingent of this population was known to Europeans as the Huns, and to the Chinese as the *Hiung-Nu*. These are the people whose incursions caused the Great Wall of China to be built. Farther west, similar populations were known as Turks. To Europeans they seemed Mongoloid; undoubtedly they were mixed—probably more Mongoloid in the eastern part of their area and more Caucasoid in the western part. This racially transitional group could have carried Caucasoid genes to the Far East, but to what extent is hard to estimate. However, the people of East Asia had acquired the idea of agriculture by about 2000 B.C., and it is probable that soon afterward they had developed population densities high enough so that the border nomads, though admittedly a chronic nuisance, could not have had a major genetic effect on a population that greatly outnumbered them. Some believe that the small features—narrow nose and small mouth—seen in some Chinese, and especially in Koreans, are an indication of admixture with a "Turkish" strain.

In Japan we encounter a distinctively non-Mongoloid race, the Ainu; they have been termed a "primitive Caucasoid" (Figure 47A). Their extreme development of body hair and beard contrasts sharply with the Mongoloids, and is excessive even by Caucasoid standards. Their heavy brow-ridges are also non-Mongoloid, and are extreme for Caucasoids. Opinion has wavered between classifying them as Caucasoids or as somewhat modified and light-skinned Australoids. This state of indetermination suggests that Caucasoid and Australoid may be closer to one another than either is to other major races. The Ainu are assumed, on good grounds, to be the earliest inhabitants of the islands of Japan. Skulls unearthed by archaeologists from a period in the second millenium B.C. resemble modern Ainu; later populations indicate a genetic intrusion of Mongoloids like those of the adjacent mainland. There is a rather broad resemblance between Chinese and Japanese, the two Asian nationalities best known in the United States. A distinctive Japanese variant is a long-faced type, which seems to be concentrated in the old upper classes. This type is also an aesthetic ideal, and appears often in Japanese art. The outline of the face is a long oval, and the profile somewhat convex. The nose is long, Mongoloid in the smoothness of its contours, but delicately acquiline. It may be that the choice of wives by upper-class males, on the basis of this standard of beauty, entrenched the phenotype in the feudal aristocrats of Japan. The broader-faced Japanese usually resemble Chinese or Indonesians (Figure 47B). The small-featured variant, which

Figure 47(a) *Above left.* An Ainu woman from northern Japan. (Courtesy Sister N. Inez Hilger.)

Figure 47(b) *Above right.* An American of Japanese ancestry: Governor Ariyoshi of Hawaii.

Figure 47(c) The small-featured face sometimes seen in Japan and East Asia: Crown Princess Michiko of Japan. (Wide World Photos.)

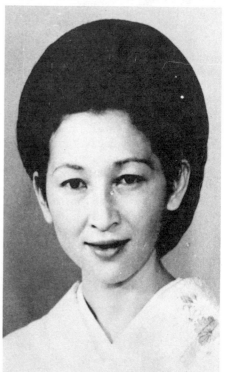

we noted in Korea, is often seen in Japan also (Figure 47C). Most interesting in Japan (and some other Mongoloid regions) is the occurrence of beard development, even though there is rarely much other body hair. Many Japanese men can raise a very respectable beard, or, like their present Emperor, a thick mustache. This ability is rare in most of the continental Mongoloids. Chinese sages were wont to train a few hairs into a wispy mustache as a sign of age and dignity, but it was never impressive by Western standards. But in Korea, Japan, and some other parts of Southeast Asia, beards are more commonly seen, although they usually do not rise as high on the face as in truly hirsute races. This is certainly understandable in Japan, if we take a realistic view of population replacements. Whoever came over from the mainland to establish the present predominant race of Japan absorbed many genes from the forebears of the Ainu, and it shows. Whether some of this hirsuteness came all the way across Asia with the Huns, or similar people, is an open question. The *Gilyak*, a tribal people on the mainland coast across from the northern islands of Japan, are bearded but their faces are otherwise quite Mongoloid. The Gilyak undoubtedly represent a similar admixture, which makes them cousins of the Ainu. It is reasonable to assume that there is a submerged Ainu-like strain in other parts of Asia also.

So far we have discussed populations in areas of Asia that are relatively open to population movements. Some of this land supports only a scant population, as in Tibet, Mongolia, and Turkestan; some—like the lowlands of China and the islands of Japan—now has some of the densest population in the world; but in no part of it are there major barriers to population movement and genetic admixture. But as we go south and west from China, this situation changes. Southern China is hilly, but not to a degree that interrupts population continuity. One who has lived in China can recognize differences in facial features in different provinces, but the differences are not great. Some "black dwarfs," distinct groups of people in southern China, are mentioned in old records. They have now disappeared as separate populations, though there are scattered groups of their relatives not far away, in Southeast Asia and Indonesia. However, in the area that includes Viet Nam, Laos, Cambodia, Thailand, and Burma we find terrain of a quite different kind. Extending southward from eastern Tibet through Burma and the south China province of Yunnan, and on into the ocean to form the Malay Peninsula and some of the Indonesian islands, are a series of steep parallel mountain ridges, between which several major rivers drain from the Himalayas into the sea. This region has remained virtually impenetrable to surface travel, particularly at right angles to the ridges. The Burma Road, which crossed this area in World War II, was notorious for its marginal passability. This mountainous core of Southeast Asia is fringed by coastal areas, including long valleys extending inward parallel to the mountains, which are fertile and support a dense population based on intensive agriculture. In this area a distinction is made between lowlanders and the upland people. The latter are called *hill tribes* in eastern India and *Montagnards* in Viet Nam (Figure 48A). Here, as in other areas of the world with similar terrain, the mountain populations often form small units, isolated from one another as well as from their lowland neighbors. In such a situation genetic differences may develop between groups living quite close together. Anyone who has to participate in the modern multinational world, where people on opposite sides of the globe are continually interfering in one another's activities, must surely envy the ability of these economically self-sufficient peoples to mind their own business and their own genetics for centuries. But it has produced a pattern of racial variation that is quite difficult to unravel. In general the lowland people of Southeast Asia fall into line with other Mongoloid groups north and south of them (Figure 48B). It will be convenient, in fact, to discuss them along with their southern neighbors, the inhabitants of the Indonesian islands. If we were to put together a mixed group of Chinese, lowlanders of Southeast Asia, and Indonesians (Figures 48C, D), it would not be at all easy to sort them out again on the basis of phenotype; though hardly an individual among them would not be recognizable as basically Mongoloid. In general, skin color becomes progressively darker as we go from north to south, just as it does among Caucasoid Europeans. Body size tends to become smaller, in breadth as well as in height. A curious variation in Indonesians is great *width* of the nose. It is a good Mongoloid nose, with a smooth, neatly angled low-lying root and a small tip, but the width across the lower part is nearly equal to the height, producing a broad triangle, as seen from the front. This variation, paralleling a similar one in tropical Africa, in a quite different major race, suggests that the wide nose may be adaptive to the tropical climate.

Most interesting, in Southeast Asia, are the small and quite different populations called Negritos (Figure 48E). Most of these peoples are found in small groups in mountainous areas on the larger islands of the Philippines; but some are in Malaya, and on the Andaman Islands. (These islands are small bits of land lying south of Burma—the tops of a submerged mountain chain in line with the great ranges of Indo-China.) The Negritos are the relatives of the "black dwarfs" of Chinese history. Very short in stature, dark-skinned, and with frizzly hair, they are quite different from the Mongoloid peoples who now predominate in this part of the world. Their name was given them because they vaguely resemble a very small version of African Negroes. However, they are much more similar to the Australoid races—Australians and Melanesians—who are geographically much closer to them, and there seems to be no serious reason to believe that they are closely related to any Africans. Because of their very small body size, they resemble some groups in Africa (who are far from typical Africans in this respect); and they also share with these groups a simple hunting-and-gathering means of subsistence. Very small body size appears to be a successful ecological adaptation by which people can coexist for a long time with neighbors quite different from themselves. The

Figure 48(a) A group of Montagnards from the hills of Viet Nam: a blend of Mongoloid and Australoid. (Wide World Photos.)

Figure 48(b) A young woman from Vientiane, Laos. (United Nations.)

Figure 48(c) A young man from the Philippines. (United Nations.)

Figure 48(d) A mother and child from Indonesia. (United Nations.)

Figure 48(e) A Negrito of the Aeta tribe from Luzon, Philippines. (From *Die Negrito Asiens*, by P. Schebesta, courtesy Verlag St. Gabriel.)

Negritos' culture indicates that they could hardly have spread over the area to their present scattered locations after the Mongoloid agriculturalists were established there, so we assume that they were an early population, since outnumbered and crowded out of most of the area. As we shall see later, an Australoid element is clearly present in the population of India, and this raises interesting questions about the role of the Australoids in the racial history of the entire area. Some early skulls from Southeast Asia appear Australoid, and it seems likely that this race, in one variety or another, once occupied the entire region of Indonesia and the tropical part of Asia, west into India. Then, in the last few thousand years, a slow southward movement of Mongoloids has entered Southeast Asia, producing populations of mixed and increasingly Mongoloid ancestry. Some of the local variations of these southern Mongoloid peoples may be the result of varying degrees of admixture with Negrito and Australoid elements.

In the hills of India and the mountain regions of Indo-China, there are enclaves of people of rather simple culture, some of whom seem predominantly Mongoloid, some Australoid, and some vaguely Caucasoid. Rather than make assumptions about a complicated pattern of population movements to account for all of these racial resemblances, we may surmise that genetic drift has been at work on a racially mixed population to produce small unique groups who favor one race or another of their mixed ancestry (Figure 48A). A similar situation appears to exist on the island of Taiwan, which has, in addition to its recent immigrants from mainland China, a number of aboriginal tribes rather isolated from one another in a mountain environment. These people range from strongly Mongoloid to a type that resembles the more Caucasoid-appearing among the Japanese. Probably an Ainu-like strain is present here, as it is in Japan, blended with a Mongoloid strain and diversified by genetic drift. Even with the larger populations of Indo-China there are trends not explicable by geographical position. The Burmese, for instance, who are farthest west, at the borders of India, are the most classically Mongoloid of the various nations in the region. The Cambodians, living in a rich lowland surrounded by strongly Mongoloid peoples, seem to show the strongest Australoid influence (Coon, 1965).

We cannot leave East Asia and the Mongoloids without some discussion of blood-group allele B, which is *the* Asian blood group. It reaches high levels—around 30 per cent, as high as anywhere in the world—in the Mongoloids. Paradoxically, the B allele seems to be *regional* rather than *racial*. It is common in the Ainu and in India among populations that differ from Mongoloids in a multitude of other traits. The supposed advantage of dealing with defined genetic traits (ones that are attributable to known alleles with known dominance and recessiveness) is that we can actually calculate the gene frequencies and resulting genotype frequencies that will result from gene flow between differing populations. This kind of calculation, however, leads us to a dilemma in the case of the distribution of the B allele in Asia. If the Mongoloids started out at some time in the past with a frequency of the B allele approximately equal to what they now have, and then bestowed the allele by gene flow on other populations that previously had not had it, they would have had to mix with the others in overwhelming numbers in order to increase the B-gene frequencies of the other populations to a level so nearly equal to their own. Such numerical predominance would have nearly obliterated the racial differences in other traits, which in total must represent a large number of genetic loci. A hypothetical population having rather noncommittal racial features, and 100 per cent B allele, mixing with Mongoloid, Ainu, and Indian—and then conveniently disappearing—might do the job better. But there is no evidence that such a population ever existed. The most attractive hypothesis to explain the situation is that the B allele is not neutral with respect to natural selection. The computer simulations of Chapter 4 demonstrated the way an allele that is selectively advantaged in many or all environments may spread from one population to another by small amounts of gene flow, and then build up in frequency wherever it has spread. Other genes introduced at the same time, by the same migrating individuals, will remain quite rare, or may even disappear altogether if they are subject to some local selective disadvantage. Even if selective effects are quite small, perhaps less than can be detected in a single generation, the final result over a few thousand years may be of such a nature that any estimate of gene flow based on simple calculation, ignoring the possibility of selection, may be totally misleading.

If the distribution of the B allele is to be explained by increase due to selection, when and how fast did the process take place? The B allele seems not to have reached aboriginal America, except its northernmost fringe, which suggests that the burgeoning of B was after the Americas were populated from Asia, possibly in the last fifteen thousand years. Did the mutation to B, from A or O, only occur once? Or had it occurred before and failed to become established, perhaps because its selective effect has not always been positive? Did some change such as the appearance of a disease, or the increase in carbohydrate in the diet following the development of agriculture, give allele B a physiological advantage it did not have before? These are interesting questions, whose answers we do not yet know.

THE AUSTRALOIDS AND PACIFIC ISLANDERS

East and south of the areas occupied by the Mongoloid Indonesians lie New Guinea, Australia, and a group of smaller islands. Crossing the archipelago east of Java, Celebes, and the Philippines, is Wallace's Line, named after Alfred Russell Wallace, the codiscoverer of evolution by natural selection, for which Charles Darwin has always been given most of the credit. This line is biologically important because it marks the limit of distribution of the higher mammals; east of it, the marsupials rule the vertebrates, except for man and other recently introduced creatures. Wallace's Line also approximates a racial boundary for man, separating the Mongoloids from the Australoids; it does so more exactly than the present political boundaries of Indonesia, which extend farther east. The Australoids take their name from the aboriginal inhabitants of Australia, who are the type population of the Australoid race, though not the only major variety. Few as their numbers are now as compared with some other races of man, they are properly recognized as a major race by virtue of their distinctiveness. The Australians, among their local varieties, agree in having dark skin, narrow heads, strong brow-ridges, and a more or less prognathous face with a wide nose. Many individuals, even women, have well-developed body hair and beard. In all these characteristics they contrast strongly with the Mongoloids, their closest long-term neighbors among other major races. The nose, though often low-lying, is not similar to that of Mongoloids in other respects. In Australians the nasal root is wide, the tip large and rounded. The end of the nose is blunt, and in many cases is depressed, making the nasal profile quite convex; though no part of the nose projects far forward.

Australia was first occupied by the human species at least fifteen thousand years ago, perhaps earlier. Man first entered this area when sea level was lower than at present, and when Australia and New Guinea were accessible, with only about fifty miles of oversea travel, from the nearest Indonesian islands. Australia is "the end of the line" in that direction, and the continent has remained nearly as isolated for its human inhabitants as for their marsupial totems. Most of the continent is arid, much of it true desert, though a narrow belt of moister climate supports forest growth along the south and east coasts. (This is the Southern Hemisphere, and wind patterns are the reverse of those in the Northern Hemisphere, bringing oceanic climate to the east rather than the west coasts.)

The Australians have been the ultimate backwoodsmen of the world. Cut off from the technological advances that had radiated out from the larger continents (agriculture, pottery, metals), and prevented by lack of resources and numbers from developing these innovations themselves, they were in a true Stone Age culture when first found by Europeans in the nineteenth century. Though we often speak of the Australians as a unit, there are local variations within the continent, which may indicate that the immigrant stocks were rather different when they arrived. The picture is confused by the long time period involved, which allows much scope for local selection and genetic drift. Some of the local differences that exist may have developed in Australia, at least in part, rather than having been imported from somewhere else.

The most distinct population appears to have been that of the island of Tasmania, off the southern coast of Australia (Figure 49A). These people are now represented by only a few mixed-blood

Figure 49(a) A Tasmanian chief's daughter, Tucanini, one of the last surviving full-blood Tasmanians. (Courtesy American Museum of Natural History.)

Figure 49(b) *Left.* An aboriginal from West Australia: Douglas Battle Crow. (Courtesy John Greenway.)

Figure 49(c) *Right.* An Australian aboriginal of north coast type: Harold Ulmari, journalism student. (Courtesy Australian Information Service.)

Figure 49(d) Two young women from New Guinea. (Courtesy Cyprian Weaver.)

survivors. Old photographs show them to be comparable in physical features to other Australians, but with frizzly hair—a trait we have observed in the Negritos and which we will encounter again in other Australoids outside the continent of Australia. The aborigines of the continent generally have hair that is straight or moderately curly. Some local trends are apparent: in the southern and extreme eastern parts of Australia, which are relatively well-watered, the natives are shorter and more hairy; in the north and in the central desert, they are taller and less hairy. In terms of outside affinities, the southerners seem closer to the Ainu, the northerners to an element we will encounter in India (Figures 49B, C). A variation concentrated in the central deserts is blond or reddish hair, which contrasts most strikingly with dark-brown skin. In some tribes this light-colored hair is very common in children, is retained more or less in some adult females, but usually turns dark in males as they grow older. The color cannot be explained by admixture; it appears to be a mutation that has become common, through selection or drift, in certain tribes. Another local variant is the presence of a fourth molar tooth, that is, an extra tooth behind the usual wisdom tooth. The occurrence of this fourth molar (which does not exceed 10 per cent in any local population) is also limited, and centers in the south-central part of the continent. The distribution of these two variants conforms to what one would expect in a large area with many local populations and slow but relatively uniform gene flow between adjacent groups (Birdsell, 1950); their centers do not coincide, and each decreases in frequency in all directions away from its center. (Although we can assign no *ultimate* specific causes for some of this local variation in Australia, this is no different from the situation in Europe, which we know so much about historically, and which has similar local variations within an area of comparable size.) The northern part of Australia has had some contact over a long period with seafarers of generally Indonesian type, which has resulted in some blood group B in that part of the continent. Otherwise the Australian aborigines have only allelles A and O.

North and northeast of Australia lie the islands of Melanesia, of which the largest, and the one which approaches nearest to Australia, is New Guinea. This is not an inconsiderable area, though it is one that is little known to the Western world. New Guinea is as long as from Maine to Georgia, as wide as from Ohio to the Atlantic coast, and has high mountains in its interior. Its climate, like that of Indonesia, belongs to the true tropics: It is hot and humid, relieved only by the coolness of altitude along its mountain spine. New Guinea, together with several groups of islands, of which the Solomons and the Fijis are the best known, is occupied by peoples most closely related to the Australians (Figure 49D). Typically, they are dark-skinned, narrow-headed, and beetle-browed. A distinctive feature is bushy hair, which lends itself to spectacular super-Afro hairdos. The combination of dark skin and bushy hair once caused them to be called "Oceanic Negroes"; they were assumed to be more or less closely related to Africans. This theory has been regarded critically for some time and appears to have been discredited by the discovery that the hair is really not very similar to that of African Negroes. The "frizzly" hair of Africa has a uniform, very fine spiral curvature, and in the Melanesians it is genuinely kinky, that is, has an irregular curvature. Thus the resemblance in the general appearance of their hair is misleading. A distinctive feature seen in some Melanesians is a convex nose, which combines the thick rounded tip, which we observed in Australians, with a somewhat more protruding bony skeleton. Because of the visual effect, early explorers thought they had found in Melanesia the "lost tribes of Israel." There is considerable local variation in skin color in Melanesia: some groups are a rather light brown. In certain areas blond hair is found, just as among their relatives, the Australians. This has sometimes been attributed to bleaching. This is an unlikely suggestion, because melanin is very resistant except to quite sophisticated chemical procedures; most folk methods of bleaching can do little more than brighten up hair that is already fairly light. However, some individuals have distinctly light skin as well as blond hair, and differ enough from their fellow tribesmen to have been called albinos, though they are by no means the pigmentless albinos of genetic literature. It is more likely that these are quite independent *blond* mutations, which may or may not be at the same genetic loci as those which produce blondism in Caucasians.

North of Melanesia lies Micronesia, consisting of many groups of small islands, which many people were hardly aware of until World War II. Guam, the largest of these islands, is smaller in area than some United States cities. Polynesia extends over essentially the whole of the central Pacific east of the International Date Line, and, except for Hawaii and New Zealand, consists of small groups of tiny islands also. With its corners at New Zealand in the southwest, Hawaii in the northeast, and Easter Island in the southeast, Polynesia covers an area as large as Africa, but considerably more than 99 per cent of it is open ocean.

It is surprising that islands so small and so widely scattered were settled by man as early as they were. In fact, they were settled relatively late, even as compared with Australia and the New World: the earliest archaeological dates are about two thousand years ago, not only for Polynesia and Micronesia, but for the smaller Melanesian islands east of New Guinea (Coon, 1965). It appears that the concept of going east into the ocean to find land, and the necessary skills for doing so, came to be shared within a rather short time by peoples of different racial groups. These included Australoids from New Guinea, who colonized the eastern Melanesian islands, and peoples from some part of Indonesia, who were the ancestors of the Micronesians and Polynesians (Figures 50, A and B). The latter two groups are not greatly different from one another, and the differences may be due to founder effect, which has also made the inhabitants of different islands *within* the two areas rather different. Both are probably derived from a Mongoloid-Australoid blend similar to that of numerous populations now

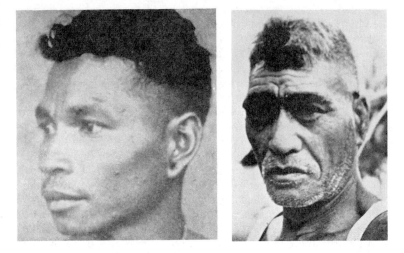

Figure 50(a) *Left.* A Micronesian from the island of Yap. (Courtesy Dr. E. E. Hunt and the Wistar Press.)

Figure 50(b) *Right.* A Polynesian chief from Mangaia, Cook Islands. (Courtesy Dr. Donald Marshall.)

Figure 50(c) Hawaii: King Kamehameha III, from a daguerrotype about 1850. (Courtesy Bernice Pauahi Bishop Museum.)

Figure 50(d) A young woman from Tahiti, Mrs. Here Tuara Thieme.

living in Indonesia and southeast Asia. Neither Micronesians or Polynesians usually show prognathism, but a wide nose and occasional frizzly hair indicate a Melanesian-like component. The Polynesians are distinct from most other Asian and Pacific peoples because of their large stature and heavy build: characteristics that were admired by early European voyagers. These large individuals often have large faces, reminiscent of American Indians (Figures 50 C and D). The body size is not difficult to account for. We know from direct observation in modern times that the largest-bodied individuals in a population tend to be the boldest in undertaking migrations to new homes. In the long process of colonizing the islands of Polynesia, self-selection of this kind must have occurred many times over, concentrating genes for large size in the descendants of the colonists.

The distribution of the B blood-group allele in these island groups is interesting. The Indonesians, as we would expect from their strong affinity to the continental Mongoloids, have high levels of it. Micronesians and Melanesians have moderate levels, though the latter are quite un-Mongoloid in most characteristics. Polynesians have less; and in the easternmost island groups of Polynesia, the B allele dwindles to an amount perhaps attributable only to recent admixture. If it is not actually being selected out in the latter area, it must have been introduced quite recently from continental Asia to the islands.

INDIA AND WEST ASIA

On a map of the world, Eurasia is a single huge continent; the recognition of Europe as a separate continent from Asia reflects only the bias of Europeans and their history-writing activities. India has been called a subcontinent. Actually, both Europe and India appear as large peninsulas extending outward from the land mass of Asia, and both, together with the large but sparsely inhabited area between them, are racially distinct from the Mongoloid Asia we have already discussed. India is rather diverse climatically. Much of it is hilly but not mountainous, and most of it is technically tropical, that is, it lies south of the Tropic of Cancer. India is in approximately the same latitude as southern Mexico and Central America, and has the same range of environments as the lowland parts of that area. There are rainforests on the west coast of India and in Bangladesh, but a greater part of India is rather dry open forest. There is desert in the northwest part, where India adjoins Pakistan. India is nearly surrounded by Mongoloids, yet its racial boundaries are surprisingly distinct. On the north of India lies the great mountain mass of the Himalayas, which we might suppose to be a barrier to human movements. But in fact the racial boundary is not the mountain mass itself. The high plateau of Tibet is inhabited

Figure 51(a) A woman from India; Professor Manesha Roy of the University of Colorado.

Figure 51(b) A modern Iranian: Mr. J. Amouzegar, Iran Oil Minister. (Wide World Photos.)

by Mongoloid peoples, who extend downward on the southern slope into Nepal and Bhutan (Fig. 46D), though not lower than about 5,000 feet altitude. On the east borders of India, the most western of the obviously Mongoloid peoples live in the hill areas between Bangladesh and Burma. Northwest of India, beginning in Pakistan, rise the mountains which rim the plateau of Iran and Afghanistan, where Caucasoid peoples have lived for thousands of years. In India, as in Asia, we can distinguish "hill tribes," self-sufficient and genetically isolated units, from the majority populations, who are village agriculturalists and urban dwellers of the lowlands. The tribal organization is obviously the older population pattern. There has apparently been a long-drawn-out, and still imcomplete, process by which tribes, one after another, have been drawn into the larger economic unit. The remaining tribes may or may not differ racially from their homogenized neighbors.

Indian society has long been divided into castes which are, at least in theory, genetically isolated from one another. Genetic studies have shown that these groups do differ from one another to some degree in gene frequencies, even within a single community. However, this does not greatly complicate regional trends in the population, either because the caste barriers have leaked considerably or because they were not developed until after local populations were fairly well blended. It has long been realized that there were at least two elements in the population of India. One of the early

Figure 51(c) An ancient Persian as shown on the walls of Persepolis, fifth century B.C. (Courtesy Iran Information and Tourism Center.)

Figure 51(d) A Kazakh (Cossack) from the western part of the People's Republic of China: he is entirely European in appearance. (*China Reconstructs.*)

discoveries of scientific language study was that there was a relation between the languages of northern India and those of Europe. The whole group was designated Indo-European, and its introduction into India was equated with semihistoric records of the arrival from the northwest of a people called the Aryans. In the light of present knowledge, it does not appear that this was by any means the first Caucasoid element to enter India. There seems to have been a much earlier component, now very widespread, of Mediterranean type, which dates back to the time of the early development of agriculture in India. There is a general trend for skin color to be lighter in the north of India than in the south, probably because of the interaction of both of these "northern" elements with an older and darker-skinned population. We can make a broad generalization about the population of India by saying that it is generally Caucasoid in features (certainly not Mongoloid), but darker in skin color than European Caucasoids (Figure 51A). Though there is some overlap, the majority of Indians, particularly in south India, would not be mistaken for Europeans, because their skin color falls outside the limits of variation in Europe. This is in spite of the fact that a quite fair skin and blue eyes occasionally occur.

A distinctive feature often observed is a "deep-set eye." (This is really a "projecting brow": the eye cannot just be pushed back into the face, because there are too many essential anatomical structures behind it.) This brow, which extends forward over the eyes and then rises rather vertically from there, is an Australoid feature, one of several indications that the dark skin of many Indians is not derived from a Negroid source. A quite Australoid-like appearance is found in some of the "hill tribes" of the east and south; these have shorter faces—sometimes prognathous—and broad noses. These tribes may not be unmixed representatives of any particular ancestral population; perhaps their various combinations of features have crystallized out of an early mixture by genetic drift. Facial features of this kind appear as individual variants within the general population, in south India particularly. Australoids evidently did extend west from Southeast Asia into India at one time, and are the people who introduced dark skins to India. The fact that this skin color has become associated with local populations in India, which are predominantly Caucasoid in other features, suggests that natural selection in the Indian climate favored and increased the genes for dark skin once they were introduced. That this has not happened in the tropical islands of Indonesia, where Australoid and Mongoloid have mixed, may be because Mongoloids have developed the second mechanism for protection of the skin against solar radiation—thickening of the stratum corneum—which has made the development of increased pigmentation less necessary. The likelihood of selection makes it difficult to evaluate the amount of the Australoid component in present-day India. It is probably considerable in areas of the south and east, but relatively small in the north and west.

The valley of the Indus River, now Pakistan, lies northwest of India. Its racial characteristics are similar to those of the adjoining part of India. The difference between the two nations is one of religion, not of physical characteristics. This is the last fertile country for several hundred miles in this northwesterly direction. Afghanistan and Iran are high plateaus interspersed with mountains, and for the most part extremely arid. This area is not easily crossed or inviting to invaders: and its population, a clearly Caucasoid one (which has been called *Indo-Afghan*) has probably not changed appreciably in six thousand years. These people are brunet white in coloring, with narrow-cheeked faces and impressive large, convex noses (Figure 51B). Some of them have broad heads; in this they resemble Mongoloids, but not otherwise. These highland Caucasoids are usually heavily bearded, in contrast with the Mongoloids. Their relatives lived, and still do, in the valleys of Mesopotamia, now Iraq. Four thousand years ago, stone carvers immortalized the type, with its stocky build, convex nose, and heavy beard of stylized curls, on the walls of Persepolis (Figure 51C). North of this high plateau lies the low desert of Turkestan, which is continuous northward with western Siberia, and opens on southeast Russia between the Ural mountains and the Caspian sea. Turkestan is now occupied by transitional peoples, carrying both Mongoloid and Caucasoid strains; they are racially similar, if not direct descendants, of the Huns, who bedeviled both the Russians and the Chinese in medieval times. In addition there are some enclaves of Mongols, vestiges of the expansion of the Mongol empire in the thirteenth century, and some peoples who look quite European (Figure 51D).

Who were the people who entered India from the north to establish the racial gradient we now see in India? Though the Middle Eastern nose is sometimes seen (usually in a delicately modified form) in Pakistan and north India, the highland people seem not to have been the principal Caucasoid element that entered India. The dry steppe lands of Turkestan, north of India and separated from it by a rugged passage over the east end of the Iranian Plateau, have been a corridor area, and many populations, some of more western affinities, have occupied it at various times. Presumably, the early Mediterranean Caucasoids of India came via this route. Because they came at a time when agriculture was beginning to replace simpler forms of subsistence, they perhaps came in small numbers and then rode the wave of population increase which occurs at such times. We know that at a later period Turkestan harbored other Caucasoid peoples, including the *Scythians,* who appear in both Persian and Greek history. They were sometimes referred to as blond (though it would not take very extreme blondness to impress the people who recorded this) and were probably genetically related to the peoples then living in northern Europe, though it would be misleading to equate them too closely with any modern European stock.

The rather mobile people of this area were, not surprisingly, often drawn to the more generously watered plains of India. The legendary "Aryans" may have physically resembled the Scythians. In any case, it is probable that the effects of these wanderers on India was more cultural than physical, regardless of the protestations of those who like to think themselves more or less purely descended from them. They may account for the greater fairness of skin and occasional blue eyes seen in northern India. Our guesses about the racial history of India would be better based if we had more information about the phenotypic results of recent mixture of Caucasoid and Australoid stocks.

There is one area remaining that can be understood in terms of its Asian neighbors—Arabia. This is a huge area with a scanty population. It lies in the desert belt of the upper tropics, and even its shores are arid, owing to a lack of on-shore winds. In a few places, mountains catch enough rain for agriculture. Arabia is largely occupied by a somewhat modified Iranian-Plateau type population, but with longer heads and facial features more like Europeans. Many people from this area have moved west into North Africa, and we will encounter them again.

EUROPE

Europe has been the subject of great interest and intensive study by physical anthropologists, most of whom in the past have traced their own ancestry to this area. Many books have been written on the fine distinctions of the various races and subraces of Europe. (Even the *races* of Europe are *subraces,* in a world perspective.) A wealth of historical records can be brought forth to guide our conjectures about gene flow within Europe and the resulting relations between regions. No less detailed a study could be made of India; in fact, anthropologists of that country are now engaged in it. The aborigines of Australia, an area about as large as Europe, are as varied as Europeans, if we look closely. For purposes of this book we must stand back and look at Europe in more general terms. The western Europeans who scattered over the world in the last few centuries found most of it to be either too dry or too hot to be much to their liking. The Spanish and Portuguese, the most southerly of the colonizing nations, were least troubled by this. Western Europe is climatically unique. Because of the scattered locations of its mountains, an oceanic climate—with ample rain and a small difference between winter and summer temperatures—is carried far inland by inshore winds from the Atlantic. As a result, the plains of northern Europe as far east as Russia, and the lands around the Mediterranean, have climates that are matched, in North America, only by a narrow belt between the Pacific Ocean and the Western mountains. This is why the Mediterranean agricultural staples, the olive and the European wine grape, are successfully grown in California but not elsewhere in the United States. Most of Europe, with the exception of the southern part of Russia and areas in the Balkans and Spain, was originally wooded, though much of the land was cleared for agriculture centuries ago, and some has been badly damaged by erosion as a result. The rest is grassland; Europe has no true desert. There are numerous centrally located mountain ranges in Europe, but many are not impressive, and they are irregularly disposed—unlike, for instance, the continuous western mountains of North America. Genes have flowed around and between the mountains for a long time, and most freely since the time of the Roman Empire, roughly the last two thousand years. The routes of freest population contact have been through the northern plains, from Ireland to Russia, and along the shores of the Mediterranean. But northern and southern zones have been by no means isolated from one another.

The genetic result of this lack of barriers within Europe is that local variations represent combinations of traits that are independently distributed, some varying principally from north to south, some from east to west. In a few places, certain trait combinations are traceable to known incursions of outside populations. Early analyses of European regional variation, emphasizing the areas best known to western European anthropologists, attempted to divide Europe into local subraces. The traditional three were (1) *Nordic,* in northwest Europe: tall, long-headed, narrow-nosed, blond; (2) *Mediterranean,* in southern Europe: short, long-headed, narrow-nosed, brunet; and (3) *Alpine,* in central and east central Europe: short, round-headed, broad-faced, variable coloring (Figures 52A and B,

53A and B). At one time it was rather fashionable to be Nordic. This particular combination of features is most common among the Scandinavians, who never glorified it. Among the Germans, who did, the Nordics are mostly outnumbered by the brunet, the round-headed, and the short. Applying this three-way classification to all Europe did not always make much sense, and other subraces were constructed to fill the gaps. These included *Atlanto-Mediterranean* in west Europe, between the Nordics and western Mediterraneans: long-headed and of mixed coloring; *East Baltic* in northeast Europe: a sort of blond Alpine, round-headed and broad-faced; *Armenoid* and *Dinaric* in the eastern Mediterranean and extending into West Asia: very round-headed, brunet, and with a large face and acquiline nose (Figure 53C). Actually, all these combinations can be fairly well accounted for by specific trends in separate traits. It is clear, for instance, that the farther north we go in Europe, the higher the frequency of blondness, and that this trend crosscuts variations in head form. It should be emphasized that we speak in terms of *frequency* of blondness, for even if we define blondness very broadly indeed, there is no living population of any size in which all individuals are blond, and there is no reason to suppose that there ever has been. The zone in which a high to moderate frequency of depigmented individuals is found extends east from the traditional Nordic area, through Finland and the Baltic states and into the westernmost part of Siberia. In the latter areas, the head form and facial features do not in the least correspond to the true Nordic type. South of the "most blond" zone, and again extending from east to west, is an area of populations in which the mixture of light and dark pigmentation is obvious, as in the traditional Alpine and the Atlanto-Mediterranean. Farther south, brunets predominate, though some blond individuals occur in the Mediterranean countries—Spain, Italy, and Greece—and even among the Caucasians of North Africa, which we will discuss later.

Another general trend can be seen in head form, which the earliest anthropologists recognized as a significant variation among European peoples. In general, long heads are concentrated in the west, broad heads in the east, with the broad heads pushing farther west in central Europe than along either the north or Mediterranean coasts. As in the case of pigmentation, there is much individual variation, but the trends show up in regional averages. The intersection of these two nonparallel trends, pigmentation and head form, essentially defines the positions of the Nordics in the northwest, the East Baltics in the northeast, the Mediterraneans in the southwest, and the Armenoids in the southeast. The other so-called local types fall into place, insofar as pigmentation and head form are concerned, in relation to these two gradients. Several subsidiary trends can be seen. In the northern tier of populations there are varieties of blondness. The amount of redness in the hair is greatest toward the west, reaching a maximum in Scotland; and as we go farther east, the hair is more likely to be an ashen blond rather than red or golden. There are also inconsistencies between hair and eye

Figure 52(a) *Left.* An American of Scandinavian ancestry: Professor Tom Dynneson, University of Texas, Odessa.

Figure 52(b) *Center.* A German from Bavaria: Professor Gottfried Lang of the University of Colorado. (Courtesy CU Photographic Service.)

Figure 52(c) *Right.* An American of Czech ancestry: Professor Dorothea Kaschube of the University of Colorado.

Figure 52(d) A young man from Russia. (*Soviet Union.*)

Figure 52(e) *Below left.* An American of Hungarian ancestry: Rose Garam Batzdorff, University of Colorado graduate.

Figure 52(f) *Below right.* A group of Lapps. (From *Within the Circle,* by E. Stefansson, courtesy Scribners.)

Figure 53(a) An American of Italian ancestry, Professor C. Camadella of Metro State College, Denver.

Figure 53(b) An American of Greek ancestry, Theodora Tsongas Ludington, University of Colorado graduate.

Figure 53(c) A Syrian, Hafez Assad, President of Syria. (Wide World Photos.)

Figure 53(d) An American of Basque ancestry, Senator Paul Laxalt of Nevada.

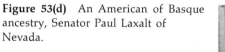

color. In the northeast, most characteristically in Ireland, blue eyes often occur with dark brown or black hair. Farther east, especially in Poland and nearby areas of central Europe, light hair may be accompanied by brown eyes. (Coon, 1939).

Facial features also show considerable local variation within the general Caucasoid pattern. A relatively straight and narrow nose, which was part of the definition of the Nordic race and is generally regarded in Europe as comely, appears most consistently in the west, from Scandinavia south to Spain. In general, a narrow face and a narrow nose accompany a narrow head. As we go east in the northern and intermediate tier of populations, we see an increasing number of turned-up noses, in which the root and bridge are only moderately projecting, and the cartilaginous tip protrudes forward. This concave nasal profile usually occurs in a nose rather short from top to bottom, in a short face. Although the turned-up nose is present in Scandinavia and Germany, it becomes characteristic in Finland and in the Baltic states, where it has become part of the definition of the East Baltic subrace. Common also among Czechs and Russians, it is a distinguishing feature of the countenance sometimes called *Slavic* (Figure 52C). This type of nose occurs in the northern blonds of eastern Europe, and in the area toward northern Russia and Siberia, where a *Ural* subrace has been defined by some anthropologists.

In the southern tier of European populations, the eastward trend of facial features is quite different. We have already discussed the ancient Caucasoid stock of the Iranian Plateau region, with its large face and convex nose. There is a clear gradient from west to east through the Mediterranean region, with an increasing frequency of convex noses, and of noses that are not only convex but massive, and set in massive faces. In this area, where artistic records go back over two thousand years, we can see this facial feature in historical perspective. The people of classical Greece seem to have lacked this Middle Eastern nose, or else they tried to ignore it in their art. But it is fairly common in modern Greeks. This is not unexpected, in view of the longstanding maritime commerce along the Mediterranean shores. North of Greece in the Balkan countries and Albania, we see it inland and even in mountain areas as the so-called Dinaric subrace. The concept of "Mediterranean" has become confused in the anthropological literature because of disagreement as to whether it should include the convex-nosed eastern Mediterraneans as well as the straight-nosed western Mediterraneans. There is, coincidentally, another trait characteristic of the Asian Caucasoids— heavy beard and body hair—which shows a similar gradient. Conspicuous in the eastern Mediterranean region, it appears less often in the west and north Mediterranean.

These various trends give us an approximate idea of the areas and environments in which some of these traits first developed significant frequencies. Reduced pigmentation clearly correlates with northern latitude, over a large area which includes much variation in other traits. We have discussed possible reasons for reduced pigmentation in Chapter 5. Whatever the cause, it is note-worthy that northern Mongoloids, from Siberia to the Eskimo homeland extending all across the Arctic coast of North America, have never developed reduced pigmentation. Although blond mutations have occurred elsewhere in the world, they never really took hold except in the northern European Caucasoids. It has been suggested that blondness—perhaps because of the effect of depigmentation on the function of the eye—is most adaptive where there is persistent cloudiness. We need to know much more about this apparently very local value of reduced pigmentation. The gradient in head form, particularly because it has attracted the attention of anthropologists for so long, has attracted many speculations. The Caucasoids, among modern races, are notable for having an extremely wide range of variation in head form. Because of the concentration of broad heads in the east of Europe, the variation is apparently continuous with the broad heads of Mongoloid Asia. To what extent is this a real genetic continuity? The total shape is not really the same: the European broad heads are usually high in the cranial vault, the Mongoloid ones more often low. The picture is complicated by the fact that in rather recent centuries there has been a shift from narrower to broader heads in more than one part of the world. It has occurred among American Indians, for example, where there is no good evidence that any new genes came in from outside. In both the Old World and the New, this change coincides with the development of agriculture and a corresponding change in diet. There seems to have been some selection in modern times that has favored an increase in the numbers of genes which enhance the breadth of the head. There has been some population movement and genetic contact between eastern Europe and western Asia for a long time. In parts of eastern Europe, we sometimes see a massive upper face that has an Asian quality (Figure 52E). There are even some surviving communities derived from Ghengis Khan's Mongols. But there is no indication that Asian influences on Europe have been so substantial, or so one-sided, that this alone would have affected head form as far west as, for instance, Germany and the Netherlands. Therefore, broad heads in Europe may at one time have been introduced from Asia or from some intermediate source, but have come to dominate parts of Europe primarily by positive selection.

Nose variations may have selective effects also, as we suggested in Chapter 6. The generally sharp and protruding Caucasoid nose is, according to general biological rules, not suited to severe cold. But in western Europe's oceanic climate, really severe cold (by world standards) does not occur. Even in the colder parts of Scandinavia, midwinter temperatures hover around 20 degrees F. *above* zero, as compared with 20 degrees F. *below* zero in northern Siberia and the Eskimo country. The moderating effect of the Atlantic Ocean rapidly fades from Finland eastward. It is possible that the East Baltic and Ural nose, with its low-lying bony portion, is an adaptation to severe cold, just as is the Mongoloid nose, but that it has developed independently and is not genetically related. The Middle Eastern nose seems to be a permanent fixture in the high plateau of Iran. We have suggested, on the basis of similar developments elsewhere in the world, that it may be an adaptation to low humidity. Its present extension into Arabia is certainly appropriate, if that is the case. Its apparent spread in the last few thousand years into the eastern and central Mediterranean region raises some questions. There has certainly been genetic contact and gene flow within the area, but there is no historical evidence that it has been extensive or one-sided. It may be significant that ecological conditions have changed in the eastern Mediterranean region during this period. Much of this country was once green, at least after the winter rains, and the hills and mountains were forested. Over the centuries since the introduction of agriculture, much of this land has been turned into rocky desert by overcultivation, overgrazing, and deforestation, with resulting erosion. If a large nose is in fact selectively favored by conditions of low humidity, it may have spread westward along the Mediterranean by the combination of some gene flow and subsequent positive selection.

Earlier, we delayed the discussion of some of the populations living between Asia and Europe. Turkestan is at present a Caucasoid-Mongoloid border area in a very clear way; it has mixed populations, some combining the wide Mongoloid face with the Middle Eastern nose, and also has interspersed populations which lean toward one race or the other. The Caspian Sea is the west boundary of Turkestan; west of it, we are in essentially Caucasoid territory. Here we come finally to the Caucasus Mountains, the mythical homeland of all of the Caucasoids. There is some blondness among these people, the heritage of the Scythians, no doubt, and the inevitable trace of the Middle Eastern nose. This region adjoins eastern Turkey, the Asia Minor of ancient history, which is as much a part of Europe as is Russia. The people of Turkey are predominantly brunet, and are mostly round-headed: seen equally often are the Middle Eastern Nose, and a straight nose similar to that of a central European Alpine. There is nothing Mongoloid about them; in fact they differ little from present-day Greeks. (Their relation to the historical "Turks" of Turkestan is tenuous.)

Two local populations in Europe have aroused long-standing interest among anthropologists: the Lapps and the Basques. The Lapps, in the extreme north of Norway, Sweden, and Finland, live by reindeer-herding in an area where few people care to bother them, and as a result have been more isolated genetically than any other population within the continent of Europe. However, they appear to be essentially *native*, despite ideas once put forth that they had some exotic Asian origin. They are small in stature, possibly in adaptation to somewhat stringent environmental conditions. But in pigmentation and facial features they are northern Europeans. Many of them are blond, though their pigmentation varies, and they have the short face and often turned-up nose of their neighbors in the Baltic states and east of them along the Arctic coast

(Figure 52F). As with many other isolated and inbred peoples, they are physically recognizable to those who are familiar with them, and they show some distinctive gene frequencies. But their uniqueness is probably the result of genetic drift and specialized selection rather than of any unusual origin.

The Basques, who live in the Pyrenees mountains between France and Spain, have been singled out for interest because they speak a language which is the sole survivor of a group of otherwise extinct languages. They do not differ physically in any major way from either their French or their Spanish neighbors (Figure 53D). However, they have a very high frequency of the Rh-negative allele. In discussing the effect of maternal-fetal incompatibility on gene frequencies in Chapter 4, we pointed out that incompatibility of this kind eliminates heterozygotes and thus tends to eliminate the rarer of two alleles. The Basques, with a 53 per cent frequency of Rh-negative, are the only known population that has passed the 50 per cent break-over point beyond which Rh-positive will be progressively eliminated. Probably their aberrant gene frequencies, as well as their retention of a language with no surviving near relatives, are both simply the result of a long period of cultural isolation and genetic drift. Another population is worth mentioning: the Sardinians, who seem to be ordinary western Mediterraneans except for an unusual frequency of the Rh chromosome CDe. In this case, their isolation in an island habitat, perhaps with an initial founder effect, has resulted in an aberrant gene frequency. No one has suggested that the Sardinians have had any unusual or romantic origin.

THE JEWS AND THE GYPSIES

Among the various populations of Europe that have ebbed and flowed over various regions of the continent for many centuries, two, the Jews and the Gypsies, are outstanding for having combined mobility with a high degree of genetic isolation, and have continued to be regarded as more or less alien wherever they have gone. In one respect they are strongly contrasted: the Jews have an unusually well-documented history, the Gypsies virtually none. The somewhat legendary early portion of Jewish history tells of an origin in the region that is now Israel, and of sojourns of at least portions of the tribe in Egypt and Iraq. We are probably correct in imagining them, by the first century B.C., as being Mediterranean Caucasians with a definite influence of the Middle East—not very different from the neighbors of the Israelis with whom they are presently at political odds (Seltzer, 1939). In 70 A.D., after the destruction of the Temple by the Romans, the Jews left Israel and moved out in various directions, some east into West Asia, some northwest into Europe, some southwest into North Africa. In these various areas they maintained a strong sense of community identity and a high degree of genetic isolation. However, at the present time, the Jews in these various areas have obviously become genetically altered in the direction of the non-Jewish populations among whom they have lived. In some cases, as in Ethiopia, Jewish communities have been entirely transformed genetically. Where they have now reassembled in Israel, the local differences in Jewish phenotype are very evident. North African, Asian, and European Jews are quite distinguishable physically as well as different culturally, and are as capable of forming prejudices against one another as any other visibly different peoples. The genetic isolation of these populations from their Gentile neighbors has clearly not been as complete as it is sometimes assumed to be. However, when we consider the length of time involved, this is not surprising. An average inflow of genes amounting to only 1 per cent per generation would dilute the gene pool by about half in the nearly two thousand years that have elapsed. Genes have gone out, too, perhaps in even larger numbers; but the effect has not been as noticeable in the larger populations. Quite possibly the genes have maintained a greater uniformity in facial features than in, for instance, blood groups, because facial appearance influenced individuals of mixed parentage in their choice of which community they joined.

The origin of the Gypsies has been inferred from their language, physical appearance, and blood groups. They are rather dark Caucasians who apparently came from India, though their name reflects an old belief that they were Egyptian. They have been small in numbers and nomadic, often living in their vehicles and making their income by trading of various kinds. Some came to the United States in the nineteenth century. At present, they are disappearing in many areas by settling down and merging with the general population. Their way of life—a biologist would call it their "ecological niche"—is not unique. In Africa and Asia we can find populations, quite unrelated to the Gypsies genetically, who have chosen a similar nomadic way of life among settled neighbors. The "Gypsies" of England are essentially English, and the "Tinkers" of Ireland, who are typical gypsies in their way of life, seem to be a genetic isolate of purely Irish origin (Crawford, 1974).

AFRICA

Africa is not a small continent. It is larger than North America, and is second only to Asia in area. In map projections showing the whole world, it comes off badly. When the round world is flattened to put it on a map, the areas nearer the poles are expanded, and the tropical regions are relatively compressed. Africa, lying right across the equator, looks smaller than it is. All of Africa is either hot or warm, but rainfall varies greatly and is the most significant factor in its climatic diversity. A rather narrow belt of the North African coast, the part opposite Spain and France, has a climate similar to the European shores of the Mediterranean, and has long had a similar agricultural economy, with wheat fields, citrus groves, and vineyards. South of this area for hundreds of miles stretches the Sahara Desert, inhospitable to travel and with a tenuous population dependent on scanty and scattered water sources. Eastward along the Mediterranean, the coast retreats southward and the desert meets the sea. Only in Egypt, where the Nile brings water from mountains far to the south, is there another concentration of settlement along the coast. The long narrow Nile Valley, with its concentrated irrigation agriculture, traverses the desert southward and is the only break in an arid and very thinly inhabited zone, a thousand miles wide from north to south, which extends across Africa from the Atlantic coast to the Red Sea and continues across the Red Sea to include Arabia. This area is not only dry but intensely hot. South of the desert area there is a rather rapid transition to the humid lowlands of the south-facing Atlantic coast of West Africa and the Congo basin: the distance from the edge of the desert to the rain forest is hardly five hundred miles. The rain forest—the African jungle of popular lore—lies right over the equator and combines heat with continual humidity. Europeans have found it virtually intolerable. East of this area is the high plateau of Ethiopia, the highest point of an elevated area that extends southward, east of the Congo rain forest, toward the southern end of the continent. Much of this southern part of Africa is grassland or open woodland which supports large herds of grazing animals, both wild and domesticated. In addition to the Sahara, Africa has one other major desert area, the Kalahari in the extreme southwest part of the continent.

Racially, Africa is Caucasoid as well as Negroid, and the boundary between the two racial groups is the great desert zone of the Sahara and the Sudan. The Egyptians are well known from ancient times, both from the skeletal remains of their early dense population and from the meticulous work of their artists (Figure 54A). These Egyptians were archetypal Caucasoids, with narrow nose, prominent nasal root, and rather small jaws; brunet in coloring, with dark eyes and hair, and skin that tanned to a warm brown in the intense Egyptian sun. We do not hesitate to call them *Mediterranean*; they were of the basic Caucasoid type of southern Europe which, despite various other influences, still predominates from Spain to Greece. For many centuries the Egyptians were essentially isolated because the peoples around them were so far fewer in numbers. The people of modern Egypt (Figure 54B) show various racial strains. Arabs, who had the heavier features and more convex nose of the Near East, though they were no different in pigmentation, moved into and across Egypt a little over a thousand years ago. Some Negroid peoples from the south have left their traces, often apparent in hair form. Northwest Africa also received incursions of Arabs, but to a lesser degree. The older population of this area, the Berbers, are more European in appearance. Some populations of

Northwest Africa show considerable blondism, with hair of various shades of brown and reddish brown, and intermediate eye color. This may be the legacy of the *Vandals*, a Germanic tribe who made a name for themselves by looting Rome in the fifth century A.D., and who went on, eighty thousand strong, through Spain to North Africa, to rule there until they disappeared by absorption. Some Negroid elements have also entered this region, by a slow infiltration all across the Sahara, where they are present both as socially separate groups and as genetically absorbed elements.

South of the Sahara, where the population begins to increase as the desert changes to grassland, the population is just as predominantly Negroid as it is Caucasoid in North Africa. The transitional zone is one of a chancy grazing economy, very vulnerable to slight fluctuations of rainfall; here, at the present time, drought and famine have reached desperate proportions. The people affected are, like their neighbors in the rain forest south of them, basically Negroid, but with indications, varying from tribe to tribe, of Caucasoid infiltration from the north and east. The rain forest itself is the home of the classical Negroes, whose physical features predominate in the populations east and south of them (Figure 55A). They are of medium to tall stature, broad-shouldered and muscular, and long of limb. They are moderately prognathous, though not as much so as Australoids, and have wide noses with a low nasal root; brow-ridges are of moderate development, generally less than in Caucasoids. The vault of the skull is characteristically narrow and rather high. Skin color, of course, is very dark; the average is a dark brown, but the color ranges to truly black, in rare cases. The hair has a very tight spiral curl, properly described as wooly.

Also in the rain forest area are the Pygmies, a distinct population that is probably rather significant in the racial history of the area (Figure 55B). These small-statured populations are scattered in enclaves through the Congo Basin, surrounded and outnumbered by Negroes of much larger body size. Adult male pygmies average, in most groups, less than five feet tall, or only very slightly more. Their small size appears to be an adaptation to environment and subsistence: they can slip through and under the obstructions of jungle vegetation, which trap a larger person like a net. They are on good terms with their larger neighbors, carrying on a regular trade by which they exchange the products of their hunting and gathering in the jungle for the agricultural products grown by their neighbors. The genetic relation is slight and one-sided: Pygmy women sometimes marry into the Negro tribes, but no gene flow enters the Pygmy communities. This one-sided gene flow serves to explain how these groups, so few in numbers, have maintained a physical difference from the tribes that surround and outnumber them. In many ways, they have extreme Negro characteristics. The nose is often actually broader than it is long, and its tip is remarkably large. Marked prognathism is common. Like their neighbors, they have the sickle-cell gene, an asset in this malaria-infested country. Different Pygmy groups differ in the skin color, some being quite dark,

Figure 54(a) *Right.* Methethy, an Egyptian official of the Fifth Dynasty, about 2500 B.C. (A painted wood statue, courtesy of the Nelson Gallery, Atkins Museum, Kansas City, Atkins Fund.)

Figure 54(b) A modern non-Arab Egyptian, Professor R. El Mallakh of the University of Colorado. (Courtesy CU Photographic Service.)

Figure 54(c) A man from Libya. (United Nations.)

Figure 55(a)   A young woman of the Fulah tribe from Guinea, West Africa. (United Nations.)

Figure 55(b)   *Left.* A Pygmy of the Ituri tribe, Central Africa. (From *Die Twa Pygmaen in Ruanda* by M. Gusinde, courtesy Verlag St. Gabriel.)

Figure 55(c)   *Right.* Ahoroab, a young Bushman hunter. (From *Kalahari,* by Jens Bjerre, courtesy Farrar, Straus & Giroux, Inc.)

others with a lighter, yellowish-brown tone. They are quite hairy, more so than their larger neighbors.

Along with the Pygmies, we should discuss the Bushmen, who live in a quite different environment, in the Kalahari Desert a thousand miles south of any of the Pygmies (Figure 55C). They are also small in stature, and are extreme in one Negroid feature, the curvature of the hair. They are distinctly lighter-skinned than any other native Africans south of the Sahara. Their facial features are somewhat Negroid but unique in detail. They have a remarkable development of the fat deposit, *steatopygia,* which also occurs in some of the Asian Negritos. To have assembled these distinctive features, the Bushmen must have been genetically self-contained for a long time. How widely they may have been distributed in the past is an open question. There is evidence that they may once have lived in the Sahara Desert as well as in the Kalahari. There are still existing two small groups in Tanzania who seem to resemble them; and occasionally other Africans, as individuals, show Bushman-like features (Coon, 1965).

We can more or less interpret the varying features of the Africans south of the Sahara and Egypt in terms of the various populations we have described. Ethiopia, a distinct and interesting area, is on a high plateau reached only by rather steep and rugged routes, which have usually protected it from foreign incursions. "Ethiopian" as we

Figure 55(d)   *Left.* A girl from Somalia, East Africa. (United Nations.)

Figure 55(e)   *Right.* A man from the Malagasy Republic, Madagascar. (Courtesy Dr. Ronald Singer and the Wistar Press.)

mentioned earlier, was the designation given to all black Africans by the Greeks, and the present nation has a long semilegendary history. As in many other parts of Africa, its racial composition is a mosaic of tribes which may differ considerably in their genetic components. The Amharas, who have generally been in political control of Ethiopia for a long time, tend to be Caucasoid in facial features, but with rather dark skin and Negroid hair. Contrasted with them and some other Ethiopian tribes are populations that are more typically Negro, hardly distinguishable from West Africans. The Caucasoid element here seems to be, like the older population of Egypt, Mediterranean rather than Near Eastern. West of Ethiopia, in the desert south of Egypt, are the Nilotics (named for their location near the upper reaches of the Nile), whom we have already mentioned as being the tallest and most linear people in the world. They are very dark of skin, and vary in facial features; some individuals are quite Negroid, others more Caucasoid with relatively narrow nose. From Ethiopia and the Nilotic region southward, east of the rain forest of the Congo, and right into South Africa, is a large group of tribes generally known as *Bantu*, in reference to their languages. Most of them, in accordance with the semidry climate, live primarily by herding. Here, as in Ethiopia, we find a mosaic of tribes, among which neighbors often differ from one another in stature and various other traits. All are generally dark brown in skin color, all have typical Negroid hair form, but some, as in Ethiopia, show Caucasoid traces in their facial features: a narrower nose, thinner lips (Figure 55D). To a degree varying with the tribe, they are taller than the West Africans. The Caucasoid strain seen in Ethiopia has obviously filtered south into a predominantly Negro population, has been picked up more or less by different tribes, and accentuated more or less by tribal inbreeding. Where there is a contrast of culture, the tribes most dependent on their cattle tend to be taller, and to look down on their neighbors—figuratively as well as literally. In South Africa, in addition to the Bantu and the Bushmen, whom we have already described, are the *Hottentots*, a people who seem to have combined skin color and body size inherited from Bantu ancestors, with facial features resembling their neighbors the Bushmen.

So far we have taken the West African Negroes for granted, as an ingredient in other populations around them. The Caucasian elements in the apparently mixed populations of Africa are no mystery: we know where they came from. The Negro element is apparently indigenous to West Africa. But what is the relation of the West Africans to the Pygmies and the Bushmen? We have already remarked, in connection with the Negritoes of Indonesia, that very small stature appears to be a successful adaptation by which populations can maintain their identity though surrounded by people different from themselves. This the Pygmies have done, and, interestingly, in a rain-forest environment ecologically similar to that of the Negritoes. But it is notable that in certain features, especially nose form and prognathism, the Pygmies seem to be *more Negroid* than the Negroes. So it has been suggested that perhaps the Pygmies are the original and unique population of Africa, and that the West African Negroes who surround them are a mixture, of very long standing, of Pygmy and Caucasian (Coon, 1965). This would accord with the fact that the West Africans are generally shorter than the more Caucasoid blends of East Africa. We would have to assume that the blending took place long enough ago that selective effects in the rain forest environment had changed skin color to something darker than the original blend would have been. (Students of these populations by no means agree on this hypothesis.) The Pygmy groups themselves, after becoming isolated in their forest enclaves for a long time, might well be expected to have diverged not only from one another but from their own ancestral type, thus making their relationships unclear. The Bushmen, too, are probably an older race than the present typical Negroes. They also are more Negroid than the Negroes in one respect, hair form. Their peppercorn hair may represent the ancestral type from which Negro hair form was derived, subsequently to be modified by mixture. The skin color of the Bushmen is as well-adapted to their desert environment as is that of the Pygmies to their shadowed forests. In a very broad sense, the two may be "ecological races" of a single basic stock.

MADAGASCAR

The island of Madagascar, lying off the east coast of southern Africa, looks small compared to its mother continent. Actually it is larger than any European nation except Russia. Racially, it is not simply part of Africa. It was settled long ago by Indonesians who came from more than three thousand miles away. This is not as surprising as it might seem. The east side of Madagascar, facing the Indian Ocean, where the Indonesians would have made their first accidental landfall, is covered with a tropical rain forest like that of Indonesia, and its dry inland is suited to the cultivation of rice. So despite the distance, this island is a logical place for Indonesian settlement. Madagascar has another element in its population, derived from Bantu Africa, which lies within three hundred miles of the island's west coast. This is the only place in the world where Negroids and Mongoloids met in any substantial numbers until African slaves met American Indians in the New World. The two racial elements have mixed, though not freely, so that Madagascar has a wide range of racial type, including many degrees of admixture between the two most distantly related of the major races of the Old World (Figure 55E).

Genetic variation in the New World is not comparable to that of the Old. Most areas of the Old World have been occupied by man for a long time, so that differences between geographically separated groups have developed over a long period of time. There, separate and genetically different populations have pushed and shoved against one another from time to time, mixing with or displacing one another in varying degrees. But until the last few centuries, they have remained in the general areas in which they developed.

The Americas were populated late. Archaeologists disagree about the exact time of the earliest arrival of man in the New World, but all agree that it was after the general racial pattern of the Old World was established more or less as it is today. In terms of the whole history of the species, the peopling of America was recent and explosive. There is little disagreement that the native populations of the Americas are descended from migrants who crossed from Asia to North America in the Bering Strait region. At present there is a gap of about fifty miles between the continents there. But during the glacial age, when much of the world's water was tied up in great masses of ice, sea level was lower, and it would have been possible for people to have moved from one continent to the other over dry land; the present location of the strait would have appeared no different from the terrain on either side of it. The entire area, of course, would have been somewhat inhospitable, by the standards of those of us who are accustomed to warmer climes; it was a treeless, cold tundra. Yet it would have offered various kinds of game for the hunter, would have been no less difficult to live in than areas where people have lived in modern times, and was certainly no more forbidding on the American than on the Asian side. The history of the glacial period is complicated, involving fluctuations in climate, sea level, and the extent of the glacial ice sheets. Yet it would have been possible, at least intermittently, for man to have come over the land bridge and down into western North America at any of various times between 65,000 and 8000 b.c. After that the sea for the last time separated the continents, and any later immigrants would have needed boats to cross over. Archaeological dates for very early human occupation in the New World are few in number and not all certain. A conservative estimate for the first occupation of North America is 15,000 b.c. (some students believe it was twice as long ago), with indications that a few scattered bands found their way to South America rather quickly. In contrast to the Old World, then, there was a period in which rapid movement into a previously unoccupied territory was possible.

Another difference between the Old and the New World is that regional diversity among New World populations is by no means so clear as in the Old World. There is a general sameness about the physical appearance of New World populations. Pigmentation varies only moderately; eye color and hair color are dark; skin color, as among the Asian Mongoloids, varies from essentially white to dark brunet, always with a marked capacity to tan. Hair form is almost universally straight, only occasionally a bit wavy. Beard and body hair are usually sparse, in exceptional cases ranging to medium in amount. Stature and head and face shape vary from area to area, but the variation is not as extreme as in the Old World. Shovel-shaped incisor teeth are consistently present in American as in Asian Mongoloids. And in a general way we can call them all Mongoloids, though none are exactly like any populations in Asia at the present time. American Indians differ most from Asian Mongoloids by often having a large nose with a strong projecting bony bridge.

There have been speculations about the origin of the American Indians ever since it was realized that they were not part of the already known populations of the East Asian islands. The theory that they are the lost tribes of Israel (an easy way of accommodating them to scriptural traditions), was suggested soon after they were discovered, and still survives in some quarters. Theories linking them, or some of them, with various European peoples have never been shown to be anything but romantic myth. The discovery of the ruined but still spectacular architecture of Central America gave rise to speculations about contacts with Old World cultures, until archaeologists painstakingly uncovered the slow and unspectacular steps by which native civilizations developed from simple beginnings in the New World. We always return to the fact that the aboriginal inhabitants of the Americas were displaced Asians, even though they have some local features caused either by a special sampling of the populations of Asia, or by changes that have occurred since the original migrations. Fifty years ago, attempts were being made to explain the composition and variation of American Indian populations in terms of a wide variety of Old World racial types, who were thought to have come from Asia in "waves of migration"—making the Bering Strait area a Grand Central Station of human races (Dixon, 1923). It was necessary to assume that the Mongoloids came last, because they are still in the entry corridor, and that they colored the American populations with a wash of "superficial" characteristics—pigmentation, hair form, and so on—which were Mongoloid. It is difficult to explain genetically how populations could be built out of one set of races and then be given a pervasive likeness to another by comparatively late arrivals. But even if we believe the explanation to be far less complicated than this, we must still consider the questions of when, and for how long, migration from Asia to North America went on, and exactly *who*, in racial terms, was occupying northeastern Asia at that time or times.

Some of the "migration" explanations assume that anyone coming over from Siberia to Alaska in glacial times would have realized that this was miserable country, and that the sooner and faster they moved south, the more comfortable they would be. This, of course, credits these prehistoric peoples with geographical knowledge they could not possibly have had. Even if they remembered that their ancestors had come from a warmer area to the south, they could not have known that traveling south into an entirely new land would bring them to a warm climate again. Therefore, their southward movement would have been not so much intended, as passively directed by the lack of resident population in that direction. Population movement into an area previously unoccupied by man is a situation we have not had to consider in relation to the distribution of races in the Old World. In the long run, most human populations must live in a state of equilibrium with their local resources, maintaining but not increasing their numbers. In the peopling of the New World, a few men with effective hunting equipment were entering an area that had the potential of feeding millions of people, even with the simplest of hunting methods. The ordinary limits on population increase were, for the time being, suspended. How fast could a relatively small immigrant group increase its numbers? And how does this fit in with the assumed length of time involved, and with the population of the hemisphere in its last pristine state—about 1500 A.D.? We must use guesses to make further estimates. Because we are trying to explain a large increase in numbers in a limited time, we will choose a minimum time, 10,000 years, and a maximum estimate of the 1500 A.D. population of the hemisphere, which is 100 million.

How fast can populations increase under good natural conditions, that is, with plenty of food but no modern medical services? A well-documented example is that of the Navaho Indians of the southwestern United States, who now have a population about 12 times what it was 120 years ago. This, in terms of "doubling time" (the easiest measure of population growth), means doubling every 35 years, that is, a mean number of four surviving offspring to each couple. This rapid increase coincided with the use of domestic sheep as a newly acquired food resource. We may compare this with the kind of increase that might have taken place in the New World after the first coming of man. A convenient figure is that 10 doublings (2^{10}) multiply a population to approximately 1,000 times its original number. Twenty doublings square the amount of increase—from 1,000 times to 1,000,000 times. Thus, 100 individuals, entering the New World 10,000 years ago, could produce a population of 100 million by doubling 20 times. This means only one doubling every 500 years. This is a very slow rate of increase as compared with the maximum potential. It is likely, given the large and unexploited food supply of two new continents, that the early increase would have been very much faster than this, later leveling off to a state where population was balanced with resources. Because, as we have said, the southward movement would have been unplanned, population near the point of entry would soon have been about as dense as the environment would bear. This would have discouraged further immigration from Asia unless the newcomers had some physiological or cultural advantages over the first arrivals. Thus it seems likely that the *genetic* make-up of the populations of the Americas was largely determined by the first migrants. Some culture traits certainly reached the New World later—for instance, the bow. But we do not have to "move in" a large new population to account for every introduction of a new cultural trait. Thus we will have to explain the genetics of the Americas almost entirely in terms of the racial composition of northeast Asia at a single period not less, probably, than fifteen thousand years ago—perhaps more.

The distribution of races in Asia at that time may well have been different from what it is today. We have mentioned the Ainu, who appear to be an older population in Japan, and who were, perhaps no more than three thousand years ago, the predominant population there. They are distinctly non-Mongoloid: in general, a heavy-featured Caucasoid. Their hirsuteness, which clearly distinguishes them from conventional Mongoloids, crops up in other Asian populations also, including some in Siberia. In the northernmost part of Asia are populations that have sometimes been called *Proto-Siberian* or *Palaeo-Mongoloid*, which lack the extreme facial flatness of modern typical Mongoloids. In general, our impression of the Mongoloid area of Asia is that the most typical Mongoloids are relatively recent and that their traits have come to dominate their present large area of occupation within, certainly, the last ten thousand years. Thus it is quite likely that the ancestors of the American Indians were either a nonmodern Mongoloid type, or a mixed one, or both, with different genetic potentialities than we would infer from modern Asian Mongoloids, particularly from the "typical" ones of Mongolia or China. It is an interesting point that the B blood group, which is frequent now in many Asian populations, not only in the Mongoloid populations, and which we suspect of having recently become abundant in Asia because of a selective advantage, is conspicuously absent from North and South American Indians. This suggests that the ancestors of the Indians had gone on their way to the New World *before* the blossoming of allele B in Asia. The Indians, therefore, may represent the peoples who were in Asia, at least in Northeast Asia, before a number of developments took place there, including the evolution of the typical Mongoloids and the spread of the B gene. Who else may have been in northeast Asia that long ago? Were there people like the present West Asian Caucasoids, with their prominent nose, a likeness of which turns up in both North and South America? Certainly it is most likely that people resembling the Ainu were there. In any case, the first migrants to the New World may not have been "just" Mongoloids, and certainly not "just" modern Asian Mongoloids.

We have not included the Eskimos in the previous discussion. They, and the related Aleuts of the Aleutian island chain, are more like Asian Mongoloids than any other American peoples (Figure 56A). Eskimos still occupy the coast of the Bering gateway, and some of them live on the Asian side of the strait. Their culture is strongly tied to the coast, their economy to the large sea mammals, and they have fine seagoing boats for hunting and travel. The

Figure 56(a) *Left.* Two generations of Eskimos. (Courtesy Fred Bruemmer.)

Figure 56(b) *Right.* A Plains Indian: Carl Sweezey (Wattan), Arapahoe artist. (From *A Guide to the Indian Tribes of Oklahoma,* by Muriel H. Wright. Copyright 1951 by the University of Oklahoma Press.)

Eskimos might have come from Asia at any time, even after the sea covered the Bering land bridge, and spread rapidly along the Arctic coasts; their way of life would not lead to conflict with hunters of land animals. Significantly, they and the Aleuts have the B blood group gene, either because of their late arrival or because they maintained contact with Asia by their seagoing craft. This is additional evidence both for the lateness of blood group B in Asia, and for the early establishment of the genetic base of the American Indians.

There are other interesting aspects to the way in which the New World was populated. When a geographically large area is being filled by a rapidly expanding population, there is a maximum opportunity for the working of genetic drift. Archaeological studies indicate that the first immigrants lived primarily by hunting, and to a great extent by hunting the large late-Pleistocene mammals of North America, some of which they are suspected of having hastened to extinction. This would have encouraged them to range quite widely, even if only to follow individual herds; and this may explain why evidences of occupation in South America seem to be nearly as old as in North America. This pattern would have resulted in early wide distribution of a thinly scattered population, which later increased in density as the hunting-and-gathering techniques changed to more fully exploit the environment. The splitting and

Figure 56(c) An Indian of the southeastern states: Allan Wright, Principal Chief of the Choctaws, 1866–1870. Mr. Wright was one-eighth English by a marriage which took place about 1775. (From *A Guide to the Indian Tribes of Oklahoma*, by Muriel H. Wright. Copyright 1951 by the University of Oklahoma Press.

Figure 56(d) A California Indian of the Maidu tribe. (Photo about 1900 by Roland Dixon, courtesy American Museum of Natural History.)

Figure 56(e) A Navajo from Arizona: Raymond Nakai, former Chairman of the Tribal Council. (Wide World Photos.)

scattering of small population groups would have repeated *founder effects* over and over again. It may well be, then, that race formation in the New World started all over again, beginning from a single early occupation. A somewhat heterogeneous population, which did not correspond to any one Old World race (or at least any one modern race) may have diversified, by genetic drift and local selection, but to a degree much less than in the Old World, because of the shorter period of time involved. This is at least as good a hypothesis as others that have been proposed to explain human variability in the Americas.

The continent into which these ancestral Americans came is climatically and ecologically as varied as all of Eurasia. As we have said, migrants from Siberia to western Alaska would not have noticed much change. However, south of Alaska, climates differ considerably on the two sides of the mountain chain that parallels the Pacific coast. The rather narrow coastal strip lying west of the mountains has an oceanic climate, with heavy rainfall and relatively mild winters, comparable to that of northwest Europe. East of the mountains, rainfall is limited: in Canada it supports a cold forest; farther south, where evaporation is greater, there is much desert and semidesert. From the Rocky mountains eastward to the Atlantic coast, there are no major elevations (the Appalachians are modest mountains by world standards), and as rainfall increases gradually, grassland gives way to woodland. The northern part of this central and eastern half of the continent is coniferous forest, with many lakes and swamps—the legacy of the continental glacier which disrupted normal drainage patterns. Southward, there is mixed forest with fertile soils, becoming subtropical, with palms and broad-leaved evergreens, along the Gulf of Mexico. North America differs from Asia by having only a small tropical portion. Climates comparable to India and Southeast Asia are found only in Mexico and Central America, where the continent tapers to a very narrow east-west diameter.

South America, like North America, has its great mountain spine, the Andes, close to its west coast. High in the central Andes lies a chilly plateau over 10,000 feet high. The greatest width of South America lies over the equator, and here, eastward from the mountains for nearly 3,000 miles, stretches the *selva*, the great rain forest of the Amazon basin, comparable to the equatorial jungle of Africa, but much greater in extent. South of this area, the rain forest gives way to drier forest and grassland in a more temperate climate. Here the continent narrows, so that this area is small in extent compared to the rain-forest north of it. This region, like the part of the United States which it resembles, is now given over to stock-raising. The small southern tip of the continent is a cool, damp area, similar to northwestern Europe.

In describing the regional variations of the American Indian, as good a place as any to start is with those of the North American dry plains just east of the Rocky mountains. These *Plains Indians* have come to be regarded as "typical" Indians by modern Americans, even though they were relatively few in numbers, and their way of life (as first encountered by migrants from the east) had been greatly altered by the horses which they had only recently acquired from the Spanish settlements to the south. However, in their physical features they do represent a distinctive and rather extreme New World type (Figure 56B). They are tall, comparing favorably with northern Europeans; in this they are unlike the generally shorter Indians of most of the rest of the hemisphere, or most Asian Mongoloids. In other features, however, they exhibit clearly both the characteristics that American Indians share with their Asian cousins, and those by which they differ. The face is large and craggy, with strong cheek bones and often a protruding, aquiline nose. The size of the face is distinctive, though this tends to escape notice because its shape is well-proportioned—*both* length and breadth being unusually great. We may observe, in front view, that the forehead seems narrow: this is because the massive face is attached to a neuro-cranium of only average size. The facial breadth they share with the Asian Mongoloids; the great length is their own. The prominent nose, as we have already said, is most unlike Asian Mongoloids, and because of it the facial contour, despite the wide cheek bones, does not appear particularly flat. Because the prominence of the nasal skeleton is in part a sex difference, the women of these Plains Indians often have a flat-appearing face, hence, an Asian cast of countenance. Also, they often have a Mongoloid eye fold, apparently in correlation with the low nasal root. We have already discussed the possible selective significance of the large external nose in western Asia and Europe, as an adaptation to low humidity. If this surmise is true, it is not unexpected that in this dry plains area, selection has promoted the same genes. Plains Indians, like all American Indians, have Mongoloid-like hair, which grows long and thick, and the characteristic Mongoloid shovel-shaped incisors.

East of the home of these Plains Indians is a wide area extending to the Atlantic Coast, which was thinly inhabited in the northern portions, but with increasing density of population southward towards the Gulf of Mexico. In the eastern and southeastern United States, the survivors of these tribes are reduced in numbers and genetically mixed to a degree that is difficult to estimate. What we know of these people—from their modern survivors, their skeletal remains, and contemporary portraits—indicates that they were basically similar to the Plains Indians west of them (Figure 56C). The face is less consistently large, and sometimes narrow in the jaw, and the nose less aquiline. There is no evidence of the low-bridged Asian nose; however, though the nose is more modest in its projection, it still has an assertive root. These populations have been described as more Caucasoid than the western Indians; the early European settlers must have concurred, for they seem not to have had a very strong feeling of racial difference toward these Indian neighbors. Some white frontiersmen went to live among the southeastern tribes, thereby complicating the genetic picture. Some selection for skin color seems to have taken place in these populations: the most southernly of them are darker in skin color.

The narrow humid strip along the Pacific coast from Alaska

south, separated from the plains by the relatively uninhabited mountain areas, is quite distinct climatically. The populations in this area, as far south as California, often had shorter faces, more pronounced brow-ridges, and considerable beard growth (Figure 56D). This suggests a concentration of an Ainu-like element in an environment not unlike that of the Ainu in Asia.

Another province, from the point of view of physical types, is the southwest United States, Mexico, and Central America (Figure 56E). This is the area of North America in which the largest numbers of Indians, both mixed and of pure ancestry, now live. These peoples are distinctly shorter than the Plains tribes, and have sometimes been supposed to be a "later migration" than other North American populations, because of their wider heads. This brings up some unanswered questions. The breadth of the head seems to have increased in this area, just as it has in some areas of Europe, without any demonstrable invasion of new peoples. It appears to be an effect of selection acting locally on a resident population. Recent study of cranial collections has shown that the most meaningful measure of the breadth of the head is not the one previously most used—the maximum breadth—but rather the breadth of the cranial base, measured low down between the ears. This is more consistently wide among Mongoloids, both Asian and American, than the breadth taken higher up. For instance, the Indians of the Plains are, like their Asian relatives, wide between the ears, but the skull vault does not bulge out above. More study will be required to ascertain just what dimensions of the head are stable within races, and which are subject to change. In the Southwestern Indians the face is wide, though not as long or massive in the jaws as in the Plains Indian tribes; the nose is less projecting, and is sometimes relatively straight. The face consequently appears flatter, more Asian, especially in the women, who not infrequently have the Mongoloid eye fold. In Yucatan, in ancient as well as in modern times, we can find profiles that combine a convex nose with a receding chin, the latter trait being most alien to the faces of North America (Figure 57A). Yet, among all the tribes of North and Central America, there are no *major* genetic differences. If a sampling of Indians from the entire area were mixed together, and we tried to sort them out by region, it would be a puzzling job, and many undoubtedly would be sorted into the wrong boxes.

From Panama south through the rain forest and tropical grasslands of the Amazon basin, we see another distinctive New World type. With a low nasal root, frequently a Mongoloid eye fold, and a lower face that is short and narrow, this face is hauntingly similar to some Southeastern Asians and Indonesians who live in a similar environment (Figure 57B). In these same populations, and mostly among males, the stronger convex nose, so common in North America, appears also, but in moderate form. But, though wide across the cheeks, these are not the massive bottom-heavy faces of North America: the chin often recedes somewhat. The populations of the cooler highlands of the Andes and of the plains of southern

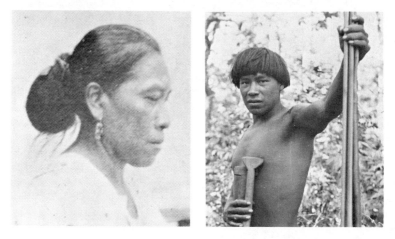

Figure 57(a) *Left.* A modern Maya Indian from Yucatan. (Photo by G. D. Williams, originally published in Vol. XIII, no. I of the Papers of the Peabody Museum. Used with permission.)

Figure 57(b) *Right.* A Camayura Indian from the Mato Grosso area of Brazil. (Photo by Dr. Edward Weyer, courtesy American Museum of Natural History.)

Figure 57(c) *Left.* An ancient Peruvian, about 500 A.D., as shown in a contemporary portrait vase. (Courtesy Linden Museum, Stuttgart.)

Figure 57(d) *Right.* A Yaghan Indian from Tierra del Fuego. (Photo by Dr. A. Lipschutz, courtesy Wistar Press.)

South America are more like North American Indians (Figure 57C, D). A very marked nasal convexity is seen in many Andean highlanders; this may be, as in other areas, a correlate of atmospheric dryness. But these highlanders would hardly be mistaken for Indians of the North American plains; they often have the narrow lower face, and receding chin, which is seen from Yucatan south.

In the New World we seem to see the process of racial differentiation only half finished, and this casts some light on the history of the development of race in the Old World, with its variation of color, size, and facial shape so much greater than the variation in the Americas. *Fifteen thousand years is not enough.*

The New and Future Races

14

THE NEW RACES

There is nothing new about the process by which the gene pools of two populations that have been separate, perhaps for a very long time, meet and mingle to a greater or less degree. The potentiality for this kind of happening is what distinguishes a single species with several races from a group of related but different species. Such occurrences have already been mentioned or implied many times in our discussion of races and their relations to one another. But there probably has been no period in history when more such "meetings" occurred in so many areas of the world than during the last four hundred years.

Biologists make a distinction between *introgression,* which denotes the entry of genes from one group into another group, which is only moderately affected by it, and *hybridization,* which denotes the formation of a new population in which the contributions of two (or more) parent groups are equally enough balanced that the new race is distinct from either of them. In plants and animals as well as in man we find *hybrid zones:* transitional areas in which mixed populations extend over a considerable distance between phenotypically different subspecies or races. We can say that a new race has been formed when the inhabitants of a hybrid zone become at least relatively isolated, eventually forming a new population in which the various genes of the parent populations are thoroughly mixed. Such a new population can be defined by its own means and variabilities. The results of the vast population displacements of recent centuries can give us some insight into how races have been formed in the past.

It is hard to know to what extent modern man has greater ability than his ancestors to maintain a sociological barrier between genetically different populations that occupy the same area. It is likely that the sociological barriers that now exist seem more formidable to us because we often fail to realize that they are, in the long run, transitory. But in spite of all barriers, the present time is a good one for observing the ways in which fusion of populations takes place. The principal driving force in recent interactions of races has been the rapid expansion of European peoples into parts of the world that were formerly less densely inhabited. The effects were not limited to the Western Hemisphere, though this was the area most affected. Simple genetic introgression from European into non-European populations was the first fruit of these contacts. The earliest contacts, as we have already said, did not produce as much genetic effect as is sometimes supposed. When strangers came to settle permanently, truly mixed populations resulted. In some cases these populations held themselves apart from both Europeans and natives, and became genetic isolates. More often the mixture resulted in introgression into one or both of the parent populations. In some cases, mixed-ancestor children were taken "home" by their European parents. Many interesting case histories could be cited: Indonesian genes in the gene pool of the Netherlands, Carib Indian in Denmark, and so on. Research workers interested in clearly identifiable traits, such as the blood groups, need to consider these events. More introgression, in general, has gone the other way. Our judgment that the B blood group was entirely lacking in American Indians is based on the fact that it is now rare among them, and is found to be rarest among the populations who seem to be of purest ancestry—even though at the present time it is hardly possible to be certain of the ancestry of many individuals whose blood might be sampled. Some workers in the field of biochemical traits have suggested that we can now ignore the visible phenotypic marks of race. However, biochemical data will become increasingly unreliable for historical inferences if field workers are not alert to the outward signs that justify question marks beside the designation of race on a data sheet.

A host of factors determined the way in which European peoples scattered over the world after the year 1500. We have already mentioned some of these. Certain diseases discouraged Europeans from settling in the deep tropics. Settlement was made easy for them where their own diseases sharply reduced native populations, as in North America. Regions where the native peoples were already agricultural, particularly where agriculture was intensive and populations high, were not attractive. Regions where vast areas were not being utilized at all, by European standards of land use, were irresistible. The nations that took part in the earlier migrations were those which were on the west coast of Europe and already had maritime traditions. In North America, for instance, early colonization came from Spain, the British Isles, and other Atlantic areas. It was two hundred years later before the nations further east—Germany, Italy, Poland, and so on—contributed as much to New World immigration. In the United States, the earlier migrants came in small craft, and many went to the small ports of the southern states. Later migrants came in large liners which could dock only in the large northern ports such as New York; and their descendants are still concentrated in the northern states (Brues, 1946b). Climate played an obvious part in choice of destination. North Europeans sought out temperate or cool climates, and the Spanish and Portuguese took over in the tropics and subtropics. Though the pattern of settlement depended to some extent on the dynastic dealings of European nations, the north-south distribution of nationalities played a clear role in the early settlement of North America: the Scots in Canada, the British and the Dutch south of them, the French in the Carolinas, and the Spanish, later ejected, in Florida. Spain and Portugal took over Central and South America, though some North Europeans went to Chile—far enough south of the equator to be in the Temperate Zone once again. Spain took the tropical Philippines, though the British and Dutch, unaccustomed to the heat, gritted their teeth and hung on in tropical India and Indonesia. The British and Dutch settled in Africa but only in the southernmost, most temperate part, and in the cooler highlands of the tropical belt.

Motivations for migration also varied. The Spanish, particularly in South and Central America, came first with the intent of finding gold or other valuable minerals, later settling or less exciting economic rewards. Notably, from the point of view of genetics, they came at first in male groups, without their own women. This initiated a halfbreed population, one that still remains as a social class (Mestizo) in much of Latin America. Most of the North European immigrants were family men who had the expectation of establishing communities entirely of their own race. The third element in the New World is African, largely from West Africa, brought during the three hundred years of the Atlantic slave trade. In the first census of the United States, in 1790, these Africans and their descendants were 19 per cent of the total population. It is not possible to discuss here all the differences in genetic composition of local populations that resulted. In the New World, local populations range from almost entirely African by ancestry (Haiti), almost entirely Caucasian (Canada), various blends of Caucasian and Indian (most of Central and South America), three-way mixtures of American Indian, Caucasian, and Negro (Brazil), to a complex society in which the component races are held more or less distinct (the United States). The degree to which various races and their mixtures have different social status varies from place to place, and is too complex to discuss here.

The history, and even the eventual degree, of admixture between the three racial components in the New World, which represent all three of the *major* human races, is not thoroughly documented. Even the original numbers of the American Indians have been estimated variously at from ten to one hundred million (Stewart, 1973). The regional distribution of the total is somewhat better agreed upon: probably about one-tenth of the total, that is, from one to ten million, lived in North America north of Mexico. (All the dense aboriginal populations lived from Mexico south to Peru.) The data on which the foregoing estimates are based are of the most dubious kind: such as accounts of early travelers who, at one moment, were confronted by hostile warriors, seeming very many, at another by a landscape in which the natives were carefully staying out of sight. But there is no question that there was a catastrophic drop in the native populations after the coming of Europeans, largely because of epidemic diseases. Some students have estimated that Indian populations at their lowest point were only 5 per cent of their numbers in the year 1492. Since then they have increased rapidly (as have the descendants of the immigrant populations); by some estimates, they have by now equalled or surpassed their original numbers. Even census data in the United States (which is more reliably documented than some other American nations) are difficult to interpret. Throughout the nineteenth century, various portions of the present western United States, where most Indians now live, were being added piecemeal to the nation. Thus the numbers of Indians recorded by various censuses cannot be taken as an indication of real changes in their numbers.

There are also difficulties in defining an Indian, because of the genetic admixture that has occurred. In Latin America, people may be socially classified as Indian, meaning that they still have a "different" way of life; or as Mestizo, meaning that they are culturally assimilated. Both may be racially mixed, and the Mestizos are genetically Indian to a degree which varies in different places. The uncertainties of statistics can be seen in some very recent United States Census data. For some time the enumerated Indian population of the United States has been increasing at the rather constant rate of about 10 per cent every ten-year census period. But from 1960 to 1970, the increase was nearly 50 per cent (U.S. Census, 1973). This does not, however, indicate a sudden surge of fertility in the Indian population. Between these two years, the Census Bureau changed from a method in which itinerant census employees recorded data on various families as they observed them, and a system in which individuals themselves wrote data on a questionnaire form. What the change indicates is that there are about a quarter of a million individuals in the United States who consider themselves American Indians, but would not be so classified by a stranger. This indicates the amount of admixture in modern Indians, as well as the fact that many Americans really do not know what Indians look like. The infiltration of Caucasian genes into American Indians has been considerable, particularly in those tribes who met European settlers early. It may be that there is almost no such thing at the present time as a 100 per cent pure Choctaw or Cherokee. Gene flow has gone both ways, perhaps in equal amounts, though the effect is less conspicuous in the much larger European-derived population. Many white Americans have Indian ancestry (Figure 58A); some claim it on uncertain evidence. A well-known bit of early gene flow was contributed by Pocahontas, who, in addition to being the subject of some possibly mythical adventures, was a real person who married an Englishman. She died young, but left one son who returned to Virginia in the early seventeenth century and started a line of numerous descendants. Now the number of any one person's descendants, on the average, increases twice as fast as the population in which those descendants live. If an average couple in an expanding population has four surviving children (and this was true for a long time in the growing United States), the population will double once a generation, but the number of descendants of any one individual will be multiplied by four in every generation. The genes, of course, are getting spread thinner all the time. A rough calculation indicates that the living descendants of Pocahontas may number somewhere in the vicinity of one million, so that a substantial number of those modern Americans who claim her as an ancestor may be absolutely right. In the state of Oklahoma, where many Indians were already farmers and artisans in the European pattern when white immigration began, genes have been mingled very freely, and perhaps 20 per cent of the culturally "white" population has in it some known Indian ancestry within the last century. This Indian component of the gene pool is spreading further—and thinner—with every generation.

In the southwestern United States, a strong Indian component is present in yet another combination. Several states in that region were originally settled as part of the Spanish occupation of Mexico, and entered the United States with Spanish-speaking populations that were largely American Indian genetically. These populations, known as *Hispano-American, Mexican,* or, more recently, *Chicano,* have remained distinct, because of language difference (Figure 58B). They are part of what is truly a new race, which extends throughout Latin America (where it is called *Mestizo* or *Ladino*). These people are a blend of Spanish and American Indian, in which the Indian component predominates. They are almost uniformly of brunet coloring, and range in phenotype from Mediterranean Caucasian (less common) to essentially Indian (Figure 59A). Chicano girls

Figure 58(a) An American of one-fourth Delaware Indian ancestry: Mr. Gary Johnson, University of Colorado graduate.

Figure 58(b) A Mexican-born American: Governor Raul Castro of Arizona.

Figure 58(c) *Below left.* An American Black: Helen Ford, Miss Black America of 1975. (Wide World Photos.)

Figure 58(d) *Below.* A brother and sister of half Caucasian, one fourth Negro, and one fourth American Indian ancestry. (Originally published in Harvard African Studies, Vol. X, Part 2. Used with permission of the Peabody Museum.)

Figure 59(a) *Left.* A Modern Peruvian, half Spanish, half Quechua Indian: Dr. A. Roberto Frisancho, University of Michigan.

Figure 59(b) *Right.* A man from Brazil showing both Indian and Negro features. (United Nations.)

often have the very long head-hair of their Indian ancestors. Individuals of first-generation Japanese-American Caucasian descent report being taken for Chicano, even by Chicanos themselves. Apparently, whether one's Asian ancestors arrived fifteen thousand years ago or only twenty years ago, does not greatly alter the phenotype!

The Negro population of the New World was brought by sea from West Africa beginning in the early sixteenth century, when the first slaves were imported to the islands of the Caribbean. Various attempts were made to use Indians for slave labor, but this was unsuccessful, probably in large part because they were in a state of disastrous morbidity because of Old World diseases. The Africans brought with them yellow fever and malaria, which hurt their masters more than themselves. During the period of the Atlantic slave trade, overland travel in the Americas was very primitive, and comparatively few Negroes reached the Pacific coast or even the highland regions of Mexico and South America. Consequently, Negro admixture is only slightly involved in the Mestizo population of Mexico or the adjacent southwestern United States, or in the western highlands of South America. Negroes became a prominent part of American populations largely in the southeastern United States, the Caribbean islands, and along the coastal regions of Central America and northern South America (Figure 58C).

The New Races **309**

Brazil is noted for a population that is a three-way hybrid of Caucasian, American Indian, and Negroid (Figure 59B). The two latter races have been geographically separated from one another for a longer period of time than any others in the world; they lie at opposite ends of the distribution of the human species. If any two segments of mankind had been long enough isolated from one another to have developed impaired interfertility, these would be the two. In the hybrid population of Brazil, it is obvious that no such impairment exists. Brazil, perhaps because of the thorough racial confusion, has not developed formalized sociological distinctions based on race. It is interesting, however, that a recent anthropological study showed Brazilians using more than a hundred words and phrases denoting the nuances of race, by which they described their fellow citizens (Sanjek, 1971). Their unstructured social system is obviously not due to a lack of interest in genetic polymorphism. In some cases in South America and the Caribbean, Negro populations have withdrawn into communities of their own, and have become genetic isolates.

In the United States, Negro slaves, from the beginning, were concentrated in the southern states. It is interesting that although Negroes had no control over their own immigration, they were eventually concentrated, as were the Europeans, in areas where the climate was similar to their country of origin—not in the northern United States or the southern, temperate part of South America. The presence of these Negroes in the United States resulted in considerable exchange of genes, in spite of a stratified social system which still persists. During the slavery period, many children were born to Negro mothers and white fathers, though society proscribed marriage between the races, and utterly condemned the reverse combination. Second and third generations of crossing produced quadroons (one-fourth Negro) and octoroon (one-eighth Negro) descendants. Because slave status was inherited through the mother, this resulted in slaves of predominantly white ancestry. In recent times, lay opinion, and sometimes legal definition, has assumed that a person of any Negro admixture at all is "Negro." An interesting study was conducted some years ago by a woman of mixed ancestry who had confidential access to families like her own (Day, 1932). She stated that it was unusual for an individual of three-quarters or more white ancestry to be *unable* to "pass for white," if he or she so desired. In Colonial days the definition of race was, in fact, rather liberal. In Virginia, for instance, a person of less than one-quarter Negro ancestry, even by the smallest fraction, was legally considered to be white. (Such a definition corresponds closely to phenotypic appearance.) The awkward fact was that such individuals might still be slaves. Stories were told of beautiful octoroon girls being sold for carnal purposes, a kind of tale which titillated the modest pornographic tastes of the nineteenth century. It was probably more common, however, for a phenotypically white quadroon to walk away to a better life with the tacit consent of a master who might be the slave's father or brother. Such individuals joined the white community and bestowed their genes upon it. Thus, although there has been much acknowledged gene flow from white to black, there has also been, from the beginning, a flow in the other direction. If the person who "passes" marries into entirely white stock, it is unlikely that Negro features will appear in the next generation. However, a later marriage of two persons who are both of minor Negro ancestry may cause a visibly Negroid phenotype to surface—the result of random recombination of genes. Because American society has maintained an irresistible pressure for every individual to be identified with one race or the other, the phenotype, as judged by the public, may determine the social affiliation of persons of mixed ancestry. This has an interesting result. Genes for traits such as skin color and hair form, which are recognized by the layman as indicative of race, will cause their bearers to join the racial community to which the genes are appropriate. But these individuals take with them genes derived from the other parent race, which do not happen to have any visible (or at least recognized) effect. Thus, social pressure maintains the *visible* differences between the races, although considerable gene flow in both directions is taking place. The results of this gene flow, of course, will never be unscrambled.

It is interesting to compare this situation with that in South Africa, where there has also been much genetic admixture between Caucasian and Negroid. In 1950, a racial classification was rigidly formalized, with a three-way distinction between *Bantu*, who are presumably pure Negro of native tribes; *White*, presumably pure Caucasian of European ancestry; and *Coloured*, who are acknowledged to be mixed. The present ratio of White to Coloured is about two to one. Classification is based on phenotype, and in general corresponds to the social affiliations into which individuals had gravitated before the classification system was codified. As a result, genetic recombinations and unexpected phenotypes become legal, rather than merely personal, problems. For instance, a child may be classified as Coloured though both parents remain legally White. To Americans, whose concepts of race have always been implicitly genetic, this is a puzzling system. The net result, like that of the uncodified system in the United States, will be to fix certain phenotypic characteristics in the legally defined "races," without any effect on genetic confusion insofar as it concerns traits that are not popularly recognized as racial.

Some genetic studies have been done, using blood-group genes, which are not involved in phenotypic race, to estimate the amount of non-African genetic material in present-day American Negroes. One estimate places the total white component at about 25 to 30 per cent, and the rate of accumulation at about 3 per cent per generation. (Glass, 1953) The inflow of genes, however, has not been constant. In the era of slavery, domestic and urban slaves acquired more white genes than field workers. After the Civil War, these two groups tended to merge into a single population. At this time the gene flow from the white population was reduced. Some Negro groups descended primarily from plantation workers have remained to this day relatively free from white admixture. One such population, known as *Gullah* (from *Angola,* the territory in Africa from which they supposedly came) still resides in coastal areas and offshore islands of the south Atlantic coast (Pollitzer, 1958). Some American Indian admixture has also entered the American Negro population (Figure 58d), though probably not as much as is generally supposed. "Indian blood" in unspecified amounts is frequently alluded to by American Blacks in describing their own ancestry. However, genetic studies indicate that it forms so small an amount of the total gene pool as to be virtually undetectable statistically. Genetic mixture in the other direction, i.e., Negro into Indian, has probably been greater (Glass, 1955).

There are some extremely interesting small population groups in the southeastern United States that have been referred to as *triracial isolates* (Berry, 1963; Thompson, 1972). Most of these consist of only a few hundred or at most a few thousand individuals, and are not considered either by themselves or their neighbors to belong to any "standard" race. They go by a variety of unique local names: the best known are probably the *Melungeons* of Tennessee (Pollitzer and Brown, 1969). These isolates appear to have genetic components derived from white, Indian, and Negro populations (Pollitzer, 1964, 1966, 1972). They consider themselves to be racially distinct from any of these, and in the days of segregated schools sometimes had their own school systems. They are usually withdrawn into secluded areas—in the mountains, or the sandy pine barrens of the Atlantic Piedmont region. They are highly inbred, as indicated by the presence of a very limited number of surnames in many of the communities. Held in low esteem by their neighbors, they take comfort in their own origin myths, which trace their ancestry variously to Phoenicians, Turks, Portuguese, or the lost colony of Jamestown. As nearly as their true history can be reconstructed, they consist of mixtures, in various proportions, of free Negroes (who had an uncertain place in society before the Civil War), remnants of Indian tribes, and whites who for various reasons had left their own communities. In some cases the triracial isolates can be traced back to the census of 1790, which listed "free persons of color." It is obvious that different proportions of the three races are represented in different isolates. They shade off, imperceptibly, into some Indian populations that still have tribal names, even though they may be more than half white, genetically. The obvious isolation, the inbreeding, as indicated by the limited number of family names, and the small numbers of most of the founding populations, make it clear that there has been much opportunity for genetic drift. This would have the effect of making these people further distinctive from one another, as well as from the "standard" races. Blood-group studies indicate that in most cases *Indian* is the smallest racial component of the triracial isolates, less important than the people themselves believe. It is difficult to know what else may have happened to these populations. Most of them are not pleased with the evidences of their Negro ancestry, and individuals who have shown a Negro phenotype may have been eased out of the communities in the past, with obvious results on the frequencies of certain genes. Facial features are quite varied, as we would expect. Hair form appears less indicative of the Negro component than the blood groups indicate. These populations may in the near future be absorbed into the general population and so lose their identity; for the most part, this would be economically advantageous to them. But they are extremely interesting to the anthropologist. In Southeast Asia we saw "hill tribes" that were difficult to assign to any of the main races of the area. It may be that these tribes originated in much the same way as the triracial isolates of the United States; and that isolation and genetic drift over a very long time period, made them the unique and puzzling genetic entities we see today.

THE FUTURE OF RACE

It is sometimes assumed that racial differences in man are on the way out. Some see this expected process as an easy, and hopefully immediate, solution to the sociological problems of race. Hopes for a "biological solution" are somewhat dimmed by the fact that the existence of a very large number of admittedly mixed-ancestry individuals in South Africa has not prevented a strongly codified system of racial discrimination. Even in Brazil, where the complex triracial blend makes racial variation an extremely complex matter, the *consciousness* of race has not disappeared. In any event, the homogenizing of a community containing more than one race is a slow process. If all aversions to marriage between races were to disappear overnight, and marriage began to take place entirely randomly with respect to race, the majority of American whites would marry other whites simply because they made up the majority of available marriage partners: the expected per cent of white-white marriages, producing racially uniform children, would be 81 per cent. In the next generation the nonmixed white marriages would be 66 per cent. For at least a hundred years there would be ample, and obvious, biological differences between individuals on which discriminatory practises could be based, if the political climate favored it. In actuality, a breakdown of genetic isolation in the United States would result in distinctly different racial blends forming in various parts of the nation. Genetic homogenization between regions would be a slow process, unless it were artificially promoted by deliberate *exchange* of large chunks of population. The internal migration pattern of the United States has always been and still is one-sided. The western states have constantly received migrants from various areas east of them, and therefore have tended to

Figure 60(a)   A boy from Ceylon. (United Nations.)

Figure 60(b)   A boy from Gabon, West Africa. (United Nations.)

approximate a random sampling of the racial stocks of the older states. Those states that have had stable or decreasing populations have undergone little or no genetic change, because few people have come to them from outside. The effect of one-sided migration makes Americans overestimate world population mobility and genetic blending. The United States has been a *receiver* of population for many decades, and its citizens are very aware of the variety of stocks it has accumulated. Countries that have *contributed* to the flow of immigration to the United States may themselves have remained quite unchanged genetically.

The prospects for the racial homogenization of the world on a continental scale are remote indeed. It is hardly conceivable that mass migrations similar to those of the last few centuries can ever occur again. Those migrations were made possible by the rapid development of areas of previously simple subsistence and low population density. The future trend will be in the direction of further equalization of economic development and population densities throughout the world, thus eliminating the motivation, even the feasibility, of substantial population movements. Even if continents were to become racially homogenized within themselves, they would differ markedly from one another. The racial average of all of present-day Africa would be quite a different race from the average of all of North America or all of South America. To reach even this stage might take hundreds of years. If and when this process is

Figure 60(c) A Cheyenne Indian boy. (Courtesy Reverend Emmett Hoffman, St. Labre Indian School.)

Figure 60(d) A group of Indonesian children. (United Nations.)

completed, race will revert to its original condition: those who live in one place will be racially alike, and those who are racially different will be geographically separated. But the *total* elimination of racial differences within the human species is a very remote prospect.

Bibliography

Abraham, S., Lowenstein, F. W., and Johnson, C. L., 1974, *Preliminary findings of the first health and nutrition survey, U.S., 1971–2. Dietary intake and biochemical findings,* DHEW Pub. No. (HRA) 74–1219–1, U.S. Government Printing Office, Washington, D.C.

Adachi, B., 1937, Das Ohrenschmalz als Rassenmerkmal und der Rassengeruch ("Achselgeruch") nebst dem Rassenunterschied der Schweissdrusen. *Ztschr. für rassenkunde, 6,* 273–307.

Allison, A. C., 1953, Cyanide smelling deficiency among Africans, *Man, 53,* 176–177.

Allison, A. C., 1954, Protection afforded by sickle-cell trait against subtertian malaria, *Brit. Med. J., 1,* 290–292.

Anonymous, 1969, Brisket disease appears to be heritable, *Colo. Rancher and Farmer, 23,* 34–35.

Anonymous, 1970, Snow monkeys of Japan, *Life,* Jan. 30, pp. 37–39.

Bajema, C. J., ed., 1971, *Natural selection in human populations,* Wiley. New York.

Baker, J. R., 1974, *Race,* Oxford U.P., New York and London.

Baker, P. T., 1966, Ecological and physiological adaptation in indigenous South Americans, IN *The biology of human adaptability,* eds. P. T. Baker, and J. S. Weiner, Clarendon, Oxford, pp. 275–304.

Baker, P. T., and Angel, J. L., 1965, Old age changes in bone density: sex and race factors in the U.S., *Human Biol., 37,* 104–121.

Baker, P. T., and Newman, R. W., 1957, The use of bone weight for human identification, *Amer. J. Phys. Anth., 15,* 601–618.

Baker, P. T. and Weiner, J. S., 1966, *The biology of human adaptability,* Clarendon, Oxford.

Balcet, C., 1942, *L'uvea nell'occhio dei mammiferi,* I.T.E.R., Turin, Italy.

Barnicot, N. A., 1964, Biological variation in modern populations, IN *Human biology,* eds. G. A. Harrison, J. S. Weiner, J. M. Tanner, and N. A. Barnicot, Oxford, New York and Oxford.

Baughman, E. E., and Dahlstrom, W. G., 1968, *Negro and white children: a psychological study in the rural south,* Academic, New York.

Baxter, J. H., 1875, *Statistics, medical and anthropological, of the Provost-Marshal-General's Bureau, derived from records of the examination for military service in the armies of the United States during the late war of the rebellion,* Gov't Printing Office, Washington.

316

Berry, B., 1963, *Almost white,* Macmillan, New York.

Beadle, G. W., and Tatum, E. L., 1941, Genetic control of biochemical reactions in neurospora, *Proc. Nat. Acad. Sci. U.S.A., 27,* 449–506.

Birdsell, J. B., 1950, Some implications of the genetical concept of race in terms of spatial analysis. *Cold Spring Harbor Symp. on Quant. Biol., 15,* 259–314, Biol. Lab., Cold Spring Harbor, N.Y.

Birns, B., Barten, S., and Bridger, W. H., 1969, Individual differences in temperamental characteristics of infants, *Transactions N.Y. Acad. Sci., 31,* 1071–1082.

Black, F. L., 1975, Infectious diseases in primitive societies, *Science, 187,* 515–518.

Blair, W. F., 1943, Ecological distribution of mammals in the Tularosa Basin, New Mexico, *Contributions Lab. Vertebrate Biol. Univ. Mich., 36,* 1–16.

Bleibtreu, H. K., and Downs, J. F., eds., 1971, *Human variation: readings in physical anthropology,* Glencoe, Beverly Hills.

Blum, H. F., 1961, Does the melanin pigment of human skin have adaptive value? *Quart. Rev. Biol., 35,* 50–63.

Blumberg, B. S., and Gartler, D. M., 1961, The urinary excretion of beta-aminoisobutyric acid in Pacific populations, *Human Biol., 33,* 355–362.

Blumenbach, J. F., 1776, *De generis humani varietate nativa,* Göttingen, Germany. Trans. of later edition, IN *This is race,* ed. E. W. Count, 1950, Henry Schumann, New York, pp. 25–39.

Bordoni, N., et al, 1973, Prevalence of dental caries in twins. *J. of Dentistry for Children,* 440–443.

Bowles, G. T., 1932, New types of old Americans at Harvard, Harvard. U.P., Cambridge, Mass.

Brothwell, D. R., 1963, *Dental anthropology,* Pergamon, Elmsford, N.Y.

Brothwell, D. R., Carbonell, V. M., and Goose, D. H., 1963, Congenital absence of teeth in humans, IN *Dental anthropology,* ed. D. R. Brothwell, Pergamon, Elmsford, N.Y.

Brown, F. M., 1942, The microscopy of mammalian hair for anthropologists, *Proc. Amer. Philosophical Soc., 85,* 250–274.

Brozek, J., 1963, Quantitative description of body composition: physical anthropology's "fourth" dimension, *Current Anth., 4,* 3–39.

Brues, A. M., 1946a, A genetic analysis of human eye color, *Amer. J. Phys. Anth., 4,* 1–36.

Brues, A. M., 1946b, Regional differences in the physical characteristics of an American population, *Amer. J. Phys. Anth., 4,* 463–481.

Brues, A. M., 1954, Selection and polymorphism in the A–B–O blood groups, *Amer. J. Phys. Anth., 12,* 559–597.

Brues, A. M., 1959, The spearman and the archer, *Amer. Anth., 61,* 457–469.

Brues, A. M., 1963, Stochastic tests of the A–B–O blood groups, *Amer. J. Phys. Anth., 21,* 287–299.

Brues, A. M., 1966, "Probable mutation effect" and the evolution of hominid teeth and jaws, *Amer. J. Phys. Anth., 25,* 169–170.

Brues, A. M., 1975, Rethinking human pigmentation, *Amer. J. Phys. Anth., 43,* 387–392.

Brues, Austin M., and Sacher, G. A., 1965, *Aging and levels of biological organization,* U. Chicago, Chicago.

Buckwalter, J. A., 1957, Disease associations of the ABO blood groups, *Acta Genetica, 6,* 561–563.

Burnet, M., 1962, *Natural history of infectious disease,* Cambridge. U.P. Cambridge, Eng.

Burt, C., 1961, Intelligence and social mobility, *Brit. J. of Statist. Psychol., 14,* 3–24.

Carbonell, V. M., 1963, Variations in the frequency of shovel-shaped incisors in different populations, IN *Dental anthropology,* ed. D. R., Brothwell, Pergamon, Elmsford, N.Y., pp. 211–234.

Castle, W. E., 1929, A further study of size inheritance in rabbits, *J. Exp. Zool., 53,* 421–454.

Catlin, G., 1844, *Letters and notes on the manners, customs and conditions of the North American Indians,* 1973 Ed., Dover, New York.

Cavalli-Sforza, L. L., and Bodmer, W. R., 1971, *The genetics of human populations,* Freeman, San Francisco, Calif.

Cavalli-Sforza, L. L., and Edwards, A. W. F., 1963, Analysis of human evolution, IN *Genetics today, Vol. 3,* ed. S. J. Geerts, Pergamon, Elmsford, N.Y.

Chai, C. K., 1967, *Taiwan aborigines,* Harvard U.P., Cambridge, Mass.

Chang, K. S. F., Chan, S. T., Low, W. D., and Ng, C. K., Climate and conception rates in Hong Kong, *Human Biol. 35,* 366–376.

Chase, H. B., 1958, The behavior of pigment cells and epithelial cells in the hair follicle, IN *The biology of hair growth,* eds. W. Montagna, and D. A. Ellis, Academic, New York, pp. 229–238.

Comas, J., 1960, *Manual of physical anthropology, English edition,* Thomas, Springfield, Ill.

Coon, C. C., 1939, *The races of Europe,* Macmillan, New York.

Coon, C. S., 1962, *The origin of races,* Knopf, New York.

Coon, C. S., 1965, *The living races of man,* Knopf, New York.

Coon, C. S., Garn, S. M., and Birdsell, J. B., 1950, *Races, a study of the problems of race formation in man,* Thomas, Springfield, Ill.

Count, E. W., 1950, *This is race,* Henry Schuman, New York.

Cowles, R. B., 1959, Some ecological factors bearing on the origin and evolution of pigment in the human skin, *Amer. Naturalist, 93,* 283–293.

Cowles, R. B., 1967, Black pigmentation: adaptation for concealment or heat conservation, *Science, 158,* 1340–1341.

Cravioto, J., 1966, Nutritional deprivation and psychological development in children, IN *Deprivation in psychobiological development,* ed. H. W. Magoun, Pan Amer. Health Organiz. WHO, Washington, D.C., pp. 38–54.

Cravioto, J., and DeLicardie, E. R., 1971, The long-term consequences of protein-calorie malnutrition, *Nutrition Reviews, 29,* 107–111.

Crawford, M. H., 1974, Human biology of the Irish Tinkers: demography, ethnohistory and genetics, *Social Biol., 21,* 321–331.

Dahlberg, A. A., 1951, The dentition of the American Indian, IN *The physical anthropology of the American Indian,* ed W. S. Laughlin, Viking Fund, New York, pp. 138–176.

Dahlberg, A. A., 1963, Analysis of the American Indian dentition. IN *Dental anthropology,* ed. D. R. Brothwell, ed. Pergamon, Elmsford, N.Y., pp. 149–178.

Daniels, F., 1964, Man and radiant energy: solar radiation, IN *Handbook of physiology, section 4, adaptation to the environment,* ed. D. B. Dill, American Physiological Society, Washington, D.C., pp. 969–988.

Daniels, F., 1968, Sunburn, *Sci. Amer. 219* (July), 38–46.

Darwin, C., 1859, *The origin of species,* Everyman Ed. 1928, Dutton, New York.

Daw, S. F., 1970, Age of boys' puberty in Leipzig 1729–1749 as indicated by voice-breaking in J. S. Bach's choir members, *Human Biol., 42,* 87–89.

Day, C. B., 1932, Negro-white crosses in the United States, *Harvard African Studies, 10, part 2,* Peabody Museum, Cambridge, Mass.

de Garay, A. L., Levine, L., and Carter, J. E. L., 1974, *Genetic and anthropological studies of Olympic athletes,* Academic, New York.

Dice, L. R., 1947, Effectiveness of selection by owls of deer-mice (Peromyscus maniculatus) which contrast in color with their background. *Contributions Lab. Vertebrate Biol. Univ. Mich., 34,* 1–20.

Dill, D. B., ed., 1964, *Handbook of physiology, section 4, adaptation to the environment,* American Physiological Society, Washington, D.C.

Dixon, R. B., 1923, *The racial history of man,* Scribners, New York.

Dobzhansky, T., 1955, *Evolution, genetics and man,* Wiley, New York.

Dobzhansky, T., 1962, *Mankind evolving,* Yale, New Haven, Conn.

Dove, S., 1974, *Eye color changes,* Term Paper for Anthropology 410, unpublished.

Dunn, F. L., 1965, On the antiquity of malaria in the Western Hemisphere, *Human Biol., 37,* 383–393.

Edinger, T., 1948, Evolution of the horse brain. *Geol. Soc. Amer. Memoir 25,* Baltimore, Md.

Edwards, E. A., Hamilton, J. B., Duntley, S. Q., and Hubert, G., 1941, Cutaneous vascular and pigmentary changes in castrate eunuchoid men, *Endocrinology, 28,* 119–128.

Erlingmeyer-Kimling, L., and Jarvik, L. F., 1964, Genetics and intelligence: a review, *Science, 142,* 1477–1479.

Falconer, D. S., 1960, *Introduction to quantitative genetics,* Ronald, New York.

Feldman, S. D., 1975, The presentation of shortness in everyday life—height and heightism in American sociology: toward a sociology of stature. IN *Life styles, diversity in American society,* 2nd Edition, eds. S. D. Feldman, and G. W. Thielbar, Little, Brown, Boston.

Fitzpatrick, T. B., Brunet, P., and Kukita, A., 1958, The nature of hair pigment, IN *The biology of hair growth,* eds. W. Montagna, and R. A. Ellis, Academic, New York, pp. 255–303.

Fitzpatrick, T. B., Szabo, G., and Mitchell, R. E., Age changes in the human melanocyte system. IN *Advances in the biology of skin,* vol. 6, eds. W. Montagna, and R. L. Dobson, Pergamon, Elmsford, N.Y., pp. 35–50.

Foreman, G., 1934, *The five civilized tribes,* U. of Okla. Press, Norman, Okla.

Fred, H. L., Schmidt, A. M., Bates, T., and Hecht, H. H., 1962, Acute pulmonary edema of altitude, *Circulation, 25,* 929–937.

Frisancho, A. R., 1975, Functional adaptation to high altitude hypoxia, *Science, 187,* 313–319.

Frisancho, A. R., Sanchez, J., Pallardel, D., and Yanez, L., 1973, Adaptive significance of small body size under poor socio-economic conditions in southern Peru, *Amer. J. Phys. Anth., 39,* 255–262.

Frisch, R. E., and McArthur, J. W., 1974, Menstrual cycles: fatness as a determinant in minimum weight for height necessary for their maintenance or onset, *Science, 185,* 949–951.

Fuller, J. L., 1967, Experiential deprivation and later behavior, *Science, 158,* 1645–1653.

Garn, S. M., 1965, The applicability of North American growth standards in developing countries, *Canadian Med. Assoc. J., 93,* 914–919.

Garn, S. M., 1971, *Human races,* 3rd ed., Thomas, Springfield, Ill.,

Garrod, A. E., 1909, *Inborn errors of metabolism,* Oxford, U.P., London.

Giles, E., and Elliot, O., 1962, Race identification from cranial measurements, *J. Forensic Sci., 7,* 147–157.

Glass, B., and Li, C. C., 1953, The dynamics of racial intermixture, *Amer. J. Human Genetics, 5,* 1–20.

Glass, B., 1955, On the unlikelihood of significant admixture of genes from the North American Indians in the present composition of the Negroes of the United States, *Amer. J. Human Genetics, 7,* 368–385.

Goodrich, L. C., 1963, *A short history of the Chinese people,* Harper, New York.

Grahn, D., and Kratchman, J., 1963, Variation in neonatal death rate and birth weight in the United States and its possible relation to environmental radiation, geology and altitude, *Amer. J. Human Genetics, 15,* 329–352.

Grande, F., 1964, Man under caloric deficiency. IN *Handbook of physiology, section 4, adaptation to the environment,* ed. D. B. Dill, American Physiological Society, Washington, D.C., pp. 911–937.

Greulich, W. W., 1957, A comparison of the physical growth and development of American born and native Japanese children, *Amer. J. Phys. Anth., 19,* 173–184.

Haddon, A. C., 1925, *The races of man and their distribution,* Macmillan, New York.

Hammel, H. T., 1964, Terrestrial animals in cold: recent studies of primitive man. IN *Handbook of physiology, section 4, adaptation to the environment,* ed. D. B. Dill, American Physiological Society, Washington, D.C., pp. 413–434.

Hammel, H. T., Elsner, R. W., Le Messurier, D. H., Andersen, H. T., and Milan, F. A., 1959, Thermal and metabolic responses of the Australian aborigine exposed to moderate cold in summer, *J. Appl. Physio., 14,* 605–615.

Hamilton, J. B., 1958, Age, sex, and genetic factors in regulation of hair growth in man: a comparison of Caucasian and Japanese populations, IN *The biology of hair growth,* eds. W. Montagna, and R. A. Ellis, Academic, New York, pp. 400–434.

Hamilton, W. H., 1973, *Life's color code,* McGraw-Hill, New York.

Hanihara, K., 1963, Crown characters of the deciduous dentition of the Japanese-American hybrids, IN *Dental anthropology,* ed. D. R. Brothwell, Pergamon, Elmsford, N.Y., pp. 7–22.

Harrison, G. A., Weiner, J. S., Tanner, J. M., and Barnicot, N. A., 1964, *Human biology,* Oxford, U.P., New York and Oxford.

Hart, C. W. M., 1954, The sons of Turimpi, *Amer. Anth., 55,* 242–261.

Henderson, A. M., Bailey, B., Drouhard, J., and Sapir, E., 1974, Unpublished data.

Hensel, H., Hildebrandt, G., 1964a, Organ systems in adaptation: the nervous system, IN *Handbook of physiology, section 4, adaptation to the environment,* ed. D. B. Dill, American Physiological Society, Washington, D.C., pp. 55–72.

Hensel, H., and Hildebrandt, G., 1964b, Organ systems in adaptation: the muscular system, IN *Handbook of physiology, section 4, adaptation to the environment,* ed. D. B. Dill, American Physiological Society, Washington, D.C., pp. 73–90.

Herodotus, ca. 435 B.C., *Works,* Loeb Classical Library, 1961 trans. A. D. Godfrey, Harvard U.P., Cambridge.

Herskovitz, M. J., 1930, *The anthropometry of the American Negro,* Columbia U.P., New York.

Hetzer, H. O., and Harvey, W. R., 1967, Selection for high and low fatness in swine, *J. Animal Sci., 26,* 1244–1251.

Hicks, C. S., 1964, Terrestrial animals in cold: exploratory studies of primitive man, IN *Handbook of physiology, section 4, adaptation to the environment,* ed. D. B. Dill, American

Physiological Society, Washington, D.C., pp. 405–412.

Hiernaux, J., 1964, Weight-height relationship during growth in Africans and Europeans, *Human Biol., 36,* 273–293.

Hirszfeld, L., and Hirszfeld, H., 1919, Essai d'application des methodes serologiques au probleme des races, *Anthropologie, 29,* 505–537.

Hock, R. J., 1970, The physiology of high altitude, *Sci. Amer., 222,* 53–62.

Hoffman, J. M., 1973, *Variation in retinal pigmentation: an anthropological perspective,* Doctoral dissertation, U. of Colo.

Holden, C., 1973, R. J. Herrnstein: the perils of expounding meritocracy, *Science, 181,* 36–39.

Hooton, E. A., 1930, *The indians of Pecos Pueblo,* Yale, New Haven, Conn.

Hooton, E. A., 1939, *The American criminal,* Harvard U.P., Cambridge, Mass.

Horvath, S. M., and Howell, C. D., 1964. Organ systems in adaptation: the cardiovascular system, IN *Handbook of physiology, section 4, adaptation to the environment,* ed. D. B. Dill, American Physiological Society, Washington, D.C., pp. 153–166.

Howells, W. W., 1973, *Cranial variation in man,* Peabody Museum, Cambridge, Mass.

Hrdy, D., 1973 Quantitative hair form variation in seven populations, *Amer. J. Phys. Anth., 39,* 7–17.

Hulse, F. S., 1968, Migration and cultural selection in human genetics, *The Anthropologist, special volume 1968,* pp. 1–27, Delhi, India.

Hurtado, A., 1964, Animals in high altitudes: resident man, IN *Handbook of physiology, section 4, adaptation to the environment,* ed. D. B. Dill, American Physiological Society, Washington, D.C., pp. 843–860.

Jerison, J. J., 1963, Interpreting the evolution of the brain, *Human Biol., 35,* 263–291.

Johnston, R. P., and R. K. Selander, 1964, House sparrows: rapid evolution of races in North America, *Science, 14,* 548–550.

Judkins, R., and Lieberman, L., 1974, Biomedicine and nutrition (diabetes), *Soc. for Med. Anth. Newsletter,* 14–17.

Karpinos, B. D., 1960, Racial differences in visual acuity, *Public Health Report, 75,* 1045–1050.

Karpinos, B. D., 1961, Height and weight of youths of military age, *Human Biol., 33,* 335–354.

Katz, S. H., ed., 1975, *Biological anthropology (Readings from Scientific American),* Freeman, San Francisco, Calif.

Kelso, A. J., and Armelagos, G., 1963, Nutritional factors as selective agencies in the determination of ABO blood group frequencies, *Southwestern Lore, 28,* 44–48.

Klasen, E., 1972, *The syndrome of specific dyslexia,* Univ. Park Press, Baltimore, Md.

Kodani, M., 1958, Three chromosome numbers in whites and Japanese, *Science, 127,* 1339–1340.

Kraus, B., 1951, Male somatotypes among the Japanese of North Honshu, *Amer. J. Phys. Anth., 10,* 347–364.

Kretschmer, E., 1921, *Korperbau and Charakter,* Springer, Berlin.

Krogman, W. M., 1962, *The skeleton in forensic medicine,* Thomas, Springfield, Ill.

Kudo, T., 1919, The facial musculature of the Japanese, *J. Morphology, 32,* 637–679.

Ladell, W. S. S., 1964, Terrestrial animals in humid heat, IN *Handbook of Physiology, Section 4, Adaptation to the Environment,* ed. D. B. Dill, American Physiological Society, Washington, D.C., pp. 625–660.

Landsteiner, K., 1900, Zur Kenntnis der antifermentativen, lytischen, und agglutinierenden Werkungen des Blutserums und der Lymphe, *Zentralblatt fur Bakteriologie, Parasitenkunde, Infectionskrankheiten und Hygiene, 27,* 357–362.

Lasker, G. W., and Lee, M. M. C., 1957, Racial traits in human teeth, *J. Forensic Sci., 2,* 401–419.

Laughlin, W. S., ed., 1951, *The physical anthropology of the American Indian,* Viking Fund, New York.

Lee, M. M. C., Chang, K. S. F., and Chan, M. M. C., 1963, Sexual maturation of Chinese girls in Hong Kong, *Pediatrics, 32,* 389–398.

Lewis, B., 1966, *The Arabs in history,* Harper, New York.

Lewis, B., 1971, *Race and color in Islam,* Harper, New York.

Livingstone, F. B., 1958, Anthropological implications of sickle-cell gene distribution in West Africa, *Amer. Anth., 60,* 533–562.

Loehlin, J. C., Lindzey, G., and Spuhler, J. N., 1975, *Race differences in intelligence,* Freeman, San Francisco, Calif.

Loomis, W. F., 1967, Skin-pigment regulation of vitamin-D synthesis in man, *Science, 157,* 501–506.

Loth, E., 1931, *Anthropologie des parties molles,* Masson et Cie., Paris.

Luria, A. R., 1966, *Higher cortical functions in man,* trans. B. Haigh, Basic Books, New York.

McClearn, G. E., and DeFries, J. C., 1973, *Introduction to behavioral genetics,* Freeman, San Francisco, Calif.

McCracken, R. D., 1971, Lactase deficiency: an example of dietary evolution, *Curr. Anth., 12,* 479–517.

McCullough, J. H., 1970, *The visual field in man and its evolution as related to facial morphology,* Doctoral dissertation, U. of Colo.

McGovern, W. M., 1939, *The early empires of Central Asia,* U. of North Carolina Press, Chapel Hill.

McKusick, V. A., 1968, *Mendelian inheritance in man, 2nd ed.,* Johns Hopkins, Baltimore.

MacPherson, R. K., 1966, Physiological adaptation, fitness and nutrition in the peoples of the Australian and New Guinea regions, IN *The biology of human variability,* eds. P. T. Baker, and J. S. Weiner, Clarendon, pp. 431–468.

Magoun, H. W., ed., 1966, *Deprivation in psychobiological development,* Pan Amer. Health Organiz. World Health Organiz., Washington, D.C.

Malcolm, L. E., 1970, Growth and development in New Guinea—a study of the Bundi people of the Madang district. *Inst. of Human Biology, Papua and New Guinea, Monograph series No. 1,* Madang, Papua New Guinea.

Malcolm, L. A., 1973, Growth and development patterns and human differentiation in Papua New Guinea communities, *IXth International Conference of Anthropological Sciences,* Chicago.

Mann, I., 1966, *Culture, race, climate and eye disease,* Thomas, Springfield, Ill.

Martin, R., and Saller, K., 1956, *Lehrbuch der Anthropologie,* Gustav Fisher, Stuttgart.

Mason, W. A., 1968, Early social deprivation in the non-human primates: implications for human behavior, IN *Environmental influences,* ed. D. C. Glass, Rockefeller Univ., New York, pp. 70–100.

Massé, G., and Hunt, E. E., Jr., 1963, Skeletal maturation of the hand and wrist in West African children, *Human Biol., 35,* 3–25.

Matsunaga, E., 1956, Selektion durch Unvertraglichkeit im ABO-Blutgruppen zwischen Mutter and Fetus, *Blut, 2,* 188–198.

Matsunaga, E., 1962, The dimorphism in human normal cerumen, *Annals of Human Genetics, 25,* 237–286.

Mayr, E., 1970, *Populations, species, and evolution,* Belknap, Cambridge, Mass.

Mendel, G., 1866, Experiments in plant hybridization. *Verhandlung Naturforscher Verein in Brunn,* vol. 4, Trans. in E. W. Sinnott, L. C. Dunn, and T. Dobzhansky, *Principles of genetics,* 1958, McGraw-Hill, New York, pp. 419–443.

Monge, C., 1948, *Acclimatization in the Andes.* Johns Hopkins, Baltimore.

Montagna, W., and Dobson, R. L., 1965, *Advances in the biology of skin, vol. 6,* Pergamon, Elmsford, Ill.

Montagna, W., and Dobson, R. L., 1969, *Advances in the biology of skin, vol. 9,* Pergamon, Elmsford, Ill.

Montagna, W., and Ellis, R. A., 1958, *The biology of hair growth,* Academic, New York.

Moor-Jankowski, J., Wiener, A. S., and Rogers, C. M., 1964, Human blood group factors in non-human primates, *Nature, 202,* 663–665.

Montagu, M. F. A., 1960, *An introduction to physical anthropology,* Thomas, Springfield, Ill.

Morris, L. N., ed. 1971, *Human populations, genetic variation, and evolution,* Chandler, San Francisco.

Morton, N. E., Chung, C. S., and Mi, M. P., 1967, *Genetics of interracial crosses* in Hawaii, S. Karger, Basel and New York.

Morton, S. G., 1854, *Types of Mankind.* Lippincott, Philadelphia.

Motulsky, A. G., 1960, Metabolic polymorphisms and the role of Infectious diseases in human evolution, *Human Biol., 32,* 28–62.

Mourant, A. E., Kopec, C., and Domaniewska-Sobczak, K., 1958, *The ABO blood groups,* Thomas, Springfield, Ill.

Nagel, U., 1973, A Comparison of anubis baboons, hamadryas baboons and their hybrids at a species border in Ethiopia, *Folia Primatologia, 19,* 104–165.

Neel, J. V., 1962, Diabetes mellitus, a "thrifty" genotype rendered detrimental by "progress"?, *Amer. J. Human Genetics, 14,* 353–362.

Newman, H. H., 1930, The fingerprints of twins, *J. Genetics, 23,* 415–446.

Newman, R. W., 1955, The relation of climate and body composition in young

American males, *Amer. J. Phys. Anth.,* *13,* 386–387.

Newman, R. W., 1956, Skinfold measurements in young American males, *Human Biol., 28,* 154–164.

Newman, R. W., and Munro, E. H., 1955, The relation of climate and body size in U.S. males, *Amer. J. Phys. Anth., 13,* 1–17.

Olson, W. S., 1966, What ever happened to hairy man?, *Science, 153,* 364.

Orentreich, N., 1969, Scalp hair replacement in man, IN *Advances in the biology of skin, vol. 9,* eds. W. Montagna, and R. L. Dobson, Pergamon, Elmsford, Ill., pp. 99–108.

Osborne, R. H., and DeGeorge, F. V., 1959, *Genetic basis of morphological variation,* Harvard. U.P. Cambridge, Mass.

Oschinsky, L., 1962, Facial flatness and cheekbone morphology in Arctic Mongoloids: a case for morphological taxonomy, *Anthropologica, 4,* 349–377.

Otten, C. M., 1967, On pestilence, diet, natural selection and the distribution of microbial and human blood group antigens and antibodies, *Curr. Anth., 8,* 209–226.

Painter, T. S., 1933, A new method for the study of chromosome rearrangements and the plotting of chromosome maps, *Science, 78,* 585–586.

Pearson, K., 1906, On the relationship of intelligence to size and shape of head, and to other physical and mental characters, *Biometrika, 5,* 105–146.

Petrakis, N. L., Molohan, K. T., and Tepper, D. J., 1967, Cerumen in American Indians. Genetic implications of sticky and dry types, *Science, 158,* 1192–1193.

Plinius Secundus, C., ca. 70 A.D., *Natural History.* Loeb Classical Library, 1963, trans. H. Rackham, Harvard. U.P. Cambridge, Mass.

Pollitzer, W. S., 1958, The Negroes of Charleston (S.C.): a study of hemoglobin types, serology and morphology, *Amer. J. Phys. Anth., 16,* 241–263.

Pollitzer, W. S., 1964, Analysis of a tri-racial isolate, *Human Biol., 36,* 362–373.

Pollitzer, W. S., 1972, The physical anthropology and genetics of marginal people of the southeastern United States, *Amer. Anth., 74,* 719–734.

Pollitzer, W. S., and Brown, W. H., 1969, A survey of demography, anthropometry and genetics in the Melungeons of Tennessee, *Human Biol., 41,* 388–400.

Pollitzer, W. S., Menegaz-Bock, R. M., and Herion, J. C., 1966, Factors in the evolution of a tri-racial isolate, *Amer. J. Human Genetics, 18,* 26–38.

Post, R. H., 1964, Hearing acuity among Negroes and whites, *Eugenics Quart., 11,* 65–81.

Post, P. W., Daniels, F., and Binford, R. T., 1975, Cold injury and the evolution of "white" skin, *Human Biol., 47,* 65–80.

Reed, T. E., 1969, Caucasian genes in American Negroes, *Science, 165,* 762–768.

Rennie, D. W., and Adams, T., 1957, Comparative thermoregulatory responses of Negroes and white persons to acute cold stress, *J. Appl. Physio. 11,* 201–204.

Rife, D. C., 1953, Finger prints as criteria of ethnic relationships, *Amer. J. Human Genetics, 5,* 389–399.

Riggs, S. K., and Sargent, F., 1964, Physiological regulation in moist heat by young american Negro and white males, *Human Biol., 36,* 339–353.

Roberts, D. F., and Bainbridge, D., 1963, Nilotic physique, *Amer. J. Phys. Anth., 21,* 341–370.

Roberts, J., and Bayliss, D., 1967, *Hearing levels of adults by race, region and area of residence,* National Center for Health Statistics Series II. No. 26, Washington, D.C.

Roe, D. A., 1974, The Sharecropper's plague, *Natural History, 83,* No. 8, 52–63.

Sanjek, R., 1971, Brazilian racial terms, some aspects of meaning and learning, *Amer. Anth., 73,* 1126–1143.

Searle, A. G., 1968, *Comparative genetics of coat color in mammals,* Logos Press, London.

Seltzer, C. A., 1939, The Jew, his racial status: an anthropological appraisal, *Harvard Medical Alumnae Bulletin,* April, pp. 3–11.

Shapiro, H., 1936, *The heritage of the Bounty,* Simon & Schuster, New York.

Sheldon, W. H., Stevens, S. S., and Tucker, W. B., 1940, *The varieties of human physique,* Harper, New York.

Sheldon, W. H., and Stevens, S. S., 1942, *The varieties of temperament,* Harper, New York.

Shuey, A. M., 1966, *The testing of Negro intelligence, 2nd ed.,* Social Science Press, New York.

Simmons, K., 1942, Cranial capacities by both plastic and water techniques with cranial linear measurements of the Reserve Collection, *Human Biol., 14,* 473–498.

Smith, M., 1964, Giving the Olympics an anthropological once-over, *Life,* Oct. 23, 1964, pp. 81–84.

Snowden, F. M., 1970, *Blacks in antiquity,* Belknap, Cambridge, Mass.

Sommers, I. G., 1949, *Histology and histopathology of the eye,* Grune, New York.

Spuhler, J. N., ed., 1967, *Genetic diversity and human behavior,* Aldine, Chicago.

Stein, Z., Susser, M., Saenger, G., and Marolla, F., Nutrition and mental performance, *Science, 178,* 708–713.

Stewart, T. D., 1973, *The people of America,* Scribners, New York.

Stout, D. B., 1946, Further notes on albinism among the San Blas Cuna, Panama, *Amer. J. Phys. Anth., 4,* 483–490.

Sutton, W. S., 1903, The chromosomes in heredity, Biological Bulletin, 4, reprinted IN *Great experiments in biology, 1955,* eds. M. L. Gabriel, and S. Vogel.

Szabo, G., Gerald, A. R., Pathak, M. A., and Fitzpatrick, T. B., 1969, Racial differences in the fate of melanosomes in human epidermis, *Nature, 222,* 1081–1082.

Tacitus, P. C., ca. 100 A.D., *Agricola, Germania,* Loeb Classical Library, 1970, trans. M. Hutton, Harvard U. Press, Cambridge.

Tannehill, R., 1973, *Food in history,* Stein & Day, New York.

Tanner, J. M., 1964, Human growth and constitution, IN *Human biology* eds. G. A. Harrison, J. S. Weiner, J. M. Tanner, and N. A. Barnicot, U.P. New York & Oxford.

Tanner, J. M., 1966, Growth and physique in different populations of mankind, IN *The biology of human adaptability,* eds. P. T. Baker, and J. S. Weiner, Clarendon, Oxford, pp. 45–66.

Tanner, J. M., 1968, Earlier maturation of man, *Sci. Amer., 218,* 159–171.

Thoday, J. M., 1973, Educability and group differences, *Nature, 245,* 418–421.

Thomas, A., Chess, S., and Birch, H. G., 1970, The origin of personality, *Sci. Amer., 223,* 102–109.

Thompson, E. T., 1972, The little races, *Amer. Anth., 74,* 1295–1306.

U.S. Bureau of the Census, 1973, *Statistical Abstract of the United States, 1973 (94th Ed.),* Washington, D.C.

Vandenberg, S. G., 1962, The hereditary abilities study: hereditary components in a psychological test battery, *Amer. J. Human Genetics, 14,* 220–237.

Vandenberg, S. G., 1967, Hereditary factors in psychological variables in man, with a special emphasis on cognition, IN *Genetic diversity and human behavior,* ed. J. N. Spuhler, Aldine, Chicago, pp. 99–134.

Vandenberg, S. G., ed., 1968a, *Progress in human behavior genetics,* Johns Hopkins, Baltimore.

Vandenberg, S. G., Stafford, R. E., and Brown, A. M., 1968b, The Louisville twin study, IN *Progress in human behavior genetics,* ed. S. G. Vandenberg, Johns Hopkins, Baltimore, pp. 153–204.

Van Thiel, D. H., Gavaler, J., and Lester, R., 1974, Ethanol inhibition of vitamin A metabolism in the testes: possible mechanism for sterility in alcoholics, *Science, 186,* 941–942.

Van Valen, L., 1974, Brain size and intelligence in man, *Amer. J. Phys. Anth., 40,* 417–423.

Vogel, F., 1965, Blood groups and natural selection, IN *Proceedings of 10th Congress of the International Society of Blood Transfusion,* Stockholm, 1964, pp. 268–279.

Vogel, F., and Chakravartti, M. R., 1966, ABO blood groups and smallpox in a rural population of West Bengal and Bihar (India), *Humangenetik, 3,* 166–180.

Von Bonin, G., 1937, Brain weight and body weight in mammals, *J. Gen. Psychol., 16,* 379–389.

Wald, G., 1945, Human vision and the spectrum, *Science, 101,* 653–658.

Walls, G. L., 1942, *The vertebrate eye and its adaptive radiation,* Cranbrook Inst. of Science Bulletin No. 19, Cranbook Press, Bloomfield Hills, Mich.

Walsh, R. J., 1963, Variation of melanin pigmentation in some Asian and Pacific peoples, *J. Royal Anth. Inst., 93,* 126–133.

Walsh, R. J., 1971, A distinctive pigment of the skin in New Guinea aborigines, *Ann. Human Genetics, 34,* 379–385.

Washburn, S. L., and Hamburg, D. A., 1968, Aggressive behavior in Old World monkeys and apes, IN *Primates, studies in adaptation and behavior,* 1968. ed. P. C. Jay, Holt, New York.

Waterhouse, J. A. H., and Hogben, L., 1947, Incompatibility of mother and fetus with respect to the agglutinogen A and its antibody, *Brit. J. Soc. Med., 1,* 1–17.

Weiner, J. S., 1954, Nose shape and climate, *Amer. J. Phys. Anth., 12,* 615–618.

Weiner, J. S., 1964, Skin color in Southern Africa, *Human Biol., 36,* 294–307.

Weiner, J. S., 1971, *The natural history of man,* Universe, New York.

Wells, C., 1964, *Bones, bodies, and disease,* Praeger, New York.

Wetzel, N. C., 1948, *Grid for evaluating physical fitness,* NEA Service, Cleveland, Ohio.

Wiener, A. S., and Gordon, E. B., 1960, The

blood groups of chimpanzees, *Amer. J. Phys. Anth., 18,* 301–311.

Widdowson, E. M., 1966, Nutritional deprivation in psycho-biological development: studies in animals, IN Magoun, H. W. ed. Deprivation in psychological development, Pan American Health Org., WHO, Washington, D.C., 1966, 27–37.

Williams, G. C., 1966, *Adaptation and natural selection,* Princeton.

Wilson, E. D., Fisher, K. H. and Fuqua, M. E., 1965, *Principles of nutrition,* Wiley, New York.

Wood, C. S., 1975, New evidence for a late introduction of malaria into the New World, *Curr. Anth., 16,* 93–104.

Wood, C. S., Harrison, G. A., Dove, C., and Weiner, J. S., 1972, Selective feeding of Anopheles gambiae according to ABO blood group status, *Nature, 239,* 165.

Wood, J. G., 1870, *Wood's natural history of man,* Routledge, London.

Woolf, C. M., 1965, Albinism among Indians in Arizona and New Mexico, *Amer. J. Human Genetics., 17,* 23–35.

Worthy, M., 1974, *Eye color, sex, and race,* Droke House/Hallux, Anderson, S.C.

Wright, M. H., 1951, *A Guide to the Indian tribes of Oklahoma,* U. Oklahoma Press, Norman, Okla.

Wyshak, G., and White, C., 1965, Genealogical study of human twinning, *Amer. J. Public Health, 55,* 1586–1593.

Yoshimura, H., 1964, Organ systems in adaptation: the skin, IN Dill, D. B., ed. *Handbook of physiology, section 4, adaptation to the environment,* American Physiological Society, Washington, D.C., 109–131.

Young, L. B., ed., *Evolution of man,* Oxford, U.P., New York.

Index

A letter T following a page number indicates a table: a letter F indicates a figure.

Because of the nature of the subject matter, references to places and regions commonly indicate *populations of* these areas.

genetics of, 31–33, 31T, 35
New World, 213
Old World, 213
phenotypes, 32T
race and, 213
Rh, 213–215, 215F, 219–220, 252
negative allele, in Basques, 283
Blood proteins, 220
Blood, skin color and, 88–89
Blood sugar, 196
Blood transfusion, 204–205
Blumberg, B. S., 220
Blumenbach, J. F., 19–21
Bodmer, W. R., 161, 188
Body build, 155, 161–175, 168F
climate and, 170–171
crime and, 173
lateral, 161–162
linear, 161–162
occupation and, 173
population differences, 162
racial differences, 169–170
speed and, 171
sports and, 173–175
temperament and, 172
tuberculosis and, 188
use of tools and weapons, 171–172
Body hair, 147–148
Body odor, 142–143, 221
Body proportions, 161–163
Body shape, *see* Body Build
Body size, 156–161, 167–169
attitudes towards, 156–157
inheritance, 160–161
nutrition and, 157–161
Body temperature, 182
Body weight, 161–162
Bohemia, skull (Neolithic), 132F
Bones, mineralization in Caucasians
and Negroes, 196
Bordoni, N., 135
Bowles, G. T., 159
"Brain damage," 238
Brain, 230F
evolution of, 68
localization of function, 130, 229–
231, 230F
size, 130–131, 228–232
body size and, 229
nutrition and, 232
racial differences, 231–232
relation to function, 130, 232
Brazil, 301F, 306, 309F, 310
Brindle trait, freckling and, 108
hair color, 99
Brisket disease, 183

Brothwell, D. R., 136–137
Brown, F. M., 146, 312
Brow-ridges, 124–125, 125F, 128
Brozek, J., 167
Brues, A. M., 102–103, 107, 128, 158,
172, 218, 305
Brues, Austin M., 229
Buck teeth, 137
Buckwalter, J. A., 218
Buriats, 255, 257
Burma, 254, 261, 264, 272
Burnet, M., 186, 188, 191
Bushmen, African, 28, 288F, 289–291
cold response, 180
skin color, 95
stature, 168
steatopygia, 153
Burt, C., 241

Calcium, 160, 196
California, 297F, 300
Cambodians, 264
Camel, 154–155
Canada, 306
Cancer of skin, and solar radiation, 91
Capillary blood vessels, response to
altitude, 183
Carabelli's cusp, 137
Carbohydrates and diabetes, 197
Carbonell, V. M., 136
Carotene, 89
Carriers, genetic definition of, 54
Castes, in India, 272
Castle, W. E., 41
Cattle, 68
altitude response, 183
Cats, eye color, 103
Caucasians. *See also* Caucasoids
body build, 169
heat response, 182
somatotype, 170
vision, 223–224
Caucasoids, 22–23, 24F, 27, 272–273F,
278–279F, 287F
Africa, 285–286, 287F, 290–291
Asia, 258, 272
Cavalli-Sforza, L. L., 161, 188, 219
Cerebral cortex, 229–231, 230F
Cerebrotonia, 172
Central America, 300, 301F
growth in, 165
Ceylon, 314F
Chang, K. S. F., 182
Chase, H. B., 98
Cherokee, gene flow into, 307

Epidemics, spread of, 186–187
Epidermis, 87
Epiphyses, 163–164
Erlenmeyer-Kimling, L., 236
Eskimos, 12, 295–296, 296F
   cold response, 180
   diet of, 91, 192
   skull, 133F
   stature, 171
   vitamin D, in diet, 91
Ethiopea, 289–290
   Jewish communities in, 284
Ethiopeans, in classical times, 10, 11F
Eumelanin, 87, 98
Eurasia, 271
Europe, 275–283
   climate and topography, 276
   eye color, 103
   skin color, 94
   stature, 168
Europeans, expansion of, 304–305
Evolution of brain, 227
Evolution of man, role of mutations, 79
Eye color, 100–105
   classification of, 102
   inheritance of, 103
   vision and, 104–105
Eye shape, 115–117, 116F
Eyebrows, 144

Face, 109–117, 120–122
   size, in American Indians, 299
   size, racial variation, 129–130
Facial expression, 110
Facial muscles, 121–122
Falconer, D. S., 47, 199
Fat, 149–155
   age of puberty and, 199
   functions of, 150–151, 154
   genetic component, 151–152
   sex differences, 152
Fecundity, 199
Feldman, S. D., 156
Female breast, racial variation, 153
Fertility, 199–201
Finger prints, 140–142, 141F
Finland, 277
Fitness, 61–62
Fitzpatrick, T. B., 99
Flatness of face, 125–126
Food requirements, body size, 157–158
Foreman, G., 198

Founder effect, 80–81, 269
   New World, 296
Fourth molar tooth, in Australia, 268
Freckling, 89, 108
Fred, H. L., 183
French, stature, 158
Frisancho, A. R., 157, 183
Frisch, R. E., 199
Fuller, J. L., 240

G-6PD, 191
Gabon, 314F
Garn, S. M., 162, 165
Gene, complex, 38
Gene, definition, 32, 37–38
Gene frequency, 50–54
Gene flow, 73–79
   between American Indian and
      Negro, 312
   between Caucasian and American
      Indian, 299, 307
   between Caucasian and Negro,
      United States, 311
   between Jews and Gentiles, 284
   between Negroes and Pygmies, 286
   evidence, in Australia, 268
   interaction with natural selection, 75,
      76F, 79
Gene pool, definition, 51
Gene, relation to trait, 38–42
Genetic changes, 57–60, 83–85
Genetic drift, 80–84, 81F, 137, 249–
      250, 264, 283, 296, 312
Genetic space, 74
Genetics, 29–85
   human, special problems, 46–48
   plants, 30, 35
   population, 49–54
Genotype, definition, 32
Germans, 12, 277, 278F, 280
Germinative layer of epidermis, 87
Giles, E., 134
Gilyak, 260
Glass, B., 311–312
Gordon, E. B., 216
Gorilla, graying of hair, 99
Grahn, D., 184
Gray matter, 229
Graying of hair, 99
Greek, 279F
Greece, early history, 10
Greulich, W. W., 169
Growth, 163–165
Guam, 269

McCullough, J. H., 128
McKusick, V. A., 47, 223
MacPherson, R. K., 194
Madagascar, 289F, 291
Magellan, 15
Magoun, H. W., 242
Maize, 194, 255
Malaria, 189–191
Malcolm, L. A., 194, 199
Manchuria, 255
Mann, I., 224
Marco Polo, 14
Martin, R., 100, 139, 153, 231
Mason, W. A., 239
Massé, G., 165
Matsunaga, E., 143, 207
Maya, 301F
Mayr, E., 93, 114, 170
Mediterranean, 273, 276–277, 280
  stature, 158
Medulla of hair, 146
Melanesia, 268–269
  age of puberty, 199
  skin color, 96
  skull, 132F
  stature, 168
Melanin
  eye, 101
  formation of, 39–40
  hair, 98–99
  skin, 87–92
  vitamin D synthesis and, 91
Melanocytes
  eye, 100–101
  hair follicle, 97–98
  origin of, 87
  skin, 87–88, 88F
Melungeons, 312
Mendel, G., 30–37
Mental traits, heritability, 235–239
Metabolic cold response, 179
Metabolism, 39
Mesomorphy, 165–166
Mestizo, 305–307
Metopic suture, 138
Mexico, 300, 307, 308F
Migration
  race formation, 250–251
  race mixture, 313–314
Micronesia, 254, 269–271, 270F
Milk, digestion of, 194–195
Monge, C., 184
Mongolia, 255
Mongols, 14, 255, 257, 274, 281
  skull, 133F

Mongoloid eye fold, 116–117, 116F
  American Indians, 299
Mongoloid face, characteristics, 126F
Mongoloids, 23, 25F, 26, 254–261,
    256F, 259F, 262–263F
  altitude adaptation, 183
  American, description, 293
  Asian, description, 26, 255–257
  body build, 169
  sacral spot in, 89
  skin color, 95–96
  sports, 175
Montagnards, 261, 262F
Montagu, M. F. A., 225
Moor-Jankowski, J., 216
Morton, N. E., 200
Motulsky, A. G., 185–186, 188, 191
Mourant, A. E., 211
Mouth, 120
Munro, E. H., 171
Muscle bulk, measurement of, 167
Mutation, 57–60, 63, 79
  evolution and, 58–59, 79
  rates, 57–58
Myopia, 223–224

Nagel, U., 239
Nasal aperture, of skull, 124, 127
Natural selection, 60–69, 65T, 66–67F,
    75, 84
  interaction with gene flow, 75, 76F, 79
  race formation, 249, 251–252
Navaho, 297F
  population increase, 294
Neanderthal Man, 8, 94, 131
Near East, early history, 9–10
Neel, J. V., 197
Negritos, 13, 26, 261, 263F, 264
  skin color, 96
  skull, 132F
  stature, 168
  steatopygia, 153
Negro, Negroid, 23, 24F, 27–28, 286,
    288–289F
  body build, 169
  cold response, 179
  growth, 165
  heat response, 181–182
  "legal definition" of, 310
  New World, 309–311
  rickets in, 92
  skull, 132
  sports, 174–175
  tuberculosis in, 188